W9-ANH-886

Table of Contents

*For our families, with love, laughter,
and respect for their incredible
courage and determination:*

Joe Hopke, and Justin and Loren Packer-Hopke

*Dan Pruitt, and Darin, Jory, and Julianna Bush,
Nadyne Neff, and Charlotte Gooding*

Challenging Kids, Challenged Teachers

Teaching Students
with
Tourette's,
Bipolar Disorder,
Executive Dysfunction,
OCD, ADHD,
and More

Leslie E. Packer, Ph.D. & Sheryl K. Pruitt, M.Ed., ET/P

Woodbine House ■ 2010

© 2010 Leslie E. Packer and Sheryl K. Pruitt

All rights reserved under International and Pan-American copyright conventions. Published in the United States of America by Woodbine House, Inc., 6510 Bells Mill Rd., Bethesda, MD 20817. 800-843-7323. www.woodbinehouse.com

Library of Congress Cataloging-in-Publication Data

Packer, Leslie E.
  Challenging kids, challenged teachers : teaching students with Tourette's, bipolar disorder, executive dysfunction, OCD, ADHD, and more / Leslie E. Packer & Sheryl K. Pruitt.
      p. cm.
  Includes bibliographical references and index.
  ISBN 978-1-890627-82-9 (alk. paper)
  1. Children with disabilities--Education--Handbooks, manuals, etc. 2. Inclusive education--United States. 3. Special education--United States. I. Pruitt, Sheryl K., 1944- II. Title.
  LC1201.P34 2010
  371.94--dc22
                                                                              2010011921

Manufactured in the United States of America

10 9 8 7 6 5 4 3 2 1

List of Figures

List of Tables

Acknowledgements

When we first set out to learn about the disorders discussed in this book in terms of their impact on school functioning, there were no textbooks to guide us. Thankfully, we had some wonderful teachers in our quest for understanding and many wonderful colleagues who shared their own expertise.

The children we have raised and the children we have worked with in our professional capacities were our first, and best, teachers. By sharing their frustrations, their hopes, and their dreams, they inspire us on a daily basis to increase awareness of the challenges they face and to identify meaningful and effective supports for them in the classroom. Special thanks to Jason Valencia for allowing us to reproduce his writing on rage attacks, to Devorah for letting us share her triumph in overcoming her challenges, and to "Nicole" for sharing the pain of her OCD. We are also grateful to the many parents and teachers we have worked with over the years for sharing their experiences, strategies, and insights, and for their enthusiastic support of our efforts to educate educators.

Many colleagues also generously shared their expertise with us: Robbyn Laufer, OTR/L and Emily Venable, OTR/L contributed to our understanding of sensory processing disorder and sensory integration issues; Rosamond Gianutsos, Ph.D., CDRS, FAAO provided feedback on an early draft of the memory chapter; Warren Walter, Ph.D. provided feedback on the chapter on Asperger's Syndrome and Nonverbal Learning Disability; Florence Cannon, M.S., CCC-SLP and Danielle Moore, M.S.,Ed., CCC-SLP clarified some of the language issues; and Janice Papolos reviewed the chapter on mood disorders. Some of the material in this book reflects earlier contributions to our understanding by Marilyn P. Dornbush, Ph.D.

and Warren Walter, Ph.D. who influenced Sherry's understanding of memory issues; Sharon Cargill, CCC-SLP, who expanded our understanding of how language difficulties affect academics and described helpful strategies; Mary Kay Jennings who contributed to strategies for assisting students with reading problems; and Colleen Wang, R.N., who contributed to some of the materials in the chapter on "storms." We also wish to thank those who read sections of the book and provided their feedback: Steve Berger, Ph.D., Gayle Born, M.Ed., Mary Jane Trotti, M.A., ET/P, and Kellie Gilpin. If we have forgotten to name any of the many people who helped us, please forgive our forgetfulness and accept our sincere thanks for your contribution. Despite our colleagues' best efforts, we may have made errors in our writing; those errors are solely ours.

We would also like to thank Jewell McClure and Judi Anderson of Parkaire Consultants for assisting us in so many ways, including cheerfully helping us stay on schedule.

Our husbands, Joe Hopke and Dan Pruitt, not only provided their encouragement and support throughout the long process of writing and editing this book, but also donated their talents and provided many of the graphics and illustrations used in this book. Our children's friends also encouraged us in their own ways, and we are grateful to Nicole Sclair for kindly providing the illustration of the brain that appears in Chapter 1.

Finally, special thanks to Woodbine House, for sharing our vision of what this book might be, and, in particular, to our editor, Beth Walker, for her tremendous enthusiasm, helpful feedback, and dedication to this project.

Making Sense of Chaos

*We must be willing to let go of the life we have
planned, so as to have the life that is waiting for us.*
—Joseph Campbell

Both of the authors have been on long journeys, as mothers and as professionals. This book was inspired by our stories.

Sherry's Story

When I got married, I dreamed of having a family and enjoying all the wonderful experiences that go with raising children. I thought about establishing traditions, family get-togethers, holidays, and wonderful vacations. And, of course, I dreamed about well-behaved children. Being a teacher in a psychoeducational setting and a behaviorist specializing in violent teenagers, I thought it would be a cinch to raise my own well-behaved children.

My sons were adorable, but even as young boys, they had some odd behaviors. My oldest would repeat actions that were not productive, like jumping off of the same piece of furniture even though he got hurt every time. Nothing would stop him. I also noticed that my children would only wear certain clothes. My attempts to put them in other clothes led to crying and screaming meltdowns. My younger son took two hours in the morning to put on his socks. He'd scream and cry the whole time because he could not get his sock seams lined up evenly inside his shoes and refused to go to school until he could. This "sock seam syndrome" as we called it was only the tip of the iceberg. After this daily ordeal, we would go down to breakfast where the toast might accidentally touch the eggs and the meltdowns

would begin again. Normal everyday events became dreaded times in our household.

School was a major source of stress for us. The teachers did not understand why the boys were late to school and why homework was not done. I would try to explain that we decided to save the younger sibling from his older brother's "storms." I know that she wanted the homework, but she had no idea what was going on in our home every night. As parents, we considered ourselves lucky just to maintain the safety of our family, our relationship with each other, and keep the house intact. As a teacher, I had never dreamed that homework would become such a low priority for us, but living in our house required us to triage situations like in an emergency room.

School personnel were not the only ones who did not understand. Family, neighbors, and friends were right there beside them. Relatives would not invite us to family occasions, and if they did, they would continually make editorial comments on our parenting. Looking back, we can now appreciate the fact that our children got rid of all the relatives we did not like, but at the time it was extremely painful and my dreams for traditions and family get-togethers fell by the wayside. Friends fell away too. Suddenly, we were isolated.

I tried to get professional help. In 1973, Tourette's Syndrome (TS) was not being diagnosed in most parts of the country unless the child was cursing, Attention Deficit Hyperactivity Disorder (ADHD) was not being diagnosed in gifted children, and neither Obsessive-Compulsive Disorder (OCD) nor depression were being diagnosed in children. Researchers had not even thought about Executive Dysfunction. So we went through my boys' childhood years without a diagnosis or effective treatment. Then came their teenage years. Everything you can imagine happened and more. I learned things I never thought I would learn, like the response time of the fire department in my county. Although I can look back now and laugh at some of what happened, at the time, there was very little laughter in our family.

We also suffered financially. I was a teacher and my husband was a carpenter. No diagnosis meant no insurance coverage and we spent most of our money going from doctor to doctor, trying to get answers and help.

When the boys were in their late teens, we finally found out what disorders had been wreaking havoc with their lives and our family. We found the disability associations that supported families in our situation. We made new friends who understood what we were going through. My sons were incredibly thankful to meet others who were experiencing the same symptoms and behaviors. They were relieved to learn that it was a medical condition—they were not bad or crazy. We were also thrilled to find out what was causing our sons' behaviors and to learn that we were not responsible for causing all of their problems. The families that we met became our closest friends and allies in a battle that had been a lonely uphill effort. I can never thank enough all of these individuals who supported us and affirmed us and made our family feel whole again.

Now I sit in my office at our clinic where parents come in with out-of-control kids and those who exhibit strange behaviors, and have the privilege of helping them through diagnosis and treatment. It is a joy to know that they do not have to go through much of what our family did.

Leslie's Story

There are some dates that I will always remember. My son's seventh birthday is one of them because on that day our lives changed forever.

My son's development had been amazing in the early years. He taught himself to read by age two and a half, and he was sensitive and polite. But by the time he was to enter nursery school, he had started doing some strange things. I still remember how his nursery school teacher called me to say that she was concerned because he kept throwing

things up in the air and when they came down, they were landing on the other children's heads. "Oh," I replied, trying desperately to believe that this was voluntary, "he's probably testing the law of gravity." But his strange behaviors continued and he couldn't seem to control them.

One night, shortly before his seventh birthday, we were out to dinner in a restaurant. As we sat there, my son suddenly started bringing both of his hands up to his face, sniffing his fingers and then licking them. My husband said "Stop it!" But our son could not stop it, and he dove under the table so that no one could see that he had to sniff and lick his fingers. Later, he told me that something in his head told him that if he did not lick his fingers, he would die. His anxiety was heartbreaking, and the next day I made an appointment with a psychiatrist.

So, there we were in an eminent psychiatrist's office on my son's seventh birthday. By the end of the appointment, not only was my son diagnosed with TS and ADHD, but my husband was also diagnosed with those disorders as well as OCD, and two other relatives were diagnosed in absentia. Within two hours, my family had gone from being "normal" to one with numerous diagnoses. My dream for my child's perfect future was shattering. As rough as it was on me emotionally, I think it was even worse for my husband. He had never been diagnosed as a child, and had had no explanation for his own peculiar behavior or his mother's demanding personality. So there he was trying to understand that he had several disorders, and worse, that he had passed them on to his son who was now suffering. The guilt was something that would continue to haunt him and would only get worse as our children's problems increased.

Eventually, my son would also be diagnosed with OCD. The severity of his ADHD, TS, and OCD would make it impossible for him to function in a regular classroom, despite his teachers' best efforts. But because he was gifted, there were no self-contained special education programs that were suitable for him, and so we wound up in federal court a few years later to get the state or district to create a program that was appropriate for him and others like him. We prevailed, but the fight to get our son the program he needed, coupled with the stress of trying to find effective treatment for him, took a toll on all of us—exhaustion, depression, and financial stress became overwhelming at times.

Then, just as we thought we might be seeing the light at the end of the tunnel, problems started to escalate with our daughter, who, up until then had been our "easy" child. In relatively short order, she went from being an honors student, second degree black belt in martial arts, and all-around "good kid" with mild TS and some OCD and anxiety issues to a "mean-as-a-snake" adolescent. I barely recognized her as my own child. She would steal, scream, storm, and in between, cry in my arms and tell me that she had no idea why she was doing these things. And so at five thirty one morning, after being up all night again trying to keep her in the house so she didn't go out and get into a dangerous situation, we called 911. She was hospitalized for almost two months in a locked psychiatric ward, and came out with a diagnosis of Bipolar Disorder to add to the list. Sitting outside that locked ward the day she was admitted and hearing the staff trying to subdue her was the worst day of our lives.

By then, it had been a decade since we had started on our bumpy road to understanding and helping our children cope with their challenges. Along the way, my husband and I lost touch with many of our friends, because their children were "normal." Some of our friends did not understand that it was easier for us to just stay home. We dreaded outings and family get-togethers because we did not know how the kids would behave or what others might say about our kids' behavior.

But that day, back in 1989, when I didn't know what lay ahead for us, I knew that educators generally didn't know much about my son's disorders and that if I did not try to get answers myself, no one else would. And so I became involved with the local chapter of the Tourette Syndrome Association and started spending most of my time trying to learn about TS so that I could help my son's teachers help him. I made a new circle of supportive friends and eventually changed my entire professional practice to focus on treating and helping children and teenagers with TS and associated disorders.

From Chaos to Awareness

It took both of us many years, but we were eventually able to make some sense of the chaos that was our children's lives. And one of the most important things we both independently realized was that teachers need support if they are to help our children. The other thing we both independently realized was that having a wacky sense of humor or developing one was one of the best coping mechanisms we could have as parents. Nowadays, when we conduct parent workshops and teacher workshops, we often tell stories about the children we have raised or the ones we see professionally, and the parents roar with laughter. Sometimes teachers may find our humor a bit surprising or irreverent because we say out loud what parents often feel but are afraid to tell them. But saying these things out loud helps parents understand that they are not alone in their frustration and that as much as we love our children, there are days that really test our patience with them.

When a child has a neurological disorder, it affects the child, it affects the family, it affects the peers, and it affects the child's teacher. But out of all those affected, it is the parents and teachers, working together, who hold the most promise of creating the kind of supportive environment and program that enable our children and students to succeed. Yes, we need great doctors who are dedicated to helping them, but on a day-to-day basis, it is the parents and teachers who can make or break a child's day—every day.

We hope that this book will help educators recognize and become more aware of what their students and families are experiencing. But from firsthand experience, we know that awareness is not enough, and so the greatest portion of this book is devoted to providing practical tools and strategies for teaching these challenging kids in the classroom.

While we try to teach our children all about life,
our children teach us what life is all about.
— Angela Schwindt

PART I

Foundations for Success

*Confusion is a word we have invented for an
order which is not yet understood.*
— Henry Miller

Overview

The disorders described in this book each have their own symptoms and often occur together. Our challenge is to help students by effectively addressing the overwhelming array of symptoms and disorders each individual exhibits—different symptoms at different times, different disorders at different times, different…everything. In Part I, we create a foundation for understanding and teaching students with neurological disorders. In Chapter 1, we help educators view the often confusing array of disorders within a neurological framework that helps explain why these students may have so many problems. In Chapter 2, we talk about what "behavior" means and how school personnel may need to reframe their thinking and language in approaching behaviors that are usually neurological symptoms and not intentional misbehavior. In Chapter 3, we provide what we call our "sanity-saving premises" for educating students with disorders that fall within this framework. By understanding and accepting these premises, teachers can avoid wasting a lot of time and energy questioning why things are the way they are, and have more energy to help the student.

Key to Acronyms in this Book

Disorders:
- ADHD: Attention Deficit Hyperactivity Disorder
- AS: Asperger's Syndrome
- ASD: Autism Spectrum Disorder
- BP: Bipolar Disorder
- CD: Conduct Disorder
- DCD: Developmental Coordination Disorder
- EBD: Emotional and Behavioral Disorder
- EDF: Executive Dysfunction
- GAD: Generalized Anxiety Disorder
- LD: Learning Disability
- NLD: Nonverbal Learning Disability
- OCD: Obsessive-Compulsive Disorder
- ODD: Oppositional Defiant Disorder
- PANDAS: Pediatric Autoimmune Neuropsychiatric Disorders Associated with Streptococcal infections
- PITANDS: Pediatric Infection-Triggered Autoimmune Neuropsychiatric Disorders
- PTSD: Post-Traumatic Stress Disorder
- SAD: Separation Anxiety Disorder
- SPD: Sensory Processing Disorder
- TBI: Traumatic Brain Injury
- TS: Tourette's Syndrome
- VMI: Visual-Motor Integration

Other Acronyms:
- BIP: Behavior Intervention Plan
- BOLO: Be On the Look Out for
- CBT: Coginitive-Behavior Therapy
- FBA: Functional Behavioral Assessment
- IEP: Individual Educational Program
- IQ: Intelligence Quotient
- OT: Occupational Therapy or Occupational Therapist
- PE: Physical Education

"Why Do Some Students Have So Many Problems?" and Other Mysteries of Life that Used to Keep Us Up at Night

What we actually learn from any given set of circumstances determines whether we become increasingly powerless or more powerful.
—Blaine Lee

As we described in the preface, our own children have numerous disorders and challenges, as do most of the children we see in our professional capacities. Despite all of their problems as children or teens, many go on to live happy and productive lives as adults. Indeed, our children and patients often tell us how having so many problems has made them more sensitive to the needs of others. But *why* do some children have two, three, four, or more conditions or challenges? There really is a reason....

Why Do Some Students Have So Many Problems?

Seasoned educators and school personnel may have already encountered students who have more than one neurological diagnosis. Although some students truly have one—and only one—disorder or challenge, the majority of children have more than one problem. And as the number of challenges increases, the student's school-related problems increase exponentially. Part of the explanation for this is that some conditions appear to be genetically or neurologically linked. For example, Tourette's Syndrome (TS) and Obsessive-Compulsive Disorder (OCD) often appear together in families. We also know that OCD and anxiety disorders "go together," and that Attention Deficit Hyperactivity Disorder (ADHD) and tics "go together." So it is not really surprising that a particular student might have tics, OCD, anxiety disorders, and ADHD.

To capture the idea of multiple diagnoses, think of blowing bubbles using a bubble wand. The bubbles may come out one at a time, but usually there is some amount of overlap with other bubbles (or in this case, disorders), as shown in Figure 1.1.

Figure 1.1. Overlapping Disorders

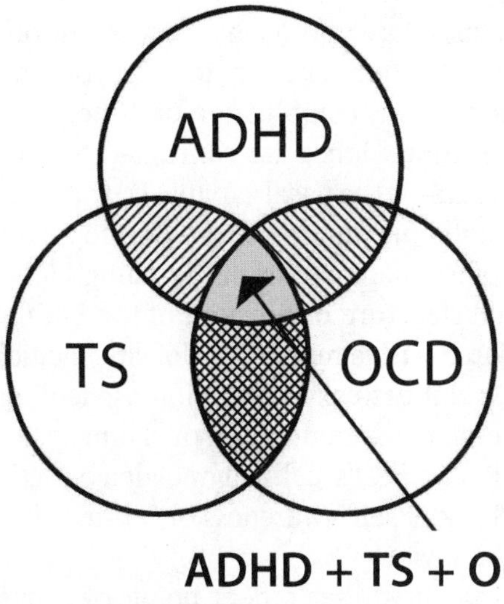

ADHD

TS   OCD

ADHD + TS + OCD

Some neurological disorders overlap, like soap bubbles. In this example, a subset of children who have Tourette's Syndrome (TS) also have features of Obsessive-Compulsive Disorder (OCD). Others have TS with Attention Deficit Hyperactivity Disorder (ADHD), and some children have all three.

Figure 1.2. Brain Structures

The frontal lobes of the brain are involved in attention, memory, executive functions, motor control, and emotional control. The basal ganglia structures connect to each other and are involved in a number of pathways that involve the frontal lobes.

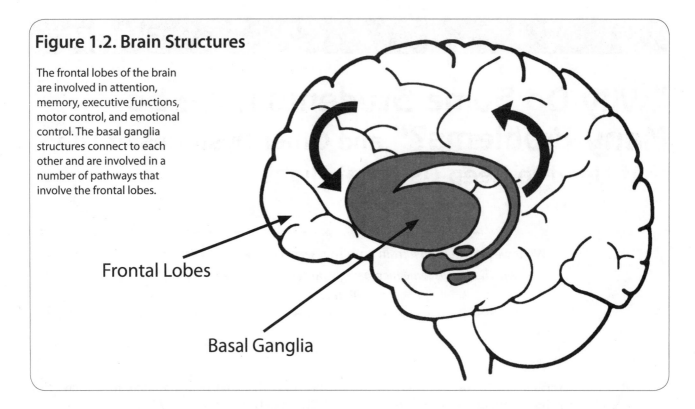

Frontal Lobes

Basal Ganglia

Brain Overview: Neuro Lite

The brain plays a role in this co-occurrence of disorders. The frontal lobes of the brain (Figure 1.2) are involved in memory, selective attention, and executive functions as well as motor control and emotional regulation. In fact, the frontal lobes are involved in every single psychiatric disorder. This helps to explain why students with a neurological disorder may have problems with attention, memory, executive functions, motor control, emotional regulation, or any combination of these.

The frontal lobes are connected to a group of structures called the basal ganglia. Dysfunction in the basal ganglia may interrupt the development or execution of normal motor skills, learning, or behavior. Abnormal structure or function of the basal ganglia is associated with a number of deficits, including:

- Inability to experience intense feelings of embarrassment, guilt, or shame
- Becoming "stuck" on one idea or activity
- Lack of self-awareness or self-monitoring of behavior
- Inability to see others' points of view
- Impairment of range of subtle emotions
- Difficulty in prioritizing tasks
- Difficulty in handling simultaneous stimuli
- Difficulty in controlling movement
- Difficulty in inhibiting responses

- Impaired visual imagery leading to impaired motor performance

If a student has one basal ganglia disorder, they are likely to have other disorders that also involve the basal ganglia. Figure 1.3 indicates disorders that involve the basal ganglia.

Almost all of the disorders described in detail in this book have been linked to dysfunction in the basal ganglia or pathways involving the frontal lobes and basal ganglia. School personnel need to screen any student with disorders that involve the basal ganglia for other basal ganglia disorders, and to remain alert to the possibility that symptoms of other basal ganglia disorders may emerge during the school year. In some cases, the school may need to refer the student to the district's psychiatrist or a neurologist to clarify the student's diagnoses.

Are These Conditions Inherited?

Research on the genetics of some of these disorders is still in its infancy, but it is clear that at least some disorders have significant genetic components. For example, ADHD is more heritable than IQ and almost as heritable as height (Banerjee, Middleton, and Faraone 2007; McLoughlin et al. 2007). Similar-

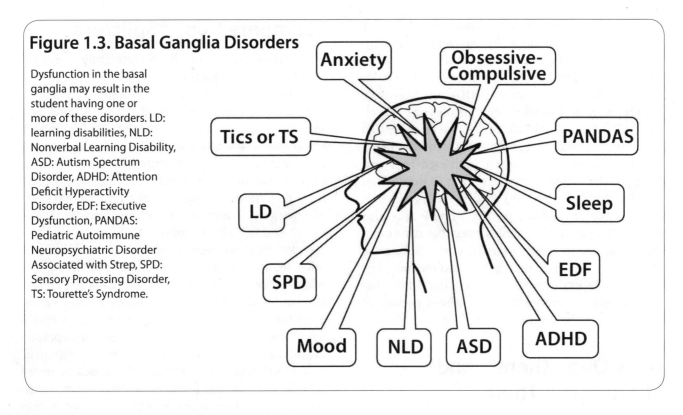

Figure 1.3. Basal Ganglia Disorders

Dysfunction in the basal ganglia may result in the student having one or more of these disorders. LD: learning disabilities, NLD: Nonverbal Learning Disability, ASD: Autism Spectrum Disorder, ADHD: Attention Deficit Hyperactivity Disorder, EDF: Executive Dysfunction, PANDAS: Pediatric Autoimmune Neuropsychiatric Disorder Associated with Strep, SPD: Sensory Processing Disorder, TS: Tourette's Syndrome.

ly, research indicates that Bipolar Disorder (BP) has significant genetic influences (Kieseppa et al. 2004) as does TS (Pauls et al. 1986).

If the student inherited a problem from a parent, the parent may not be able to remediate the problem without the school's assistance.

Not all cases of a particular disorder are inherited. In some cases, students may acquire certain problems due to prenatal or postnatal factors such as:

- head injury
- maternal smoking during pregnancy
- labor complications
- illness/infection
- medication reactions
- trauma

- toxins in the environment

Although the environment does not cause most of the disorders discussed in this book, environmental factors can exacerbate (worsen) symptoms. In some cases, environmental conditions or events may even induce or trigger disorders such as anxiety disorders in biologically vulnerable children.

Different Disorders Emerge at Different Times

Some disorders appear before the age of seven, but other disorders emerge in adolescence or even later. Disorders usually emerge at specific ages, as shown in Figure 1.4, but even then, there is variation.

Figure 1.4. Age of Disorder Emergence

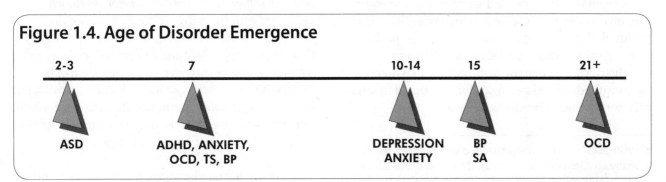

Modified from a presentation by J. Walkup, M.D., 2006. See text for explanation.

Symptoms of Autism Spectrum Disorder (ASD) are usually apparent by age two to three. Autism Spectrum Disorders include Autistic Disorder, Asperger's Syndrome (AS), Rett Syndrome, Childhood Disintegrative Disorder (CDD), and Pervasive Developmental Disorder—Not Otherwise Specified (PDD-NOS).* ADHD, anxiety disorders such as separation anxiety disorder, OCD, and tics or TS usually emerge by age seven (although they can emerge later). Mood disorders, such as depression and Bipolar Disorder (BP) tend to emerge in pre-adolescence or adolescence. OCD or BP may also emerge during or after adolescence, but can sometimes emerge in the pre-school years. Substance abuse (SA) generally emerges in adolescence, but may emerge earlier or later. Knowing when disorders tend to emerge can help school personnel know what to "be on the look out" for.

Look Over There...and There...and There

When two or more disorders appear to be linked to each other somehow, we say that they are associated disorders, i.e., they go together. Some disorders may not be genetically or neurologically linked, but may just both be present at the same time. These are called comorbid disorders. For example, a student with TS may also have diabetes, but these conditions are not necessarily associated. For that student, diabetes and TS are comorbid conditions. Although some professionals use the terms "associated disorders" and "comorbid disorders" interchangeably, we do not.

From an educational standpoint, the school team needs to apply an "If ➔ Then" approach, as in, "If the student has disorder A" then we need to be on the look out for or screen for disorder B and any other disorder known to be associated with disorder A. Screening for associated disorders may require the involvement of the school psychologist, occupational therapist, speech and language pathologist, or other school professionals. In some cases, the district's psychiatrist or physician may need to be consulted. Associated disorders are noted in later chapters as each disorder is reviewed.

---

* While PDD is the term currently used in the DSM-IV, the currently accepted umbrella term used by parents and educators is "Autism Spectrum Disorder," or ASD. We think it is best to stick with what most readers know.

"Lumpers" vs. "Splitters"

Professionals may have conflicting opinions about whether something is really part of a particular disorder or not. As one example, TS is a tic disorder but a lot of people with TS also have obsessions and compulsions. Are the obsessions and compulsions actually part of TS, or do they simply represent an associated feature? Similarly, tics and compulsions are often present in students with Asperger's Syndrome, but are they an inherent part of Asperger's Syndrome or are they associated features? And why does it matter?

We refer to those professionals who include other features as "part of" a disorder as "lumpers," while we refer to those who separately list conditions or features as "splitters." A professional who is a "lumper" might diagnose a student with Asperger's Syndrome without making additional or separate diagnoses of tic disorder and compulsions, whereas a "splitter" would list separate diagnoses or mention them as specific features. Same student, same symptoms, but the student may have one diagnosis if evaluated by a "lumper" vs. three or four diagnoses if evaluated by a "splitter."

In our opinion, "splitting" is more likely to lead to more effective treatment plans. Splitting is also more informative to teachers as it provides a more accurate picture of the student's problems that may need accommodations or interventions.

Kyle, a student diagnosed with Asperger's Syndrome, always seemed to get stuck talking about his interest in trains. He also had to have his pencils on his desk lined up in just the right way or he could not work. He had trouble transitioning from one activity to another—he just had to finish his work before he could move on. Kyle's teacher looked in a book and found that all of these behaviors were lumped under Asperger's Syndrome. Kyle's teacher was curious because she had seen some of these behaviors before in students diagnosed with OCD. Kyle's parents discussed the possibility with Kyle's doctor, who then screened Kyle for OCD. Sure enough, Kyle had OCD as well as Asperger's Syndrome, and he was referred for treatment of his OCD. Within a month, Kyle was still stuck on trains, but he was more flexible in terms of being able to transition from one activity to another, and he was able to tolerate objects on his desk not being lined up perfectly.

As suggested above, we are "splitters," and we wish more professionals were "splitters" when writing reports or evaluations for school personnel. How a teacher responds to a symptom or behavioral feature of a disorder in school depends, in large part, on whether the behavior is understood to be a tic, a compulsion, a willful misbehavior, or something else. Calling everything by one name ("It's all part of ___") often does not lead to the development of a successful treatment or educational plan, partly because it assumes that everyone knows all the possible features that can be associated with a single disorder.

"Alphabet Soup" Children

When students are diagnosed using the splitting technique, they wind up with a string of diagnoses, and teachers may be given a list of acronyms such as ADHD, OCD, TS, EDF (Executive Dysfunction), BP, etc. This may be overwhelming for the teacher and for the child and parents. Although we use diagnoses throughout this book (e.g., "If your student has ADHD plus OCD..."), in our conversations with parents, we sometimes avoid the medical terms and instead use kind, gentle humor to reduce their stress, such as describing a child diagnosed with multiple neurological disorders as having "A Little of This, a Little of That Syndrome" (Packer 2002). A kind, humorous approach to discussing these conditions with parents is often effective in communicating the child's neurologically based behavior and can help everyone take the next step in addressing the child's challenges. In our workshops for parents and educators, we talk about such clinical phenomena as "Hole in the Wall Syndrome" (Pruitt 1992) to describe children who have meltdowns and punch holes in walls, "Difficulty Waiting His Turn Syndrome" (Packer 2002), "Sock Seam Syndrome" (Pruitt 1992), "Don't Even THINK About Trying to Wake Me Up in the Morning Syndrome" (Packer 2007), and the "Just Right Syndrome" (Pruitt 1996). These terms are often readily understood by parents and educators who have seen the behavior being described. Also, these "diagnoses" help children accept a disorder and use humor as a coping mechanism.

Why Is There No One-Pill-Fixes-All?

Neurotransmitters are neurochemicals involved in relaying information from one nerve cell (neuron) in the brain to another. The disorders described in this book are associated with neurochemi-cal dysfunction as well as structural abnormalities or differences. For some disorders, we have a good idea which neurochemical is the "culprit." Transmitters that have been implicated in basal ganglia-related disorders include serotonin, dopamine, norepinephrine, and gamma-aminobutyric acid (GABA). Different disorders involve different neurochemicals, though, which is why there is no one medication that effectively treats the symptoms of all of the basal ganglia-related disorders.

To complicate matters even more, medications that make symptoms of one disorder better often make symptoms of another disorder *worse* or may have side effects that will interfere with how the child functions in school. Decisions about medication are agonizing for most parents and they need our support, not judgment or criticism, if they choose not to put their child on medication.

The amount of medication or even number of medications a student may need depends, in part, on how supportive the school environment is.

Keeping Our Eyes on the Future

Sometimes it is easy to get so overwhelmed by a student's current symptoms that we forget to inquire about the student's ability to independently perform activities of daily living (ADL). School personnel may not even know that a student still needs excessive reminders to wake up in the morning, to follow good hygiene, and to take medication. Good grades in school will not translate into independent living and success after high school unless the child has ADL skills. Parents and school staff need to review and consider the student's ability to function independently in nonacademic tasks as well as academic ones.

In the U.S., federal education law requires school districts to consider transition supports and services for students age sixteen and older. Some states require such consideration even earlier. In our experience, we have found that if a student has deficits in independent functioning, it may take *years* for them to acquire compensatory strategies. For that reason, we recommend considering transition issues even with elementary school students so that training and supports start early.

We have included a Transition Checklist (Appendix A and on the accompanying CD-ROM) to help parents and school personnel keep an eye on the future. During any annual review of the student's program and services, complete the checklist to determine if additional ADL-related goals and related services need to be incorporated in the student's plan. Although the student may not be ready to work on certain skills, the plan can indicate when those skills will be included in any planning.

Summary

Many children have more than one neurological issue, so if school personnel see symptoms of one condition or disorder, they should be on the look out for other disorders that often co-occur. A comprehensive screening requires an interdisciplinary school-based team. Remember that the student's symptoms may change from year to year and that new disorders may emerge that will also require consideration.

Adversity causes some men to break,
others to break records.
—William A. Ward

CHAPTER 2

What Do You Mean by "Behavior?"*

A word is not a crystal, transparent and unchanging; it is the skin of a living thought and may vary greatly in color and content according to the circumstances and time in which it is used.
—*Oliver Wendell Holmes*

Chapter 33 describes several pitfalls in school-home communication and strategies to promote better support and collaboration, but there is one little word—"behavior"—that deserves its own chapter at the outset of this book. That one word is the basis for much misunderstanding between parents and teachers, and this is reflected in the fact that one of the most frequent questions we get from parents and school personnel is, "How do I know if this is a symptom or a behavior?"

Would thinking of a particular behavior as a "neurological symptom" change our reaction to the behavior? If the word behavior is referenced by describing it as involuntary, as opposed to voluntary, would our approach to the behavior change? The bottom line is that how something is labeled often influences how we approach it. And in this case, the implications of language—specifically as it relates to the use of the word "symptom" as opposed to "behavior"—are significant for many people.

When someone asks "Is this behavior or a symptom?" the question implies:

- That behavior is either voluntary behavior or an involuntary symptom.
- That it is even possible for us to know with certainty whether something is one or the other, and
- That behaviors are voluntary or intentional and symptoms are not.

"It's Either a Behavior or a Symptom"

One of the greatest roadblocks to helping the student is that the parents and educators have a different understanding of the student's behavior. Parents often believe, and are frequently correct, that the behavior is actually a neurological symptom. For example, consider the situation in which a student seems to be imitating the teacher's vocalizations. The teacher and other school personnel might contact the parent and indicate that this behavior is disrespectful and that they want to target it for change. The school personnel have not necessarily indicated that they believe that the behavior is willful, but that is what the parent is likely to believe the teachers think. So the parent may respond, "You cannot do that—his imitating is echolalia (a neurological symptom)."

Were school personnel wrong in calling the imitation a behavior? No. But it really does not matter whether they were right or wrong. What matters is that the school personnel are now off to a poor start in terms of enlisting parental support for a proposed plan. And all because the word "behavior" seems to be interpreted differently by parents and school personnel and has different implications. Many parents (the authors included) have likely been burned many

---

* This chapter includes material previously published electronically as Packer LE: *What Do You Mean by "Behavior?"* on www.tourettesyndrome.net.

times by others assuming that their child's symptom is willful, bad behavior. When a teacher talks about targeting "behavior," it sets off alarm bells for many parents. In this case, the definition of terms becomes critically important: *Behavior is simply anything that the student does that can be observed or recorded.* It is as simple as that.

Calling something a behavior does not imply that it is necessarily voluntary or willful misbehavior. But the reality is that if school personnel refer to something as behavior, parents will frequently interpret that to mean that the school is implying it is voluntary, is looking to punish it, and the school has no clue about their child's disability.

When communicating with parents, it is crucial that a teacher alleviate the parents' concern as to the judgment that can accompany the word "behavior."

Consider a simple strategy school personnel can use to address this:

When contacting a parent about any behavior of concern, simply introduce the topic by saying something like, "Johnny is having some difficulty in school because he frequently imitates what his peers say and do and they are getting annoyed with him. I realize that imitating may not be a voluntary behavior on his part, but it is certainly causing social difficulties for him, and we would like to speak with you to see if we can come up with some plan to help him."

Notice what the teacher in that hypothetical example does and does not do. The teacher does:

- Provide a short objective verbal description of the behavior.
- Briefly describe the impact of the behavior on the student and others.
- Acknowledge that it may not be a willful misbehavior and that the behavior might be a symptom of the student's disability.

In our example, the teacher does not:

- Express any frustration with the behavior or convey the impact of the student's behavior on the teacher.
- Suggest that the behavior has any voluntary component to it.
- Suggest any negative consequences for the behavior.

- Suggest that the teacher totally understands the behavior.

By approaching the parent in this manner, school personnel are more likely to enlist parental support and the kind of genuine problem solving approach that is often needed.

"We Can Determine Whether the Behavior is Voluntary or Not"

Suppose that we could make a determination that a behavior is voluntary or involuntary. Does that mean if the behavior is judged voluntary, we use consequences to change it, whereas if it is viewed as involuntary, we take a different approach?

School personnel often make the mistake of applying consequences to behaviors that are not likely to be successfully modified by simple rewards and punishments (Packer 2005; DeBonis, Ylvisaker, and Kundert 2000; Burd and Kerbeshian 1992). As a result, we tend to be very cautious when we hear school personnel indicating any firm belief that a behavior is "definitely intentional" or "attention-seeking," because all too often, such pronouncements are followed by plans involving unpleasant consequences. We tend to be equally cautious when we hear parents making strong statements such as "This is a symptom!" because we hope that they are not suggesting that schools should ignore behaviors that interfere with the learning environment.

Even if a behavior is a symptom, it may require school-based intervention. But not all school-based interventions involve consequences. Asking "Is it voluntary or not?" does not lead to the best solutions. Considering all of the factors that contribute to behavior (Chapter 25) and conducting a Functional Behavioral Assessment (Chapter 26) are more productive.

"If it is 'Behavior,' Then My Child and I Both Have Some Responsibility (and Guilt)"

For many parents, learning that their child has a disorder is both a relief and a source of fear, grief, and guilt. Parents are relieved to have a name and an explanation for why their child is acting this way, and they are relieved their child's misbehavior is not a reflection on their parenting skills. But, they may also feel guilty for all the times they may have punished the child for behaviors that they now understand are part of the disorder.

Having discovered that the child has a neurological problem, parents may become very protective, as these kids are often ridiculed for their symptoms or asked to suppress symptoms that may be impossible for them to suppress. Parents are instinctively trying to protect their child from a system that tends to punish departures from set expectations for how children are to behave. Some parents, however, may go too far and not want to have any consequences for their child's behavior.

Perhaps one of the "down sides" of having a child medically diagnosed is that the parent may come to believe that because this is a neurological condition, the child cannot control very much of his behavior. As a direct consequence, the parent may stop trying to discipline the child at all for fear that the child's symptoms will become worse. Sometimes the notion of accepting the child gets taken to the extreme. In such situations, parents have essentially waived all of the rules and expectations in their home and are urging the school to do the same for behavior they view as totally involuntary or beyond the child's ability to control. Parents and teachers can become polarized in their understanding or explanation of the student's behavior and polarized over the question of whether there should be any consequences for the behavior.

Disagreement over the nature (voluntary or involuntary) of the student's behavior is the single biggest source of conflict and dispute between parents of children with neurological conditions and school personnel—as well as within families themselves.

We all recognize that we do not want to be punitive about something that the student cannot control. That does not mean, however, that we ignore behaviors that are problematic. But, keep in mind, that parents are more inclined to acknowledge that something needs to be addressed when they are not anxious that their child will be punished for a symptom that the child cannot control.

It is important for school personnel to help the parent understand what skills are necessary for the child to become an independent adult. Doing homework, being well-behaved, and socializing appropriately are three foundation skills for a happy and successful adult.

When we conduct workshops, we use a three-ring analogy (Pruitt 1996) where the inner circle is the home, the middle circle is the school, and the outer ring is the courts. We often tell parents that if they do not address a problematic symptom or behavior in the home, and if they do not allow the school to address it, the courts will address it.

To reiterate: If a student's behavior is causing significant problems for the student or others, then it needs to be addressed. Parents and school personnel can avoid arguing over nonproductive questions such as whether something is a symptom or not by focusing on the more important question of whether they agree that the behavior is not in the student's best interest, and if so, how they can best remediate it.

As we will discuss, many of the behaviors school personnel grapple with in the classroom really are neurological symptoms. Thinking of them as symptoms and approaching them as symptoms is more likely to be effective than thinking of them as wholly voluntary behaviors. Once we accept that—and accepting that can save us a lot of wasted strategies and conflicts with parents—then instead of first trying to change what the student does, we will be prepared to think more proactively about what we can do to prevent or minimize the symptom frequency or severity. By changing how we think about our students' behavior, by learning about the students' disorders and incorporating the kind of helpful accommodations and supports described in Parts II and III of this book, by creating a classroom that meets the needs of more students, and by changing the way in which we communicate with parents, we can eliminate most behavior problems and make our lives a lot easier. In the next chapter, we describe some assumptions that will serve teachers well when teaching students with neurological disorders.

Everyone thinks of changing the world, but no one thinks of changing himself.
— *Leo Tolstoy*

CHAPTER 3

Seven Sanity-Saving Premises for Educators

A person who has a cat by the tail knows a whole lot more about cats than someone who has just read about them.
— *Mark Twain*

We have developed seven premises for teachers and other school personnel that can help prevent wasted time and energy, and just may help preserve sanity:

1. Expect the student to have more than one problem (the Comorbidity Principle).
2. Expect other members of the family to have problems (the Inheritance Principle).
3. Assume the student wants to do well (the Assume Good Intent Principle).
4. Assume that we only see the tip of the iceberg (the We Don't Know the Half of It Principle).
5. Expect that what goes up must come down (the Variability Principle).
6. Expect the unexpected (the Outside the Box Principle).
7. Plan to change the environment before trying to change the student (the We Go First Principle).

1. The Comorbidity Principle: Comorbidity Is the Rule, Not the Exception

Teachers and other school personnel can safely expect that a student with one basal ganglia disorder will have symptoms of other basal ganglia disorders sooner or later. The corollaries of the comorbidity principle are:

Screen for Other Problems or Associated Disorders

For each disorder described in this book, note the list of associated conditions to be on the look out for (BOLO). By screening for associated disorders, school personnel are more likely to identify other problems that may contribute significantly to the student's school-related problems. A complete BOLO Guide is provided in Appendix B and on the accompanying CD-ROM.

Prioritize Problems and Goals

When a student has multiple challenges, the one that is most noticeable or most annoying may not be the student's biggest problem, academically. For example, a student's vocal tics may distract you while you teach, but that does not mean that they need to be targeted for intervention first—if at all. Other problems (e.g., the student's handwriting difficulties) may be a great source of frustration and underproductivity for the student and might need to be targeted first.

We use a three-pronged test to determine whether to target a problem for school intervention:

1. Is the problem the student's biggest source of interference academically, behaviorally, or socially?
2. Is this the hill I'm willing to die on?
3. Will anyone else be on that hill with me?

A student was at risk of failing a state-mandated mathematics test required for high school graduation. The math teacher contacted his mother to explain that her son knew the material but was refusing to show his work, leading to loss of points. After weeks of locking horns with the student, the teacher was ready to give up. "This is not the hill I want to die on," he told the mother.

Because her son's refusal to show his work was jeopardizing his high school graduation, the mother asked the teacher to set up a meeting that included her son, and assured the teacher that she would be on that hill with him when they tried to address the problem. At the meeting, the teacher listened while the mother asked her son to talk about why he refused to show his work. The teacher realized that the refusal stemmed from test anxiety. Showing his work would slow down his completion of the test and keep him in an anxious state even longer, so the student had refused to write out his work even though he had sufficient time available. The teacher and his mother gave him some strategies to deal with his test anxiety so that he could show all of his work. Thanks to the cooperative effort, the student succeeded, scoring 92% on the state examination.

2. The Inheritance Principle: The Apple Doesn't Fall Far From the Tree

As mentioned in Chapter 1, many of the conditions described in this book run in families. Keep in mind the Inheritance Principle and its corollaries:

These are "No-Fault" Disorders

Just as students can inherit their height, intelligence, athletic, or creative talent from parents, they may also inherit certain challenges. Treating built-in symptoms as willful misbehavior is as effective as someone swinging a chicken over their head three times and expecting the student to change their symptoms because of that.

More Than One Child in the Family May Have Special Needs

Families often have two or more children that inherited the neurological conditions. Although teachers may hope for support from the parents with the child's homework or in organizing the child's belongings, there is a good chance that the parents have other children who also require intense supervision and assistance. The sibling you have in class may actually be the parents' "easier" child! Consider these demands on the parents' energy and time when requesting support from the parents.

Darin's teacher was upset that he had not done his math homework, and contacted his parents to express her frustration that they had not ensured it was done. Darin's mother explained that Darin and his brother had gotten into a serious fight and that she thought it was more important to save the children from hurting each other than to help him with his math homework. Dealing with the boys individually and as a family had taken the entire night and they all had fallen into bed, exhausted, at three o'clock in the morning. Save the children or do the math homework? What is the priority?

One or Both Parents May Have Neurological Challenges

Nathan's teacher did not know the medical diagnosis for it, but he knew that Nathan was terminally disorganized. Nathan could never find his papers, a pencil, or his agenda, and was often late to class. If he did his homework, it would disappear into some black hole on the school bus before he ever got to school. Nathan's homework scores were affecting his grades and the teacher made an appointment with his mother to discuss Nathan's lack of organization. At the appointed time, the teacher was there, but Nathan's mother was not. With a sinking feeling, the teacher wondered if Nathan might have inherited some of his issues from the very parent he had hoped to ask for support.

• • •

A note came home from Jory's teacher, "Please help Jory organize and break down his project into manageable homework assignments so that he does not have to do his project under stress the night before." This teacher was making a tremendous assumption—that the mother's ability to plan, organize, and sequence was intact. But Jory's mother was just like Jory and did not get any diagnosis growing up, much less training or treatment. Jory's mother remarked ruefully, "I wish she had sent home instructions and a model of how to do this. Then we would have had a fighting chance."

Parents help if they can. If a parent is not providing the support needed to help the student, assume that the parent wants to, but that something is interfering. Identify the source(s) of interference and necessary supports to create a more realistic, effective, plan.

In many cases, parents have never been diagnosed or treated for their condition until their child is diagnosed. One of the implications is that the parent(s) may have gone her whole life without knowing what was causing her own issues and now suddenly discovers that she has a problem, and that her child has inherited it from her. Some parents may react by genuinely denying that their child has a problem, e.g., "I don't see any problem with Juan's behavior—he's just like I was!" And the parent is right. Her child is just like her. They may need some treatment and support to be able to help themselves and their child.

Supporting the parent in service of the child can make the difference between a successful plan for the student and one that looks good on paper but fails to achieve the desired goals. Some parents may benefit if the school psychologist can provide resources for adult-related medical or psychological services, or a referral to a family therapist. Other parents may not need treatment, but they may need the school's guidance and support as to how to help their child in the home when it comes to school-related issues. Many individualized educational plans incorporate weekly counseling or communication sessions between the school and home for two purposes: (1) so that the school personnel can suggest methods to handle homework or school-related issues, and (2) so that school personnel can let the parent know if the child is missing any work that still has to be turned in.

Weekly communication also serves a third and important purpose. Because many families are under extraordinary stress due to one or more family member having these disorders, the whole family may feel like it is under siege. Weekly communication enables the parents to let the school know when the student's symptoms are increasing, or medicine is failing, and when things are becoming overwhelming in the home. This way, school personnel can make necessary adjustments or provide additional support to the student. Chapter 33 provides additional suggestions for building home-school collaboration.

3. The Assume Good Intent Principle: "I Would If I Could, But I Can't, So I Don't"

As we've discussed, one of the most common laments we hear from students and their parents is that school personnel assume that symptoms of neurological conditions are willful misbehavior or that, somehow, the students could do something if they only tried harder or wanted to enough. Here are some direct quotes that children have told us about their sense of self-control:

"I am choosing not to, but my mind is making me!"

"My brain works so fast, that if I don't think about it, it will go on without me."

"How does it feel inside my mind? I feel like a roller coaster without any brakes."

The corollaries of the Assume Good Intent Principle are:

Assume That "She Would If She Could"

As Dr. Ross Greene says, "Children do well if they can. If they can't, it's up to us adults to figure out why so we can help." If we assume that the cause of the problems is a lack of motivation, we focus on arranging incentives instead of instruction. Providing an incentive to learn does not teach skills and will not work if the school does not also provide instruction in the skills, as well as the necessary supports and accommodations. As one common sense example: offering a student a huge reward for neat handwriting will not help if she lacks the necessary graphomotor skills.

Be curious about behavior and do not judge or assume it is willful misbehavior. Our mantra is, "Curiosity, Not Judgment!"

Design and Implement Comprehensive Assessments

The assumption that children "would if they could" changes the mode of thinking toward a functional assessment: Identify the factors contributing to the student's problems so those factors can be addressed. In some cases, it may be that a student has never been taught a skill, e.g., how to make a transition, and that a little direct instruction is all that is needed. In other cases, a comprehensive assessment may identify issues that contribute to the student's stress level in school or previously unrecognized impairments in executive functions (e.g., disorganization) that contribute to academic underproductivity. Chapters 25 and 26 discuss assessments and planning.

4. The We Don't Know the Half of It Principle: We Only See the Tip of the Iceberg

The truth is that no matter how many symptoms are visible in the classroom, we are probably only seeing the tip of the iceberg. What we may not see includes:

- Internal tics
- Sensory urges building up toward a tic
- Obsessive thoughts
- Mental rituals
- Distraction
- Fear or anxiety
- Phobias
- Stress due to effort to suppress overt symptoms
- Embarrassment
- Tingling due to panic attacks
- Feelings that the mind is jumping around
- Feelings that thoughts are racing
- Sensory overreactivity, e.g., overreaction to light touch or noise

We also may not see or learn about what is going on in the home. Many parents do not tell teachers what is really going on for fear that the teacher will think poorly of them. By taking the time to build a supportive relationship with the parent, school personnel may discover how much the family needs the school's support and assistance. The corollary of this principle is:

The Child is Usually a Lot More Frustrated with Their Behavior Than We Are

Students may choose to engage in misbehavior and get into trouble rather than acknowledge that they cannot do the work or that they cannot control their symptoms. Many will try to mask their symptoms by incorporating them into something willful,

e.g., disguising a verbal tic as a cough or sneeze. School personnel might be surprised to learn how many students go home and cry or express depression because they cannot be like their peers. The frustration we experience with the student's symptoms is nothing compared to the frustration they are experiencing with themselves.

5. The What Goes Up Must Come Down Principle: Expect Variability

One of the hallmarks of many of these disorders is variability. Educators say things like, "Well, I know she can do it because she did it yesterday. So, why can't she do it today?" The implication is that the student should be able to be consistent in her performance, at least with respect to academics. But the reality is that for many students, the amount of interference that they experience from their conditions fluctuates wildly. Some children have a few "bad hair days." The children we work with have *many* "bad neurochemical days!" For some disorders, teachers need to expect significant variability from month to month, week to week, day to day, and, in some cases, hour to hour. And keep in mind that the amount of structure, support, and consistency in classroom routines will affect the ebb and flow.

6. The Expect the Unexpected Principle: These Kids Think Outside the Box

Many of these children and teens have superior IQs, creativity, and flashes of absolute brilliance. Many of them also have an incredible sense of humor. Indeed, many students with the disorders or challenges described in this book "think outside the box." For some students, the explanation is that their creativity is the upside of disinhibition. Others think outside the box because they have no idea where the box is!

7. The Change the Environment First Principle: Change is Good. We Go First!

Even when teachers and other school personnel correctly identify a behavior that needs to be addressed, school-based plans often start with consequences for the behavior. This is not a good place to start. Using behavior techniques first is often the least successful approach to take, and, worse, runs a significant risk of backfiring. Rather than starting with trying to change the student's symptoms or behavior directly by introducing rewards and punishments, start by trying to change the environment. The National Center for Education Evaluation and Regional Assistance found strong research support for modifying the environment to decrease problem behavior (Epstein et al. 2008).

Teachers can use the Classroom Layout Checklist in Appendix C (and on the accompanying CD-ROM) to help plan their classroom, materials, and presentations so that they will meet the needs of many students with neurological disorders. Teachers can also consult chapters on the students' specific disorders to see what other elements will need to be added. Many additional helpful tips on routines that will benefit all students can be found in the chapters on Executive Dysfunction and Written Expression. Remember: The more that is set up in advance that works for more students, the fewer individual accommodations the teacher will need to make, and the fewer different plans will be required in the classroom.

Don't try to fix the students, fix ourselves first. The good teacher makes the poor student good and the good student superior. When our students fail, we, as teachers, too, have failed.
— *Marva Collins*

PART II

Disorders: Awareness, Impact, and Classroom Strategies

If a doctor, lawyer, or dentist had forty people in his office at one time, all of whom had different needs, and some of whom didn't want to be there and were causing trouble, and the doctor, lawyer, or dentist, without assistance, had to treat them all with professional excellence for nine months, then he might have some conception of the classroom teacher's job.

—Donald D. Quinn

Overview

In this section of the book, we describe a number of neurological disorders that may impair a student's academic, behavioral, or social-emotional functioning. But before describing the organization of this section of the book, we begin by introducing a way to communicate with students quickly to determine their availability for instruction and productivity.

Is the Student "Watching His Speed?"

As mentioned in Chapter 3, most of the disorders we describe have a common characteristic that complicates educational planning: variability. Symptoms may come and go (wax and wane), change in their severity, and change in their form (e.g., a student may have an eye tic one week and a vocal tic a few weeks later). To further complicate the student's life and our ability to plan, when disorders co-occur, their symptoms may fluctuate together, other disorders may emerge as time goes on, and the disorder that may be having the greatest impact on the student at the beginning of a school year may not be the disorder that is having the greatest impact on the student later that school year.

Environment as well as genetics affects the severity of many of these disorders. Consider curricular demands and classroom environment as factors affecting the student's symptoms.

For optimal learning and performance to occur, a student needs to be alert, attentive, and relatively calm or "in the zone." A useful analogy is to think of a speedometer on a car: If we are driving too slowly, we are not keeping up with traffic and we may not get to our destination on time. If we are driving at approximately the same speed as other drivers and for the road conditions, we will all arrive at the destination at around the same time as others. If we are driving a bit faster than others, but still driving safely, we will get to the destination a bit sooner. But what if we start driving significantly faster than others, or too fast for the road conditions, or way above the posted speed limits? We run the risks of accidents or speeding tickets, both of which will interfere with our reaching our destination in a timely and safe fashion.

But how does that apply to students with these neurological disorders? Most of the conditions discussed in this book are associated with dysregulated arousal level. Students with arousal dysregulation spend relatively little time in an arousal state that would be optimal for learning and performance. Instead, they spend much of their day either under-aroused or overaroused.

When students are underaroused, they are not sufficiently alert to learn and to perform. Their information processing will seem slower and they will have more difficulty sustaining their attention, initiating, persisting, and completing tasks in a timely fashion. When students are overaroused, their systems are in "overdrive" and they have difficulty thinking clearly. Problem solving is impaired, and the student experiences greater difficulty retrieving information from memory. Not only does academic functioning deteriorate, but so does emotional and social functioning. Overaroused students have a lower tolerance for frustration, more irritability, and are more likely to engage in outbursts or explosive behavior. Anxiety, fatigue, and stress can all exacerbate overarousal, as can other factors such as classroom environments that do not provide enough consistent structure and routine. For students with arousal dysregulation, having a substitute teacher can be anxiety-producing and lead to further dysregulation.

Figure 1 depicts the analogous states. Students who are not up to speed for the task demands are in the lower left zones. The student may be suffering from lack of sleep, experiencing medication side effects such as cognitive dulling, be depressed, or be experiencing symptom interference with learning or performance (such as difficulty initiating due to Executive Dysfunction). Students who are sitting at their desks staring out into space while their peers have gotten started are also in this zone, as would be a student who did not eat any breakfast and is not ready for work. They are

"STALLED" and are not moving forward acquiring new information or performing.

As the student's alertness and ability to function improves, they start to go faster, but may still be in the "DRIVING SLOWLY" zone. They are in a less than optimal state for learning and performance and may not complete tasks on time. Students who experience significant symptom interference (such as tics that interfere with reading or writing) might also be in this zone, as would be students who are so distractible that they cannot sustain their focus long enough to make steady progress.

The third zone represents an alert, attentive student—one who is keeping up with traffic and is in the "DRIVING WELL" zone for learning and performance.

When the student starts to drive faster than his peers or for the task demands, he starts to run a risk. He may be a gifted student or one who can accomplish more at a faster pace, but he may become too impulsive and his performance will deteriorate. This section of the speedometer would correspond to a "CAUTION" zone. Students who are in a hyper-energized or highly impulsive state may spend a lot of time in this zone.

At extremely high speeds, or the "DANGER" zone, the student's performance is usually impaired. This might be the case if a student is so manic or so overaroused that he cannot think, much less settle down to the task. If a task requires self-control and reflection and the student is "speeding," he may work ahead of directions, may miss important details, and may otherwise "crash" or have his engine "explode." Ideally, the student needs to be in the "DRIVING WELL" zone for learning to take place.

To help students grasp the concept of being in the optimal zone, put a speedometer strip such as that shown in Figure 1 on their desks that they can use to indicate to the teacher where they are in the zone. Coloring the bands will also help the student learn the zones, where "STALLED" might be blue, "DRIVING SLOWLY" might be blue-green, "DRIVING WELL" is green, "CAUTION" is yellow, and "DANGER" is red. Ask the students to monitor their own speed. Ask them how fast they are going and reinforce their awareness of their driving speed.

Teachers can also use a driving/speeding image, such as a traffic light, to help discreetly cue the student. A traffic light image with a green light means he's "driving well." One showing a yellow light means "caution" and that it is time to take action to get into the "green zone." And one showing red means "you are in the trouble zone." This visual cue can save a lot

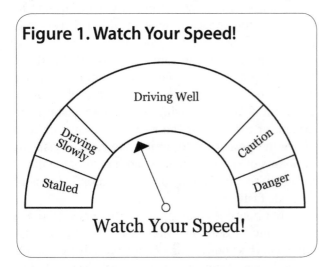

Figure 1. Watch Your Speed!

Driving Well

Driving Slowly

Caution

Stalled

Danger

Watch Your Speed!

Optimal learning and performance requires that the student be driving at the correct speed for task demands.

of words that might otherwise lead to a sensory overload and an increase in overreactive behavior.

Note that although we are trying to encourage students to be in the "DRIVING WELL" zone, there may be times when their symptom interference is so great that despite their best efforts, they will be in the "DRIVING SLOWLY" zone. Educating students about their disorders and how the disorders are affecting them can help prevent demoralization when the students are struggling. But it is also important for teachers to recognize that when students are spending a lot of time in the "DRIVING SLOWLY" zone despite their best efforts, the students probably require some (or more) accommodations. For example, if a student's tics are interfering significantly with written tasks, teachers need to provide the student with an alternate method for producing work that enables him to keep up with his peers, such as dictation or word processing.

What You Will Find in Each Chapter

Each of the disorders in this section of the book includes:
- a description of the cardinal symptoms of the disorder
- a description of specific effects or impact that the disorder may have on academics, behavior, and social relationship, noted by:

- tips and tricks that emphasize teacher- and student-friendly strategies for use in the classroom, noted by:

- short vignettes that illustrate the disorder
- cautions and pitfalls to avoid
- a list of other conditions or disorders to "be on the look out" for (BOLO), noted by:

Not every student with a particular disorder will have every type of impairment listed in the "Impact" section of each chapter. Nor will every student have every disorder listed on the "BOLO" list. Use the "BOLO" list in each chapter as a reminder of other conditions that may require screening or assessment. The decision to screen for something depends on the student's known or suspected diagnoses. For example, for a student with TS, we routinely screen for ADHD and OCD, but we may not screen for Bipolar Disorder. If we find evidence of OCD, however, then we would also screen for Bipolar Disorder and Depression. A reproducible BOLO list is provided in Appendix B and on the accompanying CD-ROM.

Additional resources in this book include:
- A glossary containing definitions of terms.
- A resources section that lists organizations that can provide additional information on the disorders.
- An appendix with useful screening tools and materials that are described in the chapters.
- An accompanying CD-ROM with downloadable charts, checklists, surveys, and forms.

Regular education teachers will be able to implement most of the suggestions and tips with no additional professional assistance. In some cases, we recommend that the teacher refer the student for further assessment by the school or district's occupational therapist, speech and language pathologist, assistive technology evaluation, psychologist, psychoeducational evaluator, or social worker. The role of related services providers is discussed in Chapter 32.

A Note on Diagnostic Criteria and Disorder Names

This book generally defines disorders as they are currently defined in the DSM-IV-TR, which is the diagnostic manual used in this country by mental health professionals (American Psychiatric Association 2000). The names and diagnostic criteria for some disorders will change when the DSM-V is eventually released. Readers can find out about these changes by consulting the DSM-V or by checking our website, www.challengingkids.com. One notable exception to our adherence to the DSM-IV-TR in this book, and as noted previously, is that we use "Autism Spectrum Disorder" instead of referring to Pervasive Developmental Disorder (PDD). Other notable exceptions are that we refer to disorders that are neither currently included in the DSM-IV-TR nor slated for inclusion in the DSM-V, such as Executive Dysfunction and Nonverbal Learning Disability.

Teachers are expected to reach unattainable goals with inadequate tools.
The miracle is that at times they accomplish this impossible task.
— Haim Ginott

CHAPTER 4

Tics and Tourette's Syndrome*

Aaron was constantly in trouble in his fourth grade class for making strange noises. His teacher sat him in the back row and told the other students to let her know if Aaron bothered them with his noises. Aaron was not invited to any birthday parties that year and no one ever called him to get together socially. When his counselor first met him, Aaron was a very sad, angry, and lonely child who did not want to go to school.

Preview

Tics are repetitive, involuntary, and purposeless movements or sounds that occur in bouts. Between 18-28% of children in education settings have one or more tics at some point in their development. For most children, tics are transient, but for the 3% of children in regular education and over 7% of children in special education settings who develop the tic condition known as Tourette's Syndrome (TS), school is much more challenging (Kurlan et al. 2002).

Description of Tics and Tourette's Syndrome

Tics are classified as either motor tics (producing movement) or as phonic or vocal tics (producing utterances or sounds). Some tics, such as spitting, are considered motor tics by some sources and phonic tics by other sources. Tics are also classified as being either simple (involving only one muscle group or sound) or as complex (involving more than one muscle group or producing meaningful utterances). Table 4.1 provides a chart of some behaviors that may be tics. It is important to note that any one be-

havior may have other causes, e.g., sniffing may be a vocal tic for one student and just an allergy symptom for another. The most common tics are simple motor tics involving the face, head, and neck region. Rapid purposeless eye-blinking is the single most common first tic. Not all students with tics develop complex tics. And not all students with tics develop Tourette's Syndrome. Like many of the conditions covered in this book, TS is more common in boys than in girls.

The complex tics listed in Table 4.1 are often initially confused with purposeful misbehavior. Complex tics that are especially likely to be misunderstood include touching, imitating others' actions (echopraxia), inappropriate sexual touching of self or others or making obscene gestures (copropraxia), imitating others' speech (echolalia) or repeating one's own speech (palilalia), and obscene or inappropriate utterances (coprolalia).

If we ask a student in a nonjudgmental but curious tone if they can stop doing something and they tell us that they cannot stop, the behavior is often a tic or some other neurological symptom such as a compulsion.

---

* There are many ways of referring to this disorder: Tourette syndrome, Tourette's Syndrome, Gilles de la Tourette's Syndrome, and Tourette's Disorder, to name a few. It is one of those "two professionals, three opinions" situations. In our many years of experience working with this disorder, we have come to realize that capitalization and apostrophes in the name are not as important as understanding the disorder. Throughout this book, then, we will refer to it as Tourette's Syndrome even though many of our colleagues now use a different name for it.

Table 4.1. Tics of Tourette's Syndrome[*]

Type of Tic	Motor	Vocal/Phonic
Simple	Eye Blinking Eye Rolling Shoulder Shrugs Head Jerks Brushing or Tossing Hair Out of Eyes Mouth Opening Arm Extending Facial Grimaces Nose Twitching Lip-licking Squinting Tongue Thrusting Arm Jerks Lip Pouting Foot Tapping or Finger Tapping Rubbing Nose With Hand	Throat Clearing Grunting Yelling or Screaming Sniffing Blowing Sounds Barking Snorting Coughing Spitting Squeaking Humming Sucking Sounds Whistling Honking Laughing Lip Smacking Simple Whistling Sounds

Complex	Pulling at Clothes
	Touching People or Objects
	Smelling Fingers or Objects
	Jumping or Skipping
	Poking or Jabbing
	Punching or Hitting
	Kicking
	Hopping
	Kissing Self or Others
	Flapping Arms
	Squatting or Deep Knee Bends
	Twirling Around
	Tensing Muscle Groups
	Thrusting Movements of Groin or Torso
	Twirling Hair
	Toe Walking
	Copropraxia:
	  Sexually Touching Self
	  Sexually Touching Others
	  Obscene Gestures
	Echo Phenomena:
	  Echopraxia: Repeating others' actions
	  Palipraxia: Repeating one's own actions
	Self-Injurious Behaviors (e.g., biting, hitting)
		Making Animal-Like Sounds
		Unusual Changes In Pitch or Volume of Voice
		Stuttering
		Repeating Phrases (e.g., "hoo boy," "shut up," "uh," "hey hey")
		Echo Phenomena:
		  Palilalia: Repeating one's own words or sounds
		  Echolalia: Repeating others' words or sounds
		Coprolalia: Uttering obscenities or socially taboo phrases in bouts or single instances

[*] Adapted from *Educating children with Tourette Syndrome: Understanding and educating children with a neurobiological disorder. I: Psychoeducational implications of Tourette Syndrome and its associated disorders* (Packer 1995).

From Tics to Tourette's Syndrome

Simple tics usually emerge during the preschool or elementary school years. A student may suddenly start blinking her eyes a lot one day, and the problem seems to intensify in frequency and severity over the next few days or weeks. Eventually, the tic starts to gradually decrease in frequency and severity, and disappears completely. This pattern of increasing frequency and severity followed by gradual remission is known as a waxing and waning cycle.

The presence of a tic does not automatically mean that the student has Tourette's Syndrome. There is a continuum of tic disorders:

- **Transient Tic Disorder** is characterized by tics that last less than a year.
- **Chronic Vocal Tic and Chronic Motor Tic Disorders** describe tics that last, on and off, for more than a year. The student has persistent or intermittent vocal tics or motor tics, but not both kinds of tics.
- **Tourette's Syndrome** (TS) involves two or more motor tics plus at least one vocal tic, where tics have been present on and off, for more than one year. The motor and vocal tics do not have to be present at the same time. The average age of onset for full-blown TS is six to seven years.

There is more than one cause of tics. There needs to be a careful diagnosis by a medical professional who is knowledgeable about tics in order to rule out other causes of the tics or other movement disorders that may look like tics before diagnosing TS.

On a practical level, pre-school or early elementary school teachers typically have no way of knowing whether a student who first exhibits simple tics will have the benign and transient tic condition or a more persistent tic condition. However, if the student suddenly seems to explode in severe and frequent tics, assume that the tics are likely to persist. Implement accommodations for the tics promptly without waiting for formal diagnosis.

The tics of TS change over time in terms of their anatomical location. A student who has an eye-blinking tic one month may develop a different tic in a few months, or the first tic may re-emerge after a period of relative calm and be accompanied by a new tic.

TS is a spectrum disorder: Some students have mild and infrequent tics while others may have frequent and/or severe tics. Some students will have a few features of other basal ganglia disorders (Chapter 1), while other students may have a number of other basal ganglia disorders in full-blown form. Even students with what appear to be mild tics may have other neurological conditions. Remember to "be on the look out" (BOLO) for symptoms of other basal ganglia-related conditions such as obsessions and compulsions, and ADHD.

*Although the media is fascinated by the involuntary cursing or socially embarrassing utterances known as coprolalia, less than 10% of students with TS have it. Coprolalia is **not** required for a diagnosis of TS.*

Although TS is not a progressive disease, tics tend to worsen during the first years after onset. The worst years in terms of tic severity and frequency are between the ages of ten and twelve (Leckman et al. 1998; Bloch et al. 2006). Tics tend to ease up after that, although some adolescents may find that their tics are becoming more complex or problematic. Tics may persist into the adult years or re-emerge in adulthood.

Middle-school or high-school students with TS often have no idea what tics will emerge or when, but there is no doubt that they will emerge at the most inopportune time. For example, a teenage girl who is asked out on a date by the boy she has been dreaming about for weeks may develop a spitting tic one hour before he comes to pick her up. Living with TS means the teens often do not know what their bodies may do next.

Do They Know They Are Ticcing and Can They Stop It?

Not all young children with tics are aware that they are ticcing, while others are acutely aware. Regardless, young students usually cannot control the tics at all. Trying to suppress a tic is like trying to suppress a sneeze or hiccup. We might delay it a bit, but sooner or later, it comes out, and while we are trying to suppress it, we probably cannot pay attention to anything else. The ability to suppress tics usually increases with age, although even older students may not be able to suppress tics at all. Even though some can suppress tics, school personnel cannot safely assume that students can suppress tics, even if the student says that they can suppress them.

Sensory phenomena are often part of the tics. By age ten, most children with TS are aware of an inner urge to tic building up that they may describe as an "itch" or inner "pressure." This is often referred to as a premonitory urge. Awareness of the urge can distract them from attending to the lesson.

Some students may not be able to suppress tics, but they may be able to modify them slightly. As children mature, some will try a hide or disguise strategy by which they try to slightly alter their tics to make them more socially acceptable. A student with tics may incorporate a tic into some behavior pattern that appears purposeful as a cover for the need to perform the tic. As an example, a student with a head jerking tic may bring her hand up to her hair as if she is brushing it back to disguise the fact that her head needs to jerk to the side.

Insisting that a student suppress or hide and disguise tics may worsen symptoms and distract the student from academic and behavioral requirements. Anecdotal reports suggest that school-based plans to decrease tics using negative or aversive consequences have made symptoms worse in a few cases (Packer 2005).

One of the fascinating aspects of tics is that although they are involuntary, students often experience them as being somewhat voluntary. A student may describe the experience as feeling the urge to tic build up and then choosing to release it. School personnel cannot, however, conclude that tics are really voluntary or that students can suppress tics if they want to or just try harder.

Factors That Influence Tic Frequency and Severity

Genetic factors, pregnancy complications, perinatal events, and environmental factors may influence the severity and course of tics or TS (Leckman et al. 1990; Müller-Vahl et al. 2008; Scahill et al. 2001; Silva et al. 1995). Some factors that affect tic severity and frequency are listed in Table 4.2.

As Table 4.2 suggests, some factors have multiple effects. A student who is asked to suppress tics may initially tic less, but the effort involved in suppressing the tics may simply delay a bout of intense tics for some students. Similarly, a student may exhibit more tics when she is first starting to relax, but once she has gotten the tics out, tics decrease as she continues to relax. Some factors worsen tics for some students and lessen tics for other students. Ask

Table 4.2. Factors That Influence Tic Severity and Frequency

Factors that Increase Tics	Factors that Decrease Tics
■ Stress (including positive events) ■ Arousal ■ Before and after performing skilled tasks ■ Starting to relax ■ Fatigue ■ Waxing cycles ■ Illness (infections) ■ Allergies ■ Caffeine (coffee, coke, tea), preserving agents, refined sugar, and sweeteners ■ Asked to suppress tics (delayed) ■ Premenstrual and menstrual ■ Talking about tics ■ Being observed	■ Distraction ■ Being nonanxiously engrossed ■ During skilled tasks ■ Exercise (some exceptions) ■ Relaxing (delayed) ■ During sleep ■ Summer vacation ■ Waning cycles ■ Nicotine ■ Asked to suppress tics (initial) ■ Talking to friends ■ Novel situation ■ Doctor visits ■ Reading for pleasure ■ Informed and supportive school environment ■ Presence and use of special talents or gifts

the parent and student about the student's tics. Do not be surprised if the student's tics worsen if school personnel try to talk to her about her tics as just talking about them seems to make them temporarily worse (Woods et al. 2001).

Time pressure is one of the biggest sources of school-related stress for students with tics or TS. This is why many students with TS require extended time on tests and a separate location for testing. Simply reducing time pressure by providing untimed tests often enables the student to work faster.

Once you've found success with a strategy, don't assume it can be removed. For example, if a student can read well with eyeglasses, we would not take the eyeglasses away, would we? Likewise, if a student does well on untimed tests, realize she may only be doing so well precisely because the test is untimed. Do not assume she will do as well on timed tests. Compare performance under timed and untimed conditions before recommending removal of an accommodation.

Even when teachers are supportive, a student's tics may go through periods of worsening simply due to the nature of the condition. Remember that a hallmark of TS is variability in tic symptoms characterized by waxing and waning cycles.

 ## School Impact

Students with TS are five times more likely than their non-TS peers to have significant rates of school and behavior problems (Abwender et al. 1996; Comings and Comings 1987). Although tics and TS may contribute to school problems, tics and TS do not by themselves significantly increase the need for special education services. The increased rate of placement in special education is likely due to the presence of other associated or comorbid conditions, especially learning disabilities, ADHD, or both (Packer 2005).

For students with TS, intelligence scores are normally distributed, but they still may experience significant tic- or TS-related school effects* of the types included in the following list. (This list does not take into account associated or comorbid conditions that also contribute to school-related problems.)

- Visual-motor integration deficits (e.g., difficulty copying from the board) (Como 2001; Schultz et al. 1998)

---

* In some cases, there is no research on a particular type of impact, and we are basing statements on our clinical experiences.

- Fine motor skills deficits (e.g., difficulty opening the milk carton) (Schultz et al. 1998; Como 2001)
- Graphomotor (handwriting) problems (Dornbush and Pruitt 1995; Packer 2005, 1997)
- Specific tic-related interference (e.g., arm tics interfere with handwritten work) (Hagin et al. 1982)
- Deficits in math calculations (Burd, Kauffman, and Kerbeshian 1992; Burd et al. 2005)
- Interference with tracking during reading
- Interference with acquisition of or retrieval of math facts
- Deficits in some types of habit acquisition (Marsh et al. 2005)
- Fatigue, frustration, irritability, or emotionality due to tics
- Homework issues due to tic interference, handwriting issues, fatigue, and frustration (Packer 2005)
- Peer rejection due to tics (Carter et al. 2000; Bawden et al. 1998; Packer 1997; Friedrich, Morgan, and Devine 1996; Stokes et al. 1991; Ohm 2006; Hollenbeck 2001; Edell-Fisher and Motta 1990; Edell and Motta 1989)
- Self-esteem issues (Ohm 2006; Hollenbeck 2001)
- Indirect interference from tics due to internal distractions such as awareness of premonitory urges
- Indirect interference with attention due to efforts to suppress tics
- Reluctance to speak in front of a group or read out loud (particularly if student has vocal tics)
- Speech dysfluencies (De Nil et al. 2005; Van Borsel and Vanryckeghem 2000)

Students who have TS plus allergies generally experience a significant tic worsening at the onset of allergy seasons (pollen in the fall and trees and grasses in the spring). Tics may also worsen right before school vacations, probably due to increased excitement over the upcoming holiday and holiday stress in families. Many students experience an increase in tics from spring until the end of school; an initial waxing cycle triggered by environmental conditions continues as the stress and excitement of end-of-school-year activities increases.

Homework is often problematic for students with TS (Packer 1997; Dornbush and Pruitt 1995;

Packer 1995, 2005). In addition to the problems already mentioned, some children come home from school and almost as soon as they walk in the door, have an explosive release of tics and emotional behaviors. Many of them are students who the teachers see as very well behaved with minimal tics during school.

Teachers are frequently surprised to find out that certain students are severely symptomatic once they are in the safety of their homes and no longer restraining their tics. Parental attempts to get the students to do homework before they've had time to release tics and restore themselves to relative calm may result in significant ticcing and emotional behaviors. For students with TS or tics, consider screening for homework-related problems and adjust homework expectations as needed. (A Homework Screening Survey can be found in Figure 23.2 and on the accompanying CD-ROM.)

Peer relationships are the biggest problem many students and parents report in terms of the impact of TS. Studies and parental surveys noted earlier strongly suggest that students with TS are at significant risk for peer teasing, rejection, and other peer problems. Although comorbid conditions certainly may contribute, research indicates that tics alone are sufficient to lead to peer problems. A reproducible handout of The Animals Inside Me, a poem that can be used as part of a peer education program for elementary age students, is provided in Appendix D.

Tips and Tricks for Helping Students with Tics and TS

- Ignore tics—**do not** comment on them publicly.
- Give students a permanent pass to leave the classroom at their discretion if the tics are overwhelming and they need to "get the tics out" in private or need to take a break.
- Extend time for reading assignments, handwritten work, tests, etc.
- Allow students with severe eye, head, or neck tics* to use books on tape or CD.
- Provide copies of board work and lecture notes for students with slow or impaired handwriting or tic interference.

- Assign a notetaking buddy when needed.
- Reduce copying from the board.
- Allow student to test in a separate location if:
  - ❑ the tics worsen dramatically during tests.
  - ❑ the student needs additional time that cannot be provided in the regular classroom.
  - ❑ her tics are distracting other students during testing.
- Add adult supervision in unstructured or less structured settings such as the cafeteria, gym, hallway, playground, and school bus if the student is being teased about tics or if there are peer problems.
- Reduce handwritten work. Allow the student to use a scribe, keyboard, voice activated software, or oral recording as a substitute for handwriting.
- Use preferential seating. Consult with students about where is best for them.
- Model acceptance of tics.
- Recognize the student's struggle.
- Provide a peer education program.**
- Allow the student to work in whatever position they feel most comfortable, e.g., lying down on the floor, cross-legged.
- Consult with the student privately about whether to call on her for reading aloud or speaking in front of class.
- Break assignments into small units and allow the student breaks and opportunities to leave the room to discharge tics in private.
- Allow students to avoid settings that are particularly stressful and where tics may distract or annoy peers (e.g., the library for students with loud vocal tics).
- Consider any medication effects and side effects in scheduling academic classes and important tests.
- Let gifted students work ahead during periods where tics have waned.
- Help the student develop a plan so that her tics do not impose on others.

---

* In our experience, even students with mild eye or head/neck tics may need books on tape or CD, particularly if they also have ADHD or OCD.

** Although there is no experimental research demonstrating that peer education programs provide significant or enduring gain in the behavior of peers or what the key elements should be, our experience has been that a well-conducted peer education program can make a positive difference. Additionally, some preliminary research suggests that proactively disclosing the TS may help prevent social rejection (Marcks et al. 2007).

- Allow a larger buffer zone around students who have large motor tics (such as arm-jabbing or kicking) or symptoms such as touching that may affect others.
- Encourage the student to let the school know what supports she feels she needs to work around the tics.
- Provide staff development on TS and ensure playground personnel, cafeteria personnel, "specials" teachers, and bus personnel are included.
- If student has complex tics involving imitation of others (echolalia, echopraxia), seat the student near a supportive peer.
- Allow the student who is going through a period of severe or frequent tics to engage in a self-selected engrossing activity, e.g., an educational computer game.

Some students with tics do not want to sit up front because they fear that everyone behind them will see their tics, etc. They may prefer to sit off to the side or in the back of the classroom. Consult with students to determine where they will feel most comfortable.

Cognitive-behavioral interventions or Cognitive-Behavioral Therapy (CBT) involves changing the individual's thoughts and behavior rather than specifically targeting their emotions. While CBT is best known in the treatment of Obsessive-Compulsive Disorder (OCD), anxiety disorders, and depression, it can also be applied to tics by using an approach known as Cognitive-Behavioral Intervention for Tics (CBIT) or the approach known as Exposure-Response Prevention that is mentioned in the chapter on OCD. Research on the effectiveness of cognitive-behavioral interventions in reducing tics continues to accumulate [cf. (Himle et al. 2007; Himle et al. 2006; Himle and Woods 2005; Piacentini and Chang 2005; Piacentini et al. 2006; Verdellen et al. 2008; Verdellen, Hoogduin, and Keijsers 2007; Verdellen et al. 2004; Woods et al. 2008; Woods et al. 2009; Woods and Himle 2004; Woods and Marcks 2005)]. If school psychologists have been trained in these techniques, they might be incorporated into a student's plan. In our experience, however, most school psychologists have not been sufficiently trained in these modalities to offer them as a service. If the student is receiving such therapeutic services outside of school, school personnel are encouraged to consult with the treating

mental health professional to determine what the school can do to support the therapy.

Associated or Comorbid Conditions

Between 60% and 90% of youth with TS seen in clinics have features of one or more additional neurological disorders (Zinner 2004; Freeman et al. 2000). The most common comorbid conditions are ADHD and OCD. Up to 75% of children and teens with TS have ADHD, and up to 60% have OCD. Approximately 25% of youth with TS have all three diagnoses. Screen for the following conditions that may be present in conjunction with TS:

- ADHD
- Obsessive-Compulsive symptoms or Obsessive-Compulsive Disorder (OCD)
- Visual-motor integration (including difficulties with fine motor control and handwriting)
- Anxiety disorders
- Sensory dysregulation
- Depression (when ADHD and/or OCD are present)
- Bipolar Disorder (when ADHD and/or OCD are present)
- Learning disabilities
- Executive Dysfunction (especially when other comorbid conditions are present)
- Working memory deficits (when other comorbid conditions are present)
- Self-injurious tics
- Sleep problems
- Speech dysfluencies, e.g., stuttering or cluttering (the absence of the normal flow of speech due to an inability to plan and organize a response, speaking in rapid spurts, or not being sure what to say)
- "Storms" or "Rages" (especially when other comorbid conditions are present)
- PANDAS (Strep infection precipitating onset of tics)
- Autism Spectrum Disorders (when several comorbid conditions are present)

School personnel may hear parents referring to "TS+." TS+ is a term Leslie coined that indicates children who have TS plus features of other conditions such as OCD and ADHD. The "+" serves as a reminder to parents and teachers that the child's greatest problems might not be from her tics or TS but from other challenges she might also face (Packer 1995). Over the years, that term has been misused by some people to suggest that everyone who has TS also has other problems, so it is important to clarify that the term TS+ is meant to encourage splitting (see Chapter 1): Teachers and parents need to be alert to "what else" the student may have.

School-Based Assessments

To obtain information about tic severity and frequency in a student who has TS, school personnel should use the Tic Reporting Inventory (see Appendix E and accompanying CD-ROM). The inventory is not scorable and is intended only for communication and sharing of information across settings—not for diagnosis. School staff can also use the Tourette Syndrome Symptom List (Harcherik et al. 1984).

Simply observing a student in the class setting is generally *not* a reliable indicator because tics are variable and the student may be suppressing tics or not experiencing tics during the time of a brief observation. If a student only has a few tics, ask the parents what tics the student has at home or reports having in school. If the student is aware of the tics, school personnel might ask the student what interference the student experiences and what supports might help. During the parent interview, inquire about homework and behavioral issues at home. Also ask about sleep problems. Surveys for homework issues and sleep problems are provided in Figure 23.2 and Appendix F and on the accompanying CD-ROM.

> *If a student with TS or tics appears to have learning disabilities, conduct an untimed assessment to determine if additional time makes a significant difference. Although some students with TS do have learning disabilities (particularly if they have comorbid ADHD), a subset of students with TS may only **appear** to have learning disabilities but really just require more time as an accommodation for interference from tics (Gallina 1990).*

Visual-motor integration (VMI) deficits and fine motor control issues are fairly common for students with TS. Even if tests of VMI indicate that a student's skills are within age expectations, the evaluator needs to ask to see a work sample because handwriting issues are such a prominent issue for students with TS. If preliminary screening suggests deficits in those areas, ask the school to arrange for an OT evaluation even if the deficit scoring does not trigger an assessment automatically. Ask the OT evaluator to specifically include assessment of handwriting speed and endurance for the types of tasks demanded by the curriculum and classroom.

Also, carefully consider any medications when conducting or interpreting psychoeducational assessments. One of the most common errors we see when reviewing school assessments is the lack of any mention of medications the student was on and how they affect performance on the assessment.

Summary

Tics are repetitive, involuntary movements or sounds that occur in bouts, wax and wane in their frequency and severity, and move around the student's body. Even when tics are not severe enough to require treatment, the child may need some common-sense accommodations and emotional support when tics worsen. Be prepared to make academic accommodations, as warranted, and take proactive steps to prevent peer rejection and to promote positive peer relationships.

Michael was worried. He had been trying desperately to hide his tics from his classmates, but now his peers were about to find out. He knew his teachers meant well when they arranged for a speaker to come in to talk with the class about Tourette's, but he did not know if his peers might make jokes about TS. During the peer program, Michael sat in the back of the classroom, waiting to hear what his classmates would say. To his relief, they asked a lot of good questions and no one made fun of him. After the program, some of them came up to tell him they now understood that he was not crazy or making those sounds or movements on purpose. They even promised to protect him if any other kids gave him a rough time.

Over the next few weeks, Michael stopped trying to hide his tics in school. To his surprise, he found that now that he was not so worried about people seeing his tics, his tics were not as bad and he was able to participate more fully in classroom activities.

CHAPTER 5

Obsessive-Compulsive Disorder

Bobby sat in the therapist's office, looking worried. He was a slender, soft-spoken child who looked like he would not harm a fly. "I know it doesn't make sense and that I wouldn't really do it," Bobby told his therapist, "but my mind keeps telling me that if I'm not perfect in music when we're playing a piece, I'll do something awful like rape somebody. And sometimes my mind tells me that if I don't do what it tells me to do, I'll die of AIDS. My mind is making me miserable."

Preview

Anyone can worry sometimes, and anyone can engage in some small rituals or habits. Some children and teens, however, worry excessively about particular themes and/or engage in ritualized behaviors over and over again. When a student spends more than one hour a day obsessively worrying and/or engaging in mental or overt rituals, the student may have Obsessive-Compulsive Disorder (OCD). Once thought to emerge in adolescence or after adolescence, we now know that in many cases, OCD first emerges in childhood and may affect as many as 1% of children and 4% of adolescents (Carter and Pollock 2000). In younger children, OCD is more common in boys than in girls (Geller 2006).

What Are Obsessions?

Obsessions are recurrent and persistent thoughts, impulses, or mental images that are experienced as unwanted, intrusive, and inappropriate. These tormenting, "over and over again" thoughts or images usually cause anxiety or distress. Obsessions are not exaggerated real-life worries. They are irra-

tional, although young children may not recognize them as irrational. In some cases, children may describe obsessive thoughts as "voices" in their heads that are different from their internal voices. Do not assume that the 'voices' represent a psychosis. In the majority of cases, it is simply the child trying to disown the upsetting thoughts by assigning them to someone else's voice.

Obsessive Themes

Certain obsessive themes tend to occur across all races, cultures, and societies. Some of the most common themes are as follows:

- Contamination fears (germs, dirt, chemicals)
- Perfectionism
- Doubting
- Having to have things in a specific order or symmetrically
- Having to have things "just so" or "just right"
- Fear of harm to family or death of self or others (violent imagery)
- Moral and religious themes, "scrupulosity" (excessive worry that you are committing a sin), or "moral policeman" (having to let people know when they break the rules)
- Needing to experience a particular sensation (such as burning or cutting)
- Sexual obsessions

Many children and teens feel a need to be perfect in their schoolwork or hobbies. The need for perfection is exhausting, as their work or results never seem quite good enough to them. Telltale signs of perfectionism obsessions are often seen in the student's handwriting, where letters are retraced or re-worked over and over, there are excessive erasures, or where there is a clear ritualized style to dotting lowercase "i's" and making the period at the end of the sentence perfectly circular, etc.

You may observe with OCD a student make a mistake towards the end of a project and tear up the entire project because it is not perfect. Or the student might give up and not hand in the work because he was "stuck" trying to perfect it for hours and hours. Students who have OCD in the presence of TS seem to have a lot of "just so" or "just right" issues, where things have to be a particular way or else they get "stuck" and cannot cope. Teachers who are not aware of the painful perfectionism may erroneously think that the student did not attempt the assignment or care about it.

Assuming good intent and being curious can help uncover problems associated with OCD.

About two thirds of children and teens with OCD have obsessions with aggression or harm themes. It is very important for teachers to know that the presence of such thoughts or obsessions is not an indication that the student is going to act on those thoughts. The reason the child experiences them as so intrusive and anxiety-producing is because they have no desire to (or intention to) engage in the behavior. Students with OCD may expend a great amount of stressful mental and emotional energy trying to ward off those thoughts. In some cases, a student may try to write the thought down on paper as a story, or poem, or drawing as part of an attempt to get the thought out of his head. In schools where zero tolerance policies are in force, this can lead to unfortunate (and unfair) consequences for the child. Collaborate with the student as to how he can safely ward off disturbing aggressive images.

The simple instruction, "Do not… " given to students with OCD may plant the image of the unwanted behavior in the student's head where it gets stuck and becomes an overwhelming urge to do precisely what you've told the student not to do. Instead of saying, "Do not touch the fire alarm," say, "When you walk down the hall, put your hands in your pockets."

Some children and about one third of teenagers with OCD have sexually themed obsessions. Teachers may find it difficult to distinguish obsessional thinking from typical pre-adolescent and adolescent preoccupation with sex. Evidence of a sexually themed obsession is not necessarily evidence that the student has been sexually molested or harmed.

Compulsions

If obsessions are intrusive and irrational thoughts loop repeatedly, how does the student ward them off? While some students may have repeated intrusive thoughts without any resulting behaviors, many students with obsessive thoughts engage in rituals or compulsive behavior. Compulsions are repetitive behaviors or mental acts that the person feels driven to perform in response to an obsession or according to rigid rules. Having to do anything over and over again frequently is an indication that the behavior is compulsive. Keep in mind that some rituals are hidden, i.e., are performed internally. There may be no overt signs. Many children who seem inattentive may actually be engaging in hidden compulsions that distract them.

Common compulsions include:
- Washing or hygiene rituals
- Counting (including counting mentally)
- Checking and re-checking (e.g., checking over and over if the door is locked)
- Saving or hoarding
- Ordering, arranging, and "evening up"
- Seeking reassurance
- Repeating activities
- Avoidance of particular settings or things
- Getting "stuck" playing video games or being on the computer
- Compulsive slowness

One might think that students with obsessive-compulsiveness would be particularly neat if they feel the need to have things "just so" or if they have contamination fears, but many appear to be quite disorganized and messy. A student who hoards may be unable to clean out his desk or schoolbag, and may accumulate all kinds of wrappers and trash. Disorganized students typically cooperate, given sufficient support in trying to clean out their desk. Hoarders, however, may resist throwing things out and may get agitated if they are pressured to do so.

Being orderly or having a filing system to find things quickly is generally a useful quality, but if the student feels significant anxiety when things are not ordered in a particular way, that may indicate a compulsion as opposed to a choice. The need for symmetry—to have things even—may also translate into evening up compulsions. In some cases, an evening up compulsion is combined with a tic. Dr. Mort Doran, a surgeon who has TS and OCD, provides a useful example of this type of combination: When he experiences a shoulder shrug tic in one shoulder, it is a tic. But when he (more consciously) repeats the same shrug with the other shoulder to "even up," that part of the sequence is a compulsion. What looks like tics in both shoulders is really one tic and one compulsion combined into one pattern.

What might be a tic in one student may not be a tic in another student or even in the same student at another time.

Compulsions are often combined together, for example repeating a word or phrase and needing to do it an exact number of times, or repeating something until it is perfect. If the behavior has a superstitious quality to it, such as "I have to say this exactly five times," it may indicate combined compulsions of repeating and counting.

If a particular situation or setting becomes associated with compulsive behavior, the student may start avoiding the situation or setting. He may fear that he will lose control and get "stuck" performing the ritual in certain school settings. A student engaged in such avoidance may appear to be oppositional when asked to go to the gym or to engage in an activity. The behavior in this case is not capricious refusal, however. It is anxiety driven.

When a student refuses to do something, be curious as to whether there is an anxiety issue due to an obsessive thought or need to perform a compulsive behavior.

Although it is not identified as a common compulsion, students with OCD are more at risk for getting addicted to electronic games. Although they usually do not verbalize any anxiety-producing thought that precedes their behavior, if we talk with them about their experience, they will probably tell us that they feel they have to keep playing. That vague sense of discomfort may be a manifestation of some "just right" or "just so" obsession. Research on Internet addiction shows a significant over-representation of adolescents with ADHD (Ha et al. 2006). Because ADHD and OCD often co-occur, compulsive Internet use or game-playing may reflect both.

Occasionally a student has compulsive slowness; they just cannot move quickly enough to get from one class to the next on time. Although slowness may be a symptom of depression in some students (see Chapter 11), other students simply appear unable to move quickly. Some possible explanations for their behavior include impaired executive functioning. For example, the student may have trouble executing goal-directed behavior, or suffer interference from intrusive thoughts or rituals, or have a hard time shifting to another activity (Hymas et al. 1991)

Be cautious about interrupting a student engaged in a compulsive behavior. If the student is "stuck," attempts to interrupt may result in fight or flight behavior. Students sometimes lash out at school personnel who try to interrupt a ritual—not because they are angry at the teacher but because they "had to" engage in the ritual.

Imagine that you are mentally counting in your head because if you do not, something terrible will happen to your family. Now imagine that a teacher tries to make you stop to take out your math book. What might you do if the teacher pushed the issue?

Compulsions vs. Other Types of Repetitive Behaviors

Not all repetitive behaviors are compulsions. Tics are an example of another type of repetitive behavior. In fact, it is often difficult to tell whether a student is engaging in a compulsive behavior or a tic or a perseverative behavior. Perseverative behavior, often seen in people with autism, is behavior that is repeated after the stimulus for the behavior is no longer present. Compulsive behaviors also need to be distinguished from stereotyped behaviors (repetitive behaviors such as arm flapping or rocking that may endure for years). The important things to remember are that not all that is "stuck" is OCD and not all that is perseverative is autistic.

Progression of Symptoms

Obsessive-compulsive symptoms may get worse before they get better, but they generally do get better. One study reported that over a decade, up to 75% of children with OCD improved significantly (Reddy et al. 2005). Even so, 70-80% of students with OCD are likely to continue compulsive behavior into adulthood. Not surprisingly, perhaps, male students with early-onset OCD and comorbid ADHD have poorer outcomes than those without ADHD or with later onset.

Factors That Influence Symptom Severity

As a general principle, anything that increases stress or anxiety may worsen a student's OCD symptoms. Other factors may also contribute to a worsening of symptoms:

- Illness, such as strep infections (see Chapter 7)
- The premenstrual period (Vulink et al. 2006)
- Waxing cycle of tics, if TS is present
- Mood disorders, if present, may worsen OCD (see Chapter 11)

The more disorders that are present, the more complex and the greater the school-related problems are.

School Impact

Nicole was a bright teenager with TS and OCD whose eye tics significantly interfered with her ability to read. When she started making a lot of errors in math calculations, her parents wondered if the tics were the problem or if something was else going on. During a phone conference, the consultant asked Nicole about the sources of interference she experienced in schoolwork and homework. Nicole readily told her about the eye and head tics but said there were not any other problems. Knowing that she was diagnosed with OCD as well as TS, the consultant gently inquired as to whether mental rituals were getting in her way when she worked on math. At the other end of the phone, she could hear Nicole sigh.

"What is it?" asked the consultant.

"It's the number four," Nicole said.

"What about the number four?"

Nicole explained, "Any math problem that has the number four in the answer, well…I can't write the number four, so I write down another number just to avoid using the number four. If the problem doesn't have the number four in it, I'll do the problem, but if the answer or work has the number four in it, then I just change it to any other number."

The consultant inquired, "Does the number four affect your reading and writing too?"

"Yes," Nicole replied, sighing again. "Sometimes I have to count how many words in a sentence have exactly four letters. And then I have to add up the number of words in a sentence and see if it's evenly divisible by four. If it's not, I have to rewrite the sentence so that it is."

Nicole was clearly impaired by her obsessions and compulsions concerning the number four, but she had not told anyone—not her teachers, not the school psychologist, not her parents, not even her prescribing psychiatrist. She was simply too embarrassed and didn't want to be viewed as crazy.

Remember that we only see the tip of the iceberg. This is particularly true with OCD.

OCD is frequently associated with significant social and academic impact. Dr. Piacentini and his colleagues surveyed children and their parents about the impact of OCD on their functioning. The biggest impact of OCD was on the students' ability to concentrate in class and on their ability to complete homework. Approximately 90% of the children reported significant OCD-related problems, and the severity of the problems correlated with the clinician's ratings of the children's OCD symptom severity (Piacentini et al. 2003). Students with OCD are also significantly more at risk for peer victimization (Storch et al. 2006), resulting in significant loneliness and depression, both of which are risk factors for suicide.

 Specific school impact of OCD may include:

- Difficulty completing assignments in class (Piacentini et al. 2007)
- Impaired concentration on work (Piacentini et al. 2007)
- Often unprepared for class (materials, books) (Piacentini et al. 2007).
- Visual-motor integration problems (Hollander et al. 1990)
- Fine motor control problems (Hollander et al. 1990)
- Handwriting issues (Mavrogiorgou et al. 2001; Stein 2001)
- Visual-spatial deficits (Hollander et al. 1990; van der Wee et al. 2006; van der Wee et al. 2003; Boldrini et al. 2005), e.g., difficulty positioning letters or words on the page or lining up numbers for math calculations

- Difficulty organizing thoughts verbally, e.g., telling a story efficiently
- Difficulty organizing a visual figure during a construction task
- Decreased speed on tasks requiring self-initiated organizational strategies
- Deficits in acquiring skills through practice (Kathmann et al. 2005)
- Impaired memory, including deficits in visual memory (Dirson et al. 1995), nonverbal memory (Penades et al. 2005), confidence in their memory (Tallis, Pratt, and Jamani 1999), retrieval or recall (Deckersbach et al. 2004), working memory, procedural memory, and strategic memory
- Controlled fluency deficits (Boldrini et al. 2005)
- Peer or social problems (Allsopp and Verduyn 1990; Piacentini et al. 2003; Storch, Heidgerken et al. 2005; Storch, Murphy et al. 2005)
- Homework issues (Piacentini et al. 2003; Piacentini et al. 2007)
- Slowed reading or impaired comprehension that can result from intrusive thoughts or hidden rituals
- Attendance issues due to rituals
- Avoidance of tasks, settings, and school, and/or school refusal
- Fatigue due to impaired sleep (see Appendix F: Sleep Survey and accompanying CD-ROM)

OCD-related handwriting issues are different than TS-related handwriting issues. For students with OCD, handwriting for complex or novel tasks may be slow and difficult. The slowness may be due, in part, to handwriting rituals that seemingly force them to go over a letter again and again or to continually erase and rewrite something until it looks perfect. While some students with OCD have slower handwriting for novel tasks, many of them perform better than their peers if the assigned handwriting activity involves repetition (Mavrogiorgou et al. 2001). Some students may get stuck blackening in a circle on a Scantron (computer) form to the extent that they cannot get beyond the first question on the exam. Some students with OCD may also have very small handwriting (Mavrogiorgou et al. 2001). Figure 5.1 depicts a handwriting sample provided by a student with OCD.

Homework is often a landmine for students with OCD. Many have trouble concentrating on

Figure 5.1. Handwriting Compulsion

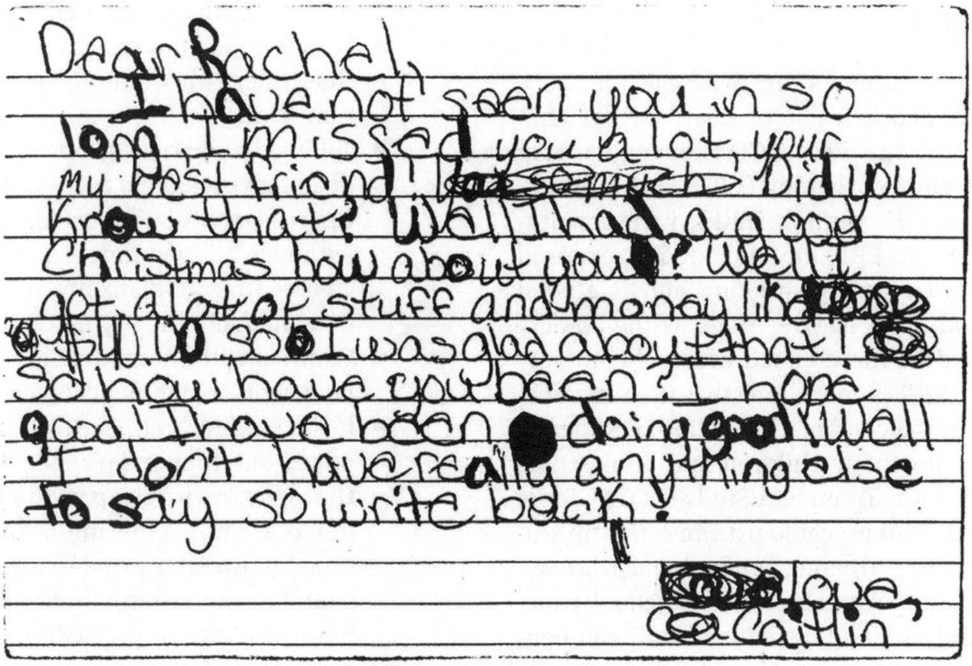
Dear Rachel,
I have not seen you in so long, I missed you a lot, your my best friend! Did you know that? Well I had a good Christmas how about you? Well I got a lot of stuff and money like $40.00 so I was glad about that! So how have you been? I hope good! I have been doing good! Well I don't have really anything else to say so write back!

love,
Caitlin

Compulsively perfecting particular letters slows handwriting and distracts from concentration on content.

homework due to interference from obsessive thoughts. If they have any perfectionistic symptoms, they may stay up all night working and reworking an assignment until it is perfect. Consider screening for both homework and sleep issues to determine if homework assignments need modification. (Surveys are provided in Figure 23.2 and Appendix F and on the accompanying CD-ROM.)

Jimmy could not leave his house for school in the morning unless the minute hand of the clock was exactly straight up on the twelve. He would wait by the door anxiously, but then hesitate because he was not sure it was exactly straight up. Inevitably, he would wait a bit too long out of doubt, and then have to wait another hour to try again. When he did get out of his house and start walking to school, Jimmy would have to cross one intersection in a square pattern exactly forty times. If a car came through the intersection after he had started the ritual, he would have to start all over again. Some days, he did not get to school until one or one thirty in the afternoon because of all his rituals. Jimmy's school team had no idea why he was so late to school so often.

Be curious about any attendance or lateness problems.

On the Importance of Treatment

Effective treatments are available for OCD. The recommended first line of treatment for children and adolescents with OCD is usually a form of cognitive-behavior therapy (CBT) known as Exposure-Response Prevention (ERP), with or without medication. In ERP, the individual is exposed to the anxiety-triggering situation and is guided in not responding to it. Over time, as the anxiety is not followed by the dreaded event, the anxiety extinguishes. ERP is more effective than medication alone, but the combination of both is superior to ERP alone for many children and adolescents (The Pediatric OCD Treatment Study (POTS) Team 2004). If the school psychologist can refer the student's parents to a treating professional who can provide such therapy, the student's school functioning can improve and the entire family can benefit. Some research suggests that ERP may actually normalize the student's cognitive functioning (Andres et al. 2007).

Tips and Tricks for Helping Students with OCD

Even though the symptoms of OCD may worsen at first, informed and caring teachers and school staff can do a lot to make it easier for the student to succeed academically and socially. The following accommodations, tips, and strategies for helping students with obsessive-compulsive symptoms are based on clinical experience.

- Try to reduce the triggers to compulsive behavior, if possible. This is more effective than trying to stop compulsive behavior once it has begun. Remember: Change the environment before trying to change the student.
- Teach students strategies to help manage OCD in the school setting. Simple relaxation techniques that all students can be taught to use are provided in Appendix G. The school psychologist or social worker can often provide students with cognitive strategies that help reduce anxiety.
- Screen for homework issues and provide accommodations as needed.
- Screen for sleep disturbance and provide accommodations as needed.
- Collaborate with the student to determine techniques that might help reduce rituals.
- Extend time for completing tasks; ensure the student understands the amount of time available.
- Taking their known symptoms into account, do not give students more work than they can reasonably be expected to complete within an allotted time. Too much work increases stress and anxiety, reducing production and increasing symptomatic behavior.
- Contract with the student about how late homework assignments will be handled.
- If the student's concentration is compromised due to interference from intrusive thoughts or rituals, provide hardcopies of lecture notes, permit the student to tape lectures, or provide a paraprofessional or notetaking buddy with carbonless paper (e.g., NCR paper) to take notes for the student.
- Provide appropriate testing accommodations:
  - ❏ Extend time for test taking.

- ❏ Break tests up into small time chunks and allow the student to take breaks between segments.
- ❏ Allow student to test in a separate location if the student's performance indicates that this reduces stress and anxiety. If the student is tested in a separate location, the proctor needs to be someone who is known to the student and with whom the student feels comfortable.
- ❏ Allow the student to write directly in the test booklet.
- ❏ Avoid Scantron (computer) response forms if the student has handwriting rituals.
- ❏ Use a multiple-choice format and allow the student to circle the correct answers instead of having to write out answers if there are significant handwriting rituals.
- ❏ Provide word banks for students with verbal retrieval and recall problems.
- ❏ Hand the student only one part of the test at a time.
- ■ Accommodate handwriting compulsions:
  - ❏ Reduce handwritten work.
  - ❏ Explore the use of assistive technology. While some students may have keyboarding rituals, other students may be able to accomplish more with the use of a notebook computer or word processor than by hand writing. In some cases, voice-activated software is advisable.
- ■ Limit the amount to be read at one time for students with silent or hidden reading rituals. If reading rituals and intrusive thoughts are severe, consider using books on tape/CD or recording the material.
- ■ Be sensitive to peer problems:
  - ❏ Identify the child's strengths and talents, and be sure to point them out to the student.
  - ❏ If the student is being ridiculed for his rituals or obsessive fears, obtain the student's permission to conduct a peer education program on OCD.
  - ❏ Give the student a permanent pass and develop a discreet signal that can be used to signal the student when he might need to take a break or leave the classroom. Be prepared with some face-saving excuses to help the student make a graceful exit (e.g., "Cindy, could you please take this note to the office for me?"). Cooperatively problem-solve with the student if the student's compulsions impinge on other students. While peers can be taught to be tolerant of noninvasive compulsions such as having to touch all of the locker handles when walking down the hall, peers are not likely to just accept compulsions that invade their privacy or their right to learn (e.g., a compulsion to touch them). The "graceful exit" (Dornbush and Pruitt 1995) and "Cooperative Problem Solving" techniques are described in Chapter 31 of this book.

Consequences Are Risky

Using any type of behavior modification plan for a student with OCD—even if the plan does not target the OCD symptoms—may actually worsen the symptoms. For example, an elementary school teacher tried to motivate a student to improve his spelling by offering him a reward if he achieved a particular grade on his next spelling quiz. That type of positive reinforcement usually sounds pretty benign, but because the student had OCD, he obsessed about the upcoming quiz. For the entire week, he worried about what would happen if the teacher could not read his handwriting and took off points for spelling when he had spelled something correctly. He worried about a variety of possibilities that were all related to the spelling quiz. What was intended as a positive reinforcer for an academic activity led to a worsening of the student's OCD.

As a general rule, do not use consequences or reinforcers with students who have OCD without first conferencing with the parents and student to ask whether consequences are likely to help or hurt. And if these methods are then implemented, monitor carefully to ensure that the consequences or reinforcers are not worsening symptoms.

 ## Associated Conditions

As with all of the conditions described in this book, it is fairly likely that the student with OCD may have at least a few features of other conditions as well. Keeping in mind that different disorders tend to emerge at different ages (see Chapter 1), what we see may be related to the student's age. For example, the likelihood of depression increases with age: 40% of children with OCD have symptoms of depression while over 60% of teens with OCD have depression. A large subgroup of students with OCD has one or more anxiety disorder diagnoses such as Panic Disorder or Social Anxiety Disorder (also known as Social Phobia). (Anxiety disorders are discussed in Chapter 6.)

The likelihood of a student with OCD developing symptoms of one or more of the following conditions is partly a result of gender. Boys with OCD are more likely to have tics, TS, and substance abuse. Girls with OCD are more likely to have skin picking, mood disorders (depression and Bipolar Disorder), Eating Disorders, and anxiety disorders [cf. (Samuels et al. 2006)]. Some of the comorbid conditions listed below are more likely to be present in teens with OCD than in children with OCD.

- Anxiety disorders including Panic Disorder, phobias
- Mood disorders (e.g., depression, Bipolar Disorder)
- Visual-motor integration deficits (including fine motor control and handwriting)
- ADHD
- Tics or TS
- Executive Dysfunction (EDF)
- Learning Disabilities (especially written expression)
- Pragmatic (Social) Language Disorder (if EDF is present)
- Working memory problems
- Processing speed problems (secondary to interference)
- Trichotillomania (hair-pulling)
- Skin picking (teens more than children)
- Eating Disorders
- Sleep problems
- Body Dysmorphic Disorder (distorted images of one's appearance)
- Sensory dysregulation
- Substance abuse disorder (especially if ADHD or BP are comorbid)
- "Rage Attacks" or "Storms"
- Autism Spectrum Disorder

School-Based Assessments

When assessing a student with known or suspected OCD, the school psychologist may find the Children's Yale-Brown Obsessive Compulsive Scale (CY-BOCS) for students aged fourteen or younger helpful. The Yale-Brown Obsessive Compulsive Scale (Y-BOCS) is appropriate for students aged fourteen or older. A newer scale, the Child Obsessive-Compul-

sive Impact Scale–Revised (COIS—R), might also be useful (Piacentini et al. 2007).

The school's evaluation will generally need to include, at the very least, assessment of:

- Handwriting
- Executive Dysfunction
- Memory issues
- Sleep problems (see Appendix F and accompanying CD-ROM)
- Homework problems (see Homework Screening Survey in Figure 23.2 and the accompanying CD-ROM)

In conducting psychoeducational assessments, evaluators need to be prepared to make some accommodations for handwriting rituals. They should also include some untimed tests to contrast to performance under timed conditions to help clarify whether the student has an actual learning disability or is simply experiencing symptom interference. Testing the student's knowledge and skills beyond the point at which some tests require that testing stop can also be helpful. Many of the students we have worked with lose their concentration despite the fact that they are capable of higher-level work. Testing beyond the limits will help clarify the student's skills.

Summary

Repetitive intrusive thoughts or rituals, or both, can significantly interfere with a student's ability to concentrate on schoolwork and to complete homework. Young students may not realize that their intrusive thoughts are irrational, but by the teen years, they are acutely aware of the irrational nature of the thoughts and are hesitant to talk about the bizarre worries or hidden rituals that plague them. OCD is potentially a seriously disabling condition for students.

Phillip was sitting in the assistant principal's office when the consultant came in. He had been sent to the office because he was neither paying attention in class nor cooperating with his teacher. The consultant watched Phillip's lips moving subtly as the assistant principal explained why he had been sent there, and she asked Phillip softly, "Are you counting in your head?" The assistant principal look puzzled by the question, but Phillip nodded his head twice quickly while his lips continued moving. "Can you signal me what number you're up to?"

"5,110," he indicated.

"What number do you have to get up to?" asked the consultant.

"150,000" signaled Phillip.

The assistant principal's expression changed from one of frustration to one of consternation and compassion. She had known that Phillip was diagnosed with OCD, but had not fully appreciated how tortuous it could be for him and how little the staff knew about his hidden rituals or compulsions. She immediately arranged for training about OCD so that Phillip's teachers could learn about Phillip's challenges. After the training, Phillip was sent from the classroom less and less, and within months, the team was able to mainstream Phillip for a portion of his day.

CHAPTER 6

Anxiety Disorders and School Refusal

Julio was terrified that he was about to lose consciousness and die. His heart was pounding, his hands were sweaty, and he felt like he had to call 911 to get help. When his teacher tried to stop him from leaving the classroom, he shoved the teacher out of the way, raced out of the classroom and the building, and ran down the city streets to get home to his mother to get help. The school suspended him from school for shoving his teacher, but Julio had no intention of returning to school anyway, as he was terrified he would have another panic attack there and that they would not help him. Julio's mother took him to see a therapist to get help for him.

Preview

Many students diagnosed with other conditions described in this book often have prominent features of anxiety but are seldom diagnosed as having an anxiety disorder. As a consequence, teachers and school personnel often focus on other aspects of the student's functioning without specifically addressing the anxiety that may be significantly impairing the student academically, behaviorally, and socially.

Anxiety is the most common form of childhood psychopathology. However, precise rates for having any one type of anxiety disorder in childhood or pre-adolescence are unknown, with estimated rates ranging from 2.6% up to 41.2% (Cartwright-Hatton, McNicol, and Doubleday 2006). Anxiety problems typically emerge before adolescence, and are relatively common in adolescents, with estimated rates of at least 10% (Garland 2001). Some estimates suggest that anxiety disorders may affect about 20% of all youth at some point in their development.

Specific anxiety disorders are more common at particular stages of development. Separation Anxiety Disorder (SAD) and specific phobias are more common in younger children aged six to nine. Generalized Anxiety Disorder (GAD) and Social Anxiety Disorder (Social Phobia) are more common in middle childhood and adolescence. Panic Disorder can occur in adolescence as well. Other anxiety disorders, described below, include anxious school refusal, School Phobia, Post-Traumatic Stress Disorder, specific phobias, and Selective Mutism.

Children and adolescents with anxiety disorders typically experience intense fear, worry, or uneasiness that is out of proportion to the situation. The anxiety usually has two components: (1) physical sensations such as headache, stomach pain, nausea, sweating, racing heart, tingling, weakness, and shortness of breath, and (2) emotions of nervousness and fear.

Types of Anxiety Disorders

Separation Anxiety Disorder (SAD)

Separation Anxiety Disorder is the most common anxiety disorder in young children. The hallmark of SAD is significant difficulty separating from parents or from home. Just the idea of going to school often provokes extreme anxiety for the student. SAD symptom severity fluctuates. In some cases, the condition persists for years or is a precursor to Panic Disorder with agoraphobia (irrational fear of going out in public places from which escape might be difficult). The average age of onset of SAD is 7.5 years. The prevalence of SAD ranges from approximately 4-5% for children aged seven to eleven years and drops to slightly over 1% for teenagers aged fourteen to sixteen years.

SAD is strongly related to school refusal, discussed later in this chapter. Up to 80% of students with school refusal report a history or presence of SAD (Masi, Mucci, and Millepiedi 2001). Childhood SAD may be a risk factor for other anxiety disorders, although what it predicts is still uncertain. Cognitive-behavior treatment (CBT), including school-based CBT to treat SAD and SAD-related school refusal, has been demonstrated to be effective.

Panic Disorder

Students with Panic Disorder experience feelings of utter terror that strike suddenly and repeatedly with no warning. The students often cannot predict when an attack will occur, and the sense of not knowing when the next attack will strike may lead them to periods of intense worry or anxiety between panic attacks.

Students having panic attacks may report that their heart is pounding, that they feel sweaty, weak, faint, or dizzy. Their hands may tingle or feel numb, and they may feel flushed or chilled. As irrational as it sounds to others, the student—like Julio in the example at the beginning of this chapter—may genuinely feel that he is having a heart attack or is going to die. The student may feel that he has to escape the premises. A panic attack or episode usually peaks within ten minutes and generally subsides within twenty to thirty minutes.

Not all students who experience a panic attack develop Panic Disorder, but a subset does. About one third of people with Panic Disorder develop agoraphobia. For teens with Panic Disorder who have experienced a panic attack in school, school avoidance or even school refusal may result because they are excessively worried about when and where the next episode will occur and their ability to easily escape.

Can you think clearly or access knowledge or skills when you are in a panicked state? Neither can your student. But even between panic attacks, the student may have difficulty concentrating or working due to interference from worry about when the next attack might occur.

Social Anxiety or Social Phobia

In the early days of middle school, Shakir was invited to hang with the guys after school near the fast food restaurant across the street, but he always made an excuse why he could not. After a month, the kids felt rejected and turned on him, teasing him at school. This pattern continued until there were no groups left that were interested in befriending Shakir. When he was referred to the school's counselor, she learned that every time he had started to cross the street, he had had an anxiety attack at the thought of having to socialize with that many kids at once. The excuses he gave the boys were a smokescreen to hide his embarrassment at being unable to handle being around that many people.

Social Anxiety Disorder is also known as Social Phobia. Social Phobia usually begins in childhood or early adolescence and has a lifetime prevalence ranging from 3-13%. Students with Social Phobia have a persistent fear of being embarrassed in social situations such as during a performance, when they have to speak in class in front of their peers, or during conversation with others. The fear is apparent in any situation where others might observe them or judge them. Social Phobia is accompanied by physical manifestations of anxiety that include palpitations, tremors, sweating, diarrhea, blushing, and increased muscle tension.

Social Phobia is not just shyness. Shyness may produce discomfort, but it generally does not produce avoidance of situations. Many children who appear shy and inhibited do not develop social anxiety disorder. Social Phobia disrupts the student's life, interfering with school or social relationships. Whereas their peers may look forward to performing in a school concert or play with a mixture of excitement and a bit of nervousness, students with Social Phobia live in utter dread for weeks before the event. To complicate their anxiety, they also worry that others will notice their extreme reactions and consider them babyish, immature, or odd.

Unlike Separation Anxiety Disorder, which has a fairly high remission rate, Social Phobia may be a life-long challenge, although it may become less severe over time. In some cases, Social Phobia (like Separation Anxiety Disorder) may lead to Panic Disorder.

Research on social anxiety in students indicates that:

- Middle school girls' sense of self-worth is diminished by anxiety due to peer victimization (Grills and Ollendick 2002).

- High school girls experience social anxiety and loneliness because of school-related victimization by peers (Storch and Masia-Warner 2004).
- High school girls are more likely to suffer severe social anxiety than high school boys (Dell'Osso et al. 2003).
- High school students with even moderate levels of social anxiety may have school difficulties and avoid social situations (Dell'Osso et al. 2003).

Although the pathways to Social Phobia are not well understood, they appear to include genetic vulnerability and family/parenting variables as well as negative peer experiences. Early disabilities may also be a risk factor for developing social anxiety as children with a history of early language impairment are 2.7 times as likely to have social phobia by age nineteen as peers without a history of early language impairment (Voci et al. 2006).

School Phobia

School phobia, a condition characterized by excessive and intense anxiety about going to school, affects up to 5% of elementary and middle school students. Young children who are school phobic may report headaches, stomachaches, or fatigue. Assuming that a physical examination reveals no underlying health problems, further assessment is indicated. Because symptoms of school phobia overlap symptoms of depression, referral to the school psychologist may be helpful. If left untreated, school phobia has potentially significant and negative long-term consequences including academic failure, impaired peer relationships, and other psychiatric or anxiety-related issues.

School phobia may sometimes be a medication side effect. Do not neglect to consult with the child's physician if a student is on medication and develops school phobia.

School phobia may also be a result of harassment or bullying at school. Do not neglect to find out whether the student is being bullied.

School Refusal

School refusal refers to student-initiated refusal to attend school as distinct from just fear or anxiety about going to school. The average age of onset of school refusal is 10.3 years. School refusal is reported to affect approximately 1% of school children across the primary and secondary school levels if a narrower definition of school refusal is used. It may affect 5-28% of students at some point in their lives if the definition is expanded to include those who attend school but have trouble staying in school.

In a number of situations, anxiety or depression may be factors in school refusal (Bernstein et al. 2001). The most common diagnoses for youth with school refusal (Kearney and Albano 2004) are:
- Separation Anxiety Disorder (22.4%)
- Generalized Anxiety Disorder (10.5%)
- Oppositional Defiant Disorder (8.4%),
- Depression (4.9%),
- Specific phobia (4.2%),
- Social Anxiety Disorder (3.5%), and
- Conduct Disorder (2.8%)

As noted by Kearney, the issue of school refusal is a complex one. Children who were classified as "anxious school refusers" were more likely to have depression and Separation Anxiety Disorder, whereas those who were "purely truant refusers" were more likely to be diagnosed with Oppositional Defiant Disorder (ODD), Conduct Disorder (CD), and depression. Other studies find that "anxious school refusers" escape anxiety by avoiding school, while ODD and CD predict pursuit of external and tangible reinforcers outside of school (Kearney and Albano 2004).[*] The assessment and management of school refusal requires a functional behavioral analysis (Chapter 26).

In a 2003 study, almost 90% of children and adolescents who had features of both "anxious school refusal" and "truant school refusal" had at least one psychiatric disorder (Egger, Costello, and Angold 2003). In our experience, school refusal is frequently associated with severe OCD, severe depression, bullying, and school failure.

[*] As discussed in Chapter 8 on ADHD, teachers and school personnel really need to incorporate lavish and tangible external or extrinsic reinforcers to motivate students with ADHD. The Kearney and Albano findings come as no surprise to us: When school is not a reinforcing place, the students will go/seek reinforcement elsewhere.

Specific Phobias

A specific phobia is an extremely intense and irrational fear of something that really poses little or no actual danger. Specific phobias usually first appear during childhood or adolescence and often persist into adulthood. Some common specific phobias are: closed-in places (e.g., tunnels, elevators), weather (e.g., thunderstorms, tornadoes), animals (e.g., snakes, dogs), insects (e.g., bees, spiders), blood, needles, heights, dark, driving, water, and flying.

These symptoms can cause social embarrassment, disruptive behavior, and an inability to follow the class routine, e.g., the student refuses to go outside for PE due to a phobia of bees. Sadly, most people do not know how painful this is and think of it as strange or willful misbehavior. Specific phobias exhibited in the home can also impair school functioning, e.g., a student who has difficulty falling asleep because of a phobic fear of the dark may be tired and unable to concentrate in school the next day.

Generalized Anxiety Disorder (GAD)

Generalized Anxiety Disorder is chronic anxiety that lasts six months or more and that pervades all aspects of the student's day. Students with GAD worry about everything, and their worry persists even when past performance indicates that there is no real basis for worry. In young children, GAD is also referred to as Overanxious Disorder of Childhood.

Symptoms of children with GAD may look like those of children with Obsessive-Compulsive Disorder (Chapter 5) in that these kids may be perfectionists, frequently doubt themselves, and seek frequent approval and constant reassurance. For some children, however, there is just a general and pervasive sense of anxiety or worry (that is, not a specific worry). GAD is accompanied by physical symptoms such as fatigue, headache, muscle tension, or aches. Students with GAD may report difficulty swallowing, have hot flashes, or feel lightheaded. They may experience nausea, trembling, restlessness, or edginess. Some children with GAD may be irritable, sweat excessively, feel dizzy, or have an acute startle reflex. GAD interferes with concentration and the ability to relax. It also interferes with the student getting a good night's sleep (Alfano et al. 2006).

Post-Traumatic Stress Disorder (PTSD)

Post-Traumatic Stress Disorder may develop when a child or adolescent is exposed to a traumatic event that involves the actual or perceived threat of death or serious bodily injury, and their response involves intense fear, helplessness, or horror. Symptoms of PTSD usually emerge within three months of the original trauma and include: persisting signs of physiologic arousal (such as difficulty falling asleep or staying asleep), irritability or anger outbursts, difficulty concentrating, excessive vigilance, and an exaggerated startle response. Occasionally, symptoms of PTSD do not emerge until years after the traumatic event. Whenever the child or adolescent is exposed to some situation or event that is reminiscent of the original trauma, the student may experience intense anxiety and distress accompanied by bodily reactivity. The student with PTSD is likely to avoid situations associated with, or which remind her of, the traumatic event. This can lead to a markedly restricted range of activities and settings, impairing social and school activities. The course of PTSD varies, and in some cases, the condition may become chronic.

Following the terrorist attacks on September 11, 2001, a survey was conducted of pediatricians to assess the impact on children. Almost two thirds of the pediatricians who responded to the survey identified behavioral problems in children directly affected by 9/11 (Laraque et al. 2004).[*]

Selective Mutism

Selective Mutism is an anxiety disorder characterized by a persistent failure to speak in social situations despite speaking in other situations. The term "specific mutism" is used to indicate a situation in which the student does not speak to school personnel, but may speak to peers and parents, both at home and in school. "Generalized mutism" refers to those situations in which the child only speaks in the home and not outside the home.

Because the child is capable of speaking and interacting in some situations, selective mutism is

---

[*] Immediately after 9/11, Leslie expected her young patients to have a worsening of their anxiety symptoms because every school in her area (New York) had someone who had lost a family member or was affected. Surprisingly, there was no significant increase in anxiety in her patients, which she attributes to the outstanding job that the schools and parents did in counseling the students and supporting them.

not due to a primary language deficit, psychosis, or lack of knowledge of social language. Selective Mutism is often maintained by well-intentioned family, friends, and teachers or other school personnel who readily interpret the nonverbal gestures and behavior. Not surprisingly, children with specific or generalized mutism display high levels of social phobia and significant deficits in verbal and nonverbal social skills at home and in school (Cunningham, McHolm, and Boyle 2006).

The symptoms of selective mutism tend to improve over time, but, like other anxiety diagnoses, the presence of selective mutism predicts higher future rates for phobic disorders and other psychiatric disorders (Steinhausen et al. 2006). Treating anxiety improves academic performance and school functioning during the course of treatment (Wood, 2006).

School Impact

As suggested by the descriptions of the disorders, anxiety disorders may have significant negative impact:

- High anxiety can impair academic performance (Muris and Meesters 2002).
- High anxiety is a risk factor for substance abuse, depression, and adjustment problems post-school. Substance abuse and a history of anxiety disorders predicts early school withdrawal (Van Ameringen, Mancini, and Farvolden 2003).
- Teenagers with high anxiety express higher levels of stress, anger, sadness, fatigue, and an urge to eat. They also experience stronger smoking urges and more tobacco use, although the relationship between anxiety, depression, and smoking is different for adolescent boys than it is for girls (Dudas, Hans, and Barabas 2005).
- Anxiety can lead to school attendance problems including school avoidance, school refusal, and/or withdrawing from school early. The more anxiety diagnoses the student has, the greater the risk of leaving school early.
- Social phobia is associated with reduced visual memory scores (Vasa et al. 2006).
- Anxiety disorders may be associated with lowered linguistic abilities and reduced cognitive flexibility (Toren et al. 2000).
- High anxiety can impair self-esteem.

- High anxiety can impair peer relations as well as limit the student's ability to form or maintain close personal relationships.
- Severe anxiety can negatively affect a child's thinking, decision-making ability, and perception of the environment.
- Anxiety can significantly interfere with concentration and learning.

Tips and Tricks for Helping Students with Anxiety Disorders

The following tips and strategies can help students with anxiety disorders:

- Do not force, but positively reinforce the student for staying in an anxiety-provoking situation. If the student's anxiety is so intense that she really cannot tolerate the situation, allow her to leave the situation and go to a designated "safe person" or a "safe place." The safe place may be another part of the classroom or another designated location in the building.
- For students who leave the classroom too frequently, gradually introduce some limits on how often or when the student may go to the "safe person" or "safe location," but only do so after consulting with the parents, student, and any treating professionals.
- For students with panic attacks, provide a permanent pass so that the student can make a graceful exit from the classroom without being conspicuous. The ability to make a graceful exit is important to the student's self-esteem and peer relationships. (See Chapter 31 for more on graceful exits.)
- Provide lecture notes and copies of board work as an accommodation for material missed while the student is out of the room or for impaired concentration due to interference from anxious thoughts.
- Extend time on classwork and homework as well as on tests.
- Accommodate late arrival to school due to sleep problems or separation anxiety. Do not punish a student for being late to school if she has separation anxiety, school avoidance, school phobia, or school refusal.
- If the student has Separation Anxiety Disorder:

- ❑ Have a "check-in" ritual for the child when she arrives at school (counselor, nurse, office). Having the responsibility to report to a particular individual and being greeted warmly by school personnel for showing up may increase the student's likelihood of entering the school building.
- ❑ Try to have a motivating activity for the student to do after the check-in procedure (such as feeding the class pet, helping the teacher set up the classroom, playing with a friend before class, computer time, etc.)
- ❑ Provide positive reinforcement for compliance with the check-in procedure.
- ❑ At the start of any program to help the student reduce anxiety, encourage the student to bring in a "transitional object" from home (something that makes her feel safer, like a favorite stuffed animal) and encourage her to take a favorite book or drawing or object from school back home (school-to-home transitional object).
- ❑ Pre-plan with the student when she will be allowed to call home, e.g., "Finish this worksheet and then you can call home and tell Mom that you got your work done." Dealing with separation anxiety by allowing the student to call home to report success tends to be more effective than a "cold turkey" approach of "You cannot call home at all." As an alternative plan, have the parent and student pre-determine what time the student may call home.
- ❑ Encourage parents to tuck into their child's lunch bag or notebooks cheery notes like "I'm so proud of you for making it through to lunch today. Have a great time with your friends!" or "When you come home today, I hope you'll tell me about something exciting you learned in school today!" Positively reinforce time spent in school or time spent on tasks. Use in-school reinforcers such as the opportunity for more time on the computer, lunch in the classroom with a special friend, extra recess time, or time to read or draw.
- ❑ Encourage parents to systematically increase the amount of time that the stu-

dent is separated from them in the home or outside of school.
- ❑ Suggest to the parents that someone other than the parent takes the child to school. This sometimes makes it easier for the child to separate and enter school.
- ❑ Provide in-school counseling to support cognitive interventions that can help the student replace anxious thoughts with more positive ones; collaborate with treating therapist if student is getting cognitive-behavior therapy.

Before the child calls parents from school, coach parents how to respond if the student calls crying, and begs to be taken home. One strategy we have used is to teach parents to say, "I understand that you are having a rough time right now. I'd like you to call me back in one hour to let me know how you're doing." If the child persists, crying, "Take me home NOW!" the parent might then say, "I know that you're upset, so please call me in an hour. Please put your teacher on the phone now and I will tell her that I want you to call me in an hour."

- ■ If the student exhibits school refusal:
  - ❑ Expose the student to school gradually—starting with a few hours.
  - ❑ Have a "check-in" ritual for the child when they arrive at school (counselor, nurse, office), as described above.
  - ❑ Set up an engaging activity for the student to do after the check-in procedure, such as feeding the class pet, helping set up the classroom, playing with a friend for a few minutes before class, or providing some computer time. This provides positive reinforcement for completing the check-in.
  - ❑ Provide in-school counseling to support cognitive interventions that can help the student replace anxious thoughts with more positive ones; collaborate with therapist if student is getting cognitive-behavior therapy.
- ■ Provide test accommodations:
  - ❑ Have someone the student knows test the student in a separate location.
  - ❑ Extend time.
  - ❑ For students that have trouble retrieving language, provide a word bank.

- School personnel can teach students simple relaxation techniques that can be used in school, e.g., yoga or breathing techniques (see Appendix G and the accompanying CD-ROM).
- If school avoidance is the result of academic difficulties leading to anxiety, address any learning disabilities and provide added academic support.

If the student's plan calls for a check-in ritual, ensure that there is an alternative person available to support the check-in ritual in case the assigned staff person is absent!

- For students with social anxiety (social phobia):
  - ❑ Provide added adult support during interactions with peers.
  - ❑ Allow the student to eat lunch in the classroom with a few friends.
  - ❑ Provide added adult support during transitions, for example, changing classes.
  - ❑ Provide the student with specific instructions as to what to do in a novel situation such as "When we go on the field trip tomorrow, you can help by checking off each student's name as they get on the bus."
  - ❑ Allow the student to observe others giving their oral presentations or engaging in an activity before asking the student to give her presentation, etc.
  - ❑ Carefully match the student with other students for small-group instruction and activities.
  - ❑ Use coaching and "Instant Replay" (Chapter 31) to teach the student what to do in social situations. For example, "Look at the bridge of the other person's nose when she is talking to you" or "Take turns talking."
  - ❑ Include peer interactions as part of academic assignments, e.g., "Think-Pair-Share" activities (see "Decreasing Hyperactivity" section in Chapter 8) or working on tasks with peers.
  - ❑ Provide social skills training in a small group. Many students with social anxiety do not need social skills training, but the small-group experience can build their confidence and enable them to feel more comfortable with peers.

- Plan and prepare staff to respond in an agreed upon fashion to phobic reactions and incorporate accommodations or interventions into a plan.
- When the student is calm, talk about what to do when the student feels panicky or highly anxious, e.g., use diaphragmatic breathing for ten breaths, think about how your friend would handle this situation, go for a walk in the hall, come back and resume work.
  - ❑ Use coaching or direct instruction and "Instant Replay" (Chapter 31) to teach the student how to respond to anxiety-producing situations, e.g., "If you cannot find your pencil, raise your hand and I will give you one," "If you make a mistake, make an X through it and I will know not to read it." With younger students, role-playing with puppets may be helpful.
  - ❑ Use coaching, "Cooperative Problem Solving," and "Instant Replay" (Chapter 31) to help the student implement anxiety-reducing strategies.
- Reduce unnecessary exposure to anxiety-producing situations until the student is better prepared to handle those situations, e.g., if a student experiences significant anxiety about public speaking, allow the student to tape record the presentation or to present it only to the teacher, etc.
- Incorporate stories or books that deal with anxiety into the student's reading.

If a student is frequently using the "graceful exit" pass to leave one—and only one—class, initiate a Functional Behavioral Assessment (Chapter 26) to determine if curricular modifications or special education services are required. It is important to determine if something is going on in the class that is leading to social anxiety or avoidance.

Other School-Based Interventions or Supports

The Role of the School Nurse

For students whose school anxiety or avoidance might increase their asthma symptoms or is a consequence of their asthma or any other medical condition, including the school nurse in the planning and supports can make a positive difference. School nurses play an important role in conducting groups, educating students and their parents, and coordinating with the student's physicians.

School-Based Therapy

If school psychologists are well trained in cognitive-behavior therapy (CBT), suggest that the student meet with the school psychologist. This is an effective individual or group-based intervention for anxious students on its own or used in conjunction with other supports and interventions. Providing parent education and training can boost the clinical anxiety-reducing benefit for the students (Bernstein et al. 2005).

The "Worry Hill" program by Aureen Wagner, Ph.D. provides a clear explanation of anxiety and how parents and school personnel can help a child overcome anxiety (Wagner 2005).

For school refusers, school-based CBT may have to wait until other interventions have been successful in getting the student back into school. When a student is not attending school due to school refusal, the first step is to conduct a Functional Behavioral Assessment (Chapter 26) to determine the function that the refusal serves and so that meaningful interventions can be developed. Even if the school refusal is thought to be anxiety-related, a more refined analysis of the type of anxiety is required. For example, if a student is socially anxious, then the plan will need to deal with peer issues, whereas if a student is avoiding school due to a specific phobia, a different approach will be required.

Some students who have been absent from school for long periods of time (due to hospitalization or other factors) may also experience significant anxiety upon returning to school and may need to be slowly exposed again to the school setting. For such students, asking the student to attend school for a specific class or a small amount of time each day may be an effective approach. As the student becomes more comfortable, the amount of time can be gradually increased. To prevent additional stress that can increase the student's anxiety, provide 1:1 tutoring in the school setting for work missed. This way, the student can catch up and feel less anxious about attending classes while increasing the amount of time they spend in the building. If the student cannot tolerate spending that much time in the building, provide 1:1 tutoring in another setting (such as the public library) each day to supplement time spent in class. This way, the student is not in the home and is still getting instruction. In extreme cases, the school may need to provide the supplemental 1:1 tutoring in the home.

For students with whom cognitive-behavioral interventions may be particularly challenging, consider starting with a more behavioral approach. For example, the school psychologist or counselor can teach the student relaxation techniques (Appendix G), and then teach the student to use the techniques when she encounters an anxiety-provoking situation. The student practices acting as if she were not anxious ("make believe" or "be an actor"), e.g., "Act as if you were your best friend, Julie. How would she handle this?"

Associated or Comorbid Conditions

Approximately half of anxious adolescents have other disorders. The most common comorbid condition is depression, with anxiety emerging first developmentally and depression emerging later. The following conditions tend to occur at higher rates in children and adolescents with anxiety disorders:

- Other anxiety disorders (e.g., social phobia)
- OCD
- Mood Disorders (e.g., depression or BP)
- Memory problems
- ADHD
- School refusal
- Unexplained headaches, stomachaches, muscle/joint pains, nausea or gastrointestinal symptoms, etc.
- Substance abuse or alcohol abuse
- Eating Disorders
- Sleep problems
- Executive Dysfunction (EDF)
- Pragmatic (Social) Language Disorder (Social language deficits caused by verbal EDF)
- Sensory dysregulation
- Learning Disabilities
- Processing speed deficits (may be secondary to interference)

School-Based Assessments

A number of clinical scales can be used by the school psychologist to assess anxiety, e.g.:

- Spence Children's Anxiety Scale for children ages eight through twelve
- Revised Children's Manifest Anxiety Scale for ages six to nineteen
- Beck Anxiety Inventory for Youth for ages seven to fourteen.

Parents who are concerned about their child's anxiety issues may ask the school to assess the student to determine if any accommodations or school-based interventions are needed. In some cases, the school's assessment may trigger a referral to an outside mental health professional for evaluation and treatment.

Assessments for anxiety disorders are more helpful if they include both timed and untimed measures of performance, review of attendance records, review of how often the student might be leaving classes and/or going to the nurse's office, and screening the student for sleep and homework issues (see Appendix F and Figure 23.2).

Summary

Anxiety disorders are the most common childhood psychiatric disorder. Students may experience any of a number of different types of anxiety disorders, but all impair a student's ability to concentrate, enjoy school, and socialize with peers. Students with anxiety disorders may need accommodations in class, for tests and homework, and support for transitions and social situations. In more severe cases, they may require Behavior Intervention Plans, in-school clinical services such as counseling, and for students who are social phobic, social skills training in small groups. The school psychologist, counselor, or special education teacher can coordinate in-school services.

Julio's school team asked his therapist to advise them about what to do when Julio had panic attacks. She recommended arranging for Julio to go see a "safe person" when he felt panicky and that school personnel cue Julio to use certain techniques she had taught him in therapy. In her first meeting with Julio, the therapist had talked with him about panic attacks, instructed him in a simple breathing relaxation technique that she encouraged him to practice daily, and suggested an alternate thought

to concentrate on when he started to have his next panic attack. They spent the remainder of the session practicing what he would think and do if he felt he was going to have another panic attack, and how he would practice the skills at home each day. His mother was taught the techniques and was asked to help her son with "practice panic drills." Somewhat to everyone's surprise (including the therapist's), Julio did not have any more panic attacks in school or at home, and at last follow-up, two years later, he was still panic free.

CHAPTER 7

PANDAS (The Strep Connection)

Julie's teachers knew her as a model third grade student who had good grades, good behavior, and friends. But when Julie returned to school after being absent for a day due to a strep infection, her teachers were stunned to see that she was displaying severe tics and was extremely anxious. Julie went to the doctor and came back to school diagnosed with TS and OCD. Julie's mother had a history of OCD and anxiety disorders, but until that day, no one had ever seen any signs in Julie.

Preview

Almost 300 hundred years ago, physicians knew that some patients experienced bizarre movements or symptoms following infections such as rheumatic fever. The topic was never really investigated systematically, though, until there was a resurgence of interest in the 1990's following reports that some children had an acute onset of tics, obsessions, and compulsions following a strep infection, or an acute worsening of their symptoms if they already had a history of tics, obsessions, and/or compulsions. The relationship between strep infections and tics, obsessions, and compulsions was called "PANDAS," an acronym for "**P**ediatric **A**utoimmune **N**europsychiatric **D**isorders **A**ssociated with **S**treptococcal infections."

The "Strep Connection"

PANDAS is very controversial and not everyone is convinced that it should be considered a distinct and unique disorder (Singer and Loiselle 2003; Hoekstra and Minderaa 2005; Kurlan 1998, 2004; Swedo et al. 1998; Swedo, Leonard, and Rapoport 2004). Professionals do agree, however, that some children who are already symptomatic have acute worsening of symptoms following a streptococcal infection, and some children who had never had symptoms suddenly explode in tics, obsessions, and compulsions following an infection. Some clinical researchers have reported that PANDAS may also cause worsening of anxiety, mood problems (Leslie et al. 2008), sleep problems (Matsuo et al. 2004), and ADHD symptoms (Leslie et al. 2008). The flare-ups may occur almost immediately after onset of the infection or shortly thereafter. Unfortunately, they may continue long after the active infection has disappeared.

Based on available research, it appears that a small subset of children with TS or OCD get acute exacerbations of their symptoms following an infection and a small subset of children who never had any tics or obsessive-compulsive symptoms but who have a family history of TS or OCD will have an acute-onset of TS or OCD following an infection. Lest we alarm parents, it is important to emphasize that not every child who has tics or obsessions and compulsions will have an acute exacerbation following a strep infection, and not every child who has a parent with either of these disorders will suddenly develop TS or OCD following an infection.

What Teachers Need to Know

Symptoms of children who have tics or TS (Chapter 4) or obsessive-compulsive problems (Chapter 5) may worsen when the child is ill. Although any kind of infection or other severe illness may trigger this kind of severe eruption or acute worsening of symptoms, strep seems to be a common infectious culprit.

Although this discussion has focused on strep, which is one type of bacterial infection, the same types of patterns have also been observed following other types of bacterial infections and even viral infections. Some researchers talk about PITANDS, an acronym for **P**ediatric **I**nfection-**T**riggered **A**utoimmune **N**europsychiatric **D**isorders," to include both bacterial and viral infections.

There is not much that teachers can do if a child is having a PANDAS-related flare-up of symptoms other than to be supportive and make even more accommodations. Nothing indicates that treating the infection stops the symptom flare-up once it has begun although treating the infection is important for other health reasons. Even after the infection is gone, the flare-up may persist and everyone may just have to ride out the rough period.

John was scared when his normally mild symptoms of TS and OCD suddenly worsened dramatically after an ear infection. Not only was he in physical pain from his new head and neck jerking tics, but he did not know if his tics were going to be like this for the rest of his life. He was also concerned that other students would make fun of him. His parents agreed that he could stay home until they could meet with his teachers the next day to come up with a plan for him in school. They also reassured John that what he was experiencing was just a temporary worsening from a recent infection and that his symptoms would eventually ease up.

When John's teachers heard what had happened, they immediately agreed to arrange for peer education to make sure that John felt as comfortable and accepted in school as possible. They also worked with John's parents to determine what accommodations he might need for reading and writing activities and homework. When John returned to school, he was relieved to find that his classmates thoughtfully offered to take notes for him, read to him, and that they made a point of including him in lunch time and recess social activities.

CHAPTER 8

Attention Deficit Hyperactivity Disorder

*For students with ADD, school too often starts with failure
experiences and goes downhill from there.*
— Ronald E. Reeve

Preview

Out of all the disorders described in this book, Attention Deficit Hyperactivity Disorder (ADHD) has accumulated the most research and generated the most controversy. It is the most common diagnosis out of those covered in this book: 7.8% of children aged four to seventeen in the U.S. have been diagnosed with ADHD, increasing to almost 15% of sixteen-year-old boys and 6% of eleven-year-old girls. ADHD is diagnosed about two and a half times more often in boys than in girls (CDC 2005).

ADHD appears to run in families. The genetic contribution to ADHD is greater than the genetic contribution to IQ and nearly that of the genetic contribution to human height. Environmental factors such as parenting or teaching do not cause ADHD (Barkley, 2003).

Families are often under great stress when a child has any neurological challenge. ADHD, in particular, takes a significant toll on marriage. Parents of children diagnosed with ADHD in childhood are almost twice as likely to divorce before their child turns eight years old (Wymbs et al. 2008).

Subtypes of ADHD

The three subtypes of ADHD are:
- **Primarily inattentive,** where attentional difficulties are the primary problem.

Students with this subtype have difficulty focusing on nonself-selected tasks.
- **Primarily hyperactive-impulsive,** where motor activity and impulsivity are the primary problems.
- **Combined,** where inattention and hyperactivity-impulsivity are both significant problems.[*] Students with the *combined subtype* are at greater risk of academic, behavioral, and social-emotional difficulties.

Although the majority of students with ADHD are in regular education settings, the majority of students in self-contained education settings may have ADHD (Bussing et al. 1998; Dery et al. 2004). To complicate matters, a significant minority of students with the combined subtype are also diagnosed with Oppositional Defiant Disorder (ODD) and Conduct Disorder (CD). Students with these additional problems are at even greater risk for placement in school programs for behaviorally or emotionally disturbed students. Left untreated, the outlook for students with ODD and CD is poor in terms of criminal behavior, personality disorders as adults, substance abuse disorders, depression, and more parent/family disorders.

---

[*] The diagnostic criteria and subtypes are expected to change when the DSM-V is released in a few years. The present discussion is based on the DSM-IV-TR.

In contrast to students with the combined subtype, students with the *inattentive subtype* face an increased risk of anxiety disorders but not ODD or CD. Compared to students with other subtypes, these students are more likely to have speech/language problems, fall behind in academics, have more problems with math, suffer greater rates of anxiety problems, and have learning disabilities. The *combined subtype* accounts for 50-75% of children and teens diagnosed with ADHD. The least common subtype is the primarily hyperactive-impulsive type.

Students with ADHD often require significant accommodations and interventions in school if they are to succeed academically and socially. Just because the diagnosis may be fairly common does not mean it can be treated lightly. A diagnosis of ADHD needs to trigger a comprehensive school assessment.

Impact of ADHD

Social Impact and Outcomes

Students with ADHD often have significant social problems. Students with the primarily inattentive subtype of ADHD are rated by teachers and parents as being socially passive and having deficits in social knowledge. Although these students are not seen as having problems in emotional regulation, they are often neglected and rejected by their peers because they are withdrawn and sometimes anxious.

The "2/3's Rule"

As a rule of thumb, Russell Barkley, Ph.D. suggests that adults treat students with ADHD as if they were 70% of their chronological age in terms of their self- and emotional control (Barkley 1991).

This may be a somewhat optimistic estimate, as many of these students have more than one disorder and are not even at the 2/3 level when it comes to emotional regulation and social skills.

Students with the combined subtype tend to be actively disliked by their peers. By fourth grade, 70% of children in this subtype are rejected by peers and have no reciprocal friendships. Peer rejection often occurs within the first two hours of interaction (Weiss and Hechtman 1993). Further, 40-70% of teens with ADHD engage in oppositional or aggressive behavior towards teachers and peers. Those

with comorbid ODD or CD also engage in more sensation-seeking activities. During adolescence, many of these peer-rejected students with ADHD eventually associate with peers who engage in more problematic behavior patterns.

The peer problems encountered by students in the combined subtype are not just the result of the students being more impulsive or hyperactive. Aggressive behavior and emotional dysregulation contribute significantly to the problems. Students with ADHD are generally able to understand the emotional expressions of their peers, but they may not pay enough attention to the peers' behavior. Those with comorbid ODD or CD are even more at risk for misperceiving others' anger and/or responding angrily or aggressively to their peers. The peer rejection that began in the elementary grades worsens in adolescence.[*]

Consider these alarming statistics on adolescents with ADHD:

- 75% have social relationship problems
- 25-33% of teens with ADHD will have a diagnosed antisocial disorder, and up to two-thirds of that subgroup will be arrested

Criminal activity:

- 31% run away from home (vs. 16% of peers)
- 20% engage in breaking & entering (vs. 8% of peers)
- 74% get into fist-fights (vs. 53% of peers)
- 39% carry a weapon (vs. 11% of peers)
- 22% commit assault with a weapon (vs. 7% of peers)
- 16% set fires (vs. 5% of peers)
- 22% are arrested for a felony (vs. 3% of peers)

Sexual activity:

- Begin sexual activity on average one year earlier than their peers without ADHD
- Have more sexual partners, spend less time with each, and are less likely to use contraception
- Have significantly more teen pregnancies than their peers without ADHD (38% vs. 4%)
- Are treated for sexually transmitted diseases (STDS) more than their peers without ADHD (16% vs. 4%)

---

[*] Many of the statistics in this section are from (Barkley 1998; Barkley 2003).

Persistence of Problems in Adulthood:

For the majority of teens with ADHD, problems will persist into adulthood (Mannuzza, Klein, and Moulton 2003). Comparing a community sample of adults with ADHD and non-ADHD controls, adults with ADHD:*

- Complete, on average, two to three years less schooling; only 17% complete college (compared to 26% of non-ADHD peers)
- Are less likely to be employed (52% vs. 72% of non-ADHD peers)
- Tend to hold lower-ranking occupations
- Are fired from their jobs and change jobs more often than their non-ADHD peers
- Suffer from poor self-esteem and social skills deficits
- Are more likely to be arrested (37% vs. 18% of non-ADHD peers)
- Are more likely to exhibit an antisocial personality and other personality disorders
- Are more likely to have a substance use disorder
- Are more likely to divorce (28% vs. 15% of non-ADHD peers)

Academic Impact

Although estimates vary across studies, it seems clear that the majority of students with ADHD have academic problems in the elementary grades that continue into adolescence:**

- 50% require academic tutoring or extra help
- 25-45% are retained at least one year
- 25-50% are placed in special education
- 40-60% are suspended from school (compared to 18% of non-ADHD students)
- 10-18% are expelled (compared to 5% of their peers)
- 30-40% drop out of school (compared to 9% of non-ADHD students)
- Have a lower class ranking (69th percentile) and grade point average (1.7 vs. 2.6 for peers) if they do stay in school

Young adults with ADHD-combined type and young adults with ADHD-inattentive type were both

less likely to have graduated from college and were more likely to have received special educational placement in high school.

Do not assume that mild symptoms mean mild academic problems. Even having relatively mild ADHD symptoms nearly doubles the probability of grade repetition and is associated with 8-10% lower math and reading test scores relative to average test scores for U.S. children (Currie and Stabile 2006).

Students with ADHD also often have:
- Handwriting problems
- Problems copying from the board
- Learning Disabilities (LD) - 19-90% of ADHD cases, depending on how LD are defined, have:
  - reading disabilities - 16-39%
  - spelling disorders - 24-27%
  - math disabilities - 13-33%, especially mental computation problems
  - written expressive language problems - 65%
- Speech and language problems, e.g., pragmatics, word retrieval problems, reduced verbal fluency
- Story recall problems
- Excessive speech
- Impaired memory (e.g., procedural, strategic, and working memory)
- Executive Dysfunction

Remember the Variability Principle

These children do well twice and we hold it against them the rest of their academic careers.
— Sam Kuperman, M.D.

A student with ADHD varies widely in sustained focus and productivity. On a neurological level, the student's brain is like a power grid that is usually "browned-out." When the student's brain is "browned out," she will have difficulty attending and working at a normal pace. Occasionally, when the topic is particularly interesting or on a "good neurochemical" day, brain activity is boosted into a more "normal" zone and she can pay attention.

---

* Many of the statistics in this section are from (Biederman et al. 2006).

** Many of the statistics in this section are from research conducted by Barkley or reviewed by Barkley [cf. (Barkley 2003)].

Stimulant medications used to treat ADHD increase focus by essentially boosting the students' levels of the neurochemicals.

Some of the variability in performance is due to failure to pay attention to details, but there are other factors at play. Some students with ADHD have visual tracking deficits (Munoz, Armstrong, Hampton, & Moore, 2003). The inability to pay attention to details and deficits in visual tracking can result in what are erroneously called "careless errors." Situational and task factors, such as those listed below, also contribute to variability in academic performance and symptoms. Each of these variables has implications for classroom structure and management:

- Time of day
- Task complexity
- Demands for self-restraint (e.g., staying seated, remaining quiet while teacher speaks)
- Low stimulation levels
- Insufficient extrinsic reinforcement
- Absence of adult supervision
- Stress

ADHD or Gifted—or Both?

Children or teens may have ADHD and be intellectually gifted, although the similarity in some of the features of both conditions may make recognition of either or both difficult. The confusion between ADHD and giftedness becomes apparent when we consider the behaviors that have been associated with each condition, as illustrated in Table 8.1.

ADHD-gifted boys seem more similar to ADHD boys than to gifted boys in terms of their learning characteristics, physical difficulty with handwriting, difficulty getting started on reading texts, lack of enjoyment for reading, and difficulty with routine math. The only learning characteristics ADHD-gifted boys shared with gifted boys without ADHD are their dislike of handwriting and long worksheets and enjoyment of science and "hands-on" activities (Moon 2002).

Giftedness does not appear to be a protective factor and seems to predict poorer psychosocial skills and family difficulties (Moon et al. 2001). Gifted students with ADHD may find interactions with their gifted non-ADHD peers are problematic because of their social and emotional immaturity. Thus, gifted students with ADHD are likely to be more impaired than students with ADHD-only. Further, their giftedness may mask some of their deficits and result in the school not identifying them as being entitled to, and in need of, accommodations or special education services.

Gifted students with ADHD have different needs than ADHD students who are not gifted. An

Table 8.1. Comparing ADHD and Giftedness

Behaviors Associated with ADHD (Barkley, 1990)	**Behaviors Associated with Giftedness** (Webb, 1993)
Poorly sustained attention in almost all situations	Poor attention, boredom, daydreaming in specific situations
Diminished persistence on tasks not having immediate consequences	Low tolerance for persistence on tasks that seem irrelevant
Impulsivity, poor delay of gratification	Judgment lags behind development of intellect
Impaired adherence to commands to regulate or inhibit behavior in social contexts	Intensity may lead to power struggles with authorities
More active, restless than normal children	High activity level; may need less sleep
Difficulty adhering to rules and regulations	Questions rules, customs, and traditions

Source: (Webb and Latimer 1993)

appropriate program is one that both nurtures the talent of gifted students with ADHD and that also addresses any disabilities (Niehart 2003).

> *Accommodations that are often recommended for children with ADHD may exacerbate problems if the child is also gifted [Moon, 2002, as cited in (Niehart, 2003)]. For example, shortening work time may frustrate a gifted student with ADHD who is interested in the activity and capable of more high level work.*

ADHD and Safety

One too often overlooked consequence of ADHD relates to safety. The statistics on teen sexual behavior, sexually transmitted diseases, and unwanted pregnancies are only part of the story. Children with ADHD have more accidents than their peers without ADHD, have more serious injuries, including injuries to multiple body regions and head injuries, and are more likely to require hospitalization in intensive care units (DiScala et al. 1998). Walking (pedestrian accidents) and bicycling pose significantly greater safety risks for youth with ADHD than their peers without ADHD.

School personnel supervising students on the playground, in the gym, on the school bus, or in less structured settings need to be informed that particular students may need more supervision and guidance to protect their safety. Field trips may also pose safety concerns and may require added adult supervision.

Guiding Principles for Educating Students with ADHD

The needs of students with ADHD vary to some degree depending on the subtype of ADHD that they have. (Refer to Table 8.2 on page 58.)

> *If we lose our composure when a student breaks the rules, the student will be distracted by our emotional response and will be more focused on our behavior than on her own behavior. By remaining calm, we increase the likelihood that the student will notice or reflect on her own behavior.*

Tips and Tricks for Helping Students with ADHD

Students with complex behavior or symptom management needs require highly trained school personnel to design and implement management strategies. Ask the student support team, school psychologist, special education department, and related services for additional expertise. Some school systems have access to neuropsychologists and behavior experts. Other important sources of information are the volunteer organizations that have experts available on a particular disorder. Some of these resources are provided in the resources section of this book.

Fostering Attention

Seating:
- Seat the student directly facing the board or screen if she must copy from it.
- For direct instruction of new skills, use traditional row arrangement of desks.
- Seat the student close enough to enable frequent and discreet refocusing or assistance.
- Seat the child with attention problems close to the main area of instruction and away from potential distractions such as windows, doors, etc.
- Seat the student next to a good role model in terms of work pace, focus, and behavior.
- Reconfigure desks for different types of tasks requiring different levels of activity. Students with the hyperactive-impulsive and combined subtypes of ADHD typically learn best in environments in which they can move around and respond actively during or between activities. Combine both elements (teacher-directed instruction and opportunities for movement and active engagement) by having clearly defined classroom spaces. Creating multimedia learning centers based on themes can also provide students with areas for appropriate movement and activity. The configuration of the classroom desks can also be altered for specific types of activities:
  - ❑ Have the students move their desks into a circle for group discussions to promote more participation by more students.

❑ Have the students move their desks into clusters for cooperative group-learning activities. To reduce off-task and impulsive behavior, seat the student with impulsivity in a cluster with good role models but try to allow the students some element of choice as to how they group their desks for cooperative learning activities.

Working Privately with the Student with ADHD:
- Walk around the classroom during times when the students are reading and discreetly touch the page or place in the book where the student's attention needs to be focused.
- Privately consult with the student and ask whether the student would find it more helpful to be called on randomly or to be

Table 8.2. Guiding Principles for Teaching Students with ADHD

Principle	Implementation
Externalize important rules about behavior.	Post the rules for behavior in the classroom with their rewards and fines. Actively teach the class rules the first day and week of classes.
Introduce new learning in the morning.	Introduce new and complex material mid-morning when students experience optimal arousal (have better focus).
Externalize important information about academic tasks.	Use a smartboard, whiteboard, or overhead projector to visually emphasize important information. Provide hard copies of instructions and notes.
Externalize steps in multi-step sequences.	Provide visual cues or organizers for multiple-step sequences.
Use cognitive cues to preserve the sequence in multi-step tasks.	Use and teach the use of mnemonics that preserve sequence, such as "**D**oes **M**cDonald's™ **S**ell **B**urgers?" for the steps in long division (**D**ivide, **M**ultiply, **S**ubtract, **B**ring down).
Externalize sources of motivation and reward lavishly.	Incentives help, so figure out what will motivate the students (e.g., homework passes).
Teach strategies to compensate for impaired executive functions.	Approach impaired executive functions (Chapter 9) from the perspective of teaching life skills that the student needs to remain organized and successful.
Add adult supervision.	Add adult supervision to reduce impulsive or hyperactive behaviors that may lead to injuries in the gym, cafeteria, on the playground, and on the bus.
Provide assistance at the point of performance when it is needed.	Check for comprehension after giving directions. For example, ask the students to complete one math problem and then go over it with them before continuing.
Expect variability in performance.	Capitalize on the good days or hours to teach new material, and use the more difficult times to consolidate or rehearse previously acquired skills.
Enforce rules consistently and calmly.	Providing the consequence consistently and evenhandedly is more effective than providing a major consequence inconsistently.

pre-cued or told in advance that she will be called on.

- Develop a private joke or signal with students to use to help them reconnect or refocus.

Encouraging Focus and Filtering Distractions:

- Give the student some degree of control. This decreases impulsive behaviors, reduces task avoidance, and increases performance. Providing students with some degree of choice also serves as cognitive stimulation. Asking, "OK, which would you prefer to do first—spelling or math?" may redirect students whose attention has wandered or whose behavior has started to become disruptive.
- Break a thirty-minute lesson plan down into two fifteen-minute lessons. The time between the lessons can be used for a reinforcement activity or to connect the lesson information to something meaningful in the student's life.
- Use group-based rewards with younger students to foster attention, such as the "Count Down to Recess" (Chapter 28) where the class can earn extra recess time by being attentive during an instructional unit.
- Reclaim wandering attention by judicious use of phrases such as, "Now this is really important...."
- Use a smartboard, an overhead projector, or a PowerPoint™ presentation to focus attention. (Note: Students with sleep problems may fall asleep if the room is too dark.)
- Employ multi-sensory and hands-on activities.
- Hold an interesting object during presentations, which encourages students to look at you.
- Provide a quiet "office" in the classroom that students can go to when they are having trouble filtering out distractions.
- Allow students to use headphones with white noise or familiar music to help filter out distractions.
- Allow students to wear hats to filter out visual distractions when needed.
- If students have a number of math sheets or work sheets to do, add noninformational color to the later sheets to boost attention.
- Monitor the noise level in the room and reduce it when necessary.

- Remove distractions like rubber bands.
- Provide a few "free desks" so that students who are having trouble sustaining their focus can get up and move to another desk.
- Create a super-stimulating classroom environment so that if the student's attention wanders, it wanders to something academically relevant and enriching.* When stimulation from the educational activity is greater than stimulation from other sources, there are less behavioral problems and more on-task behavior and productivity. When the environment is more stimulating than the planned activity, inappropriate behaviors are more likely.

A teacher recognized that she had a room full of students with distractibility and impulsivity issues and decided to make the best of the situation. She set up her classroom so that no matter where the students looked, they saw something academically challenging. As part of her approach, she changed a display on her desk every week so that the students always had something different to look at. She added more stimulation by presenting the display as a weekly puzzle to solve. The "weekly challenge" gave the students something productive to contemplate while they waited for her attention.

Self- and Peer Monitoring:

- Teach self-monitoring techniques to boost on-task behavior. Use direct instruction plus reinforcement to teach self-monitoring skills.
- Employ peer monitoring to improve on-task behavior and use group-based contingencies, as described in this chapter and in Chapter 28.
- While teenagers with ADHD are doing academic work, seat them in front of a mirror. The mirror serves as a monitor to get them back on task.

---

* Experienced teachers may remember when, years ago, a stripped classroom (Hewitt's Engineered Classroom) was considered better for students with ADHD. They were surprised to learn that the stripped classroom produced more behavior problems than the stimulating classroom environment. In our experience, if the classroom is not visually stimulating, students with ADHD become more hyperactive and seek stimulation, e.g., outside the window, under the radiators, or wherever. By changing the displays on the bulletin boards regularly and by introducing academic puzzles strategically around the classroom, the students find something enriching no matter where they look, and are less likely to create their own stimulation that may be disruptive.

Other Techniques:

- Show students a sample of what a completed project looks like at the beginning of your presentation of a big project.
- Provide sufficient review of old material before introducing new material.
- When giving multi-step directions introduce one direction at a time, then pause or provide a filler before introducing the next direction.
- Check for comprehension.
- Allow as much early morning natural light into the classroom as possible.
- Use color-highlighting to direct attention to important instructions or operational symbols in math.

Learning to go to an "office" (e.g., a carrel in the classroom) to facilitate concentration is a life skill for students with ADHD. Make sure going to this location is a positive experience and is distinguished from any aversive intervention such as a teacher-directed time out.

Decreasing Impulsivity

The following are some strategies for dealing with students who have "Difficulty Waiting Their Turn Syndrome":

Working with Other Students:

- Set up learning activities with peers. Peer attention is a more potent reinforcer for the behavior of boys with ADHD than is teacher attention (Northup et al. 1995). Cooperative learning activities also permit the student with ADHD to be more verbal and active than would normally be allowed in a teacher-directed activity and to work at a faster pace. Boys with ADHD particularly enjoy learning and participating in small groups. Small group activities allow immediate feedback from peers. This approach boosts motivation for students with ADHD to participate, helps students who find it hard to get started, and helps peers see the student with ADHD in a more positive light.
- Use class-wide peer tutoring. When peer math and spelling tutoring activities are used, academic engagement increases and fidgetiness decreases. Peer monitoring can also be an effective strategy as long as the students take turns being the peer monitor. Students with ADHD may benefit from being put in the position of monitoring others' behavior when the monitoring system is tied to a group-based reward.
- Use group-based behavior management techniques like the "Good Behavior Game" where one of the target behaviors is "raising your hand and waiting to be called on before answering."

Give Students Tools:

- Use techniques that enable students to quietly signal that they need assistance without disrupting class (e.g., a paper cup on the student's desk that gets turned over to signal that help is needed, or a tug on the student's ear, etc.).
- Use "talking passes" or a "talking object" so that only the student who is in possession of the pass or object can be speaking.
- Teach and reward self-monitoring techniques (Chapter 28).
- Teach "Turtle" self-monitoring technique: When the teacher says "Turtle!" students will freeze and monitor themselves to find out if they are doing what they are supposed to be doing (Chapter 28).

Routines and Transitions:

- Have predictable routines. Have the daily routine prominently posted where all students can see it.
- Use checklists and check off each item as it is done. Use direct instruction to teach transition skills if student has difficulty making transitions and acts impulsively during transitions (Chapter 9).
- Prompt or cue transitions verbally.
- Provide adult support in proximity to the child for changes in routine and during transitions.

Other Techniques:

- Reward correct responses. Use check marks to indicate correct answers on tests instead of X's to indicate incorrect answers.
- Decrease impulsive errors by having student cross out wrong answers instead of circling correct answer.
- Teach students acceptable delay-filling techniques to help:

❏ the student who needs more time to respond (e.g., saying "I was thinking about that."), and

❏ remain as patient as possible (e.g., doodling) while having to wait for the teacher or peers.

- Teach "Blurt Blocker" techniques to decrease impulsive answering (Chapter 31).
- Model delay before responding by pausing before responding to students' answers to show them how to delay impulsive responses.

Most students with ADHD have had enough red ink to last a lifetime.

Decreasing Hyperactivity

- Arrange for an empty desk so that the student can switch desks or tables if she needs to get up and move around.
- Alternate quiet activities with more opportunities for movement.
- Use multi-sensory activities.
- Incorporate more large muscle movements or actions in learning activities.
- Collaborate with the student to pre-plan a safe place or refuge that the student can go to if she has a need to 'chill' or just get out of the classroom. Ensure that the student's input is obtained as to what spot works best.
- Encourage students to make a "graceful exit" (Chapter 31) by providing the student with a permanent pass so that she can leave the classroom to go to the refuge when needed.
- Allow more opportunities to move around.
- Do not punish misbehavior by taking away recess; the student needs the opportunity to expend excess energy.
- Allow the student to use calming manipulatives.

If a student needs calming manipulatives, make sure that the manipulatives do not make noise or roll or are otherwise disruptive.

- To reduce hyperactivity, add color to work sheets that require sustained attention.
- Add color or stimulation to activities involving acquisition of new information.
- Use cooperative learning activities such as Think-Pair-Share (Lyman 1981).

Think-Pair-Share can be used at all grade levels and for all aspects of the curriculum. We love this approach because it gives students acceptable opportunities to move and talk. As such, it can augment and yet provide relief from lengthy presentations that are difficult for hyperactive or impulsive students to sit through. It can also be used at the very outset of a presentation to get the students more interested in the topic.

To use the Think-Pair-Share method, pose an open-ended or challenging question to the class. For example, before introducing the history of World War I, the teacher might ask, "Why do countries go to war?" Or before starting science lab, the teacher might ask, "What do you think will happen if…?" Give the students thirty seconds to one minute to think about the question and their individual answers.[*] Then instruct the students to pair off (switch the pairings each time the technique is used) and to share their ideas with their partner. Give them a few minutes to share their ideas, then reconvene the class as a whole and ask each pair to report on their ideas or randomly call on pairs to share what they came up with. Having each student be able to report on their partner's ideas as well as their own reinforces the importance of listening to each other. Once this part of the activity is completed, segue into the presentation, e.g., "We've heard a lot of good ideas about why countries go to war. Now let's find out what happened in World War I."

Modifying Materials and Presentations

- Use worksheets that allow sufficient space for large, sloppy handwriting.
- Color-highlight important instructions and teach students to routinely color-highlight important instructions.
- Color-highlight math operational symbols and teach students to highlight math operation symbols.
- Check for comprehension in multi-step sequences after the first or second step.

---

* Some teachers are taught to allow thirty seconds, but we prefer one minute because students with the conditions described in this book: (a) have retrieval problems and will be embarrassed that they cannot come up with their ideas or thoughts quickly, and/or (b) have an initial anxiety reaction and need time to think and not just react anxiously. If your question is really complex, you may want to allow even more individual think time.

- Provide cognitive cues for multi-step sequences and teach students to generate their own helpful sequence-preserving mnemonics (e.g., "**S**he **M**ade **H**im **E**at **O**reos" preserves the sequence of the Great Lakes from left to right as well as providing reminders of the names of the lakes).
- Provide study guides, outlines, partial notes or complete notes, and copies of any overheads or power point slides.
- Use a visual organizer (concept map or "mindmap") and a template to help students organize their materials and thoughts for written expression tasks. (See Chapters 9 and 19.)
- See the tips and strategies section of the Executive Dysfunction chapter (Chapter 9) and Chapter 17 on handwriting problems for other tips.

Testing Accommodations

Students with ADHD often require testing accommodations. A description of accommodations is provided in Chapter 22. Also see the testing accommodations that may be required for students with impaired handwriting (Chapter 17). Because many of the most problematic behaviors and challenges associated with teaching students with ADHD are attributable to the student's Executive Dysfunction, teachers and other school personnel are encouraged to see Chapter 9 of this book for many other important tips and strategies for Executive Dysfunction.

Associated or Comorbid Conditions

The vast majority of children and teens who have ADHD do not have just ADHD. Over two-thirds of clinic-referred children and teens have one or more comorbid conditions. Many of the associated conditions listed below are discussed in other chapters in this book. One of the most common comorbid conditions is Executive Dysfunction (EDF) (Fuggetta 2006). Any student diagnosed with ADHD needs to be screened for EDF.

- Developmental Coordination Disorder (DCD)
- Fine motor planning deficits (e.g., difficulty tying shoes, opening milk carton or locker)

- Graphomotor (handwriting) problems
- Learning Disabilities (LD)
- Executive Dysfunction (EDF)
- Memory deficits, e.g., working memory
- "Storms"
- Processing speed deficits
- Conduct Disorder (if child has combined subtype of ADHD)
- Speech and language disorders
- Depression and dysthymia
- Bipolar Disorder
- Anxiety disorders
- OCD
- Antisocial Personality Disorder (teens)
- Substance abuse
- Enuresis (urinary incontinence)
- Sleep problems
- Autism Spectrum Disorder (ASD)
- Tics or TS
- Sensory dysregulation

School-Based Assessments

Many schools use the Conners' Parent and Teacher Rating Scales Revised (CTRS-R) (Conners et al. 1998) to screen for ADHD and as a convenient tool for reporting on a student's symptom severity in school when communicating with the student's treating professionals. The CTRS-R does not, however, address the comorbid conditions or other problems that require screening and that are listed in the BOLO section above. The teacher or building team not only needs to screen for the disorders listed in the BOLO list above, but will find it helpful to use the Organizational Skills Survey, Homework, Survey, and Sleep Surveys (found in the Appendices and on the accompanying CD-ROM). Finally, it is very important to screen for peer relationship problems, including assessment of the quantity and quality of the relationships.

Consider any medications that may influence performance on the assessment or on classroom functioning. When scheduling assessments for students who are taking medications for ADHD, school evaluators need to consider whether to test the student during the period of optimal medication or to test after the medication has worn off. Make sure any written report of an assessment or evaluation specifically states whether the student was on medication and how the medication might have affected performance on the assessment.

Remember that if the student is off medication, any academic testing will be testing the student's attention and not necessarily the student's knowledge or skills.

Summary

ADHD is frequently confused with Executive Dysfunction. From a practical standpoint, teachers cannot cure the core symptoms of ADHD: distractibility, impulsivity, and hyperactivity. School personnel can directly instruct and remediate some of the executive skill deficits by using tried and true learning disability techniques of direct instruction and practice toward mastery. Teachers and other school personnel need to expect variability in the performance of a student who is diagnosed with ADHD and be prepared with environmental supports and strategies to reduce problems associated with difficulties in attention, motoric hyperactivity, and impulsivity/disinhibition. The vast majority of students diagnosed with ADHD will also have other comorbid or associated disorders that will affect school functioning.

At the beginning of Justin's sixth grade year, his teacher called Leslie and said, "Your son doesn't seem to know he has a desk and chair. He's constantly in motion in the classroom. Do you want me to try to get him to sit at his desk?" Leslie replied, "If it's not bothering you or the other students, I wouldn't target that. Personally, I wouldn't care if he lies on the floor breakdancing while doing his work as long as he does it!" Leslie and the teacher agreed that they would not comment on his hyperactivity but just focus on his productivity and increasing the quality and quantity of his work.

Several months later, Justin's teacher called and said, "Eureka! He's discovered that he has a desk and is voluntarily sitting at it."

There are often many problems to target. Focusing on academic productivity rather than on decreasing hyperactivity is often more effective.

Remember the Outside the Box Principle (Chapter 3). Some of the students that make us want to pull our hair out have incredible creativity and talent that will serve them well in the future. An adult with ADHD told us how he was always in disciplinary trouble in school because he would daydream about computer games and did not really care about the classwork. His school years were miserable and he decided not to pursue college. Instead, he formed his own company to make computer game software. It became the third biggest company of its kind in the country. Likewise, Michael Flatley, creator of River Dance, flutist, and Golden Gloves champion, also spent his youth in trouble: "I can go back to when I was six years old. I was always getting in trouble for dreaming, and the things I got in trouble for dreaming then are the things I'm doing today."

CHAPTER 9

Executive Dysfunction

I love deadlines. I like the whooshing sound
they make as they fly by.
— Douglas Adams

Jill was really looking forward to the tryouts for the cheerleading squad. Every day, she rushed home and practiced for hours to perfect her routine. But on Thursday, Jill's world flipped upside down. "What happened to you?" her friend Tina asked her in first period class. "How come you didn't show up for the tryouts?" Jill looked stricken. "What are you talking about?" Jill demanded. "Tryouts are next Wednesday." "No, they're not," said Tina. "They were yesterday."

Preview

Although all teachers are aware of two of the foundations of learning—attention and memory—the third foundation, executive function, is less well recognized. Yet it is crucial to learning through its direct effects and through its influence on working memory. We begin by defining the executive functions:

> Executive functions are control processes.
> They involve inhibition and delay of
> responding. They can be divided into the
> realms of initiating, sustaining, inhibiting/
> stopping and shifting. Another important
> aspect of executive function is planning
> and organization, which requires "attention
> to the future." (From *Attention, Memory
> and Executive Function*, Chapter 15, Martha
> Bridge Denckla, M.D.)

Think "absent-minded professor," "terminally disorganized," (Packer 1995) or "clueless" (Dornbush and Pruitt 1995). In other words, if your student experiences Executive Dysfunction (EDF), he has a great deal of trouble "getting his act together" (Denckla 2007). Executive Dysfunction is the most underdiagnosed and underestimated impediment to students using their IQ points for success. It does not matter how "bright" or intellectually gifted a student may be—if he is disorganized or otherwise "clueless," his accomplishments will not be commensurate with his intellectual potential.

Hallmarks of Executive Dysfunction[*]

A student with EDF may have significant problems with any or all of the following:
- Setting or appreciating longer term goals
- Planning
- Pacing work so that assignments are completed on time
- Getting started
- Using feedback to adjust behavior

---

[*] Even though there are as yet no uniformly agreed-upon criteria for diagnosis, we agree with educators that school personnel need to screen for the types of deficits described in this chapter so that an appropriate program of supports, accommodations, and interventions can be developed.

- Sequencing
- Self-monitoring
- Inhibiting behavior
- Sustaining effort and focus
- Executing and completing projects
- Making transitions and shifting cognitive sets flexibly (switching quickly and smoothly from one focus of attention to another)
- Organizing materials and workspace (including locker and book bag)
- Prioritizing
- Regulating emotional responses

If this list looks a lot like manifestations of ADHD (Chapter 8), that's because there is tremendous overlap between what is considered ADHD and EDF. We view these disorders as associated, but distinct. Symptoms of EDF are not exclusive to students with ADHD; there are many non-ADHD disorders that are also associated with EDF.

Considering the hallmarks of Executive Dysfunction, think about a long-term written project that you might assign. What does a long-term project involve?*

- Picking topic
- Planning assignment
- Estimating time
- Getting started
- Gathering materials
- Breaking assignment into parts
- Determining deadlines
- Evaluating performance
- Self-monitoring
- Producing a completed or finished product

Is it really any wonder that a student with EDF is unsuccessful? And is it any wonder that so many students with ADHD and EDF "crash and burn" in middle school, where there is a greater demand on the executive functions (Langberg et al. 2008). Langberg also provides a review of studies investigating interventions for EDF in middle school settings (Langberg, Epstein, and Graham 2008).

Setting Goals

Most of us have many goals. Some goals are short-term, such as "I want to watch my favorite show tonight." Other goals are longer-term, such

---

* From *Educators Handbook*, Tourette Syndrome Foundation of Canada, 2001.

as the young newlywed who hopes to buy a house, or the adolescent who dreams of being a physician. Students with EDF often seem to lack long-term goals. They also have difficulty remembering academic long-term goals, even though the teacher has clearly outlined goals and expectations. Because the student does not retain clear goals, they may seem to not care about their grades or academic deadlines. They live in the "here and now." In a sense, students with this type of EDF suffer from what might be called "future myopia" (Barkley 1997).

If you don't know where you are going, you'll end up someplace else.
— *Yogi Berra*

In other cases, students with EDF may have unrealistic goals. For example, when one of Sherry's sons was asked to write his first paper on any topic of his choice, he decided on the topic, "The Universe." When asked how long the paper was supposed to be, he said, "Three pages." This student was classified as intellectually gifted, but the discrepancy between his intellectual ability and his common sense was enormous.

 ## Tips and Tricks for Setting and Maintaining Goals

- Frequently remind students of the long-term purpose or goal.
- Establish subgoals with their own deadlines.
- Explicitly and frequently relate subgoals to a larger goal.
- When introducing the next step, review older material and concepts and preview new material to relate it to the larger goal. Explicitly point out the connection between the current or intermediate step and the long-term goal.
- Use "thermometer" charts that indicate progress toward the goal at the top.
- Hold weekly (or more frequent) meetings with the student to review the goal or intermediate goal and progress towards it.
- For larger projects, check to ensure that intermediate deadlines are entered in the student's planner.
- Use direct instruction to teach students how to "chunk" larger projects into subgoals and

intermediate deadlines, but, in the meantime, provide that chunking for them.

When it comes to "chunking" and establishing intermediate deadlines, use small chunks with individual deadlines and require that the student check in frequently. If the first intermediate deadline is set for two weeks away, the student will likely delay starting and totally forget about the project until the night before the first deadline—or worse, the day after it is due.

Planning

Some students may have little difficulty in appreciating a goal or even setting their own goals, but lack the planning skills required to achieve their goals. Planning may include activities such as:

- Considering different ways to reach the goal and evaluating each approach.
- Developing a sequenced set of specific steps towards the goal.
- Identifying the materials needed to complete the project.
- Considering whether materials can be obtained in time and are not too costly.
- Revising the plan, if needed.
- Establishing intermediate deadlines so that the entire project is completed by the final deadline.

Tips and Tricks for Planning

Teach students the mantra of "Plan Your Work and Work Your Plan."[*]

When helping your student prepare for a project, provide him with index cards that have been pre-punched with holes. Ask the students to put each step on one index card, and then put all the index cards in order. Put the cards on a ring to keep them in order and to prevent them from being lost. Because students may not include all steps they need to complete the project, help them track steps and identify anything they might have skipped. Using index cards makes it easy to add steps in the sequence or to re-order the sequence.

After reviewing the steps with the student and ensuring that the sequence is complete, ask the student to complete a project planning sheet that lists each of the steps and the due date for each step. A project planning sheet will be most helpful if it includes sequenced steps and intermediate deadlines and a section for materials that need to be obtained. To calculate the intermediate due dates, have the student work backwards—enter the date the project is due first (the "turn in" day), then work backwards to figure out when each step will need to be done by to meet that deadline. Monitor the student's plan to make sure that the student is meeting the intermediate due dates. *Source: (Dornbush and Pruitt 1995)*

Time Issues and Pacing

Many students have time-related issues. Some have poor time sense, i.e., time seems to move too quickly sometimes and too slowly at other times. Other students may have a different type of time problem—they may not accurately estimate how long it takes to complete a task. As a consequence, they'll often wait to start a major project until the night before it is due. In some cases, it may be that their sense of time is intact but that the students cannot keep all of their various assignments or tasks in mind long enough or well enough to add up all of their assignments for the night to determine how much time they need to allow. Students who fail to pace themselves, allow sufficient time, or keep track of time so that work is completed by a deadline create much frustration for parents and teachers.

As part of school-based screening, include information about a student's time-related difficulties.

Tips and Tricks for Time Issues

- Teach students to externalize time, i.e., not to rely on their inner sense of time but on external devices. For example, have the student use a multi-alarm programmable wristwatch to set reminders. A cell phone can also be programmed for reminder alarms. Start with inexpensive devices as the student with EDF is likely to lose at least a few watches or devices before they develop the habit of using them reliably.
- Provide checklists and prioritized "To Do" lists.

---

[*] Adapted from a quote from Norman Vincent Peale.

- Use direct instruction to teach students how to create their own checklists and prioritized "To Do" lists.
- Teach student to estimate how long a task will take and then have them check the accuracy of those estimates (see Chapter 23).
- Provide students with some information about how much time something may take so they can check their progress, e.g., "This worksheet will probably take you about fifteen minutes total."
- Teach students to allow more time than they think is needed for any project.
- Use a "countdown" timer or clock positioned on the student's desk to help the student keep track of time. (Note: Use a silent clock; a noisy clock may distract the student or others and may increase anxiety for anxious students to the point where they work more slowly.)
- Model allowing more time for tasks.
- Establish intermediate deadlines for big projects and monitor progress towards the intermediate deadlines.

Teach students the mantra of "Do it now, not later!" (Pruitt 1995) because "later" probably means never. "Do it now" applies to entering project dates in a planner, completing subtasks, and actually completing the assignment.

- Teach students the use of time management tools. Being able to set a repeating function on a computer, PDA, or cell phone is especially helpful for routine activities. For example, set "Spelling Quiz" to repeat on Fridays, and set "Study for spelling quiz" to repeat on Thursdays.
- Write the due date for each assignment clearly at the top of each assignment and teach students to write due dates on the top of their homework assignments.
- When going over homework assignments for the day or monitoring the student's agenda or planner, remember to include intermediate deadlines for big projects.
- Use direct instruction to teach students strategies that improve their efficiency. For example, teach the student test taking skills such as whether to tackle short answer or essay questions first. Not everyone is

born knowing how to take tests, and some students will need extra instruction and rehearsal on test taking skills.

> **About "five-minute warnings"**
>
> Although five-minute warnings may seem sensible, these warnings may not work if the student loses track of time or has no concept of how long (or how short) five minutes really is. Clocks that show the passage of time are helpful.

I still remember the day it finally dawned on me that asking my son, "Justin, would you please take out the garbage in five minutes?" was simply not going to work, and that I might as well be saying to him, "Justin, would you please take out the garbage sometime before the end of your life?" He simply had no concept of five minutes or could not accurately keep track of time while he was engrossed in something. He needed a reminder system that did not involve me nagging him. That is when we convinced him to set timers for himself. He is now a young adult and if he remembers to set a timer or reminder for himself on his watch or cell phone, he is successful, but if he procrastinates setting a reminder, he will forget and the task will not get done. Learning to set reminders is a life skill.

Use reinforcers to help the student work in a timely fashion, but do not just offer an incentive or reward without also providing some device or strategies. At the beginning of any program, incorporate some rewards for just using the reminders and techniques.

Initiation

Students with EDF often have difficulty getting started on tasks. These cognitively based problems are often misinterpreted as oppositional behavior or lack of motivation. For some students, difficulty getting started may be due to anxiety issues. We have encountered students who explain their "last minute" approach to big projects by saying that they work best under pressure. We tell them that research shows that students who procrastinate typically earn poorer grades when they get to college and are in courses with lots of deadlines (Tuckman 2005).

For other students, what may appear as an oppositional refusal to start working may be more of a learned helplessness response following repeated incidences of the student starting work but not being able to complete it due to EDF.

When a student with EDF is confronted with a large task that he cannot comprehend and deal with quickly as a whole, his reaction may be one of initial anxiety, followed by fear or even terror, then depression. He tries to escape the "yucky" feelings, but in doing so, may use the strategy of escaping the project or work that generated the anxiety.

Over time, the student may just quit sooner and sooner until he no longer even starts projects. If we assume the problem is primarily motivational, we might try offering positive inducements for starting or negative consequences for not get started. But a motivational approach is unlikely to be successful if lack of motivation did not cause the problem and you do not remediate the real problem.

The student may not be able to verbalize exactly why he cannot seem to get started. But his behavior is a form of communication about the problem. It is up to school personnel to be detectives to figure out what is interfering with initiating.

To understand the interference, ask questions such as:

1. Does the student have a plan for his work?
2. Is the student able to start the task promptly once the start signal has been given? And if not, is it because he is unable to change tasks or because he does not know how to start?
3. Does the student have the organizational skills needed?
4. Does the student have a learning disability that interferes with performing the task?

Tips and Tricks for Initiation

- Break the task down into smaller units.
- Have the student develop routines for getting started. Use direct instruction to teach the "how to start" sequence of skills, which might include such simple steps as:
    1. Write your name at the top of the page.
    2. Note whether it is homework or classwork.
    3. Put the due date at the top of any homework.
    4. Read the directions and highlight important words.
    5. Check to make sure you understand the directions.
- Check for comprehension. If students do not understand the task, they either do not get started, or start impulsively and on the wrong track.
- Collaborate with students to see what supports they need to get started.
- Instruct students to do just one problem or the first step and then signal you or come to you to have you check their work. The short-term check is also a good opportunity to incorporate some verbal praise about initiating behavior, e.g., "I like how you started so promptly."
- For younger students, incorporate external positive reinforcers for getting started within a reasonable amount of time. At the beginning, providing concrete and tangible reinforcers for every time the student starts a task may help boost task-starting behavior. Later on, contingencies can be added in so that the reinforcer or token is only earned if the task is initiated within a certain amount of time.
- Incorporate strategies to reduce the student's anxiety. (See below and Chapter 6.)

For highly anxious students, reduce anxiety and prevent problems by privately telling the student ahead of time, "We are going to be starting a big project later today, but don't worry, I will go over all the steps with you and check in to make sure that you are understanding the steps as we go along."

To help one anxious student who was having difficulty getting started, the teacher placed a therapist-created visual reminder on the student's desk to use his "BRAIN," (Figure 9.1 on the next page) and a checklist to self-monitor his use of the strategy.

Using Feedback

Students with EDF may have difficulty using feedback. An inability to use feedback effectively in academic tasks is evident in written expression tasks, where the student may strongly resist all requests to accept editing. But the deficit is also apparent in social interactions, where students with EDF may not seem to know how to adjust their behavior when giv-

Figure 9.1. Use Your BRAIN

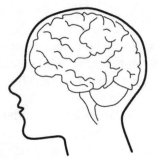

Use Your BRAIN!

B = Breathe out once slowly.

R = Read or listen to the instructions.

A = Ask a question if you don't understand the instructions.

I = "I can do this!!"

N = Now get started!

© 2008, L. E. Packer, Ph.D.

This "BRAIN" cognitive cue can help anxious students get started on tasks more quickly.

en peer feedback in verbal or nonverbal form. Telling a student with EDF, "You are playing too rough" or "This paragraph is confusing, please clarify" is as helpful as saying, "You are doing something wrong." Clues or feedback that would normally be sufficient are not sufficient for a student with EDF.

Tips and Tricks for Using Feedback

- Provide specific feedback as to what to do. For example, instead of saying, "This is sloppy," say "When you write, leave more space at the end of each line." Similarly, telling the student, "You are going to run out of time" does not tell the student what he needs to do to finish on time. Does he need to work faster or leave out some details he was planning to include? Be specific.
- Praise students lavishly when they learn from feedback, e.g., "I am really impressed with how well you responded to your peer editor's suggestion by adding more examples to this section."
- Create a buddy system where the student can observe modeled behavior by a student or paraprofessional who is willing to explain his actions as he responds to others' feedback.

Sequencing

Some students have difficulty arranging things in order over time or in space. Students with EDF may seem to be impulsive, for example, leaping to a step without having done preliminary steps that are important to success. But consider that it may not be impulsivity that is causing their problem. Deficits in working memory make it difficult for a student to both hold information and manipulate it, and the more steps that there are, the more likely it is he will skip or miss a step. If by some miracle the student can hold more than one thing in memory, then the student has to organize it while floating all the steps in memory. For students with EDF, this can be overwhelmingly difficult.

Sequencing deficits may appear as difficulties in:
- Planning steps in order.
- Telling a story in chronological order.
- Answering questions fluently.
- Following multi-step directions in the correct order.
- Putting things in order.
- Multi-step math problems.

Tips and Tricks for Sequencing

To help the student follow sequences:
- Provide external cues.
- Place written and/or visual cues on the student's desk.
- Use cognitive cues that help the student retain the order of information or steps (discussed below).
- Teach students to create their own cognitive cues.

An external visual cue can be something as simple as a strip of paper taped to a student's desk to remind the student of everything that needs to be checked when editing written work. (A simple math editing strip is depicted in Chapter 20; editing strips for written expression are depicted in Chapter 19.) An external cue may also be as simple as a checklist of steps to follow that is placed on the student's desk, with the student instructed to check off each step as it is completed. Visual or symbolic cues represent the sequence of the steps. Figure 9.2 provides one such example for long division.

Mnemonics such as "HOMES" are verbal cues that facilitate retrieval of information (in this case, the names of the Great Lakes), but mnemonics do not necessarily provide any information about the

order of the elements or content. When it is important to remember sequence or order, use verbal cues that have the order built in. The cue, "**E**very **G**ood **B**oy **D**oes **F**ine," represents the notes on the lines of the treble clef in order. When mnemonics preserve sequence, they are cognitive cues.

Returning to our example of the sequence of long division (**D**ivide, **M**ultiply, **S**ubtract, and **B**ring down), the following cognitive cues both preserve the sequence of steps in long division:

> "**D**irty **M**arvin **S**mells **B**ad"
> (Dornbush and Pruitt 1995)
>
> "**D**oes **M**cDonald's **S**ell **B**urgers?"
> (Source unknown)

Similarly, to remember the Great Lakes in a specific order:

> "**S**arah **M**ust **H**ave **E**ighteen **O**reos" preserves the order of the lakes from west to east as well as the names (**S**uperior, **M**ichigan, **H**uron, **E**rie, **O**ntario).
>
> "**S**cared **H**arry **M**eets **E**vil **O**gre" preserves the order of the size of the lakes from largest to smallest area as well as the names of the Great Lakes.

A list of other content-related mnemonics can be found in Appendix I and on the accompanying CD-ROM.

Self-Monitoring

Self-monitoring relates to a student's ability to see him as others see him and to evaluate his own performance and production rate. Self-monitoring checklists or interventions can also be used on a class-wide basis.

Tips and Tricks for Self-Monitoring

An Individualized Approach

An individualized form for self-monitoring is depicted in Figure 9.3 on the next page. The checklist is an adaptation of a checklist that a consultant created for a middle school student with EDF. The form was one element of a comprehensive intervention plan to address organizational and academic goals

---

Figure 9.2. Visual Cue for Long Division

A symbolic depiction of the sequence of steps in long division. The symbols represent divide, multiply, subtract, bring down, and then go back to the beginning of the sequence and do it all again (Dornbush and Pruitt 1995).

Figure 9.3. Self-Monitoring Form

Self-Monitoring Form

Name: _____

Date: _____

Instructions: Fill this out at the end of the day and take it to _____. Rate yourself on how you did, where 1= "didn't do at all," 3= "average," and 5= "excellent and did it without reminders." If something didn't apply for the day, just leave the line blank.

ITEM	1	2	3	4	5
I requested this form from aide.					
I recorded all my homework assignments completely and accurately.					
Packed up all materials for homework at end of class period or day.					
I entered long-term project deadlines or test dates in planner.					
I worked on breaking down long-term projects or studying for tests into intermediate deadlines and entered these deadlines in my planner.					
I showed my teacher(s) intermediate work towards big project.					
I remembered to go to school nurse to take in-school medication today.					
I conformed to school code of conduct by acting appropriately.					
I cleaned out folders, book bag, desk, locker today (circle which ones you did).					

Self-monitoring form for a middle school student.

in his Individualized Education Program (IEP). This chart helped encourage the student to think about organizational skills on a daily basis, with the ultimate goal of having him take more responsibility for organizing himself.

The student used this form to earn points towards a reward he had selected.

At the end of each day, the student was to request this form from the classroom paraprofessional. If he did not request it, he would be cued to ask for it, but would not earn full points for the first item on the checklist if he required cueing. He would then complete the form, review it with the paraprofessional* or teacher and then turn it in. Completed forms were sent home at the end of each week so that his parents could see his progress and reinforce his efforts.

The student rated himself on each of the items in the chart in terms of how well he thought he had done on that task for the day. If something was not possible (for example, if he had no dates to enter in his planner), he could just put a line through the item.

In reviewing the form with the paraprofessional or teacher, his first goal was to match his perception of his performance to the staff's perception. If they agreed on how he did, he earned points (e.g., one point for each item if his evaluation of his performance matched theirs). Positive reinforcers were initially based on the student earning an agreed upon number of "match points." It was important that the first goal not relate to performance on the items because it might have led to him scoring himself unduly high to earn points. By reinforcing accuracy in self-reporting first, the student was able to earn rewards even though he might not yet be completing specific items on the chart independently. Once he was reliably assessing his performance, he then began earning points if he scored well on the items on the chart using a graduated approach over weeks. By recording the data daily, the data provided an additional means of determining whether the student was achieving his IEP objectives for organization and self-management.

This type of self-evaluation form helps a student reliably evaluate his own performance by adult standards, provides a daily reminder of things that are important for him to do, shapes organizational skills, and provides one last opportunity for the day to get assignments recorded and necessary materials packed.

---

* As used here, the term "paraprofessional" is interchangeable with "paraeducator" or "classroom aide."

Tips and Tricks for Checking Work

Many of the disorders described in this book are associated with varying levels of impulsivity. Your students can help remedy this by checking their work as another form of self-monitoring. Tips and tricks include:
- Reinforce accuracy over speed.
- Allocate separate time during classwork and tests for students to check their work.
- Provide editing strips (see Chapters 19 and 20) or checklists that remind students of each important step in checking their work.
- Have students cross out incorrect answers instead of circling correct answers on tests.
- When grading student work, place check marks next to correct answers instead of X's next to incorrect answers.

Simply permitting more time for quizzes or tests is generally not sufficient to help impulsive students focus on accuracy and check their work.

Inhibiting Responding

Impairment in inhibiting behavioral responses is one of the core symptoms of both EDF and ADHD. Deficits in inhibition are also associated with other conditions discussed in this book, e.g., tics, manic episodes. As part of planning for the student with inhibition problems, teachers need to determine whether the student knows the rules and is just unable to follow them, or needs instruction in the rules—or both.

Repeating rules over and over again to a student who already knows the rules is a waste of time and unlikely to be successful. As Barkley has said, "the problem… is not one of knowing what to do but one of doing what you know when it would be most adaptive to do so" (Barkley 1997).

Tips and Tricks for Inhibiting Behavior

When school personnel think about trying to get a student to inhibit some behavior, it may not be because inhibiting that specific behavior is the final goal, but is viewed as setting the stage for the student to start achieving the "real goal." Goals such as "student will sit in his seat" are not as helpful as directly specifying and addressing what we want the student to be accomplishing. If "sitting in his seat" is viewed as a means to some larger goal such as improving academic output, then we suggest rewriting the goal to something like, "Will complete more classwork within allotted time." That type of goal construction is more likely to lead to more direct approaches to boost productivity.

Engage the Student in Developing the Behavior Plan

Whenever possible, engage the student in the process of developing a plan to help him manage his disinhibited behavior. Even if the school team is not conducting a Functional Behavioral Assessment (Chapter 26), any plan is more likely to be successful if we get the student's input and commitment to the plan. A "Cooperative Problem Solving" approach that can be used to engage the student is described in Chapter 31.

Provide any interventions and supports at the point of performance. Preparing students for what might happen later in the day or the next day is not as effective as working with them when they are in the situation or when they are motivated to accept assistance and suggestions. The majority of the work needs to be done in the classroom or in the settings and situations where the problems with inhibiting behavior occur.

It is also important to note that reward-based systems or "Cooperative Problem Solving" may not work if the class is so unstructured and has too few environmental supports. Designing a classroom that incorporates visual cues and routines is an essential ingredient that precedes other interventions oriented to inhibiting behavior. (See Appendix C: Classroom Layout Checklist and the accompanying CD-ROM.)

Add Adult Supervision

Because students with behavioral disinhibition are at greater risk of accidents, planning for the student needs to include added adult supervision. Activities or settings that are most problematic include the playground, cafeteria, bus, gym, and field trips.

Structure the Classroom to Promote Inhibition

State regular classroom rules positively. Figure 9.4 illustrates positive elementary school classroom rules that we have seen.

Simply posting classroom rules in general terms is not sufficient for many students with EDF, however. The first day of classes and during the first week

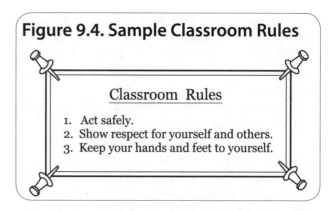

Figure 9.4. Sample Classroom Rules

Classroom Rules

1. Act safely.
2. Show respect for yourself and others.
3. Keep your hands and feet to yourself.

of school, allocate time for direct instruction of the classroom rules, using the "Say, Show, Check" method for young students. To do this, tell the students the rule or expectation, demonstrate it in action while they comment on it, and have them rehearse or demonstrate the behavior while the teacher observes and provides feedback and reinforcement. A booster session may be needed following an extended vacation or if the class behavior seems to deteriorate.

If there is a group- or individual-based reward system in conjunction with the classroom rules, teach the reward system in conjunction with teaching the rules. Some students may need specifically individualized rules and some may require more structure and support to comply with the rules.

EDF is best remediated through direct instruction. For example, if a student has been asked to be respectful to the teacher, does the student really know what that means? A student with EDF might be turned around looking at the bulletin board while listening to the teacher's lecture. At some point the teacher notes the behavior, feels ignored and disrespected, and says to the student, "You are not listening, Daniel." The student argues with the teacher and says, "Yes, I am!" The argument persists until the student gets sent out of the room. The student will not understand what happened because the teacher said, "You are not listening." Daniel *was* listening, and with his EDF he only hears that. He does not know that he appeared to be disrespectful because he was not watching the teacher. She did not say what she really meant and he did not pick up on the implication. The teacher can never assume that students with EDF will pick up on any implied information not directly stated.

If, however, the teacher remembers that the student has EDF and may just not know how to act like a respectful listener, then the interaction goes very differently. The teacher moves next to Daniel and says the following in a nonjudgmental tone:

Teacher: "Daniel, are you listening to me?"
Student: "Yes, I am."
Teacher: "I appreciate that but I think it is important to learn how people feel when you are turned around and facing away from the speaker. In social language that says, 'I am not listening and do not care about what you are saying' and is a sign of disrespect. I am afraid that others will not know how much you are truly interested in what they are saying and will get mad at you for acting like that. Let's practice facing toward the speaker so the person speaking will feel important and respected."

Establish Classroom Routines

The importance of consistent classroom routines cannot be stressed enough in any discussion of behavior management, and it is the very students who need routines the most—those with EDF—who often have the most difficulty learning the routines. Developing a habit involves frequent rehearsal, and students with ADHD and/or EDF tend to lose interest if the activity is no longer novel or stimulating. To promote learning of classroom routines, incorporate:

- Active movement on the students' part
- Some novelty
- Color
- Humor (when possible)
- External reinforcement contingent on successful compliance with the routine

One way to promote mastery of a routine is to incorporate more stimulation. For example, when teaching young students the routine of turning in their homework, elementary school teachers can create color-coded bins—one for each subject area's homework papers and use "bells and whistles" to indicate when it is time to turn in assignments.

Many teachers walk around to collect homework, in part because it may reduce the likelihood of students becoming unruly after they get out of their seats to turn in their homework. While we understand this rationale, such strategies do not teach students the more active response of turning in work, which they will need for the future. As adults, their employers will not come to them to get their work; they will have to remember to go hand it to the boss.

Instead of collecting homework, then, consider a routine where a novel audio signal cues students that it is time to place their homework in the appropriate homework bin. Because some students may not

return to their seats promptly, use direct instruction to teach getting up quickly and quietly, turning in the work, and then quickly and quietly returning to seats. Provide positive reinforcement for compliance.

Sustaining Focus and Effort

The inability to sustain focus can be due to a variety of causes, including EDF. To address difficulties in sustained attention, consider the physical layout of the room, classroom structure and routines, materials and presentation factors, and individualized strategies.

Tips and Tricks for Sustaining Focus and Effort

In addition to the tips in the chapter on ADHD (Chapter 8):

- Decrease delays during presentations. The longer students have to wait, the more difficult it will be for them to sustain their attention.
- Review old material and skills and then preview new material to show where it will "fit in" with the previous material and overall goals. Many students have difficulty sustaining focus and inhibiting responding to distractions because they do not really understand how what they are doing relates to previous material and skills.
- Check for comprehension. Allow a few extra minutes at the beginning of each activity to check on students who have attention or comprehension problems.
- Use concrete and real life examples that are meaningful to the student.
- Externalize and boost motivation to attend by using procedures such as "Countdown to Free Time" (see Chapter 28).
- Establish a classroom routine to get students' attention, such as "Give Me Five!" (Chapter 28).
- Pause and create suspense by looking around before asking questions.

Executing and Completing Projects

Students with EDF are less likely to complete work, and the longer the task takes to complete, the more steps, the more organization and time management required, and the less interesting the subject is, the less likely the student is to complete it. For tips on written expression and big projects, refer to Chapter 19.

Apart from difficulties in completing classwork, students with EDF also experience tremendous difficulty in completing homework. Homework issues related to EDF and other factors are considered in Chapter 23.

Identify the role of executive function in the student's difficulties in completing projects and homework. When the impaired executive skills have been identified, review methods in this chapter and book to address the specific deficits.

Making Transitions

Difficulties in making transitions are a major source of school problems for students with EDF. In some cases, difficulty shifting may be due to compulsive behavior or obsessional thinking. In other cases, perseveration or cognitive rigidity may interfere with making quick and easy transitions. In other cases, the difficulty in making a transition or shift may represent the student's difficulty in mentally putting on the brakes for what he is doing so that he can mentally reorganize to start the requested activity. What may appear to be uncooperative or oppositional behavior in response to a transition instruction is often a result of cognitive difficulties.

Saying "Hurry up!" to a student who is dysregulated or who has EDF and is having difficulty only increases arousal levels, results in greater dysregulation, and slows down transitioning even more.

Tips and Tricks for Transitions

The following techniques promote faster and smoother transitions:

Early Warnings

One of the simplest and most effective techniques to combat trouble during transitions is to give advance warnings. For example, let your students know that in fifteen minutes they are going to lunch. Then give them a ten minute warning. Five minutes later give one last warning. This allows the students with transition issues enough time to shift from work to lunch. As noted in an earlier example,

however, five-minute warnings do not work for some students and they will need to see external reminders of time.

Direct Instruction

The time spent making a transition is one that is significant to teachers, as the average elementary classroom makes between eight and ten transitions of about eight minutes each per day. That adds up to one entire day per week of instructional time spent on—or lost to—transitions.

The trick is to use direct instruction. Starting in the earliest school grades, most students can be taught how to make a transition using a simple lesson like the one below, which is adapted from Rathvon (1999). Teachers will need a sign, a stopwatch, and a recording sheet (the latter two are needed only for the optional timing and recording for the Beat the Clock enhancement). The sign can be a simple one, like that shown in Figure 9.5.

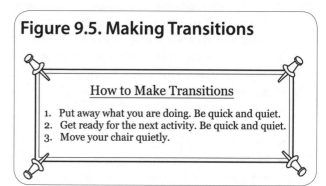

Figure 9.5. Making Transitions

How to Make Transitions

1. Put away what you are doing. Be quick and quiet.
2. Get ready for the next activity. Be quick and quiet.
3. Move your chair quietly.

A simple sign with the directions for how to make a quick and quiet transition.

During the instructional activity, tell the students that they are going to learn how to make a transition:

- Define "transition time" (or a more age-appropriate word) as the time it takes to change what we are doing. Ask them to repeat the definition. If they repeat it accurately, say "Right, [transition time] is the time it takes to change what we are doing." If they do not get it right, just repeat the definition and have them repeat it again.
- Tell them the two important things about making good transitions: being quick and being quiet. Ask them to repeat aloud what is important about making good transitions.
- Go over the rules on the sign. Read them to the class and discuss each one briefly. Have the students repeat the three rules.

- Now demonstrate how to make good transitions. Start with a seated activity and talk out loud as you model a transition. For example, "It is transition time. I need to get ready for math. I put away my spelling book quickly and quietly. Now I take out my math book quickly and quietly."
- Tell the class that they are going to see more transitions and ask them to comment on what you are doing as you are doing it. Model quick and quiet transitions from one activity to another at your desk. Then model some transitions that involve you getting up from your desk and going to another part of the classroom. For example, "It's transition time. I need to go to music. I am putting away my spelling book quickly and quietly. Now I am moving my chair quickly and quietly, and lining up at the door quickly and quietly."
- Model a few more transitions, having the students comment on what you are doing and how you are doing it.
- Now have the class practice transitions. Cue them by saying "It is transition time. Get ready for math. You will need ____." Provide feedback and praise.

The whole lesson will probably take less than twenty minutes. It may need to be repeated occasionally, particularly after vacations.

If you want to speed up transitions after the class has the habit of making (relatively) quick and quiet transitions, you can introduce a "Beat the Clock" component whereby the group can earn rewards for completing transitions before the buzzer sounds. If you have anxious students, this may not be a good idea—speeding up transitions via "Beat the Clock" may backfire for anxious students.

Provide Support for Transitions

Although you can teach transition skills as a group activity and cue the group as a whole, some students require individual cueing. Stand close to the student and softly cue the transition. Consistent with the guiding principle of externalizing motivation, contingencies can also be established for individual rapid and quiet transitions.

Having a consistent classroom routine and a visual display of the routine can also facilitate transitions. Have the weekly and daily routines prominently posted and get in the habit of checking off each item

as it is completed. If the daily routine changes, be sure to point this out to the students. For some students, having their own individual daily schedule on their desk that they can check off is necessary and helpful.

Organizing Materials, Belongings, and Workspace

Disorganization is often the most prominent symptom of EDF. These are the students who never record all their assignments, who lose their materials, planners, and belongings, and on those rare occasions when they manage to complete an assignment, they cannot find it. Their backpacks are like a black hole—things go in but never come out. Notes you send home are never returned, and when you call the parent, you find out that they never got the note.

Because so many students have organizational deficits that impair school functioning and homework, we have developed a simple screening tool that we encourage teachers to send home during the second month of school for parent completion and return. Reproducible copies of the Organizational Skills Survey are provided in Appendix H and on the accompanying CD-ROM.

If you send the Organizational Skills Survey (Appendix H) home and it is not returned to you, then that is a pretty good indication that there may be a problem—either with the student or with the parent—or both. You will need to follow up.

 ### Tips and Tricks for Organization

Physical Layout and Structure
- Use a color-coding system. Use one color for each subject, e.g., blue for science, green for math, etc.
- Set up color-coded bins in the classroom to coordinate with the system. Encourage students to get into the routine of dropping their work into the color-coded bins.
- Set up a mailbox for each student.

Classroom Structure and Routines
General:
- Have the daily routine prominently posted where all students can see it. Check off each item as it is completed.

- Teach students to immediately mark each paper as either classwork or homework.
- Teach students to routinely color highlight important instructions on handouts.
- Set up a weekly routine for cleaning out desks.
- Set up a weekly routine for cleaning out folders and book bags.
- Assist older students with cleaning out their lockers on a weekly basis.
- Have all students bring in an extra supply of pens, pencils, tissues, or whatever they tend to lose or use up most frequently.
- Schedule a date on which students check their "stash" of supplies and write notes to replenish. Follow up to see that they have.
- Use a separate communication system for communicating with parents, like a separate folder or notebook—not the student's planner. (See Chapter 33.)
- Provide students with their own to-do lists taped to their desks. Eventually, students need to be taught how to create their own to-do lists, but when first starting, provide them with the to-do list and ensure that it is taped to the desk and clearly visible. (Do not use a small index card that may get covered up—use a big sheet of paper!) Have them check off items as they are done.
- Provide study guides, outlines, and copies of any overheads.
- Break down large projects into smaller units, etc.

Schedule a swap meet! Students come in with a stash of extra supplies and you send home an extra set of books.

Homework-related:
- Create homework buddy teams that check each other to ensure assignments are recorded and necessary materials packed up (for younger students).
- Follow a consistent daily routine for recording homework assignments and packing books and materials. Allow extra time to record assignments, and verbally cue when it is time to record assignments.
- Cue students to record homework due date at top of assignment if the date has not been indicated already. Ensure that they note it.
- Follow a consistent daily routine for turning in homework and notes from parents.

- Set up a system for students to get the daily homework assignment if they forget to take their planner home, e.g., assign homework buddies, send assignments home by email, or post assignments to a classroom website.
- Schedule brief weekly meetings with each student to give them a list of whatever assignments or signed notices are missing. Place that list in the communications notebook or folder for the parents' attention.
- If possible, provide an extra set of books to be left at home.
- Set up a system to submit homework from home, as described below.
- (Other homework-related tips are provided in Chapter 23.)

All too often, the very environmental supports and cues that helped the student in elementary school are abandoned in middle or high school because the students are presumed to have mastered the skills by then. For students with EDF, however, the absence of visual and verbal prompts results in deteriorating functioning or "crashing and burning."

Simply accept that even though the student should know to record their assignments, and even though you have clearly written the assignment on the board, some students still require a verbal prompt, "OK, everybody record the assignment now." Say this towards the end of class rather than first thing, as disorganized students are the ones who arrive late and miss the cue, or who will be busy unpacking and miss the prompt. Learning to allow a few extra minutes each day to allow students to record and pack up can reduce stress on everyone.

Teach the students the mantra of "Record it or Regret it!"

Students with EDF simply cannot count on their memory, despite their best intentions. The "record it or regret it" mantra is used in conjunction with the "do it now, not later" mantra. Remember that if you give an assignment verbally because you are out of time or have a revision and do not write it on the board, call attention to it, and allow sufficient time for disorganized students with handwriting issues to record it.

Students with EDF often are overwhelmed by book bag and locker chaos. You may need to sit down with the student and make a list of exactly which books they need to grab at which times of day and which books are to be put into the locker at

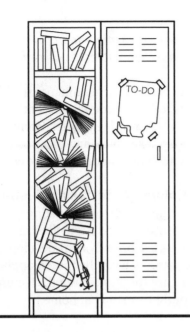

which times. Color-coding helps, as it enables them to "grab all blue and all green for morning classes" or "grab red and yellow for afternoon." Post the list on the inside of their locker.

Make sure that the pages of the student planner are large enough to accommodate sloppy handwriting! See Chapter 17, Handwriting Issues, for the relationship between handwriting issues and organizational deficits.

"The Dog Ate My Homework"

For students who seem to lose their homework between home and the classroom, work cooperatively with them on a plan of action. Can they fax a backup copy of their homework to the school at night? Can they email an assignment to the teacher or themselves at school as a backup? Think creatively, but engage the student in solving his problem and have him take some responsibility for getting the assignment turned in. Taking some responsibility, however, does not translate into penalizing the student for failure to turn in work. If you penalize a student who has done his homework but lost it or forgot to bring it in, you penalize him for doing homework as well as for not turning it in. In this situation, it makes more sense to reward the success than to penalize the failure.

Remember that you can boost performance by adding external rewards (e.g., a lottery the student's name is entered in for each homework assignment submitted). But the rewards only work if

the student has the skills and supports to engage in the desired behavior.

Prioritizing

Prioritizing involves:
- Ranking ideas in the order of importance.
- Putting things in order of the dates they are due.
- Assessing the value of the activity.

What happens when a student cannot prioritize? He may waste time working on small projects and run out of time for more important projects. An older student may have difficulty deciding what to record when taking notes because everything may seem equally important or unimportant. The student may have difficulty determining how much detail—and which details—he needs to include in written expression and whether he is providing the most important information when telling a story orally. He may make "poor choices" due to lack of prioritizing skills (e.g., going out to a movie instead of staying home to study for the final exam).

At home and in school, the student with prioritizing deficits may fight every fight as if it is the most important battle. Parents and teachers need to prioritize when it comes to picking and choosing battles with a dysregulated student who has EDF.

Sometimes, the failure to prioritize is simply age-appropriate behavior. For example, a teenager may easily view going out with his friends that night as much more important than an upcoming test in school for which he is supposed to study. Similarly, a young child may demand that he be given more time to finish a drawing he is making even though the entire class is lined up at the door, waiting to go to music class. But if a student repeatedly exhibits such problematic behavior, be curious as to whether it might indicate EDF.

Tips and Tricks for Prioritizing

- Tell the student the priorities in order if assessment indicates that he cannot prioritize properly.
- Tell students what information or material need to be memorized because they may not figure it out on their own.

- Provide study guides, outlines, partial or full notes, and copies of any overheads.
- Employ some verbal cues and strategies. When trying to decide which homework assignment to make a priority, ask the student: "Which assignment is worth more points towards your final grade?" "Which assignment is due first?" The answers to these questions may help the student determine which task to make more of a priority or to tackle first. Unfortunately, these questions are less likely to work if asked by parents unless the teacher has sent something home to parents with the answers to those questions, because the student with EDF will probably answer, "I don't know" to both of those questions!
- Cue the students with phrases such as, "Now this is important…." or "One of the things that will absolutely be on the test is…."
- Teach students with EDF how to create their own to-do lists, then how to prioritize the items on their to-do lists. In the interim, provide them with a prioritized daily to-do list.

Prioritizing When Taking Notes

As suggested above, prioritizing deficits impair students when it comes to note-taking, as everything may seem equally important to them. Teachers can assist students by providing direct instruction on note-taking skills that incorporates clues as to how to prioritize material, and then providing verbal cues during presentations (such as the "Now, this is really important" preface). No one system of note-taking is successful for every situation. Different students have different styles, just as teachers do. Consider the following two approaches to note-taking for students with EDF.

Mindmapping

A mindmap is a visual method of organization that shows the 'shape' of the subject, the relative importance of information and ideas, and the way that information relates to other information. Because less writing is involved, more information can be represented on one piece of paper, which may foster comprehension of the big picture. (See Chapter 19 for an illustration of a mindmap.) Because handwriting is an issue for many students with the types of conditions covered in this book, they may find this system more attractive to use than a more traditional method of note-taking or outlining.

Even when using a mindmap, provide students with skeleton notes in outline form.

Consider creating a mindmap first in terms of its major points to help guide the student's note-taking and research. Alternatively, the student can simply read the books, take notes, and then "sort" them into piles, after which the mindmap can be constructed.

Two Column Note-taking System

Another approach to note-taking that has some attractive features is the system illustrated in Figure 9.6. This is based on a system developed by Garneau Collegiate. As with the mindmapping system, students can use this system to take lecture notes in class or to outline or study at home.

Regulating Emotional Responses

Students with EDF have difficulty regulating their affect (mood), emotional responses, and arousal level, which partly explains why they may spend so little time in the "DRIVING WELL ZONE" (discussed in the Overview to Part II). To complicate social-emotional aspects, students with EDF may experience problems with emotional control if they have not internalized speech to the same degree as their non-EDF peers. Without self-talk, emotionally driven responses are disinhibited. Because they do not have that protective delay that allows them to reflect and to match their response to the situation, they overreact and tend to react more aggressively than the situation calls for.

---

*Anyone can become angry, that is easy . . .
but to be angry with the right person, to the right
degree, at the right time, for the right purpose,
and in the right way. . . This is not easy.*
— *Aristotle*

As we described in the Introduction to Part II, students can be taught vocabulary and imagery to help them identify whether they are "at the right speed" for task conditions and task demands. When a teacher sees a student struggling, the teacher might say something like, "I think you are going too

Figure 9.6. Two Column Note-Taking System

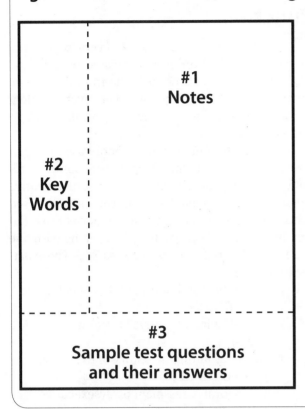

#1 Notes

#2 Key Words

#3 Sample test questions and their answers

Directions:
- Have the students create a crease two inches from the left margin of their note paper. Have them create a second crease two inches from the bottom of the page, and then unfold the paper.
- Direct them to use the area marked #1 ("Notes") to take notes from the book or in class.
- Have them use the area marked #2 ("key words") to note key words, or new vocabulary words from class or from the book. In the area marked "Notes" directly opposite the word, they should write the definition of the new word or enter notes about the new concept or key word.
- Instruct the students that while everything is still fresh in their minds, use area #3 to predict and write down several sample questions they think will be on the next test.

Developed by Garneau Collegiate, and reproduced with the permission of the Toronto District School Board.*

* Retrieved from http://marcgarneauci.com/Students_Services/reading_notetaking.html.

fast. Are you getting too close to the red zone? Remember to take a break and use one of our strategies (e.g., relaxation breathing or going to get a drink of water) to lower your speed so that you stay in the green zone and do not get a speeding ticket or worse—crash!"

The optimum use of this "Watch Your Speed!" program is seen when a student comes up to a teacher and says that he is "racing" and he needs to make a "pit stop" at the counselor's office to get help slowing down, or that he is not fast enough and needs to use his strategies to boost his speed.

In addition to considering EDF as a source of a student's emotional dysregulation, teachers and other school personnel need to inquire about two other sources of emotional dysregulation: sleep problems (Chapter 14) and medications (Chapter 24). Both of those factors may be causing or contributing to emotional dysregulation.

Tips and Tricks for Emotional Regulation

For students with problems in arousal and emotional regulation, here are some techniques or suggestions to consider:

- Provide added adult supervision where needed, e.g., during unstructured time such as lunch and recess, on field trips, or in any other situation in which the student tends to get overaroused.
- Schedule the most challenging academic activities for mid-morning, if possible, when most students are at their optimal arousal level for learning and performance.
- Have prominently posted classroom rules for behavior that include rewards for good behavior and fines for punishable offenses.
- Have group-based and individually-based reinforcement contingencies for prosocial behaviors.
- Use role-play to prepare students for any anticipated difficult situations and cues or prompts at the point of performance.
- Prepare students for any activities or transitions that are likely to be problematic or stressful.
- Teach problem solving skills using the P.L.A.N. technique and conduct an "Instant Replay" afterwards to review the students' performance and outcome (see Chapter 31 for a description of these techniques).

- Use "graceful exits" to help students leave the room so that they can go calm themselves if you see warning signs that they are over-aroused or about to explode (see Chapter 31).
- Schedule breaks and opportunities for active movement.
- If students do lose control and have an emotional "storm" or "rage attack," give them an opportunity to calm themselves before asking them to engage in any academic work (see Chapter 15).

EDF and Social Skills

Not surprisingly, students with EDF often experience significant social impairment. Some impairment may be due to verbal executive deficits that affect language and communication skills (see Chapter 18), but the same deficits that affect academic functioning may also affect social functioning, e.g., the failure to plan ahead, the inability to shift flexibly, and the inability to organize social plans. EDF also affects social functioning through its impact on the ability of the student to take the perspective of others. The impact of EDF on social skills is described in more detail in Chapter 34.

Associated or Comorbid Conditions

EDF usually occurs along with another condition or disorder. Screen for:

- ADHD
- Autism Spectrum Disorder
- Brain Injury (e.g., acquired brain injury, traumatic brain injury)
- OCD
- Anxiety disorders
- Mood disorders (e.g., Depression or Bipolar Disorder)
- "Storms"
- Memory deficits, e.g., working memory deficit
- Nonverbal Learning Disability
- Learning Disabilities: written expression, math calculation
- Verbal Executive Dysfunction (e.g., practical social language skills, pragmatics)
- Handwriting deficits
- Language problems
- Sensory dysregulation

Assessing Executive Functions

As described in Chapter 1, every psychiatric or neurological disorder is associated with frontal lobe impairment, and because the frontal lobes are involved in executive functions, whenever a student has any diagnosed neurological or psychiatric disorder, we need to screen for EDF.

In our experience, most school-based psycho-educational assessments do not incorporate sufficient screening for EDF or assessment of executive functions. Neuropsychologists and qualified licensed school psychologists may use a number of tests that tap into specific executive functions, along with one of several batteries of tests to assess EDF. These batteries include:

- Developmental Neuropsychological Assessment (NEPSY)
- Delis-Kaplan Executive Function System (D-KEFS)
- Behavior Rating Inventory of Executive Function (BRIEF)
- Behavioral Assessment of Dysexecutive Syndrome (BADS-C)

Each has its limitations, but in our experience, if schools use the BRIEF battery, teachers and parents will have a better understanding of any executive skills deficits that may be impairing functioning. When school personnel use the BRIEF battery, students are less likely to be described as "lazy and unmotivated" and more likely to receive the EDF supports and strategies they need.

The fastest and easiest way to assess student challenges is pretty straightforward:

1. Look in their desks, bookbags, and lockers at school or their closets or desks at home.
2. Ask parents to complete the Organizational Skills Survey (Appendix H).

If you find a chaotic mess of books, papers, and other materials, refer the student for a BRIEF assessment or some other neuropsychological assessment. Figure 9.7 depicts our shortcut assessment for organizational deficits.

Summary

EDF is one of the most serious sources of academic impairment for students. For each grade level

Figure 9.7. The Dreaded Bookbag

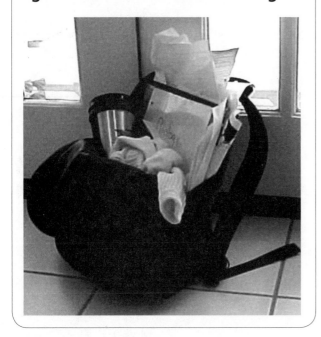

An easy way to screen for organizational problems. To administer the test, simply look in the student's bookbag. An alternate version for older students involves looking in their locker. Photo credit: Colleen Wang.

and curriculum, success depends on the executive functions the student must possess to master the curriculum. These skills are sometimes referred to as the "hidden curriculum" because they are necessary but not directly taught. EDF also significantly affects behavior and social-emotional functioning. Executive Dysfunction can rob one of friends, the ability to get a job or even an interview, and the ability to create a successful family.

Chantal was never prepared for class. Her teacher understood her challenges and tactfully provided her with a pen, paper, or whatever she needed, but she was concerned that Chantal was not learning how to be prepared. Chantal had an idea, and asked her teacher if she could bring a box of supplies to leave in her homeroom so that she could start the day prepared and come back to homeroom on her lunch break to get more supplies if she needed them. The teacher agreed and complimented her on taking some steps to help herself. Chantal was excited and proud that she now had supplies when she needed them. Two months later, she beamed when she was given the "Most Improved" certificate from one of her teachers.

"Perhaps the most valuable result of all education is the ability to make yourself do the thing you have to do, when it ought to be done, whether you like it or not; it is the first lesson that ought to be learned; and however early a man's training begins, it's probably the last lesson that he learns thoroughly."
— Thomas H. Huxley

CHAPTER 10

Memory Deficits and Slow Processing Speed*

Carrie said, "I study and study and I still get bad grades on my tests. My parents know I study because they see me but the teacher does not think it's possible I can study this hard and still make bad grades. I get to the test and all the answers are gone from my head. Just using flashcards does not seem to make them stick in my head no matter how many times I look at those stupid cards. Why bother studying when I make the same grade whether I go to all that effort or not? I'm quitting!"

Preview

Memory is one of the three foundations of learning, the other two being attention and executive functions. There are different types of memory and different stages in the memory process. Some types of memory may be intact while other types are impaired for a particular student. Regardless of whether the student has a primary memory issue or is experiencing memory interference due to symptoms of her neurological disorder(s), it is important for school personnel to assess and address memory issues.

Students with memory impairments associated with their neurological disorders experience great inconsistency in being able to perform on a memory task. It is the combination of memory issues and neurological disorders that causes memory to appear variable. Sometimes the inconsistency is misinterpreted as insufficient attention or motivation. It is more constructive to recognize that students with memory impairment need to try harder

and use different strategies than other students who do not struggle with memory issues. When viewed in this light, the students are heroes when they succeed rather than slackers when they fail.

Some students with neurological disorders have a slow processing speed, which decreases their ability to act on information quickly so that it can be stored in memory before it is lost. Slow processing speed further confounds the ability to learn in an efficient manner. Slow processing speed has been noted in people with OCD, depression, Bipolar Disorder (even in remission), and especially the inattentive type of ADHD.

Types of Memory and Stages of the Memory Process

Short-Term Memory

Short-term memory is the memory used to temporarily store and act on information in a conscious way while it is processed and manipulated. Immediate memory is the first stage of short-term memory. Immediate memory cannot hold much information. Symptoms that interfere with registering information impair immediate and short-term memory. Immediate memory is generally intact for the people with the disorders covered in this book.

Working memory is the second stage of short-term memory. Working memory is the product of attention, memory, and executive function. It allows the student to hold verbally presented information in mind while drawing upon or retrieving older information or rules to apply to the new information. For ex-

---

* Some of the material in this chapter is based on material published in (Dornbush and Pruitt 2009)

ample, if a teacher asks a student to add four digits, the student must keep those four numbers in mind while applying the rules of addition. The most common effect of working memory deficits is an inability to follow multiple directions. Working memory does not apply solely to academic tasks, however. It also affects behavioral and social-emotional functioning. Working memory is often (but not always) impaired in the people with the disorders described in this book.

Computer Random Access Memory (RAM) is a useful analogy for working memory. RAM provides temporary work space for running computer applications, much like a scratch pad provides temporary space for doing arithmetic calculations. It may help to think about students with working memory deficits as having very little RAM or a smaller scratch pad compared to their peers. Another useful analogy is to think of everyone else having a large desk available so that they can keep necessary files out and readily available while the students with working memory deficits only have small desktops and can only look at one file at a time.

Long-Term Memory*

Long-term memory is exactly what its name suggests: It stores information over a long period of time. As material is rehearsed over and over, those memories become consolidated, or stored in long-term memory. Psychologists often talk about the storage of memories in terms of encoding processes. Consolidation can happen in a short time or may take place over a more extended period.

Long-term memory is comprised of explicit memory and implicit memory. Explicit memory involves conscious awareness of retrieving past learning or experience in a current memory task, e.g., the student realizes that she knows an answer on a test because she studied that material the previous evening. Implicit memory involves no conscious awareness of how past learning or events relate to the current memory task, even though it influences it. Riding a bicycle is an example of using implicit memory. While a person is riding a bicycle, she is using information from past learning but is not consciously making an effort to retrieve past learning. Explicit memory is sometimes referred to as declarative memory and is discussed more below.

Prospective memory is memory for what has to be done later or in a different place. The role of prospective memory is becoming increasingly appreciated in terms of its impact. For example, if students do not remember that they need to do homework that night, it will not get done. While traditional views of memory focus on the management of past information, prospective memory focuses on retaining information for future use or in a different place. Prospective memory allows a person to keep his eye on future needs, e.g., remembering the relationship between doing homework and future job success. Many students do not even remember to think about the future.

An example of a time-based prospective memory challenge is demonstrated by the student who has an appointment with a guidance counselor at two thirty and needs to remember to ask her teacher to be excused to go to the counselor's office. A place-based example of a prospective memory challenge is remembering to ask one's parents (at home) to sign a permission slip to return to the teacher in school the next day. Students with prospective memory deficits need to be directly taught compensatory strategies for how they can remember what they are supposed to do in the future or in a different place.

Metamemory is awareness of memory and knowing how to use it. An important metamemory skill is the ability to accurately predict what we are likely to remember and what we are likely to forget. Students with poor metamemory frequently fail to keep appointments or fail to meet academic responsibilities because they believed they would remember something and did not use a compensatory strategy like writing it down. Some students (particularly those with Executive Dysfunction) do not activate verbal rehearsal or visualization strategies without direct instruction. Students with metamemory deficits need to develop a more accurate understanding of their memory weaknesses so they can develop compensatory strategies.

The special education teacher, counselor, or school psychologist may be able to help the student appreciate why she needs to learn compensatory strategies, can provide her with a setting and support for developing compensatory strategies, and can generate some useful accommodations for teachers to employ with the student as part of the student's plan. One such compensatory strategy is for the student to learn the mantra, "Write it or regret it" (Pruitt 1995).

Declarative memory is explicit memory for facts and knowledge (i.e., information that can be

---

* There are different types of long-term memory, and some of the types of memory described in this section may be viewed as part of short-term memory by other sources.

declared). Students with the disorders described in this book have generally intact or strong declarative memory. Declarative memory is made up of semantic memory and episodic memory:

Semantic memory is memory for the meaning of words, concepts, and knowledge that is unrelated to specific experiences, e.g., remembering the meaning of vocabulary words or remembering that a peach is a fruit and not a vegetable. Semantic memory is usually intact in this population, although students with Nonverbal Learning Disability or an Autism Spectrum Disorder may have some impairment in this area.

Episodic memory is memory for the flow of events in time. Episodic memory is usually quite good in this population. Autobiographical memory is one form of episodic memory. Students will be able to tell us in amazing detail all about a trip they took over a year ago, despite the fact that they cannot remember where they put an important note from their parents fifteen minutes ago.

Do not be misled into thinking that students have an adequate or wonderful memory for academics just because they have strong autobiographical memory and can report every pitch and play in a baseball game they attended three years ago. What appears to be an inconsistency in memory is understood as consistent once the specific memory disorder is understood.

Strategic memory is the memory used for learning and remembering to use strategies. An example of strategic memory is the ability to remember how to plan and organize a term paper or how to structure an essay. Students with strategic memory deficits may seem to be unable to generalize or apply any strategies they have been previously taught, especially from one year to the next. Strategic memory is impacted by Executive Dysfunction.

Denny was dejected and frustrated. A high school sophomore with an IQ well into the Superior range, his written expression had never reflected all of the wonderful ideas and insights he had. "Why do they assume that I can remember how to write an essay?" he asked the school's consultant. "Each year, it's like I have to start all over again to learn how to write. I feel so stupid." In a way, Denny was right. Each year, his teachers had to re-teach him how to organize and develop an essay. And each year, his teachers had used their own favorite methods for teaching the skills. Denny had never had one system that was used in all his courses and across all years. Denny's teachers were asked to use one—and only one—system for organizing an essay, and Denny started taking a graphic essay organizer with him from class to class. Sometimes we need to explicitly teach and practice skills which need to become implicit.*

Procedural memory is implicit memory for how to do something. When someone performs a sequential act again and again, the rehearsal results in more efficient memory for the activity so that it can be performed automatically. How to ride a bicycle involves procedural memory. Once mastered, the skill becomes automatic. As one example, even if one has not ridden a bicycle in years, the skills do not need to be learned over again.

Students with the disorders described in this book often have deficits in procedural memory. As two examples, simple morning hygiene routines never become automatic, and handwriting skills never become automatic (see Chapter 17).

Retrieval is the ability to access remote semantic memory, i.e., the ability to pull a specific target word or words from memory. Students with word retrieval problems may feel embarrassed when called on in class to answer questions if they have not been able to retrieve the word they want quickly. For students with word retrieval problems, wait until they raise a hand to indicate that they are ready to answer the question.

Word retrieval issues impact student performance on fill-in-the-blank tests—these students have difficulty retrieving the words within the allotted time. A word bank can offset the difficulty with retrieval on the fill-in-the-blank tests. Retrieval is mentioned in more detail in Chapter 18 and is frequently remediated by a speech and language pathologist. Any activity that increases the student's vocabulary can promote retrieval, e.g., encouraging the student to work on easy crossword puzzles.

Fluency of retrieval is the ability to produce examples again and again (e.g., being asked to retrieve the names of all 50 states). Simple word retrieval, by contrast, might be remembering the name of the capital of the State of Massachusetts.

Table 10.1. Impact of Disorders on Different Types of Memory

	Usually Spared	Often Impaired
Short-Term Memory	Immediate Memory	Working Memory
Long-Term Memory	Declarative/Explicit Memory ■ Semantic Memory ■ Episodic Memory	Prospective Memory Metamemory Procedural Memory Strategic Memory

Word retrieval is not a memory disorder but results in an inability to use what has been stored. Word retrieval problems are a language deficit and are discussed in Chapter 18. It is mentioned in this chapter because it looks like and is frequently confused with a memory disorder.

Table 10.1 provides a summary of the different types of memory discussed above with an indication as to whether they are likely to be spared or impaired in students with the disorders discussed in this book.

Symptom Interference

Symptoms of different disorders can directly or indirectly impair the student's ability to memorize information. ADHD (Chapter 8) significantly impacts memory, beginning with the ability to attend to material and resist distraction. Students with ADHD may have reduced visual-spatial short-term memory, although it is not clear whether this deficit is secondary to attention deficits that interfere with the material being encoded and consolidated. Any hyperactivity further hinders focus—the student misses information because moving interferes with the student being cognitively at the right place at the right moment. ADHD has also been linked to deficits in free recall of verbal material (e.g., retrieval of items in a list), procedural memory, and working memory.

Tics (Chapter 4) can also interfere with concentration, and therefore, memorization or remembering. Tics or the awareness of the urge to tic building up can make it difficult for the student to attend to what the teacher is saying, and some information may be missed. Even if information is taken in, tics may still interfere with consolidation or storage of the information. TS may also result in nonverbal memory deficits.

Obsessions (Chapter 5) can also interfere with students' ability to attend to, and memorize information. Repeating thoughts that get stuck in their heads reduces the students' ability to attend to what the teacher is saying. These students have less "free memory" to store the new information. For example, if a young student irrationally fears that her mother will get hurt if she does not keep rehearsing "Mary Had a Little Lamb" over and over again in her head, then she cannot fully attend to the lesson plan and has diminished available memory for storing new information. Compulsions similarly interfere with attention and memory. When students are stuck repeating mental events or stuck on a topic, they may be less able to acquire and memorize new information. In addition to deficits in working memory, OCD has also been linked to impaired nonverbal memory and to reduced confidence in memory.

Mood Disorders (Chapter 11) have their own way of impairing students' memorization. Depression slows thinking to the point that holding onto information to memorize it becomes overwhelming. Information is lost before students can encode and transfer it to long-term memory. Depression can also impair the will to even initiate memorization. Mania puts the mind into such a racing state of thoughts that holding onto anything is sometimes impossible. The student whose thoughts are racing cannot slow down to rehearse the material sufficiently to store it in memory.

A student with sensory dysregulation (Chapter 12) who is overwhelmed by environmental stimuli has difficulty attending to the job at hand, such as learning or rehearsing new information. The classroom that seems relatively quiet to the teacher may seem painfully loud to the student who over-registers the sound of the ticking clock or the other students' pencils scraping across their papers. Similarly, if the student is so acutely aware and troubled by a tag on the back of her sweatshirt that rubs against her back, she is unable to rehearse and memorize new information.

Sleep increases storage of information in long-term memory. Sleep disorders (Chapter 14) make it difficult to learn and rehearse new material and to form new memories. Fatigue, which may be due to sleep disorders, medication side effects, or just inadequate sleep during the teen years, results in information being forgotten before it is stored and memorized.

Executive Dysfunction (Chapter 9) has its own impact on memorizing material, particularly through its contribution to working memory, procedural memory, strategic memory, prospective memory, and metamemory. The lack of specific executive skills also impairs memorization. For behavior to be goal-directed, the student must simultaneously understand the goal and maintain it in working memory. This requires executive functions such as developing and initiating a plan of how to organize and sequence the material to be memorized, and then sustaining the effort while inhibiting other responses. Another type of Executive Dysfunction— difficulty in prioritizing—can also impair the student's ability to memorize the most important facts. Instead, these students may devote their energy to unimportant details. Students use self-monitoring, another executive function, to consciously evaluate their method for memorizing and its effectiveness. If students have difficulty with self-monitoring, they may not accurately estimate how well they are doing at memorizing the material. Sequencing deficits, if present, also negatively affect procedural memory.

Students with EDF will need to be explicitly told that they need to memorize material. Without such explicit instructions from the teacher, the students may not figure out that they are supposed to memorize the material.

Slow Processing Speed

Slow processing impairs the ability to consolidate information in long-term memory. Even if the student has a normal memory capacity, slow processing speed interferes with memory capabilities. Whether it is a reading task or listening to verbal information during direct instruction, the student who processes slowly needs more time than her peers. If the material is paced too quickly, she will lose new information because she is still processing earlier information. An analogy of slow processing is that of a computer that has an older processor or operating system. The computer may have a large hard drive that is capable of storing tons of information, but the user's ability to work quickly is limited by the slow processor.

When presenting material, pause between units to allow extra time for processing and consolidation into memory. Talking slowly is not necessarily the best strategy. Instead, it is often more helpful to simply pause between thoughts to allow the student time to "catch up" with the idea.

There used to be little to do about processing speed other than to allow extra time. Now there is a research validated program, Fast ForWord,* that can increase processing speed in some students. This program seems to work mostly for students and families that can use the program on their computers on a consistent basis while being monitored by a healthcare professional, e.g., a speech and language pathologist who is trained in Fast ForWord.

Tips and Tricks for Helping Students with Memory Disorders and Slow Processing Speed

Reducing the Impact of Memory Disorders

- Relate new information to previously learned material, e.g., go on a field trip to a nature center then teach about animals seen there.
- Spend sufficient time reviewing old concepts and skills before introducing new ones. Make explicit connections between what students have already learned and what they are about to learn.
- Teach students how to use mnemonics and cognitive cues to help memory storage and retrieval (see Chapter 9).
- Teach math tricks to help students memorize math facts.

---

* See www.scilearn.com.

- Use music or rhythm to help establish sequences, e.g., "The ABC Song" for learning the alphabet.
- Reduce complexity, e.g., break up a lesson into manageable units with breaks. The breaks can be fun, reinforcing games for previously covered material.
- Provide a syllabus that emphasizes key points.
- If your student needs to memorize items on a list, start with ones that are already meaningful to him. Explain how unfamiliar items relate to previous learning.
- Create silly stories that contain words that the student is trying to memorize. Humor makes things easier to remember.
- Teach the students to review information immediately before a test, in addition to studying beforehand.
- Teach students to write down all memory strategies on the back of the test sheet before beginning the test.
- Provide visual as well as verbal information for students with working memory problems.
- When expected to write an essay, provide templates or graphic organizers to assist in written expression for students who have working memory and strategic memory problems.
- Use a "trick book" or strategy book to collect strategies for a student who has strategic memory problems.
- Teach students who have working memory and prospective memory problems to "Write it or regret it!"
- Promote metamemory to justify the use of memory "prostheses" such as agendas, to-do lists, etc.

If students write memory strategies on the back of the test, then they do not have to hold onto the mnemonics at the same time that they take the test. This is important for students with working memory deficits.

Accommodating Students with Slow Processing Speed

- Use untimed tests or allow extra time.
- Do not call on students unless their hands are raised.
- Do not assume the student does not know something just because she cannot formulate an answer efficiently.
- Use multiple choice tests.
- Provide word banks for fill-in-the-blank tests.
- Screen for neurological disorders that may impair processing speed such as the inattentive type of ADHD, depression, and anxiety disorders.

 # Associated or Comorbid Disorders

If a student has memory impairment or slow processing speed, school personnel should also screen for:

- ADHD
- Handwriting and VMI deficits
- Mood Disorders
- OCD
- Anxiety Disorders
- Sleep Disorders
- EDF
- Pragmatic (Social) Language Disorder
- Expressive Language Disorder
- Learning Disabilities
- Sensory dysregulation
- Autism Spectrum Disorder

Students with memory or processing speed impairment may be at risk for a reactive depression, i.e., they may come to feel that they are not as capable or smart as their peers and they may lose their motivation to try.

Summary

Memory deficits and slow processing speed are two disorders that can confound students' ability to learn even if they are bright and usually understand the material. If the two are both present, this can lead to a real struggle. Encoding becomes more difficult and studying for a test can be a real nightmare. Memory strategies that help compensate for memory disorders and extra time for students with slow processing can offset these difficulties and allow the student to succeed.

Mrs. Johnson noticed that Carrie seemed smarter than her grades demonstrated. She also observed Carrie was starting to give up on her schoolwork. She asked Carrie to come in after school and tell her what the problem was. After Carrie told Mrs. Johnson that she was frustrated by her inability to remember and recall facts and figures, Mrs. Johnson helped her come up with mnemonics and other memory strategies. Carrie was able to use these strategies to improve her grades. Mrs. Johnson was so pleased to see Carrie change her attitude and finally succeed and demonstrate how much she knew.

CHAPTER 11

Mood Episodes and Mood Disorders (Depression and Bipolar Disorder)

Any teenager can have a bad day or week, but when Annie changed overnight from being a sweet and anxious freshman in high school to someone who was "mean as a snake," her teacher became concerned. Over the next weeks, Annie became more and more disrespectful, started cutting classes, and had more and more trouble focusing. What surprised her teacher the most was how wonderful their relationship had always been and how tough Annie had suddenly become. At first, the teacher was hurt and angry, but quickly realized that there had to be something wrong because there was no reason for their good pupil-teacher relationship to have deteriorated with no precipitating event. Had Annie started taking drugs or was something else going on? The teacher called Annie's parents to report her observations and to ask if Annie was also having trouble outside of school.

• • •

Logan was normally a well-behaved second grade student, but his behavior was becoming increasingly inappropriate. He had become very impulsive and was having difficulty focusing on his work. Of even greater concern, he seemed to be using a lot of sexual references in his conversations with peers, he had his hand down his pants frequently during school, and he had rubbed up against his teacher in a sexual way. Concerned that perhaps he had been exposed to sexually inappropriate behavior or material in his home, his teacher went to the principal to report her observations and concerns.

Preview

Once thought to only occur in adolescents and adults, we now know that even young children can suffer from mood disorders. The symptoms of mood disorders vary with age, but may include hypersexuality and irritability, as seen in the examples above.

Like other disorders described in this book, mood disorders are heritable. Some research indicates that if one parent has Bipolar Disorder (BP), the risk of the child having BP is 15-30%. When both parents have BP, the risk increases to 50-75%. If one child has BP, a sibling has a 15-25% risk of also having BP.

Types of Mood Episodes

The building blocks of mood disorders are mood episodes.

Major Depressive Episodes

The features or symptoms of a depressive episode can best be remembered by the mnemonic, **THE SAD FACES***

THE SAD FACES
Too serious
Hallucinations (hears "voices")
Excessive guilt ("It's all my fault")

Sleep disturbance
Appetite disturbance
Down mood

Feels worthless
Agitation
Concentration impaired
Energy loss
Suicidal thoughts

---

* This mnemonic is an adaptation of the mnemonic "SAD FACES + GSW" (author unknown).

Another mnemonic is:

D = Depressed mood
E = Energy loss/fatigue
P = Pleasure lost
R = Retardation or excitation
E = Eating changed (effect on appetite, weight)
S = Sleep changed
S = Suicidal thoughts
 I = "I'm a failure" (loss of confidence)
O = "Only me to blame" (guilt)
N = No concentration

Source: (Blenkiron 2006)

A student in a depressive episode may exhibit or report some or all of the following:

- Withdrawal from peers
- Neglect of personal grooming/hygiene
- Frequent complaints of boredom, headache, stomachache
- Loss of enjoyment in activities
- Sad appearance
- Difficulty concentrating
- Tiredness
- Loss of energy
- Extreme irritability
- Absenteeism
- Failure to turn in classwork or homework
- Easily agitated
- Walks and moves more slowly
- Frequent complaints that things are "too hard"
- Aggressive and/or disruptive behaviors
- Feelings of guilt or worthlessness
- Talks about killing self or having thoughts of suicide
- Reports of "hearing voices" (auditory hallucinations)

Although most lay people associate "depression" with a person who seems "sad" or "blue" or "down," be aware that many students in the throes of a depression may appear more irritable and aggressive than sad.

What school personnel witness may be partly dependent on the student's age or developmental level. In very young children, loss of enjoyment in fun activities, sadness, and irritability/aggression may be the most sensitive indicators of a depressive episode (Luby et al. 2003). In adolescence, depressed girls report more guilty feelings, body image dissatisfaction, self-blame, self-disappointment, feelings of failure, concentration problems, difficulty working, sadness/depressed mood, sleep problems, fatigue, and health worries than depressed boys. Adolescent boys report more loss of enjoyment, depressed morning mood, and morning fatigue (Bennett et al. 2005).

An episode of depression is not diagnosed unless a number of symptoms are present and have lasted at last two weeks. The symptoms either represent a change in behavior or a noticeable worsening of symptoms that may have already been present. An episode of depression generally lasts for months. School personnel will almost certainly need to implement a number of accommodations and supports for the student, and the sooner, the better.

In a study of over 2,600 thirteen-year-old students in Australian high schools, failing academic performance was associated with a five-fold increase in likelihood of a suicide attempt (Richardson et al. 2005). Students who are in a depressive episode need treatment. If school personnel detect behavioral or mood changes in a student and if the changes last two weeks or more, do not assume that the parents know. Contact the parents to inform them so that they can get their child assessed by a health care professional.

There are a number of pathways to depression:

- Genetics
- Stressful life events (including child abuse, family issues, trauma, and failure)
- Other medical conditions
- Substance abuse (e.g., cannabis, hallucinogens, inhalants, alcohol*)
- Side effect of some medications

School success and school connectedness are two factors that can protect a student from depression. School connectedness is the extent to which students feel accepted, valued, respected, and included in the school. School connectedness is also associated with general functioning. To a lesser extent, connectedness also correlates with the severity of anxiety symptoms (Shochet et al. 2006).

An episode of depression usually reoccurs within five years.

---

* Many teachers and parents do not seem to appreciate the exponential effect that alcohol has on increasing depression.

Quick Facts and Statistics on Depression

- Up to 12% of all children under age thirteen experience major depression.
- One in ten teenagers experiences major depression each year, but fewer than half receive treatment.
- Depression is associated with greater rates of smoking, alcohol, and drug abuse.
- Substance abuse increases the risk of suicide in depressed adolescents.
- Depression increases the risk of suicide.
- Most suicidal adolescents are not identified as at risk by school officials.
- Suicide is the third leading cause of death in those aged ten to twenty-four in the U.S. and the second leading cause of death in that age group in Canada.
- Across all age groups from five to nineteen, girls think about suicide more often, are more likely to attempt suicide, and have a higher rate of suicide attempts requiring medical treatment than boys, but boys are more likely to complete suicide.
- School failure can lead to depression and to an increased risk of suicide.

Possible Warning Signs of Suicide

- Talks about suicide or death
- Writes or creates pictures depicting or describing suicide or death
- Has a specific plan to commit suicide
- Has a history of a previous suicide attempt
- Makes suggestive comments, e.g., "Things will be different soon" may not indicate optimism but intention to commit suicide
- Exhibits out-of-character impulsive and risk-taking behaviors
- Puts things in order and "tidies up loose ends." In children, this may take the form of cleaning their room (if it is not their habit), catching up on all their schoolwork, etc.
- Gives away treasured objects
- Says "I Love You" and "Good-bye"
- Demonstrates a sudden lifting of mood or even a euphoric state, which may indicate relief at the thought that the suffering will be over soon

Refer students engaging in alcohol or substance abuse for screening for ADHD and mood disorder. Many of these students may be self-medicating because they have not been properly diagnosed and treated.

Mania

Mania is another type of mood episode. The features of a manic episode are euphoria (elevated mood) or irritability and at least three of the following (or four, if the mood is irritable):

- Inflated self-esteem or grandiose thinking, e.g., "I'm perfectly able to start training in a new sport today and make the next U.S. Olympic team."
- Decreased need for sleep; may be up all night and not feel tired
- Pressured speech, more talkative than usual
- Marked flight of ideas or feeling that thoughts are racing
- Increased distractibility
- Increased goal-directed activity or psycho-motor agitation
- Increased, excessive involvement in pleasurable but risky activities, e.g., unrestrained buying, sexual indiscretions, or jumping from high places

A student in a manic state may be unable to attend school because the symptoms are either so severe that they pose a risk to the student or they interfere with the student's ability to function in school. If school personnel note that a student seems to be "revving up," the school needs to promptly contact the parents and ask them to report it to the child's doctor, who may be able to adjust medications to prevent a full-blown manic episode.

A manic episode may be part of one type of Bipolar Disorder, discussed later in this chapter, although it is important to note that not all students with Bipolar Disorder will have manic episodes and not all students with manic episodes have Bipolar Disorder. Mania can also be a result of substance use or a medical condition such as hyperthyroidism.

When mania presents as euphoria as opposed to irritability, the euphoric mood may manifest as what can be called "The Giggler," i.e., the student who giggles incessantly and inappropriately. We realize that it may be difficult to determine when giggling is a sign of mania as opposed to normal behavior in pre-adolescent or adolescent girls, but we are referring to a significant/noticeable change in behavior. Similarly, the irritability may make a normally pleasant student seem "mean as a snake."

Mania seriously impairs the student's ability to learn. Students with the primary experience of euphoria may refuse treatment because they feel so good. Students in the beginning stages of a manic episode may need added adult supervision to address safety issues in addition to other accommodations they may require.

Some of the symptoms of mania may look remarkably like features of Attention Deficit Hyperactivity Disorder (ADHD, see Chapter 8), and many students may actually have both disorders.

The following features of mania distinguish it from ADHD:

- *Grandiose thoughts.* Students in mania think they can accomplish a lot, while students with ADHD often have a disheartened view of what they can actually accomplish.

- *Sleep patterns.* Some students in mania or mixed episodes may report that they are up all night but are not tired. Students with ADHD who do not get enough sleep generally report being tired.

- *Racing thoughts, rapid and pressured speech.* If the student's speech is much faster than normal, ask the student if he feels that thoughts are racing around his head. Even students with mania as young as six can tell us that they feel like their thoughts are suddenly racing.

- *More goal-directed behaviors.* ADHD students with Executive Dysfunction (Chapters 9 and 10) generally have difficulty starting and completing tasks. A student in a manic episode may start and finish an incredible number of tasks, moving from one to the other as each is completed.

- *Pleasurable, but high-risk behaviors.* Although students with ADHD may seem sensation-seeking, students in a manic episode engage in behaviors that may lead to pain, arrest, or other problems. Hypersexual behavior, for example, may indicate a manic episode. In adolescents, this behavior may manifest as increased sexual drive, increased sexual references and jargon, and/or increased self-stimulatory (masturbatory) behavior. In younger students, this behavior manifests as a fascination with private parts, an increase in self-stimulatory behaviors, a precocious interest in things of a sexual nature, and attempting to rub up against adults (like Logan in the vignette at the beginning of this chapter). In one study of manic youth, 43% had symptoms of hypersexuality (Geller et al. 2000).

Some school personnel mistakenly interpret the hypersexuality of mania as emotional disturbance or sexual misconduct by the family. It is important for the school to ask parents to report the sexually inappropriate behavior to the child's doctor, who can determine if it is part of mania.

School personnel need to consider the safety of other students and personnel if a student engages in sexually inappropriate behavior, even if it is due to mania. If a student who is known to have a mood disorder engages in sexually inappropriate behavior, the team needs to consider the accommodations and supports the student needs, including whether the student needs to work individually with a teacher (and away from peers) while their medications are adjusted. Collaboration with the child's parents and doctors is crucial.

- *Psychotic thoughts.* In severe mania, the student may have psychotic thoughts that are somewhat consistent with their mood (euphoric or irritable). Psychotic thinking is not part of ADHD.

Hypomania

A somewhat milder form of mania is known as hypomania ("under or below mania"). A student with hypomania, or "Mania Lite," has a milder mood disturbance that produces less impairment, fewer symptoms, and does not require hospitalization. Students with hypomania experience it as a very pleasurable state with increased energy and creativity. If it stops there, it can be a positive experience. Not all hypomanic episodes progress into the impairing state of mania. In this case, hypomania is unlike other disorders described in this book because it can actually be associated with enhanced productivity.

Mixed Episode

Some students may experience both mania and depression simultaneously. A student is in a mixed episode if he has symptoms of both a full manic episode and depression daily for about one week with significant impairment in functioning. Just as mania or major depression may require hospitalization to protect the student's safety, mixed episodes may also necessitate hospitalization.

*Janice Papolos, co-author of **The Bipolar Child**, suggests that a mixed episode state may be the most dangerous of all mood states and have the highest risk of suicide because the child may have suicidal thoughts combined with the increased energy of mania to act on those thoughts.*

Types of Mood Disorders

Depression

The mood disorder known as "depression" is synonymous with "Major Depressive Episode," discussed in the previous section of this chapter.

Dysthymia

A milder, but longer lasting form of depression is dysthymia (Dysthymic Disorder). A student may be diagnosed with dysthymia if he has been "down" or had irritable mood plus at least two other depressive symptoms for at least a year with the symptoms causing significant impairment or distress. Students who suffer from dysthymia may be less impaired than students in a major depression, but they suffer for longer.

A student with persistent "blahs" may have dysthymia.

In a significant percentage of cases, dysthymia is an early marker for future problems such as depression or Bipolar Disorder (Kovacs et al. 1994). For this reason, it is important for school personnel to refer students for assessment by a qualified mental health professional if they suspect a student may be dysthymic.

Some students with dysthymia occasionally plunge into a full depressive episode. When these two conditions occur together, some people refer to the student as having a double depression. Students who suffer from dysthymia with intermittent periods of major depression are truly between a rock and a hard place.

Bipolar Disorder

The mood disorder known as Bipolar Disorder was formerly referred to as "Manic-Depression." It is also sometimes referred to as "Bipolar Depression."

The term bipolar suggests that the student experiences mood swings between two opposite poles on a mood continuum. In fact, mood swings do not necessarily occur as opposites, but the term Bipolar Disorder (BP) is still used to denote mood disorders wherein the individual has significant mood swings or cycles.

A student suffering from Bipolar Disorder may appear to be in a pleasant mood one minute and then suddenly turn cold and mean the next minute. For some students, these mood episodes, or swings, may cycle very rapidly and can be very disconcerting to school personnel who cannot understand the student's "Jekyll and Hyde" demeanor.

There has been a tendency to diagnose some youth with chronic severe irritability and ADHD as having Bipolar Disorder. There has also been discussion of creating a new mood disorder called Temper Dysregulation with Dysphoria when the diagnostic criteria are revised in the DSM-V. For now, we simply note that if a child or teen does not have clear cycles in their mood and there is no family history of BP, a diagnosis of Bipolar Disorder may not be appropriate (Carlson 2007). That said, there is no debate that children with severe and persisting irritability with outbursts are at significant risk of future problems and are in need of early diagnosis, treatment, and school-based supports.

Students may have any of a number of BP subtypes.* BP subtypes vary in terms of how high the highs are and how low the lows are:

- Some students have a history of at least one hypomanic episodic and at least one major depressive episode, but no manic or mixed episodes. This subtype seems to be the most common one in adolescents. Students with this subtype have periods of euphoric or irritable mood with a few hypomanic symptoms, but they generally will not be impaired dur-

---

* On a practical level, school personnel need to know what to expect for a particular student. By asking the student's parent (or the student, when appropriate) what types of mood swings the student experiences, what the student's behavior looks like when he is experiencing mood problems, and how often these problems occur, school personnel will be better prepared to meet the needs of the student.

Table 11.1. Bipolar Disorder Patterns by Age Group

Children	Adolescents
■ More mixed episodes; fewer discrete episodes of depression and mania ■ Very rapid cycling ■ Really irritable ■ Explosive outbursts ■ Somatic complaints (headache, stomachache) ■ Overly sensitive to rejection	■ More distinct episodes of hypomania and depression; not as much mania or mixed episodes ■ Rapid onset of symptoms ■ Psychotic thoughts that are consistent with type of mood (depressed or euphoric)

(Packer 2004)

ing those periods. When they cycle into major depression, there is significant impairment.

■ Some students have at least one manic episode or at least one mixed episode. Some of these students may also have major depressive episodes.

■ Some patterns of BP do not fit neatly into the preceding descriptions and are currently referred to as Bipolar Disorder—NOS ("Not Otherwise Specified"), although that may change in the future DSM-V.

As surprising as this may seem, young children with BP are more likely to have manic episodes than adolescents.

As with depression, the type of patterns and symptoms school personnel see vary as a function of the student's age. In young children (ages three to seven), the most prominent behavioral changes are that of aggression and irritability (Danielyan et al. 2006). By age three, problems with mood, sleep disturbances, hyperactivity, aggression, and anxiety are evident in 75% of those who are subsequently diagnosed with BP.

Mood episodes where irritability is a prominent feature (such as irritable mania or a mixed episode) account for about half of the first mood episodes of BP (Faedda et al. 2004). Table 11.1 depicts some of the differences in Bipolar Disorder symptoms as a function of age group.

Cyclothymic Disorder

Just as Dysthymia is a chronic but milder form of Depression, the disorder known as Cyclothymia is a chronic mood disorder that is a milder form of Bipolar Disorder. Cyclothymia is characterized by

periods of hypomania that cycle with periods of depressive symptoms that are not severe enough to be considered major depression. Cyclothymic Disorder causes significant impairment.

Mood Disorders and Safety

Students with depression or BP are at increased risk of harm for any of these reasons:

■ Impulsivity due to mania or mixed episodes may lead to accidents or suicide attempts.

■ Hypersexuality due to mania may lead to unwanted pregnancies or sexually transmitted diseases.

■ Slowing down of movement associated with depression may prevent students with depression or BP from reacting quickly to avoid harm, e.g., reacting too slowly to an oncoming car when crossing a road or failing to duck when something is thrown at them in physical education class (PE).

■ The student's school team may need to add adult supervision in less structured settings to ensure student safety.

School Impact

Having described all of the serious symptoms that students may experience, it may come as a surprise that not all students with depression or BP will require special education services. Some of them will do well if they get some accommodations for their symptoms. Others may require special education services or even a smaller, more supportive setting during very difficult times. Some students may require a treatment facility if they pose a danger to themselves or others.

Some of the deficits noted below persist even when the student is in a normal (euthymic) state. Even when the student appears fine, he may have impaired working memory and other sources of interference with learning and productivity (Dickstein et al. 2004; Lagace, Kutcher, and Robertson 2003).

 Mood disorders impact many areas of functioning:

Motoric:
- Deficits in motor coordination
- Fine motor skills impairment
- Difficulty in sequencing complex motor acts
- Deficits in handwriting
- Psychomotor retardation (moves and speaks slowly)

Executive Functions:
- Perseveration or cognitive rigidity
- Problem solving deficits
- Impaired planning and organization
- Deficits in sustained attention
- Deficits in attentional set-shifting (flexibility in transitions)
- Impaired verbal fluency
- Deficits in written expression
- Impaired response inhibition

Memory and Processing Speed:
- Impaired working memory
- Impaired verbal memory and retrieval problems
- Deficits in declarative memory
- Delayed facial recognition
- Impaired processing speed

Social-Emotional:
- Impaired ability to read emotional cues in others' faces
- Agitation
- "Short fuse"
- Irritability or "mean as a snake" behavior

Other:
- Lower math achievement scores
- Impaired alertness due to sleep problems
- Difficulties due to medication side effects

Some of these issues are common to students with depression and to students with BP; some are not. For example, adolescents with BP in remission demonstrate significantly lower achievement in mathematics compared to those with major depressive disorder in remission.

Tips and Tricks for Helping Students with Mood Disorders

For a child who has marked "swings" or distinct episodes, the school may need to incorporate a "Plan A" and "Plan B," depending on the mood. A child who is usually an ultra-ultra-rapid cycler or in a more chronic mixed episode, however, may only need one plan for the vast majority of the time.

Typical Accommodations

- Accommodate medication side effects (see Chapter 24).
- Accommodate sleep-related impairment (see Chapter 14).
- Reduce and adjust homework (see Chapter 23).
- Accommodate impaired concentration, focus, memory, and slowed processing speed (see Chapters 8 and 10).
- Provide testing accommodations. Provide word banks for fill-in-the-blank tests or multiple choice formats instead of formats that require retrieval of verbal information from memory. Remember that even when the student's mood seems normal, some of the memory problems persist.
- Permit student to leave the room to go to a pre-arranged safe place or person.
- Schedule Resource Room* as the student's first period of the day to give him a "gentler," more slow-paced start to the day and to give him time to get organized or prepared for classes.
- Schedule Resource Room as the student's last period of the day to give him a chance to get started on any homework and to ensure that he'll have all assignments recorded and necessary materials packed up.
- Allow students more time if they have psychomotor retardation.
- Use preferential seating.

---

* As used here, we are referring to a pull-out related service in a separate classroom with a low student:teacher ratio.

- Acknowledge the student's feelings without disputing them. Saying "Yes, it can be frustrating when..." is more effective than saying "Cheer up, it's not so bad!"
- For students who are in an irritable depression or irritable mania that is not severe enough to require hospitalization or absence from school:
  - allow them to work independently instead of in a small group, unless the small group experience improves their mood.
  - arrange a discreet signal to cue them when they need to remove themselves or take a quick break to restore themselves to calm.
  - help them make a graceful exit (Chapter 31) if their behavior is beginning to be disruptive to others or hurtful to others.
  - teach them the importance of reparations (Chapter 29) and allow "do-overs" so that the students can restore their relationships or resume their work.
  - provide creative but safe activities to allow the students to express their ideas and feelings (e.g., art, creative writing, music, dance).

Do not punish a student who is in a depression or a manic episode for failure to complete homework. Simply acknowledge that the student is going through a rough time, ask the student what he thinks can be reasonably managed, and then agree to work out a catch-up plan when things are going more smoothly.

Other Accommodations and Supports

- Provide in-school counseling. Students with significant mood disorders may require in-school counseling on a regular or as-needed basis to assist with:
  - helping to recognize how their condition is affecting their ability to deal with academics and peer relationships.
  - developing self-advocacy skills.
  - developing strategies to work around or manage the impact of their symptoms in school.
  - seeking adult assistance or support when needed for difficulty coping.
  - dealing with feelings and frustration.
  - communicating needs.
  - learning anger management skills.

- Assign a gatekeeper/liaison. A student with significant mood-related problems and/or frequent changes in medication may be best accommodated if someone on the student's team is the parents' liaison. The liaison can quickly disseminate information to the school staff on the student's changing status or changing medication. The liaison can also promptly report changes in the student's functioning to the parents. Use case management as necessary.
- Adjust student's school day as needed. Some students may not be able to arrive at school on time. Others may be unable to tolerate a full day of school without having a "meltdown" or becoming more depressed.
- Use the Resource Room (external classroom) to help transition a student returning to school following hospitalization, etc.
- Provide referrals to mental health services or agencies.
- Educate peers.

In our experience, one of the more difficult issues to deal with regarding depression is the reactions of peers who may say things like "Snap out of it!" or "Stop feeling sorry for yourself!" Educating students about depression and Bipolar Disorder helps the student suffering from it and also helps other students recognize when that student might need help or when a peer or family member might have a mood disorder and possibly be at serious risk of suicide. Students who have participated in peer education programs report that they find it valuable to know what they can say or do to help a classmate or friend who is in a depression. In some cases, students have approached school personnel to alert them that a student is depressed or suicidal.

Dealing with "Storms," "Rage Attacks," "Meltdowns," or "Explosive Outbursts"

Students with depression or BP may have "meltdowns," "storms," or "rage attacks." See Chapter 15 for some techniques to prevent trouble and learn what to do when they occur.

Addressing Self-Harm Intentions or Thoughts

If a student has thoughts of serious self-harm, follow the school's policies and procedures, but ensure that the parents are contacted promptly. Advocate for an immediate referral to a psychiatrist or suggest that the parents take the child to a hospital emergency room.

Once the student has been assessed and treatment initiated, the student's physicians may indicate that the student can return to school. If thoughts of self-harm are still present, the school needs to provide additional interventions, but the nature of the plan depends on whether the self-harm is related to depression or if it is related to anxiety, a compulsive behavior, or a complex tic or mania. To determine the underlying issues:

- Have the student clarify self-harm vs. suicidal thoughts with the help of a school psychologist or social worker. Help the student develop a safety plan for each type of situation or risk (e.g., what will the student do if he has intrusive thoughts of cutting or killing himself, etc.).*
- Encourage the student to consider how his suicide would affect the important people in his life, i.e., family, friends.
- Encourage the student to identify important and available sources of support in his life (e.g., friends, parents, a teacher, clergy) and how he might reach out to them for support if he is feeling suicidal.
- Teach the student noninjurious ways of expressing depression and hopelessness (talk, writing, music, art, etc.)
- Devise a school safety plan for crisis situations together with staff and parents. The plan should include who the student will contact, what the student will do if that person is not available, which school personnel are responsible for contacting the parents, under what conditions the team may need to place a 911 call, etc.
- Determine, along with staff and parents, which staff member will be responsible for monitoring the student's status and emotional functioning in school. Determine a schedule and means of home-school communication, including who the parent may contact if there are particular concerns or a change in the student's status.

---

* Recent research on cutting suggests that approximately half of all adolescents engage in cutting at some point, so cutting may not be the best indicator of how much danger a student may be in.

- Develop, together with the parents, a suicide prevention plan to be used at home. Include strategies such as having a parent go for a walk with the child when the child is feeling particularly depressed, having the child take a relaxing warm bath, going for a swim with the child, encouraging the child to read a favorite book, watch a funny movie, or call a friend to go out. Provide parents with emergency telephone numbers, referrals to mental health resources, and include professionals who can provide private therapy for the student.
- Focus on a better future. Working with the school psychologist or social worker, encourage the student to identify goals for the next four years. Include discussion of goals for a career, a personal relationship with peers or romantic interest, and family oriented goals. Have the student record these in a personal journal.

Assisting with Social Interactions

- Assign the student to work in cooperative learning groups or with a supportive peer. If possible, also arrange for a homework buddy.
- Help the student arrange for socialization with peers outside of school (e.g., the student may attend sports events, school concert, after school clubs). Monitor to ensure that the student attends and follows up on the plan. Create more opportunities for peer interactions.
- Assist the student with interpreting facial expressions if his interpretation is impaired during a mood episode.

Depression: Associated or Comorbid Conditions

If a student is diagnosed with depression, school personnel also need to screen for:

- Suicidal thoughts
- Other mood disorders (especially dysthymia, BP)
- Sleep disorders
- Anxiety disorders
- ADHD (Biederman et al. 2005)
- OCD

- EDF (including pragmatics)
- Substance Abuse Disorder
- Processing speed deficits
- Memory problems, e.g., working memory deficits
- Word retrieval problems
- "Rages" or "Storms"
- Sensory dysregulation

Bipolar Disorder: Associated or Comorbid Conditions

If a student is diagnosed with Bipolar Disorder, school personnel also need to screen for:

- Sleep disorders
- "Rages" or "Storms"
- Suicidal thoughts
- Substance Abuse Disorder
- ADHD (Hazell et al. 2003; Reich et al. 2005; Rucklidge 2006)
- Obsessive-Compulsive Disorder (Masi et al. 2004; Zutshi, Kamath, and Reddy 2007)

In our experience, if OCD is present with depression or BP, but is not detected and treated, the treatment plan for the mood disorder may fail. Be sure to screen for OCD.

- Anxiety disorders, especially phobias and panic (Altindag, Yanik, and Nebioglu 2006; Keller 2006; Otto et al. 2006; Zutshi et al. 2006)
- EDF (Frangou et al. 2005; Shear et al. 2002)
- Delayed facial recognition (McClure et al. 2003)
- Learning Disabilities, especially math (Lagace, Kutcher, and Robertson 2003)
- Visual-motor integration problems (if co-morbid disorders are present)
- Memory disorders, e.g., working memory impairment
- Word retrieval problems
- Sensory dysregulation
- Developmental Coordination Disorder (if ADHD comorbid)

may suffer from mood disorders such as dysthymia, depression, and Bipolar Disorder. To help the student function successfully, accommodate symptoms while recognizing that neurocognitive deficits persist even when mood appears normal. Provide direct instruction on strategies to manage symptoms and protect important peer relationships.

Remember Annie from the beginning of this chapter? When her teacher contacted her parents, they reported that they had seen changes too, and her doctors were trying to help her with medication. Unfortunately, Annie's behavior continued to worsen and become more impulsive. She was hospitalized for almost two months for Bipolar Disorder. After discharge from the hospital, she was not ready to return to school and was placed in day treatment to help her learn to manage her symptoms and keep herself safe. When Annie finally returned to her high school, her school team made accommodations for her medication side effects, gave her testing and homework accommodations, in-school counseling, and time in the resource room to help her get organized and caught up if she missed classes or had trouble concentrating in class. With the help of her family, therapists, and teachers, Annie not only graduated from high school on time, but she completed college four years later.

Summary

It is only within the past decade or so that professionals have become aware that young children

CHAPTER 12

Sensory Dysregulation and Sensory Defensiveness

Parker was sitting at his desk quietly working on his math worksheet. His teacher walked around the room to see how the students were doing, offering help and a "good job!" to the children. As she came up behind Parker, she patted him lightly on his shoulder, saying, "Good job!" Parker jerked violently at her touch and looked distraught, yelling "Owww!"

Preview

Some students overreact or underreact to sensory events. Their abnormal reactions can mimic willful misbehavior. Recognizing signs of sensory dysregulation—overreactivity as well as underreactivity—leads to more effective accommodations and school-based services and interventions.

We recognize that there is currently controversy over whether sensory dysregulation, often referred to as Sensory Processing Disorder (SPD), is a genuine and verifiable disorder. In our experience, students who have sensory defensiveness that interferes with their academic, social, and behavioral functioning can be referred to an occupational therapist trained in sensory integration for assessment and successful treatment. Regardless of anyone's views on the theoretical controversies, the important thing is to recognize and accommodate symptoms that interfere with functioning.

Sensory Regulation

In the course of normal development, the brain integrates and organizes sensory input from the environment. Sometimes, the brain does not efficiently accomplish this task. This leads to sensory dysregulation resulting in overreacting or underreacting to environmental sensory stimuli. Sensory dysregulation can interfere with cognition, behavior, socialization, and feelings of competency in handling changes in expectations or routines. If the normal course of sensory integration is delayed or interrupted, the child may be hypersensitive (overreactive) or hyposensitive (underreactive) in any one or several of the senses.

If children are hypersensitive, they may exhibit avoidant behaviors. Hypersensitivity is most often associated with sensory defensiveness. Sensory defensiveness is defined as a "constellation of symptoms that are the result of feeling alarmed, defensive or negative about a harmless sensory experience; an overreaction to normal protective senses sometimes appearing as behavior that is irrational" (Wilbarger and Wilbarger 1991). If sensory data are not integrated and processed efficiently, hypersensitivity can be the result. Hypersenstive children are sometimes referred to as "sensation avoiders."

In contrast, a student who experiences hyposensitivity (a "sensation seeker") may seek out intense levels of stimulation, but not all sensation seekers are hyposensitive. Sometimes, a hypersensitive child may seek intense input to help calm her sensory system. A "crasher-banger" (Pruitt 1992) is a term for a student who is extraordinarily forceful in her movements and and needs to crash into objects to regulate her sensory system. Both hyposensitive and hypersensitive students may be crasher-bangers. In other words, you cannot always tell from the behavior whether the student is hyposensitive or hypersensitive. An assessment by the occupational therapist will help identify and clarify the nature of the student's sensory issues.

Our sensory systems include:

Tactile — the sense of touch. We explore the world tactically through our hands (discrimination) but we also perceive sensations around us, such as someone standing too close or touching us. Our tactile system is essential for helping us determine the types of input touching our body, and how we should respond to that input. A student who is tactically defensive (hypersensitive) might have an aversion to light touch or particular textures. A student who is hyposensitive might seek out tactile input, e.g., putting objects in her mouth or bumping into walls and people.

Auditory — the sense of hearing. A student who is hypersensitive has auditory defensiveness, or oversensitivity to sound, which may cause her to respond to a whisper as if it were a scream. A child with an under-responsive system typically has functional hearing but her brain fails to register or respond normally to everyday auditory input.

Vision — the sense of sight. The function of our visual system is not only to look at people and objects, but use our peripheral vision to know what is next to us as we move through space. If processing is impaired, the student may have visual defensiveness, e.g., oversensitivity to incoming visual stimuli. A child with a hyposensitive system seems to be unaware of people and things within her environment.

Olfactory — the sense of smell. If processing is impaired, the student may have olfactory defensiveness, e.g., oversensitivity to smell. An oversensitive reaction to scents has the potential to affect a student's ability to focus on schoolwork and activities, food preferences and eating habits, as well as ability to participate and enjoy social events. A student with an under-responsive system may not detect that they are offending others by poor hygiene.

Gustatory — the sense of taste. If the student is hypersensitive, she may overreact to the taste of substances in the mouth. A student who is hyposensitive might constantly put things into her mouth, such as her fingers, school supplies, or food. It is important to note that there are other reasons students might put things in their mouths, such as self-calming, anxiety, underarousal, or overarousal.

Vestibular — the sense of movement and awareness of one's body and the effect of gravity. The vestibular system responds to the position of the head in relation to gravity and accelerated or decelerated movement. If the student is hypersensitive, she may experience vestibular defensiveness or gravitational insecurity, i.e., an oversensitivity to movement and its relationship to gravity. Students with vestibular defensiveness may be terrified of playground activities that involve their feet leaving the ground or they may become car sick on field trips. A student with a hyposensitive vestibular system may crave movement, such as spinning her body around and around for lengthy periods of time.

Proprioception — the sense and awareness of the movement of muscles and joints. This information enables the brain to know where each part of the body is and how it is moving. If a student has hypersensitivity in this system, she may overreact to information coming from her muscles and joints. Although it is theoretically possible to be hyposensitive to proprioceptive input, in most cases, the problems appear to be due, instead, to low muscle tone or joint weakness. In contrast to other modalities of sensory defensiveness, proprioceptive defensiveness does not typically trigger a "fight or flight" response.

Table 12.1 identifies the senses and associated symptoms of hypersensitivity and hyposensitivity. In some cases, a single outward behavior may be associated with both types of sensitivity. Each student can have a different repertoire.

Levels of Impairment

Wilbarger and Wilbarger define three levels of sensory defensive responses: mild, moderate, and severe. Students with mild impairment can function reasonably well but may appear quirky and become irritable in response to sensory stimuli. Treatment for such students can make the difference between a mildly unhappy and somewhat rigid student and a happy, confident one. Moderate or severe impairment frequently affects multiple areas of a student's

Table 12.1. Symptoms of Sensory Hypersensitivity and Hyposensitivity

Sense	Hypersensitivity	Hyposensitivity
Tactile	■ Cannot stand being touched lightly ■ Strongly reacts—fearfully, anxiously, or angrily—to unexpected touch ■ Hates to be tickled ■ Does not like to touch messy, gooey substances ■ Wants labels in shirts removed ■ Will not wear turtlenecks ■ Is irritated by seams in socks and clothes ■ Avoids substances of any kind on hands ■ Hates washing face ■ Hates brushing teeth/hair ■ Hates substances on skin, e.g., rough textures ■ Hugs too tightly or avoids hugging ■ Does not want to be held, even as an infant ■ Avoids groups ■ Overreacts to touch even when it is expected, e.g., when students are lined up ■ Wears shorts in winter ■ Wears coats or long sleeves in summer ■ Picky eater, sometimes with a very limited repertoire of foods ■ Toe walker ■ Overreacts to pain ■ Gags easily on things like runny food, toothpaste	■ Does not use correct pressure and control when touching, e.g., touches objects or people too hard or hugs too tightly ■ Loves to roughhouse ■ Seeks out messy activities ■ Loves rough textures ■ Craves strong input from environment, e.g., strong touch ■ May have difficulty with fine motor skills ■ May have high pain threshold, e.g., does not react to injections or cuts ■ Unaware of being bumped ■ May not notice dirt on skin ■ May not notice that clothes are backward or twisted around on their body ■ Puts things in mouth excessively ■ Craves touching certain objects
Auditory	■ Angered by loud noises not chosen by the student ■ Covers ears in noisy situations, such as cafeteria, halls, PE ■ Reacts strongly to sudden loud noises, such as fire alarms and vacuums ■ Bothered by sounds that others cannot hear, such as the hum of fluorescent lights ■ Upset by chairs scraping on classroom floor ■ Avoids loud public places ■ Covers ears or reacts strongly when public address announcement system is in use ■ Frequently asks others to be quiet, sometimes in an angry voice ■ Grinds teeth	■ Always turns volume up too high ■ Speaks loudly; unaware of normal volume levels ■ May not respond at first when name is called ■ Difficulty following directions ■ Does not know where sound is coming from ■ Difficulty following conversations ■ Makes noises and sounds ■ Seems not to notice certain sounds ■ Subvocalizes or talks out loud when thinking

(continued on next page…)

(Table 12.1. continued...)

Visual	■ Reacts strongly to visual stimulation ■ Is oversensitive to light ■ Avoids eye contact ■ Irritated and distracted by fluorescent lighting ■ Trouble reading under fluorescent lights ■ Likes darkened rooms	■ Does not notice major stimuli in the visual field ■ Loses place a lot (trouble tracking), e.g., reading, copying from the board ■ Has trouble positioning in the visual field, e.g., writing on the lines ■ Difficulty orienting a visual image in space ■ Trouble with puzzles ■ Relies heavily on other senses besides the visual sense ■ Does not notice subtle visual differences, e.g., the difference between a plus and a minus sign ■ Cannot locate items in the visual field ■ Dislikes cutting and pasting
Olfactory	■ Reacts strongly to smells, such as those in the cafeteria, PE, bathroom ■ Avoids going to the bathroom due to smells ■ Reacts very strongly to perfumes ■ Talks about smells more than usual ■ Cannot handle certain spices even in moderation ■ Experiences a great many foods as having a bad smell; unwilling to eat many foods	■ Underreacts to smell to the point of not wanting to wash ■ Does not understand people's reaction to body odor ■ Unable to detect bad smells when needs to (smoke, gasoline) ■ Sniffs food and other items frequently ■ May leave unclean objects around due to failure to appreciate others' reactions to the odor
Gustatory	■ Reacts strongly to certain tastes ■ Likes bland food ■ Cannot stand the taste of certain foods ■ Cannot handle certain spices, even in moderation ■ Chokes often	■ Craves oral input; frequently puts things in their mouths (pencils, shirt sleeves/collars) ■ Detects no difference in taste of different foods ■ Wants extremely spicy, salty, chewy, or sour food ■ Craves sweets ■ Drools excessively
Vestibular	■ Is often carsick ■ Difficulty walking up and down stairs ■ Trouble with activities that require balance, such as riding a bike ■ Appears clumsy ■ Is afraid of movement ■ Avoids heights, e.g., stairs, getting up on low stools, playground equipment ■ Has fear of falling ■ Avoids being upside down or swinging ■ Dislikes moving fast or erratically	■ Craves spinning, e.g., turns swing in circles over and over without ever getting dizzy ■ Loves to swing high ■ Likes to jump ■ Likes to be tossed high in the air ■ In constant motion, always running, fidgety ■ Craves scary rides at amusement parks that make most kids dizzy and even sick ■ Thrill seeker to the point of being too risky ■ Bruises often and breaks bones ■ Runs rather than walks ■ Likes sudden, fast movements

Proprioception		<ul><li>Bumps into walls and people</li><li>Constantly moving in seat</li><li>Chews on everything</li><li>Uses atypical pencil grip</li><li>Appears clumsy</li><li>Drops things often</li><li>Cracks knuckles a lot</li><li>Grinds teeth</li><li>Wears heavy clothing</li><li>Likes heavy hugs</li><li>Likes to jump from high places</li><li>Behaves like "a crasher-banger"</li></ul>

life. Students with moderate or severe impairment need a complete evaluation by a neuropsychologist and an occupational therapist. They also usually require a comprehensive treatment program by a multidisciplinary team. The school's occupational therapist can provide direct services to the student as well as help teachers provide a sensory diet—a program of sensory activities that promotes more normal responses to sensory information.

 ## School Impact

In terms of specific school impact, sensory dysregulation may lead to a variety of problems, depending on the type of sensory defensiveness or dysregulation. Note that some of these overlap with other symptoms from other disorders but the symptom is from a different cause, e.g., a student who is distracted by the seams in socks may be distracted by a compulsion to have the seams "just so" whereas a student with sensory dysregulation may be distracted by the rough texture of the seams against the skin.

Academic Deficits:
- Demonstrates reading problems, e.g., tracking place on page
- Has difficulty copying from board (tracking)
- Has tracking deficits in math
- Inability to edit work efficiently
- Handwriting issues
- Has difficulty following two and three step directions, especially ones related to moving through space
- Looks at only one side of the page or one half of material
- Writes on only one side of the paper or organizer

Avoidance:
- Avoids school settings and activities
- Avoids playground equipment
- Avoids loud peers, games, cafeteria, or assemblies

Sensory Defensiveness:
- Demonstrates disruptive behavior due to overstimulation, e.g., yelling, running away, aggression
- Is distracted due to sensory issues, e.g., teacher's perfume, sound of student's writing
- May react loudly and angrily to stimuli, e.g., loud noises such as custodian cutting lawn

Motor/Movement/Physical Problems:
- Confuses left and right side of body
- Fidgets constantly
- Is always moving
- Is always out of seat
- Is clumsy
- Falls out of chair (difficulty with balance, stabilizing posture, and knowing where body is in space)
- Has poor desk posture
- Demonstrates weaker muscle tone; tires more easily than most children
- Confuses left and right side of body
- Shows difficulty getting from one place to another
- Uses the middle cubby rather than one on the left or right because she avoids crossing the midline
- Cannot physically play peer games
- Has issues with moving through space; bumps into things

Attention Deficits:
- Has an impaired ability to concentrate on work (distracted by stimuli)

Social-Emotional-Behavioral Impact:
- Unpredictable and intense outbursts that seem disproportionate to the situation
- Avoids busy or loud settings and activities, e.g., parties, sports, games, PE
- Avoids peer interactions
- Has difficulty playing with peers
- Does not recognize personal space of peers
- Displays excessive anxiety
- Frustrates easily
- Is inflexible

Tips and Tricks for Helping Students with Sensory Dysregulation

Tactile

- Avoid touching the student lightly. Use firm pressure to the shoulder or back instead of light touch or avoid touch altogether.
- Seat students with sensory issues away from others and near the teacher in group activities, but try to position the student's desk so that she can see who is moving near her and might come into contact with her.
- During group activities (circle or rug time), seat a young child with sensory issues next to a quiet child who is unlikely to touch her.
- During group activities, seat children with sensory issues to the side or in back of the group or near a wall.
- Allow the student to avoid lining up in close proximity to others. Assign the student to be in charge of the back of the line so that being at the back of the line is both acceptable to the student who needs to avoid contact, and even desirable.
- Do not surprise the student with unexpected touch. If necessary, approach the child from the front to give a visual cue that touch is coming.

Auditory

- Muffle the sound of chairs scraping by putting tennis balls on feet of chairs.

- Cover PA system so that it is not as loud.
- Be aware of some student's reaction to even pencils moving across paper and adjust seating to avoid proximity to noise.
- Have student close to the teacher when going into noisy settings such as cafeteria, physical education, or assembly.
- Seat student so that most noise and movement is in front of her and not coming at her from behind, which might surprise and alarm her.
- Seat student away from fluorescent lights if she hears the hum, or turn off lights and use natural lighting where possible.
- Seat student away from clock if the ticking sound is loud to her.
- Warn student of practice fire drills if at all possible.
- Allow the student with sensory issues to use sound canceling headphones.
- Use white noise machines to block extraneous noises.

Visual

- Seat students with sensory issues near windows for natural light.
- Avoid fluorescent lighting when possible. Provide an incandescent lamp near or on the student's desk to offset the disturbing effect of the fluorescent light.
- Reduce unnecessary teacher and student movements during lessons.
- Seat student so that she is not facing busy visual displays on the walls of the room.
- Do not rapidly move electronic pointers for overhead slides.
- Use highlights and colors to cue students as to locations of classroom supplies or to locate items on the student's paper.
- Allow students to wear visors if fluorescent lights are visually distracting to them.

Olfactory

- Do *not* wear perfume or scented lotions.
- Avoid using smelly liquids around students.
- Avoid using scented markers.
- Be aware of impact of cleaning products on some students.
- Be aware that chemicals used on school grounds may also trigger strong sensory reactions.

- Have student sit away from science experiments involving strong smells.

If students crave strong smells, they may require added adult supervision during chemistry labs.

Gustatory

- Allow students to chew gum or something safe if they crave input to their mouths.
- Let student drink from a water bottle to allow for oral input.
- Let the student suck and/or chew on a straw if it is calming.
- Be aware of student's eating restrictions, e.g., cannot eat tomatoes or cucumbers.

Vestibular

For sensation avoiders (hypersensitive students):
- Seat student with sensory defensiveness at the front of the school bus to help avoid motion sickness.
- Watch students with sensory defensiveness carefully when they are exposed to a lot of sensory information from the environment, e.g., hallways.
- Be near and monitor students during physical activities involving balance, especially swinging or activities in which their feet leave the ground.

For sensation seekers * *(hyposensitive students):*
- Allow the student to sit on a seat cushion or on a ball chair, or allow the student to sit on a baffled camping pillow filled with a small amount of air. This allows for movement without leaving the desk.
- Allow the student to sit on a rocking chair or take a rocking chair break prior to starting an academic task.
- Suggest some rhythmical, sustained movement (e.g., marching, washing desks, or bouncing), which can be organizing to the central nervous system.
- Provide organized movement breaks periodically during academic study times.
- Ask the student to erase the board or run notes to other teachers to allow her to get some extra movement.

- If possible, let the student run around the playground when unable to settle down.
- Never discipline a "sensory seeker" by taking away recess privileges or physical education—it will intensify the random movements, fidgeting, and outbursts.

Proprioception

- Allow the student to utilize a nonrolling, quiet squeeze toy for fine motor calming input.
- Allow student to hang from playground equipment; suggest five minutes of hanging from a rope or a climbing activity towards the end of recess, right before she returns to class.
- Have student push against an immovable object for resistance.
- Have student carry heavy items such as books from one place to another.
- Use a pillow that gives feedback and resistance on the student's desk chair.

Some students may wear too much clothing for the season because the weight of the clothing calms them or because it protects them from unexpected light touch that is registered by the hair on their skin. Other students wear too little clothing for the season because they are always hot or cannot tolerate the sensation of clothing touching their skin. This is a good example of how the same sensory defensiveness may lead to two different strategies in two different students.

Other Recommendations

- Allow children to occasionally have a piece of hard candy while doing deskwork. This is a calming technique and increases the student's attention.
- Have selected music playing that can help students with focus, e.g., classical music such as Mozart. If students with ADHD are too distracted by the music, then allow students who need the music to use earphones. Note that some students have a very strong negative reaction to music and may react emotionally if their peers are listening to music.

---

* Some of these suggestions are from Kari Hall. Downloaded from http://www.spdnetwork.org/aboutspd/tips.html.

Associated or Comorbid Disorders

Symptoms of sensory dysregulation may mimic symptoms of inattention, impulsivity, and hyperactivity. They may also look like symptoms of OCD (e.g., the child who keeps smelling things or the child who cannot tolerate sock seams and compulsively pulls up her socks). Or sensory dysregulation may be comorbid with one or more of these disorders. If a student has sensory dysregulation, also screen for:

- ADHD
- Developmental Coordination Disorder
- OCD
- Anxiety Disorders
- EDF
- Handwriting and VMI deficits
- Learning Disabilities
- Bipolar Disorder
- Autism Spectrum Disorder
- "Storms"
- Sleep problems

To complicate matters, sometimes what starts out as a sensory defensive reaction can become an obsession or a compulsion that takes on a life of its own.

School-Based Assessments

The school's occupational therapist is the primary professional in screening for sensory dysregulation, and in providing services to the student and information and strategies to the school personnel and parents. The classroom teacher, other school personnel (including the cafeteria monitor), and the student's parents can also provide valuable clues regarding sensory issues by their observations and reports.

Summary

Sensory dysregulation affects many students and impairs their ability to be available to learn, behave appropriately, and socialize. Many times students with sensory defensiveness are seen as behavior problems, overreactive, and melodramatic. Pediatric occupational therapists with sensory integration and sensory defensiveness training treat sensory defensiveness. Treatment usually enhances the student's ability to function more normally in response to sensory stimulus.

Sam could not handle being in the halls, cafeteria, or at PE. He kept complaining about the noise and people hitting him when they were only brushing up against him and touching him lightly. After ongoing therapy via a tailored sensory diet from the school's occupational therapist and receiving specialized treatment in desensitizing his tactile and auditory systems, Sam was able to tolerate everyday events better and his behavior at school and home improved significantly.

CHAPTER 13

Asperger's Syndrome and Nonverbal Learning Disability

To me having AS means that I will always be a little remote, a little bit removed from the people around me. I will frequently forget to communicate with the people around me and thus create a plethora of misunderstandings. I am as headstrong and stubborn as a rock, and I get tired very quickly from too much social interaction. I had to be trained how to interact with people among a million other little things.
— *Erika L. Peterson, describing life with Asperger's Syndrome**

Some of the disorders described in this book occur at higher than expected rates in students with Asperger's Syndrome (AS) or Nonverbal Learning Disability (NLD). For example, tics or Tourette's Syndrome (TS), Obsessive-Compulsive Disorder (OCD), anxiety disorders, and Executive Dysfunction are often reported in students with AS or NLD. Based on currently available research, however, it does not appear that AS or NLD occur at higher than expected rates in TS, OCD, ADHD, or Mood Disorders.

In discussing TS, OCD, and other conditions, we do not recommend routinely screening for AS or NLD. If a student is diagnosed with AS or NLD, however, then we strongly recommend that school personnel screen for tic disorders, ADHD, OCD, anxiety disorders, sensory integration issues, and mood disorders as well as Executive Dysfunction and memory deficits. Although AS and NLD are not a primary focus of this book, we are including this chapter so that educators are more likely to recognize symptoms and refer those students for further assessment.

ASPERGER'S SYNDROME

Asperger's Syndrome is an Autism Spectrum Disorder (ASD), and is one of a number of conditions that are currently classified as Pervasive Developmental Disorders (PDD) in the DSM-IV-TR (American Psychiatric Association 2000).

Description of Asperger's Syndrome

The following mnemonic identifies some of the cardinal characteristics of AS:

A= abstractions confuse them
S= speech atypicalities (staccato and pedantic)
P= perspective of others lacking
E= eye contact missing
R= rigid, narrow interests
G= gait can be distinctive
E= Executive Dysfunction
R= reciprocity of emotions lacking
S= socially impaired

© Challenging Kids, 2006.
Adapted from www.psychjam.com

---

* From Peterson, EL: A.S. Retrieved online from http://www. freestyle.mvla.net/galleries/2006-2007/p4-documentary/ books/ErikaP.pdf, December 24, 2007.

For many years, students with AS were often referred to as odd, or as geeks or nerds. Many of these students were diagnosed with ADHD without a diagnosis of AS, which only became its own diagnostic condition in 1994. Students with AS may have comorbid ADHD, but there are distinct differences between AS and ADHD:

- Students with AS have highly restricted interests (e.g., maps, trains), whereas students with ADHD have a more typical range of interests.
- Students with AS hyperfocus on a particular interest and details in general, whereas students with ADHD tend to miss details in areas where they have no interest.
- Routines calm students with AS and they adhere to routines inflexibly, while routines tend to bore and irritate students with ADHD, who have difficulty learning routines.
- ADHD is not associated with significant differences between verbal and performance IQ measures, whereas AS is associated with significant performance deficits relative to verbal IQ.
- Novelty and risk-taking behaviors are exciting to many students with ADHD, but are rarely experienced as positive by the student with AS.

Impact of Asperger's Syndrome

Communication Deficits

In terms of development, language skills generally appear on time or even early in children with AS. Young children with AS tend to have a well-developed vocabulary, but early strengths tend to mask some of the true language problems to come. Their prosody (rhythm of language) is frequently affected and the level of pitch and intonation may be awkward. Many children with AS are described as pedantic or "little professor" in their communication style.

To the surprise of others, the student with AS may repeat verbatim a phrase learned in a movie or on TV with the exact accent, intonation, and phonation of the original source. Unfortunately, it is not always appropriate to the conversation. Students with AS are often impaired in their understanding of the social rules of language (pragmatics), which significantly impairs their peer relationships.

Students with AS interpret language very literally. They may also have trouble retrieving words. A comprehensive speech and language assessment is crucial when assessing students with AS.

Narrow Interests

Students with AS overfocus on their area(s) of interest. They have an intense preoccupation to the exclusion of other areas and the interests of their peers. Their preoccupation with a particular topic may last for weeks, months, or years. Some develop a tremendous knowledge base in their area(s) of interest.

Seven-year-old Stewart was so absorbed with snakes that his teacher contacted his therapist in desperation. "I can't get him to focus on any of the academics," the teacher reported. "All he wants to do is draw snakes or talk about snakes or read about snakes. Help!" The therapist empathized with the teacher and suggested as a short-term solution that the teacher try to integrate the curriculum around Stewart's perseverative interest in snakes. "Instead of asking him to do regular math problems, tell him to do snake math: If he has one snake and gets two more snakes, how many will he have altogether, etc.?" the therapist suggested. "And when he needs to write a sentence, let him write a sentence about snakes. That will enable you to determine if he understands the mechanics of writing."

Although we do not want to reinforce a perseverative interest, teachers may need to be creative and "go with the flow" for a short period to get the student participating in activities. Once the student is participating and earning reinforcement, you can try gradually bringing him around to other topics.

Rigidity and Perseveration

Students with AS are typically inflexible and rigidly adhere to routine. These features resemble the compulsiveness seen in OCD (Chapter 5), and it may be difficult for school personnel to distinguish between AS-related perseveration (stuck) and OCD-related compulsiveness. Outwardly, the behaviors may appear the same: the student may be unable to make transitions, have trouble completing work in a timely fashion, and may become agitated or difficult if there is an attempt to interrupt them. It is important to screen students with AS for OCD to determine if treatment of obsessive-compulsive symptoms is needed.

Cognitive Deficits

A neuropsychological evaluation is helpful in identifying cognitive strengths and deficits in students with AS. One of the most common cognitive deficits is in the domain of verbal executive skills, where students with AS often have significant difficulty in cause and effect relationships. This deficit not only impairs the student academically but has significant impact on social development and peer interactions. Additionally, slow processing speed, if present, results in needing more time and perhaps repetitions for students to be able to grasp a concept. Students with AS tend to have excellent rote memory skills, but may have deficits in other types of memory. Include screening for memory deficits when assessing students with AS.

Do not be misled by the student's strengths in rote memory skills and vocabulary. Students with AS have difficulty understanding inferential material.

Motor Skills

Students with AS often have poor coordination. Many of them probably would meet the diagnostic criteria for Developmental Coordination Disorder, but that diagnosis is currently not supposed to be made when an Autism Spectrum Disorder such as AS is diagnosed. A stiff or awkward gait is commonly observed, although there does not seem to be one "signature" gait observed in all children with AS. Some students with AS appear to fall forward as they walk. Students with AS also have impairment in fine motor skills and handwriting, although there is no one pattern of handwriting deficits that appears common to all.

Emotional Difficulties

In situations with excessive stimulation, students with AS are likely to become overaroused and emotionally deregulated. Some of the dysregulation may be due to sensory defensiveness (see Chapter 12), and some may be due to inflexibility and need for predictable and rigid routines. Many AS students need more down time than even other students with neurological disorders. This helps them regulate their emotions and other neurological responses to overarousal. Having a neurological disorder can be exhausting. Planning such breaks into the student's daily schedule can help prevent social-emotional difficulties or "storms" (see Chapter 15).

Another common emotional challenge is the inability to recognize and reciprocate the emotions of others. This can cause additional social issues and relationship difficulties when it comes to meeting the needs of others, as described below.

Social Interaction Difficulties

Students with AS generally experience significant difficulty with social interactions, due to a number of factors such as:
- Inability to take the perspective of others
- Deficits in understanding the rules of social interaction
- Inability to read nonverbal social cues such as body language and facial expressions

For such students, making and keeping friends is a struggle and frequently a losing battle. They may not understand why we cannot read their minds and hearts even though they are unable to read ours. Because students with AS tend to be concrete thinkers and interpret things in black/white terms, the truth becomes more important to them than feelings. In other words, students with AS often do not develop the important social skill of the little white lie, and may be tactless in their comments to others. The social inflexibility of students with AS also poses significant challenges in social situations as they may be unable to cope with unanticipated events or people reacting in unexpected ways. These situations increase stress levels and agitation, leading to more peer problems.

Students with AS frequently miss a listener's nonverbal cues. The tendency to go on and on talking about their particular area of interest combined with a failure to make eye contact may lead to listener frustration and reduce others' attempts to socially interact with students with AS. Even when the student with AS *does* make eye contact, the student often misinterprets facial expressions and may respond based on an incorrect perception of others' emotional state. For example, the student with AS may misinterpret a bored expression as interest and be encouraged to continue going on and on about one topic, or the student may misinterpret a neutral expression as anger and act accordingly. Alternatively, the student with AS may stare inappropriately at a person.

Stewart was in his therapist's office. His therapist asked him, "How can you tell if the other kids are interested when you are talking about snakes?" Stewart thought about it, and said, "Um... because they're not talking?" The therapist asked him if that could just be politeness, and Stewart agreed that perhaps his peers were just being polite by not interrupting him. "So how can you know if they're really interested or just being polite?" his therapist asked.

Stewart began working with his therapist to try to monitor how others were reacting to his talking about snakes. If others asked him a question about what he was saying, he would take that as a sign of interest. But if no one was responding and he had been talking for thirty seconds or more without a pause, he would ask his peers if he was boring them or if they wanted him to continue.

Because Stewart wanted to make friends, he was responsive to learning strategies for managing his perseverative interest in snakes and being thoughtful of his peers' needs. His teacher assisted him by developing a private signal that she used with him when he was starting to go on and on about his interest to others' frustration.

Students with AS have a limited range of facial expressions and gestures, which creates more difficultly during the teenage years. These students also have difficulty in gauging appropriate physical proximity for different types of relationships, i.e., how close they are supposed to stand to a teacher, friend, or family member.

Social skill deficits are the most impairing and distressing aspect of life for most students with AS, and the impairment worsens as the students age and the gap between their skills and their peers' skills becomes more obvious. Young children with AS are more inclined to play alone, which may, in part, result from their narrow focus of interests, but may also be due to avoidance of the stresses associated with interactive play. As they mature, many will become loners.

For students with significant social interaction difficulties, being alone may help them avoid stress and find a sense of calm. Becoming aware of when the student needs this time to refuel can enable you to assist the student in making a graceful exit. For too many students with AS, however, being alone is not a choice but an unhappy result of impaired and unremediated social skills.

To help students with AS succeed socially, provide a designated place and method for downtime so that they can restore themselves to a more balanced state.

Students with AS may have difficulty with co-operative play, especially sharing any object of focused interest. This hampers friendships that are often built on common interests. The inability to share such an object makes the student appear selfish to peers, when, in fact, the lack of sharing is just a lack of understanding about how the reciprocity of friendship works. This egocentricity can be remediated with instruction and practice. Students with AS are frequently surprised to see themselves appearing uncooperative in a videotaped interaction with others, because that was not their intent.

Stewart brought a new book on snakes with him to his therapy session. He was very excited about it and wanted to tell the therapist all about it. Instead, the therapist asked him to put it aside while they worked, and told him that if he was able to focus on their work, they could look at the book together for a few minutes at the end of the session. When it came time to talk about the book, Stewart opened it and started talking, but did not offer to let the therapist look at it or hold it. Through direct instruction and practice, the therapist taught Stewart to offer to let her look at his possessions.

Students with AS also need guided practice and rehearsal of social rituals such as demonstrating affection. Although the student may intellectually understand the importance of communicating positive feelings, he may not necessarily understand that saying just one kind remark is not enough to maintain a relationship. Nor may the student know when would be an appropriate time or situation to show fondness for a friend. As one adult with AS once lamented, "My wife shouldn't have to hold up a sign that says 'Hug me!' I should know when she needs to be hugged, but I just never seem to recognize the situations."

Tips and Strategies for Students with Asperger's Syndrome

The following tips and strategies are organized by area of difficulty.

Transitions:

- Stick to a structured routine as much as possible.
- State clear expectations and rules.

- Cue potential changes or transitions.
- Provide direct instruction on how to make a transition. Do this discreetly for middle school and high school students.
- Use visual organizers for daily routine and highlight any changes in routine. Consistent structure and routine reduces stress for the student with AS. The organization and consistency of the classroom environment is one of the key factors in managing the student's deficits.

Academic Production:

- Allow extra time for handwritten work.
- Utilize word processors for ease of production.
- Recognize and praise good rote memory skills.
- Assist with cause and effect deficits in reading comprehension.

Speech and Language Deficits:

- Arrange for a speech and language assessment to determine the student's need for speech and language services to address deficits.

Most students with AS require speech and language services to promote social and academic skills. Students with AS need direct instruction, practice, and feedback for acquisition of social language. Small-group practice is helpful.

- Pause between instructions to allow for execution.
- Allow extra time for slow processors before repeating question or instruction (count to fifteen in your head).
- Check for comprehension.
- Write down instructions.
- Use short, direct, and concrete verbal cues.
- Teach the student to use their verbal skills to help analyze a social situation, as described in the section of this chapter on Nonverbal Learning Disability.
- **Do not** use slang or idiomatic speech. A sarcastic, "Oh, that was great!" may inadvertently positively reinforce an inappropriate behavior.
- When the student behaves inappropriately, tell him in a nonjudgmental tone using clear, short statements. Then tell the student how to behave appropriately also using short, clear nonemotional statements.
- Provide instruction and assistance to expand vocabulary. When a word has more than one meaning, tell the student which meaning is being used.
- If the student tends to get frustrated frequently and does not communicate that appropriately, coach the student what to do and say to request help, e.g., "Raise your hand, wait to be called on, and say, "Can you please help me with this?"

Visual Needs:

- **Do not** use meaningful looks to signal information to a student with AS. Instead, use a privately prearranged signal.
- To help students with AS with writing tasks, incorporate visual cues and graphic organizers (see Chapter 19 on Written Expression).
- To help students with a sequence of operations, use visual editing strips (see Chapters 19 and 20).
- To help students pay attention, use props during instruction.

Sensory Overstimulation:

- If establishing and maintaining normal eye contact is too difficult for the student, teach the student to focus between the speaker's eyes on the bridge of the nose where there is less sensory stimulus. It will still look like normal eye contact to others but will be easier for the student with AS.
- Ask the student to teach us how we will know that he is attending to our presentation, e.g., using the eye contact technique listed above.
- Avoid situations that might produce "sensory overload" for the student.

Stress Reducers:

- Provide clear expectations and rules for behavior.
- Teach the student to make a graceful exit to go to some safe place or person (see Chapter 31).

- **Do not** lock horns with the student if the student is perseverating. Provide some graceful and face-saving techniques to end the exchange.
- Use "Instant Replay" and "Cooperative Problem Solving" to address problematic behaviors (see Chapter 31).
- Allow the student to leave the classroom five minutes early to avoid sensory over-stimulation from being in the noisy, crowded halls between classes.
- Educate the student's peers and school personnel about AS.

Social Skill Deficits:

- Foster social skills by direct instruction and teach the student how to interact through social stories, modeling, role-playing, and video self-modeling.
- Be sensitive to peer rejection and bullying. Added adult supervision in settings like the playground, the cafeteria, the school bus, and the halls may be needed.
- **Do not** expect skills learned in one setting to generalize to another setting. Teach skills and rehearse them in a variety of settings. Use verbal cues to emphasize similarities between situations.

Students with AS may not generalize skills learned in one setting to other settings without training and rehearsal across settings. Have parents also provide such training to promote generalization to nonschool settings.

- Work with the student to plan what to say or do in upcoming situations that may be difficult for the student. Afterwards, quickly review how the plan worked (see Coaching and "Instant Replay" in Chapter 31).
- Help the student with AS identify and understand the impact of ritualistic behavior on social interactions.
- Provide direct instruction and written text cues to improve quantity and quality of social interactions.
- Teach recognition of social cues and how to respond.
- Provide social skills groups that teach and permit guided rehearsal with support for social skills such as turn-taking and show-

ing interest in what other people want to talk about or do.
- Arrange for a mentor to advise the student on social "do's" and "don'ts."

 ## Associated or Comorbid Conditions

- OCD
- Language Disorders (e.g., pragmatics)
- NLD
- Executive Dysfunction
- Working memory deficits
- Anxiety disorders
- Handwriting (dysgraphia)
- Coordination problems (even if diagnosis of Developmental Coordination Disorder is not supposed to be made)
- Sensory dysregulation
- "Storms"
- ADHD
- Tics or TS
- Depression
- Sleep Problems

Diagnostic Confusion

As explained in Chapter 1, there is overlap in the features of neurological disorders. The core feature of AS and other disorders on the autistic spectrum—the inability to take the perspective of others—is also found in other disorders covered in this book (e.g., severe EDF). As always, a comprehensive evaluation is necessary along with an understanding of the other disorders that share features with Asperger's Syndrome.

AS is more likely to be misdiagnosed or incompletely diagnosed than many of the other conditions described in this book except for mood disorders. Based on our clinical experience, the misdiagnosis happens two ways: misdiagnosing EDF with OCD and/or mood disorders as AS or failing to diagnose AS in the presence of ADHD.

If an undiagnosed student has an uncoordinated gait (e.g., he appears to be falling forward as he walks), a lower performance IQ, difficulty making friends, and if the student also has narrow interests, consider speaking with the school psychologist about a referral for evaluation and assessment. We also recommend screening all students with AS for NLD, described below.

Summary

Students with Asperger's Syndrome may benefit from early intervention services to promote positive outcomes. Although students with AS may have strong academic skills, failure to remediate social and communication deficits may lead to impairment as adults. Social skills have everything to do with being an adult, acquiring a job, friends, and a family. Teach social skills in a group setting and train parents on how to promote rehearsal and generalization of the skills at home. With proper social skills and communication services, many students with AS are able to lead productive and satisfying lives.

NONVERBAL LEARNING DISABILITY

Preview

Nonverbal Learning Disability (NLD, formerly abbreviated NVLD) is a disorder characterized by significantly lower performance IQ and an inability to interpret the emotions of others, resulting in significant social impairment. NLD is often confused with Asperger's Syndrome. They can occur together but have distinguishing constructs. NLD has a very distinct neuropsychological profile with strengths and weaknesses. The name of this disorder is often misleading as it cannot be remediated using a traditional learning disability approach. The following material is influenced primarily by the pioneering work of Byron Rourke, who developed the neuropsychological profile of NLD.*

NLD is a very serious disability with a guarded outcome for success. Students with NLD pose even more of a challenge in the classroom than students with other conditions described in this book because of the severity of their social-emotional impairment. To complicate matters even more, the older the student gets, the more of a challenge the teacher will face. The student may become quite agitated over not having a normal teenage social life and he may

also suffer from anxiety and mood disorders. Students with NLD are at a higher risk for depression due to their social difficulties.

Description of Nonverbal Learning Disability

Although there is considerable variation across individuals, students with NLD exhibit a pattern of relative impairment in social perception, visual-spatial abilities, and mechanical arithmetic, combined with well-developed verbal skills and rote memory. Their inability to "read between the lines" and interpret nonverbal social cues significantly impairs development of successful social relationships. Students with NLD have a pattern of deficits in:

- Interpersonal relationships
- Social judgment
- Emotional stability
- Executive functions, e.g., organization and planning skills
- Visual and tactile perception, memory, and attention
- Early fine motor skills, e.g., writing, cutting
- Oral motor planning (praxis), e.g., planning motor movements of lips
- Rhythm of speech (prosody)
- Word meaning (semantics)
- Concept formation and problem solving
- Study skills
- Mathematics, especially math calculation
- Reading comprehension
- Science
- Ability to handle novel situations

Strengths

One of the most significant strengths of a student with NLD is a relatively higher verbal IQ. Other areas of relative strength include:

- **Auditory and verbal attention.** Students with NLD have a greater ability to attend to sounds than to visual stimuli. This is also true in the area of memory where auditory and verbal memory or memory for sounds is a strength. The verbal area is also stronger in the cognitive area but only in certain ways as will be pointed out in the weakness section.

- **Auditory perception.** Auditory perception includes the ability to hear and identify the

---

* A listing of Dr. Rourke's books and articles can be found on his website at http://www.nld-bprourke.ca/NLD.BIBLIO.BPR. BooksPlus.html.

distinct features of a sound, to distinguish the primary sounds, to memorize a sound and blend multiple sounds, and hold onto enough sounds to understand the whole of what words are being said. Because students with NLD have superior auditory perceptual skills, they are good phonetic readers through their ability to sound out words. They are often also superior spellers who can easily read or spell those words that follow the regular phonetic rules.

- **Verbal reception.** Students with NLD have a superior ability to take in words with accuracy. These students are able to repeat what is said, associate it to previously learned information, and store it in long-term memory.

- **Rote memory.** Rote memory is an area of strength for students with NLD. But as with students with AS, superior rote memory skills means that although the students can link new material with previously learned information, they may not be able to use this information for inferential reasoning.

- **Correct volume.** Students with NLD use the correct volume when speaking unless they are overstimulated. At such times, students are usually unaware that they are speaking too loudly.

- **Fine motor skills.** Fine motor skills are an area of relative strength in handwriting activities, but *only in the later developmental stages*.

Weaknesses

Nonverbal skills (as assessed in standard IQ tests) are one of the cardinal weaknesses of students with NLD. Other areas of weakness include:

- **Visual Attention.** Students with NLD cannot attend as well to visual, written, or printed material as they can to orally presented material. One consequence of deficits in visual attention is difficulty engaging in academic tasks that require them to carefully edit or check their work.

- **Tactile attention.** Students with NLD have problems with tactile attention (awareness of information being transmitted to the brain from the skin). Because of this, these students have a hard time paying attention when coming into contact with a person or object. This deficit affects social functioning as well as academic functioning, e.g., holding someone's hand too hard.

- **Visual-motor integration (VMI).** Visual-motor integration is the ability to integrate the visual image of letters and shapes with the appropriate motor response, e.g., to be able to draw/reproduce a visually presented shape. VMI is a deficit area in young students with NLD, but is not an issue in older students with NLD with respect to handwriting or graphomotor skills. Handwriting in younger students is usually sloppy, although it does improve in later years. The student with NLD may be physically awkward and have trouble learning coordinated sequential motor movements that require bilateral coordination such as skipping or riding a bicycle.

- **Visual perception.** Visual perceptual skills include discriminating visual information and interpreting it. Students with visual perceptual deficits may have difficulty picking out the primary visual image from the background, memorizing individual as well as multiple images, and holding onto enough images for sufficient time to allow transfer to memory (as would be required in copying from the board). Visual perception also entails the ability to orient or position a visual image in space correctly, as would be required in reading or distinguishing the letter 'b' from 'd.' Visual closure is the ability to identify familiar objects as a whole from the parts, e.g., not having to read every letter in a word to recognize the word. Visual closure permits more efficient reading. Not all students with NLD will have all of these problems.

- **Visual memory and tactile memory.** Students with NLD have deficits in visual memory and tactile memory due, in part, to deficits in attention. However, even when they can attend normally, they remain weak in visual and tactile memory. For example, the student with NLD will correctly spell phonetically regular words, but phonetically irregular words are difficult due to this visual memory deficit. Students with NLD may also have impairment in immediate memory for faces (Rasmussen, 2005) (Liddell & Rasmussen, 2005).

- **Poor sense of direction.** Students have difficulty with finding a place when walking or driving, e.g., they may get lost getting from one classroom to another, even if they have gone there before.

- **Difficulty with mechanical arithmetic.** Deficits in the mechanics of math calculations are one of the hallmarks of NLD. The visual spatial problems described earlier cause serious problems in lining up math problems. Deficits in visual attention lead to errors such as mistaking a subtraction symbol for an addition symbol or omitting dollar signs or decimal points in answers. Maintaining sequences and procedures are difficult in math across the board, including problem solving sequences in word problems.

- **Speech**. Speech is the ability to verbally communicate. Oral motor praxis is the ability to plan movements of the muscles in the lips or mouth to produce sounds clearly. Students with NLD may have oral motor apraxia, which results in unclear speech. Such students are usually "late talkers." The normal rhythm (prosody) of speech may also be impaired, resulting in robotic speech production or in sounding overly serious.

- **Language**. Language is a systematic means of communicating by the use of sounds or conventional symbols or gestures. It involves the ability to receive information, process it, store it, and respond to it. The efficient use of language results in effective communication. Semantics (word meaning) can be delayed in a student with NLD, even though he is proficient at decoding or sounding out words.

  Lack of flexibility in language creates difficulty for students with NLD in identifying all the possible solutions to choose from when attempting to understand a situation and make a decision. Problem solving, predicting outcomes, and inferring cause

and effect relationships may be daunting tasks for the student with NLD and impair his performance in academic subjects, e.g., literature, social studies, and science.

Verbal executive deficits and working memory deficits impair the student's ability to float a number of possible solutions in mind. Putting all the pieces together, seeing how they connect, and integrating them with previous knowledge is compromised.

Humor is a difficult area due to the language deficits. Multiple meanings, e.g., puns and word plays, along with teenage jargon, are quite difficult for the student to understand. Sarcasm is always misinterpreted, and frequently taken literally.

Students with NLD have difficulty identifying things that do not fit or are inappropriate in a situation. This causes an inability to think on their feet and leaves students with NLD relying on habitual responses rather than appropriate language responses in new situations. Novelty, in general, is an anxiety producing situation with added impact when more complex language demands are present.

Students with NLD may also be hyperverbal and verbose, causing further inefficiency in language communication. Not surprisingly, language impairments associated with NLD pervasively impact social relationships.

- **Socialization.** Socialization is probably the most difficult area for students with NLD and their family members. The student with NLD relies more heavily on verbal than nonverbal skills, which might lead us to erroneously believe that verbal skills are an area of strength that can successfully be tapped to assist in social skills. Unfortunately, in our clinical experience, this does not appear to be the case and using verbal strengths may be of only minimal help. Socialization deficits are related to a number of factors in NLD:
  - ❑ Social language skills (i.e., pragmatics) are affected by Verbal Executive Dysfunction (Chapter 18) and working memory deficits (Chapter 10); impaired pragmatics is probably one of the biggest deterrents to friendships.

❏ Social reciprocity is missing. These students are unable to converse with the right rhythm and tone.

❏ Talking too much without understanding the impact on the listener is consistently a problem.

❏ Impulsivity due to self-regulatory deficits from Executive Dysfunction (Chapter 9) can cause social missteps.

❏ Social perception is frequently askew because nonverbal cues are either missed, misread, or misinterpreted.

❏ Behaviors that suggest excessive familiarity may be observed long before familiarity might be appropriate in a developing relationship.

❏ Facial expressions often do not match the emotion being felt by the student or the emotion of the person interacting with the student.

These problems can lead to social isolation and to the student with NLD being bullied. These students are likely to withdraw socially as they get older and have painful experiences that reinforce an inability to make and keep friends.

Students with NLD have such pervasive problems that, in addition to any school supports and related services, it is key to involve an outside professional who specializes in working with students with NLD.

To add to the challenges they already experience, students with NLD also have limited self-awareness and may not recognize their own strengths and weaknesses. This can result in making unrealistic choices or setting unrealistic goals, as seen in career or vocational choices. Good transition programs can prepare these students for making a realistic vocational choice.

Increasing Difficulties over Time

Whereas students with some of the disorders covered in this book experience symptom improvement or overall improvement over time, students with NLD may experience more impairment over time due to two factors. The first is that although symptoms may not worsen per se, the student feels the effects of the condition more keenly as the demands and complexity of the school environment increase. They fall further behind in academic functioning as difficulties in inferential thinking becomes more important and as rote memory and decoding skills become less important. They stand out more socially because their social skills deficits are more likely to be noticed as their peers mature and develop in a more typical fashion.

The second factor contributing to worsening over time is that some symptoms first emerge or worsen in adolescence. Students with NLD must handle multiple adjustments as they continue through school. These students may be hyperactive in the very early school years. This can continue through elementary school. Any novel or difficult situation that arises can disrupt the student's ability to be successful in the current school setting. A sudden change in routine or getting feedback of a mistake or error can also precipitate a crisis for some students. Making sure the student is supported in very small, successful steps is the best chance the student has to maintain a stable, calm approach to school.

During adolescence, these students experience an increase in anxiety and mood disorders such as depression. As anxiety and mood disorders increase and social withdrawal becomes acute, emotional problems, temper, and the risk of suicide can result. It is important to make sure there is constant monitoring and appropriate, timely intervention.

Below is a mnemonic for remembering some of the cardinal deficits of NLD:

N= no friends
L= lower performance IQ
D= deficits in math

Tips and Strategies for Nonverbal Learning Disability*

General tips for improving comprehension and performance

■ Provide more content and classroom structure than other students might need.

■ Begin by addressing and directly teaching organizational strategies.

---

* Some of the material in this section is based on suggestions from Jean Foss (2001, ERIC EC DIGEST #E619) and the NVLD website but modified, added to, and adapted for this use by the authors.

- Work with part/whole relationships by giving student the "whole" (big picture) first and then teaching the individual parts.
- Work to integrate verbal and nonverbal processes with cognitive strategies, e.g., "**E**very **G**ood **B**oy **D**oes **F**ine" is a cognitive strategy for remembering the notes on the lines of the treble clef.
- Use the student's verbal strength to analyze and mediate information as an intervention, e.g., have the student link the information in the lecture to previously learned vocabulary.
- Teach the use of self-talk to provide direction for completing tasks.
- Use direct skills instruction for academics and social instruction.
- Relate new concepts to previously learned information.
- Teach problem solving with use of a mnemonic to assist memory and retrieval.
- Make explicit connections between content and real life situations, e.g., if teaching measurement, student could go to store to compare one quart of milk, a half-gallon, a gallon, etc.
- Present information in more than one modality, e.g., have the student feel a ball while discussing "sphere" and have the student write "a sphere is smooth and round all around." Have the student roll the ball while saying, "Spheres can roll because they are round all around."

Using direct instruction and guided rehearsal

- Be clear and direct in addressing weaknesses.
- Gain a commitment from the learner to collaborate and to ask for help to improve the weakness.
- Include a clear explanation of the contexts in which the skill you are trying to teach can be applied.
- Begin a lesson with what is most familiar, and teach in a sequential step-by-step fashion.
- Provide instruction to directly associate and integrate verbal labels and description with concrete objects, actions, and experiences, e.g., teach that the word "position" is in the word "preposition" and that the majority of prepositions describe the position of a person or object in space.
- Provide specific sequenced verbal instructions, teaching the learner to verbally self-direct so that the student eventually internalizes this process.
- Make cause/effect relationships explicit whenever possible.
- Teach the student how to externally (e.g., on paper) identify the different steps necessary to establish cause and effect.
- Encourage the student to use multisensory steps to aide in integration, both receptively and expressively (read it, see it, hear it, touch it, say it, write it, do it). Write down the steps to refer to for use.
- Identify opportunities to generalize and practice new skills in situations that are similar to each other, e.g., waiting your turn to talk is the same social skill as waiting your turn in the cafeteria line. Directly teach the similarities in the situations to promote greater generalization.

Modifications that contribute to a supportive academic environment

General:
- State clear expectations.
- Establish performance expectations based on knowledge of what the student is able to complete or produce, given the nature of the tasks and the time available.
- Provide structure and written directions about priorities for completing multiple tasks.
- Arrange with other teachers to stagger the demands for products (papers, projects, tests, etc.), so that they are not all due at the same time.
- Modify homework assignments as needed.
- Modify testing in both time requirements and content.
- Provide templates or graphic organizers to assist with organization of written material. (See Chapter 19 on Written Expression.)
- If possible, provide a second set of books to be left at home.
- Ensure that the student has extra pencils and paper at school.
- Coach time management skills.

Specific:

- Preview reading tasks; have the student look at the questions and then explain the questions and note that this is the important information in the chapter.
- Add further explanations to the "hows" and "whys" of reading comprehension, especially in middle and high school content areas.
- Define all vocabulary before a lesson and before reading material.
- Provide story starters for written expression.
- Monitor science and social studies projects for organizational problems.
- Waive foreign language requirements.
- Modify art for fine motor and visual perceptual deficits.
- Modify physical education activities, e.g., if the student cannot sequence motor movements for the activity, the student can be the score keeper.
- Encourage the use of computers.

Modifications that facilitate socialization

- Be sensitive to situations that have high potential for the student to behave inappropriately.
- Facilitate group activities to avoid victimization and bullying.
- Intervene to prevent behavior that might lead to criticism, teasing, or ostracism.
- Act as a buffer and support to facilitate the most positive outcomes possible.
- Help the student to anticipate the kinds of situations that might prove difficult.
- Plan in advance alternative responses they might have in difficult situations.
- Engage the student in a collaboration in which the teacher signals when the student makes a social error and the student agrees to immediately stop the behavior. Discreet signals can be used to alert the student to lower their voice, for example.
- Arrange structured social activities (through elementary school); coach the child in how to participate, and signal the child discreetly if he behaves in a way that is likely to lead to peer rejection or peer problems.
- Provide verbal mediation (e.g., self-talk) for nonverbal experiences and teach the children to use verbal mediation to interpret and guide their own experiences.
- Teach students through direct instruction to interpret facial expressions, gestures, and other nonverbal aspects of communication, including the *intensity* of others' reactions.
- Teach them through direct instruction to watch for and interpret indications from others that they are talking too much, or that the communication is ineffective in some way.
- Teach them through direct instruction how to self-monitor their understanding when communicating.
- Teach them how to ask clarifying questions but to also limit their questions to the two most important questions and to then give others a turn to talk.

Behavioral supports

- Provide peer and staff awareness training.
- Pair student with good role models.
- Identify a safe person and place for the student to go to, as needed.
- Follow a consistent schedule to reduce anxiety over change and novelty.
- Allow for downtime without constant academic demands so that the students can recharge their batteries.
- Use the graceful exit plan as needed.
- Avoid sensory overstimulation and plan with the student how the student can handle novel or overwhelming situations.
- Teach the student anxiety-reduction and relaxation strategies (see Appendix G).
- Use "Instant Replay" and "Cooperative Problem Solving" techniques for improving behavior and social skills (Chapter 31).

Assessment

In addition to screening for the disorders listed in the "Comorbid and Associated Conditions" section, school personnel need to do the following:

- Have a Speech and Language Pathologist test the student for comprehension, semantics, oral motor praxis, prosody difficulties, auditory memory, and pragmatics. The school psychologist can also test for memory.
- Have an Occupational Therapist test for difficulties with tactile perception, visual

perception, complex psychomotor, visual and tactile memory, and early graphomotor skills or deficits. The school psychologist can also test for visual-motor integration and visual memory, but as noted in the chapter on handwriting, standardized tests of visual-motor integration are not sufficient to screen for handwriting issues.

- Check for difficulty in reading comprehension with the "how" and "why" questions.
- Test mathematics in both calculation and reasoning for learning problems.
- Have a physical therapist screen for gross motor problems as needed.

Comorbid and Associated Conditions

NLD frequently occurs with other disorders and may share features with many other neurological disorders. Note that language issues and learning disabilities, even though part of NLD, deserve separate assessment, diagnosis, and remediation.

- Asperger's Syndrome (Autism Spectrum Disorder)

- Executive Dysfunction
- Memory deficits
- VMI deficits
- Early handwriting issues
- Sensory dysregulation
- OCD
- Anxiety disorders
- Depression
- Language disorders
- Learning Disabilities (especially reading comprehension and math calculations)
- Sleep problems
- "Rages" or "Storms"

Summary

Students with NLD need early intervention services. Students with NLD suffer greater academic impairment than students with Asperger's Syndrome, especially in mathematics. The most significant deficit, however, is the inability to develop and maintain social relationships. Students with NLD are at a greater risk for not having friends than any other disorder in this book, including Asperger's Syndrome.

Failure to remediate social deficits in students while in school leads to serious problems in adult-

Table 13.1. Comparing Features of Asperger's Syndrome and Nonverbal Learning Disability

Asperger's Syndrome	Nonverbal Learning Disability
No language delay	Early speech and vocabulary delayed
Semantic-pragmatic deficits	Complex verbal communication skills impaired (not just semantic-pragmatic deficits)
Clumsiness; gross motor is generally within normal limits	Significant gross motor deficits
Fine motor skills impaired	Fine motor problems; dysgraphia (early) with improvement with age
Visual-perception within normal limits	Visual-perception problems
Poor social judgment	Severely impaired social judgment
Hyperfocused on details	Difficulty with attention to visual details
Restrictive, perseverative interest(s)	Unrestricted interests

Adapted from a chart by S. Sands, S. Schwartz in the May/June 2000 New York University Child Study Letter.

hood because social skills impact getting a job, enjoying friends, getting married, and having a family. Social skills need be taught in a group setting (Chapter 34 provides additional strategies). Parents of students with NLD need to be trained in how to promote rehearsal and generalization of skills in the home. The student with NLD needs help developing a healthy ego, employing outside assistance from a professional who specializes in youth with NLD.

CHAPTER 14

Sleep Problems

Tommy was yawning in first period science and his head was down on his desk again. He had been doing this for two weeks. His teacher called his mother to suggest he not be allowed to stay up late watching TV or playing video games. Tommy's mother was thankful for the concern, but said, "I guess I should have told you or told Tommy to tell you... he's been having trouble falling asleep and he's up until 3:00 a.m. almost every morning. Even when he does fall asleep, he wakes up frequently and tells me he's having bad dreams. I wish he could get a good night's rest."

Preview

Most of the disorders described in this book either have sleep problems as symptoms or sleep disorders are listed as comorbid. Sleep-related problems in children and adolescents may be one of the most neglected contributors to academic and behavioral problems in school.

Quick Facts for Educators about Sleep

- Many teenagers need nine hours of sleep—more than younger children and adults.
- Teenagers' biological cycles push them towards later bedtimes and later rising times.
- Sleeping late on the weekends does not make up for lost sleep during the week.
- Sleep disorders contribute significantly to academic, motoric, behavioral, and social-emotional difficulties, but not all sleep disorders have the same impact.
- Sleep disorders are fairly common in children.

Overview of Sleep Problems

The results of one of the first studies to examine common sleep problems in elementary school children found that 37% of the children had at least one type of significant sleep problem, and approximately 10% of the children had significant problems with daytime sleepiness (Owens, Spirito et al. 2000).

Adolescents also suffer from sleep problems. In one study, students who described themselves as doing poorly reported going to bed later and getting less sleep than students who described themselves as earning A's and B's. Not surprisingly, students who got less than eight and one quarter hours sleep per night during the school week and who were up late on the weekends reported increased daytime sleepiness, depressive mood, and sleep/wake behavior problems. The investigators concluded that overall most of the adolescents surveyed were not getting enough sleep, and their sleep loss interfered with daytime functioning (Wolfson and Carskadon 1998).

In another study of youth aged eleven to seventeen years, investigators found that 17% of youth reported poor quality sleep, 6% reported difficulty falling asleep, 7% reported daytime tiredness, and 5% reported experiencing daytime sleepiness almost every day (Roberts, Roberts, and Chen 2002).

Sleep problems correlate with behavior, attention, and hyperactivity problems. Parents of over 800 children aged two to fourteen years completed surveys on sleep problems and behavior. The investigators found that children at high risk for sleep disorders were two to three times more likely to engage in bullying and other aggressive behaviors when compared to children who were not at risk for these sleep disorders (Chervin et al. 2003). Although such results do not prove which came first—the behavioral problems or the sleep problems—the significant relationship indicates that sleep issues need to be part of school-based screening. If problems are detected, schools may wish to refer the parent to the student's pediatrician to discuss a sleep study.

Adolescents require about nine hours sleep per night, but generally do not get that much sleep due to homework demands, social engagements, and early school start time.

Some of the most common types of sleep disorders are insomnia, Restless Legs Syndrome (RLS), Periodic Limb Movements of Sleep (PLMS), and sleep-disordered breathing (SDB). All of these conditions may contribute to a poorer night's sleep, but they do not all have the same effect on daytime functioning. From a practical standpoint, teachers may wish to screen all students for sleep problems, so that parents may be given helpful resources and so that the school can make any necessary accommodations, as described later in this chapter.

Sleep Problems and Neurological Disorders

Attention Deficit Hyperactivity Disorder

Children with ADHD have more difficulty falling asleep than their non-ADHD peers (Hvolby, Jørgensen, and Bilenberg 2009; Owens, Maxim et al. 2000), although there are conflicting data about whether they have more trouble staying asleep. A recent survey of parents found that over 70% of children with ADHD had sleep problems, with almost 45% reporting moderate or severe problems (Sung et al. 2008). Unmedicated children who are newly diagnosed with ADHD have significantly more Periodic Limb Movements during sleep, significantly more awakenings and overall less sleep than their non-ADHD peers (Picchietti et al. 1999). Sleep problems correlate with children being late for school or missing school and their daily functioning (Sung et al. 2008).

Mood Disorders

Depressed patients commonly complain of difficulties falling and staying sleep, and report awakening early in the morning. Any parent of a child or teenager with depression is well aware of the difficulties of getting depressed children to school in the morning. Depressed adolescent boys may be more severely sleep-disordered than depressed adolescent girls (Robert et al. 2006), and suicidal depressed adolescents are significantly more likely to report insomnia than nonsuicidal depressed adolescents (Barbe et al. 2005).

Hypomania and mania are features of Bipolar Disorder, and are also associated with sleep disturbance (Mehl et al. 2006). Sometimes the first warning sign that a child or adolescent is going into a hypomanic or manic phase is that she goes without sleep for one or two nights but does not report feeling tired. A recent review of the literature on sleep problems in children with Bipolar Disorder suggests that students with part-day manic cycles and chronic mixed conditions have trouble falling asleep (but not a decreased need for sleep), whereas students with days-long manic cycles or chronic mania experience a decreased need for sleep (Staton 2008).

Tourette's Syndrome

For most children or adolescents with Tourette's Syndrome (TS), tics decrease significantly or disappear totally during sleep. But that does not mean that the student is getting a good night's sleep. Research on unmedicated children and teens with TS found it took these children longer to fall asleep, and they had prolonged wakefulness after sleep onset (Kostanecka-Endress et al. 2003). The severity of tics during the day correlated positively and significantly with the number of awakenings during the night. On a practical level, our experience indicates that children or teenagers with Tourette's often have trouble fully relaxing to fall asleep, and sleep onset may be delayed because they first have to "get their tics out." So the child or teen may lie down to go to bed and may tic explosively or vigorously for an hour or more. Tics may also be awakening the child from sleep for short periods throughout the night.

Obsessive-Compulsive and Anxiety Disorders

Although early research has produced equivocal results [cf. (Papadimitriou and Linkowski 2005)], a recent study found that 92% of children with OCD experienced at least one sleep-related problem, with the total number of sleep-related problems being positively correlated with OCD severity and anxiety severity (Storch et al. 2008). Our experience has been that children and teenagers with OCD may stay up late into the night working to get a paper perfect, for example, thus shortening their total amount of sleep. Other children and adolescents with OCD may have time consuming rituals that they must engage in at night that prevent them from getting to sleep at a reasonable hour. The rituals may be requiring that toys be lined up just so, extensive, time consuming hygiene rituals, the bedding arranged in a particular way, or extensive good night rituals involving a parent. Individuals suffering from Panic Disorder and Generalized Anxiety Disorder also experience sleep problems (Papadimitriou and Linkowski, 2005).*

Autism Spectrum Disorders

Sleep problems have long been noted in children with autism [cf. (Allik, Larsson, and Smedje 2006; Liu et al. 2007; Paavonen et al. 2008)].** Of particular note for educators is one report that some sleep measures are significantly correlated with the child's nonverbal functioning (Elia et al. 2000).

School Impact

Sleep-related problems may contribute to:
- daytime sleepiness
- impaired attention
- impaired memory
- increased hyperactivity
- increased impulsivity
- bullying
- aggressive behaviors
- poorer performance in sports
- accidents, such as car crashes
- depressed mood

In addition to the sleep problems described above, some children and adolescents also suffer from sleep-related side effects of medications that are used to treat their disorders. Stimulant medica-

---

* The same laboratory investigation, however, failed to objectively confirm subjective reports of sleep problems in patients with Post-Traumatic Stress Disorder or Obsessive-Compulsive Disorder.

** Subjective reports may not be confirmed by objective laboratory methods, as reported in several studies on sleep disorders in children and young adults on the autism spectrum (Tani et al. 2004; Wiggs and Stores 2004).

tions used to treat ADHD can cause insomnia, while some of the medications used to treat tics and ADHD can cause tiredness.

Screen for sleep-related problems in all students. A simple survey that teachers can send home with students for parents to complete is included in Appendix F and on the accompanying CD-ROM.

Tips and Tricks for Helping Students with Sleep Problems

- If the student is falling asleep in class, consult with the student's parents and physician as to whether to allow the child to sleep in school or not. If the physician recommends allowing the student to sleep, inquire as to how long and inform the parents of where the student will be allowed to sleep.
- If the physician advises, encourage the student to get up and move around or take a walk. If the student is genuinely tired, the activity will not wake them up and they will fall asleep again, but for other students, the exercise may be enough to boost their alertness.
- Allow students with significant sleep disorders or medication-related morning problems to start school later in the day.
- If student's endurance is significantly impaired by sleep disorders or medication-related problems, shorten her school day.
- Alternate quiet sitting activities with opportunities for movement and activity.
- Allow students to work standing up if it helps them fight off sleep.
- Provide a home tutor at a time that is best for the student in terms of alertness. Having a tutor arrive at four o'clock in the afternoon if the student is invariably asleep at that time simply makes no sense.
- Provide testing accommodations such as flexible scheduling.
- Reduce homework or extend time on homework.
- Encourage students to include protein in their breakfast, and allow protein snacks during the school day.

- Open the blinds in the classroom to allow in as much natural light as possible.
- Avoid darkening the room in the morning, e.g., to use overheads.

Provide parents with information on establishing good sleep habits. A reproducible copy of Sleep Hygiene: "DO's and DON'Ts for Establishing Good Sleep Routines" is provided in Appendix J and on the accompanying CD-ROM.

Associated or Comorbid Disorders

Because sleep disorders are associated with so many disorders, it would be simple to say "Be on the lookout for everything!" but if a student has significant sleep problems, at the very least, screen for mood and anxiety disorders.

Summary

Sleep-related problems are part of, or related to many other disorders discussed in this book. Teachers and school personnel need to screen for sleep-related problems that may significantly impair attention and memory, increase hyperactivity, impulsivity, and be-havior problems, or lead to mood deterioration. Sleep problems contribute to academic and behavioral difficulties, over and above symptom interference from the disorders with which they co-occur, and may require their own accommodations. Because sleep problems are more common than widely recognized, we recommend that teachers routinely screen all students for sleep problems, using the Sleep Survey provided in the Appendix (and CD-ROM).

A therapist once observed a special education class where four out of five boys were sound asleep at their desks at ten-thirty in the morning. After investigating further, the therapist contacted the boys' parents to inform them. None of the parents had been aware that their children were having difficulties staying awake in school. It turned out that all of them were on the same medication for ADHD, a medication that causes drowsiness as a side effect. One of the first changes the therapist suggested to the teacher was that he try to make his presentations more exciting. By providing more stimulation in the classroom, the increased interest level helped the boys overcome their tiredness and stay awake. At least one student had a medication reduction to offset his tiredness, and from that point on, the teacher worked with the parents and the boys to figure out how to help them stay awake in school.

CHAPTER 15

"Rage Attacks," "Storms," or "Meltdowns"

Why do children explode? Because they can't think of anything better to do.
—Ross Greene, Ph.D.

"He's like Jekyll and Hyde since coming back from winter recess," Frankie's teacher told the school psychologist. "There are days when he comes in and I can see him start to get wound up. Then, in a flash, he's just exploding—cursing, picking up his desk and slamming it down into the floor, knocking everything off his desk, yelling things that don't make any sense. And when he's like that, there's nothing that I can do that will get him to calm down. It's like watching a volcano erupt and just wondering when it's going to run out of steam or lava. Of course, I can't teach and the other students can't learn while all this is going on. But I really feel badly for him because I can see that the other children are becoming afraid of him and backing away from him."

Preview

"Rage attacks," "storms," or "meltdowns" are not recognized diagnostic terms, but anyone who is parenting or teaching a child or teen who suffers from these explosive outbursts can immediately relate to those terms. Regardless of what one chooses to call them, we are talking about sudden, out of control explosive outbursts that appear—to the observer and to the child experiencing it—to be without warning and totally out of proportion to any triggering event.*

---

* The explosive outbursts we are describing in this chapter are not wholly consistent with what the DSM-IV calls "Intermittent Explosive Disorder."

Thankfully for teachers, most storms or rage attacks do not occur in school, and some teachers are shocked to learn that their very well-behaved student is having total meltdowns when he gets home from school and is smashing things or putting holes in the walls at home. The fact that children suppress these explosive outbursts in school and have them at home is not an indication that the parents are too lenient with the child in the home. Rather, it is generally an indication that the parents have done a good job of teaching their child to respect the teacher and the school. If parents report that their child is having storms at home but there are no storms in school, we recommend:

1. Begin figuring out what additional supports or accommodations the student might need in school to reduce stress in school that is being let out at home.
2. Inquire as to whether the storms only occur over homework, if they occur as soon as the student walks in the door, and if they occur during school vacations. Work with the parent and student to figure out what elements of the school program may need to be modified.
3. Work with the parent to determine if the child needs homework modifications to reduce their stress, and
4. Thank the parent for teaching their child to respect the school.

These Episodes Are Not Tantrums

Storms or rage attacks are not tantrums. Tantrums are goal-directed behavior. The purpose of a tantrum is to get someone who is not doing what you want him to do, to do what you want. If there is no one around, a tantrummer generally stops tantrumming because without an audience, his tantrum doesn't work. Or as soon as we give in to the child or student and give him what he wants, a tantrummer will stop the tantrum. A storm or rage attack does not stop, even if we were to say, "OK, I give up—you can have ...." Nor is it obvious what the goal of a storm or rage attack might be. In our experience, these episodes do not appear to be voluntary behaviors that would be modifiable by applying consequences after they occur.

A storm is generally out of character for the child or student. At the beginning of this chapter, we provided a teacher's perspective. Now read the words of Jason Valencia, a young adult who tries to describe what it is like to experience these storms. He starts by giving his background, and then describes the experience.

"I am twenty-one years old. I have TS + OCD + ADD + Panic Attacks + Depression and, yes...I have what I, personally, identify best as 'rage.' It doesn't matter to me if rage is officially accepted as part and parcel of TS or not, nor do I care what others name it. However, as part of my own neurological picture, I have attacks of rage—not anger...I have that too, but different from the unreasonable sudden outbursts. I know this from deep within; I have always known this. However, I have not always understood it. Finding out that, for me, rage is a part of my overall symptoms, was a great relief in comparison with the years I spent agonizing over my 'evilness.' I was not 'born bad;' I am neither aggressive nor dangerous. Getting past the 'why' of my rage allowed me to concentrate on the 'hows' of controlling it. Learning the reason was the gift that prompted me to deal with it."

● ● ●

I move confidently through the day's routine, hanging out with friends, watching a good movie on cable, or searching out my niche on this planet, a necessary pursuit even non-Touretters relate to. But I do have Tourette's Syndrome. For me, these times are the calm before the storm. Yes, just the calm before the storm...until, abruptly, a comment is made to which I take offense, or a person gives me a dirty look, or so I interpret it. Black clouds of anger permeate my head and darken my mind; the cloudburst is on its way... the pressure begins to build, as harsh winds of the oncoming tempest wipe away trees of reason that only moments before stood calmly and reassuringly in my head. From somewhere deeper, a lightning bolt strikes...running through my body with terrifying speed and electricity, causing my hand to lash outward at any object near to me. Torrential rains pour from my mouth, a mix of hate-filled words combined with obscenities that would make Madonna blush.

In the distance I hear the faint calls of others, telling me to calm down. But how can I calm down in the middle of this storm with its somber clouds and suffocating winds? 'Dear God, please let it stop!' I cry out when, finally, the winds diminish to a dizzying breeze of confusion. My mouth closes as downpour becomes a meager sprinkle, until only droplets remain on my hate-soaked tongue.

As gray clouds drift off to some subconscious region to await the next storm, I step out of myself to survey the damage, if any. But what makes my blood run cold are the reactions of those near to me. They only stare in shocked silence, and then it hits me... they never saw the storm coming; never suspected the damage it might cause to their feelings or cherished belongings. They never saw the storm coming, they only felt it. They only felt my rage."

Jason's description of his storms really captures so many of the elements we hear over and over again from the children who experience them, their parents, and the schools:

- the children's sense that the storm just takes over them and that they cannot stop it once it has started,
- the speed with which a child goes from being okay to being in a storm,
- the fact that a storm is usually out of proportion to any trigger in the environment,
- the disconnect between what the child is doing and their ability to observe their own storm behavior, and
- the dismay or remorse that many children feel for hurting feelings or property. However, not all children or teens who have storms feel remorse, largely because they do not remember what happened during a storm.

Figure 15.1. Pathways to Explosive Behavior

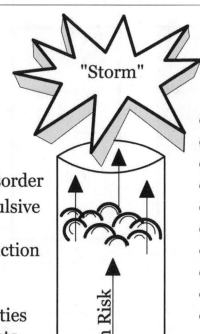

"Storm"

- Depression
- Bipolar Disorder
- Attention Deficit Hyperactivity Disorder
- Obsessive-Compulsive Disorder
- Executive Dysfunction
- Sleep Disorders
- Fatigue
- Learning Disabilities
- Social Impairments

- Anxiety
- Autism/Asperger's Syndrome
- Sensory Defensiveness
- Complex Partial Seizures
- Brain Injury
- Difficult Temperament
- Language Processing Deficits
- Medication Side Effects
- Over-arousal
- Nonverbal Learning Disability

Storm Risk

Pathways to explosive behavior are varied, but the more comorbid conditions or risk factors the students have, the more likely they are to have "storms." Adapted and modified from material presented by Ross Greene, Ph.D., by L. E. Packer, Ph.D., and Colleen Wang, R.N. (1999), revised 2007 by L.E. Packer.

Pathways to Storms, Rage Attacks, or Meltdowns

There is no one pathway or diagnosis that is associated with these outbursts. Figure 15.1 depicts a number of different conditions or pathways that may make students more vulnerable to having this problem.

A number of clinical disorders or conditions have been linked to an increased risk of explosive outbursts. The greater the number of disorders a person has, the higher the risk is. Other factors can also lead to explosive outbursts.

If a student is having explosive outbursts in school, school personnel need to arrange for a comprehensive evaluation and Functional Behavioral Assessment (Chapter 26) so that all of the pieces of the puzzling behavior can be identified and addressed.

Anyone can get pushed past his breaking point, but students with neurological disorders or challenges seem to have a lower threshold. One way, perhaps, to visualize the difference in thresholds is presented in Figure 15.2 on the next page.

Whereas a typical student remains within a relative "calm zone" for much of the time, and can stay in a "rumbling" or pre-explosive state for a certain amount of time, the student with neurologically based dysregulation tends to stay calm for less time and is more likely to become dysregulated sooner. Unlike the typical student who can stay a bit dysregulated without totally losing control, the student with neurologically based dysregulation tends to "go from zero to sixty" in a matter of moments or minutes, and spends more time in explosive outbursts than the typical student.

There may be precious few moments between when a student becomes dysregulated and before he totally loses control. Pre-plan some "rumbling interventions" that can help restore the student to calm.

Figure 15.2. Dysregulated Children vs. Average Children

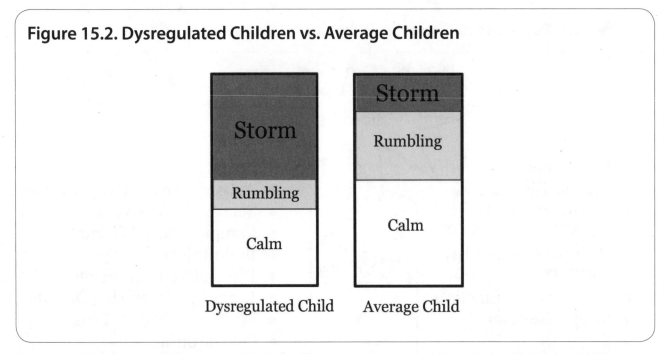

Hypothesized (based on experience, not research) relative differences in the amount of time typical and dysregulated children stay in a calm state and a "rumbling" state before they have an explosive outburst or storm (Packer and Wang 1999).

Even though some students will seemingly go "from zero to sixty" in a nanosecond, not all students will lose control as soon as they become dysregulated. Some may be able to control their symptoms for minutes, or even hours. When students attempt to control their dysregulation or attempt to avert a storm, they experience a great deal of stress suppressing their symptoms, which can lead to a more intense storm or meltdown if one does occur.

Over time, and through consultation with the student's parents, and by observing the student, school personnel will probably begin to recognize the signs that the student is in the rumbling stage and getting ready to "blow." Implementing the rumbling interventions described later in this chapter may help avert the storm.

Factors That Influence the Frequency and Severity of Storms

Some of the pathways to storms were identified in Figure 15.1, and as noted earlier, the more neurological conditions the student has, the greater the likelihood of a storm. In general:

Stress → Overarousal → Explosive Build Up → Storm

Source: (Pruitt 1987)

Therefore, any type of stress buildup—whether it is due to academic issues, social or peer issues, illness, fatigue, time pressures, frustration due to handwriting issues, or medication side effects—can contribute to an increased likelihood of a storm.

If a student tends to have storms in school, using the "Watch Your Speed!" approach to signal the student when he is "racing" and encouraging him to monitor his own "speed" may help prevent problems. Take proactive steps as soon as school personnel or the student recognizes that the student is in the "CAUTION" zone (see the overview to Part II).

Rumbling: Warning Signs of an Impending Storm or Rage Attack

Based on our experience, here are some signs that a student may be in a rumbling stage and close to having a storm:

- If the student suddenly seems unusually reactive or overreactive to touch, noise, etc.
- If the student suddenly becomes very loud, as if he cannot modulate the volume of his voice, even if not yelling
- If the student seems to start pacing a lot or exhibits an unusual and rapid buildup of motor activity or fidgetiness

Figure 15.3. Recipe for a Storm

Recipe for a Storm

- Assume that the student's behavior is voluntary disrespect towards you, and respond accordingly.
- Back the student into a corner—literally or figuratively.
- Grab or attempt to restrain the student.
- Move the student into a small space.
- Push or shove the student in an effort to remove the student from the class or situation.
- Keep talking when the student is already over-aroused.
- Give the student work that is too difficult if he has a low frustration tolerance
- Touch the student.

- Become angry and show your displeasure by facial expression, tone, or body language (e.g., roll your eyes, sigh, or make faces).
- Act scared of the student.
- Embarrass the student in front of his peers.
- Raise your voice to make sure you have the student's attention, or if he still does not cooperate, become even louder.
- Use sarcasm.
- Physically prevent the student from leaving the room if he needs to get out of there to go calm himself.
- Decide that you have to show the students who's in charge and order the student to comply with your rules.

That should do it!

- If the student's frustration tolerance plummets to the point where demands have to be met "NOW!" and the student cannot tolerate waiting or being told "Not now"
- If the student appears "stuck" and cannot let go of a thought, demand, or behavior at the same time that you or the environment are demanding or insisting on compliance
- If the student appears very agitated
- If the student appears very anxious

Any of the above signs may indicate an impending storm, depending on the student's pattern and history. Once teachers learn the student's warning signs, implement the interventions below as soon as the signs appear.

Tips and Tricks for Preventing Storms: Rumbling Interventions

- Allow the student to make a "graceful exit" while saving face (see Chapter 31 for "graceful exit" strategy with face-saving). Do not order the student to leave the class-

room, as that will likely produce additional emotion and dysregulation. Have some pre-planned excuses or a system in place that the student has helped plan.
- Let the student go to someone he trusts, such as the school nurse, the school psychologist, or a trusted staff member. It is important that the student be actively involved in determining who the "safe person" will be.
- Let the student go to his safe place where he can calm himself or "chill" if he wants a self-imposed timeout. Some students do not really need to talk with anyone; they just need to go find a place to "re-group" and restore calm. For some students, the safe place may be an office in the school building. For others, it may be a stairwell, or even a closet. Again, the students should be involved in determining where their safe place will be as only the students know where they feel safest. Make certain that school faculty and staff are aware of this arrangement so they do not inadvertently engage the student when he is going to his safe place.
- If a student is in the rumbling stage, do not "lock horns" with him—disengage!

Even if it seems as if the student is intentionally challenging the teacher's authority in the classroom, engaging in a battle of wills or locking horns with a dysregulated student on the brink of totally losing control is a surefire way to ensure a storm.

- Encourage and promote physical activity to dissipate the buildup of tension:
  - ❑ Ask the student to do something that requires large muscle use—like washing the blackboard, lifting heavy cartons of books, or lifting furniture to move it.
  - ❑ Encourage or allow the student to take a walk around the halls or building to dissipate energy.
  - ❑ If the gym is available, allow the student to run around the gym, "shoot hoops" for a while, or engage in an activity that will burn off energy and distract him.
- Allow the student to go lie down in the nurse's office to read a self-selected book.
- Allow the student to get engrossed in a computer program or academic game.

If an aide or paraprofessional is required to accompany the student while he walks in the halls, advise the aide to just walk quietly with the student and not touch him, try to make eye contact, or try to get him to talk. If the student initiates conversation, the aide should respond by validating the student's feelings. The aide needs to be told not to try to reason with the student but to simply validate his feelings if he verbalizes feeling upset or angry.

From experience, we know that some teachers will have concerns about allowing a student to go play a computer game or read a book at such times, as it seems like the school is reinforcing the student for becoming dysregulated. Further, they may be concerned that the student will become more dysregulated over time if dysregulation leads to a break from schoolwork or fun activities. In our experience, when a student is about to have a storm, the priority has to be preventing the storm. We do not believe that students are being manipulative when they are that dysregulated, and we believe that by allowing them to calm themselves, teachers are teaching them that there are things that the students can do for themselves in the future—whether it is to step out of the room for a few minutes, go "chill," or to distract themselves with interesting activities.

Some of the best preventive measures are the ones developed over time. These are things that the teacher can access when need be:

- Develop rapport with the student. Try to spend thirty minutes alone with the student at the beginning of the school year to get to know him. Information and insight gained about the student can serve as a bond or bridge that can be used later.
- Develop a private joke with the student. If the student sees you as someone who laughs with him, it will be easier for him to accept your guidance and support when it is really needed.
- Learn to recognize the warning or rumbling signs for that student. Does the student tend to get sweaty, agitated, and red in the face before a storm or does he generally clench his fists, etc.?

When a Storm Appears Inevitable

There may be times that a storm is inevitable. Once a storm begins, there is generally nothing that can stop it, and attempts to intervene might make it worse. During a storm, the student may scream, curse, hit walls, throw things, slam desks, and/or destroy property. School personnel may fear that these energy releases may endanger the physical safety of the student or others. Usually, however, the student is trying very hard not to hurt anyone during a storm, and as long as people keep their distance, there is generally little risk of physical injury to others.

If it becomes impossible to prevent the storm, the teacher needs to immediately shift focus to protecting the health and safety of the student, other students, and himself.

Some tips from our experience:

- Keep some physical distance from the student. Attempts to restrain the student may lead to injury for the student or school personnel.
- Avoid providing any additional sensory input as it will maintain or worsen the storm.
- If necessary, remove the other students and personnel from the immediate area instead of trying to remove the student.

- Do not take storms personally. Most verbal outbursts during a storm or rage attack need to be viewed as just "mental debris."
- Remember that the storm must just run its course and that if anyone attempts to stop the storm or shorten it, it will probably only make it last longer.

When a storm is coming at you, do not try to overpower it or reason with it—move in the opposite direction while protecting the safety of the student, peers, and yourself.

After a Storm

After the storm, a student may have no memory of what was said or done during the episode. The student may be tired and want to sleep—allow this. If the student does not want to sleep and just wants to be left alone, allow the pursuit of a self-selected calming activity. Allowing such activity is not reinforcing the "storm" and is important in enabling the student to restore calm and focus.

Some students will remember what they said and did during a storm, but others won't, or are so embarrassed that they will not discuss it. Our best advice is to take the student at his word on this. Defensive behavior is common to students due to embarrassment and fear of being out of control. Putting the student on the spot or demanding an explanation or apology immediately after a storm may rekindle the storm. Give the student time to fully recover. A student who is recovering from a storm is not ready to have a meaningful conversation about what caused the storm, what they could have done differently, what the teacher could have done differently, etc. There is a time and a place for such discussion, but not right after a storm.

Make sure the fire is out before trying to sift through the ashes.

Aftermath and Reparations

If a student experiences incoherent meltdowns, the entire team should implement a functional behavior assessment to determine what environmental changes and related supports need to be provided to reduce the likelihood of these types of episodes (see Chapter 26). Preventing a storm is actually much easier than trying to stop one that has already started, so be proactive.

Because teachers and most school personnel are trained to apply consequences to unwanted behavior, it is understandable that teachers would ask after a storm, "What are the consequences to the student? What disciplinary or other measures need to be employed?" Our answer is simple: punishing a child for neurologically based dysregulation is unlikely to cure the child's neurology or to teach the child not to become dysregulated. Neither of us has ever met a child or teen who enjoyed storms. Most of them are mortified by them, worry about their loss of self-control, and are painfully aware that their peers are backing away from them. Artificial punishments are simply not as powerful as the actual consequences to the child of loss of control. When we talk about "storm cleanup," we are talking about restoration and reparations.

In our experience, it is appropriate and helpful to use natural consequences and reparations as a strategy for dealing with this situation, but it must be done within the context of a lot of positive behavior supports. We suggest that when the student is ready (not during the potential rekindle stage), the student needs to take steps to repair any relationships that may have been damaged and to engage in reparations. If the student put a hole in a wall, the student needs to repair the hole. If people were cursed at, the student needs to apologize for any hurt feelings. And as part of the reparations and restoration, the student is encouraged to tell others what steps he is taking to ensure that it will not happen again. (Reparations are discussed in Chapter 31.)

If a student has physically injured others as part of a storm, then school personnel need to determine if the injury was the result of someone putting themselves in the path of the storm or if the student actually assaulted someone. If the latter, then a Functional Behavioral Assessment needs to be conducted (see Chapter 26).

When Storms Only Take Place at Home

As suggested at the beginning of this chapter, school personnel may never see a student storm in school, but the student may be having storms at home. In our experience, if a parent reports that their child is having these storms at home, then school personnel should work closely with the student's parents and the treatment team to determine if there are any school-related factors that need to be addressed. Consider these statements from actual parents who described their experiences with their children:

".....he tore off towel bars, broke his brother's toys, threatened me, etc.—out of control anger. Finally he was able to speak and it was that school kids tormented him and he was being scrutinized so much at school that he did not want to go anymore. I told him I would help fix school and I still update him as I try to fix things for him at school."

● ● ●

"This sounds very much like my ten-year-old son. We, too, had a problem with being tormented at school. This led to rages and waxing of his tics. When he finally told us what was going on and we took steps to correct it, he became his normal sweet self. And I can't emphasize enough the importance of remaining calm during his rages. This makes a distinct difference in the amount of stress I experience and helps him calm down much faster."

● ● ●

"..... The attacks are completely out of character—my son has never been involved in a playground fight, has never harmed an animal, etc. No one who knows him would ever consider him to be a child prone to violence—except during these rage attacks. If there is a big disagreement, true anger, he handles it in a completely different way than the way he handles a small frustration in these rage attacks. And when these attacks are over, he can remember what happened and feels just horrible about it. And he can't understand why or how it happened any more than anyone else around him can."

● ● ●

"My son's eyes would glaze over and he could not reason until the attack passed. He would have no direct memory of the attack, and afterwards he was filled with shame and self-loathing. It has been the hardest part of his disorder to deal with by far! I did begin to see a connection between his Obsessive-Compulsive Disorder and the rages. For my son, the rages were always triggered by an unfulfilled obsession or compulsion. It wasn't obvious, though, that he was obsessing on whatever it was. He did not have the self-awareness or verbal skills to express this stuff. I am speaking of his rage attacks in the past tense. He has really worked on self-control, and he now tries to stop it before it escalates to a rage attack

by leaving the situation, being alone, etc. He is now fifteen years old, and I am seeing real changes."

School-Based Assessments

If a student is having storms or rage attacks in school, then a comprehensive assessment is needed that includes, at a minimum:

- Functional behavior assessment (Chapter 26)
- Speech and language assessment, including pragmatics (social language)
- Handwriting assessment
- Learning Disabilities assessment
- Executive Dysfunction screening
- Screening for: depression, Bipolar Disorder, Obsessive-Compulsive Disorder, Asperger's Syndrome/Autism Spectrum Disorder, sleep disorders, and anxiety disorders
- Conducting an A-B-C analysis (Appendix O) as part of the Functional Behavioral Assessment (see Chapter 26)
- Classroom observations for settings and tasks or situations that have been associated with storms
- Consideration of student's medications and possible adverse effects
- Careful history-taking interview with parent(s) about similar behaviors at home, history of any sensory integration issues, relevant family history, and current stressors

In most cases, unless the student is already diagnosed with a condition that may be associated with storms, a referral for a psychiatric evaluation at public expense may be warranted. In some cases, a referral to a pediatric neurologist or a sleep disorders clinic may be needed.

Summary

Storms or rage attacks are associated with a number of neurological disorders, and the more conditions a student has, the greater the likelihood of this type of problem. In most cases, storms just serve to release energy, are not person- or other-directed, and are self-limiting. School personnel working with students with such problems will need to work closely with the parents, the student, and the treatment team to identify all of the factors that may be increasing stress or leading to explosive outbursts.

When Frankie, who we described at the beginning of this chapter, continued having meltdowns in school some mornings, his school team decided to conduct a Functional Behavioral Assessment to help them determine the function of these storms and so that they could teach Frankie an alternative replacement behavior. After days of recording observations on A-B-C forms and interviewing Frankie's parents and school personnel, the team realized that they had not yet conducted an actual interview with Frankie. As part of the interview, the school psychologist asked Frankie, "Do you have any ideas as to what is causing you to have some bad mornings?" Frankie answered, "Yes, some mornings my teacher wears perfume."

The psychologist checked Frankie's records and noted that his mother had reported that he had moderate sensory defensiveness, including for olfactory (smells). At the psychologist's suggestion, the teacher stopped wearing all cologne for the next three weeks. Frankie's hypothesis appeared correct: Once the teacher stopped wearing the new cologne she had received as a holiday present, his behavior reverted to his normal morning behavior.

CHAPTER 16

Oppositional Defiant Disorder

Some children and teens give new meaning to the expression, "Just Say "No!" But whenever we hear a parent, a teacher, or any health care professional talk about a child or teen having "Oppositional Defiant Disorder," we shudder. Simply put, we are unconvinced that there really is any such disorder or that you will ever see a "pure" case of what is called Oppositional Defiant Disorder (ODD) without there being some other diagnosis or condition that can account for the student's seemingly oppositional behavior. For example, there is a body of research on students diagnosed as ADHD + ODD. These students are more likely to have "storms" (Chapter 15) and to develop personality disorders and other problems as adults. In our experience, many of the children and teens diagnosed as having ADHD+ODD have other problems as well, such as unrecognized depression, OCD, or other neurological disorders. Indeed, a number of studies find that ODD predicts depression and other problems.

In our experience, teachers are wise to assume that their students "would if they could, but can't, so they don't" (Chapter 3). Taking this point of view is more likely to lead to the type of Functional Behavioral Assessment (Chapter 26) that will identify the causes and factors that maintain what appears to be willful oppositional behavior. Once the correct cause of the oppositional behavior is identified and treated or addressed, it is amazing how their ODD often appears to be "cured."

For teachers who are struggling with a student who appears seriously oppositional, here are just a few hypotheses to consider and explore:

- Does the student have any obsessive-compulsive tendencies? Students with obsessions and compulsions can get "stuck" and be unable to cooperate with you until they have completed a mental ritual or until something is "just so" for them.
- If the student is diagnosed with ADHD or has a diagnosis of, or features of an autism spectrum disorder (such as Asperger's Syndrome), has the school district arranged for an assessment of neuropsychological functioning to determine if the student has Executive Dysfunction (EDF)? Students with EDF may have significant difficulty making transitions and students with ASD often perseverate or get "stuck."
- Has the student been assessed for specific learning disabilities or academic difficulties? Some children and teens would much prefer you think them oppositional than to admit that they do not understand what is going on, what you want them to do, or how to do it.
- Is the student chronically irritable? Severe irritability has been used to diagnose ODD, but irritability may also be a symptom of depression or other conditions such as inadequate nutrition, poor sleep, or home variables. Quickly throwing a label of ODD on such students does not necessarily lead to a more complete assessment and appropriate treatment.

Remember: Being curious about behavior and not judgmental is more likely to lead to better understanding your student's behavior and designing appropriate supports and interventions to assist the student to be successful.

PART III

Academic Issues: Awareness, Impact, and Classroom Strategies

Children often misbehave when they have difficulty with an assignment. They are afraid to ask for assistance. Their experience has taught them that to request help is to risk rebuke. They would rather be punished for acting up than ridiculed for ignorance. A teacher's best antidote to misbehavior is a willingness to be helpful.

— Haim Ginott

Overview

The neurological disorders described in Part II often have significant academic impact. The types of academic impact that top the list are visual-motor integration and handwriting issues, difficulties with written expression, and homework issues.

Difficulties with these skills are not the whole story, however. This section also discusses the impact of these disorders on language and reading. It also includes a review of how classroom teachers can accommodate medication side effects, adjust classroom and homework assignments, and create a classroom environment with routines that proactively reduce some of the most problematic symptoms of these disorders.

CHAPTER 17

Handwriting and Visual-Motor Integration Issues

Marco's teacher felt like she was pulling teeth trying to get Marco to write the assigned paragraph. She knew that he had a wealth of information on the topic, but he would not write more than one sentence.

Preview

Approximately 70 to 90% of children with neurological disorders we see have handwriting difficulties, compared with 10-30% of the total elementary school population [cf. (Karlsdottir and Stefansson 2002)].These difficulties stem from visual-motor integration deficits, fine motor control deficits, and/or handwriting (graphomotor) deficits.

When the student is engaging in disruptive or symptomatic behavior, these handwriting concerns can seem minor, but, in fact, these deficits significantly contribute to frustration that may lead to disruptive or symptomatic behaviors. Screening for and addressing these issues through educational planning reduces frustration and related outbursts.

Overview of Handwriting and Dysgraphia

Handwriting (graphomotor skills) is a complex neurodevelopmental process, and students with writing difficulties—dysgraphia—may suffer serious academic impairment. Symptoms of dysgraphia may include:

- Illegible handwriting even when the student is attending to writing and making great effort;
- Inconsistent spacing between letters within and between words;

- Inconsistency in staying within lines of the page or margins;
- Mix of uppercase and lowercase letters within a word;
- Mix of print and cursive;
- Inconsistent letter sizing;
- Cramped or unusual grip on writing instrument, which may be accompanied by:
  - Abnormal wrist, body, or postural positioning
  - Abnormal amount of pressure used in writing;
- Slow and labored writing or fast and impulsive writing;
- Large handwriting.

For many students, writing never becomes a fluent, automatic process. Students with dysgraphia exhibit a lot of "in air" time during writing (as opposed to "on paper" time). They may use many segments in constructing letters and their writing indicates many direction reversals in the formation of the letters. Investigations into predictors of handwriting difficulties have identified several factors that correlate significantly with handwriting quality. The most notable of these is deficits in visual-motor integration (Maeland 1992; Weil and Amundson 1994).

"Visual-Motor" Is More than Just Vision and Motor

Visual-motor integration (VMI) skills enable the student to integrate the visual image of letters and shapes with the appropriate motor response, e.g., to draw/reproduce a shape that has been displayed. VMI is more than using visual perception appropriately, and it is more than using fine motor skills appropriately. Neurologist Martha Denckla once said that the hyphen in "visual-motor" reflects the executive function aspect of integration. No matter what one calls it, VMI is more than the sum of vision and motor.

Even if a student's visual acuity is normal, we need to determine if visual perception (the ability to accurately interpret visual information) is adequate. Visual perception includes:

- **Visual discrimination** — distinguishing the edges of a visual stimulus—somewhat like sharpening a camera lens for focus.

- **Visual single item memory** — memory for one visual stimulus, e.g., memorizing the letter "a."

- **Visual sequential memory** — memory for a series of items, such as letters and digits, presented visually, e.g., memorizing the spelling of sight vocabulary.

- **Visual figure-ground** — finding the primary object in the visual field, e.g., the squirrel on the tree in the "Highlights® Magazine" drawings or the words on the page as opposed to the background.

- **Visual form constancy** — maintaining the shape of a stimulus in visual memory without loss or distortion until it can be encoded for long-term memory storage or be copied down on paper, e.g., copying from a book or from the board.

- **Visual-spatial relations** — accurately positioning objects in space, e.g., writing on the line or keeping a letter in the proper spatial relationship to another letter. Students with learning disabilities commonly experience impaired visual spatial relationships. This is seen in students with dyslexia. Number and letter reversals are a common symptom of this type of problem.

- **Visual closure** — detecting the ending of one word or visual form while looking at the next word or form. Visual closure is essential for efficient reading and includes the ability to read some words by shape or pattern recognition rather than by individual letters. An inability in this area causes very slow, inefficient reading.

For the purposes of the students discussed in this book, the emphasis in this chapter will be on fine motor skills. Fine motor skills are involved in the motor part of visual-motor integration. Students use fine motor skills in planning and using the body's smaller muscles efficiently. If a student cannot plan and organize finger movements, he may be said to have fine motor apraxia. Apraxia is the inability to plan and execute skilled movements. Some students, particularly those with ADHD and those with eye tics, may have reading problems due, in part, to impairment in making smooth, small muscle tracking movements with their eyes. The student uses fine motor skills to hold a writing utensil with an appropriate tripod grip to stabilize it in the hand, while controlling the larger muscles in the wrist, arm, and shoulder to stabilize the hand.

Some of the warning signs that a student may have VMI problems include inability to finish written work within an appropriate amount of time or avoidance of written work. There is also a significant discrepancy in grades when tested orally as opposed to when written answers are required.

The fact that the student may have intact and adequate visual and motor skills does not mean that the student can integrate them efficiently.

Other Sources of Handwriting Impairment

The following issues may also impair the ability to write and complicates handwriting challenges:

- Students with deficits in tactile perception may not feel where the pencil is in their hand.
- Kinesthesia and proprioception contribute to awareness of movement and the position of joints. If there is impairment, students may use a death grip on the pencil to get more sensory input or they may exert so much downward pressure when writing that the pencil goes through the paper. Some students with impaired kinesthesia may not use enough pressure in their grip on the writing utensil and will constantly drop their writing utensil or have it fly out of their hands.

Contrary to what many school personnel may have been taught, the type of pencil grasp— dynamic tripod grasp vs. atypical grasp—does not affect legibility (Dennis and Swinth 2001). Type of grasp does, however, affect how easily a student tires when writing. An inefficient, uncomfortable grip may lead to writing avoidance.

- Difficulties with bilateral coordination can also impair handwriting. We use bilateral coordination in crossing the midline of the body—defined by an imaginary line drawn from the top of the head straight down through the body—dividing the body in half. When students copy from the board or a book or write from the left side of the page to the right, their writing hand crosses the midline of the body. Some students position themselves at their desks so that they do not have to cross the midline as they write. These students may be providing a practical solution to a coordination problem. With that in mind, remember that not all students can reasonably be expected to, or directed to, sit up straight at their desks and face forward.

- Executive Dysfunction (Chapter 9) may also contribute to impaired handwriting. The planning aspects of motor skills reflect an executive component. Students with dysgraphia frequently tell us that writing is labor-intensive for them, in part, because they have to consciously think about how to plan the formation of letters and words. In the process of focusing on *how* to write, they often lose the content or wind up so frustrated by the process that they write a sentence or two and then balk at writing any more.

Because writing is not automatic and because they may have executive deficits as well as VMI problems that contribute to illegible writing, students who try to write neatly may have to write very slowly so that they can focus on neatness. This is similar to the students who decode so slowly that they lose the content of what they are reading. If asked to write more quickly, they can often do so, but legibility suffers and they may neglect to apply spelling, punctuation, and capitalization rules—even though they know them. For older students, the realities of notetaking and pacing of classes requires faster handwriting, and any attempts at legibility generally fall by the wayside.

Students with handwriting impairment, and in particular those who also struggle to organize and sequence their thoughts, strongly resist editing their work. For these students, consider the use of assistive technology.

For the reasons cited above, written expression generally does not provide an accurate indication of the student's knowledge of a particular content area. Handwriting issues also negate the rehearsal or memory storage benefits that most students derive by writing out facts or by completing homework assignments that ask them to formulate and express an idea.

Assessment and Referral

Most regular education teachers can assist the majority of students with handwriting issues, but when a student's handwriting continues to be illegible despite added instruction and rehearsal, consider referring the student for occupational therapy services (Hammerschmidt and Sudsawad 2004). An occupational therapist is the visual-perceptual-motor therapist and handwriting specialist in the school.

If a psychoeducational assessment is conducted before any referral for occupational therapy evaluation, watch for some red flags of handwriting issues that seem to be often overlooked. First and foremost, psychologists or other evaluators need to directly inquire as to whether the student seems to have handwriting issues. Ask to see at least one long paragraph or a one-page writing sample, depending on the age. One-sentence samples often do not demonstrate many of the writing problems that occur when extended writing or writing under time pressure is required.

School psychologists who are assessing students as part of a comprehensive evaluation generally use some tests that are directly correlated with, and predict handwriting issues. Tests such as the Purdue Pegboard, the Bender-Gestalt, the Beery-Buktenica Developmental Test of Visual-Motor Integration, and the Bruininks-Oseretsky Test of Motor Proficiency all tap into fine motor control or VMI. The Bruininks-Oseretsky provides a measure of VMI that is somewhat sensitive to neurocognitive (organizational) deficits. The Jordan Left-Right Reversal Test and Trials tests from the Halstead-Reitan Neuropsychological battery may also provide helpful information. Students with the disorders covered in this book often test out over a year below expected age level on one or more of the tests school psychologists use in comprehensive evaluations. Unfortunately, being a year below expected level on tests of VMI generally does not trigger a referral to a school-based occupational therapist, even when specific evaluations of written language indicate significant problems with written expression.

Although a significant percentage of students with these disorders do score significantly below normal on tests of VMI, many students who score within normal range have significant graphomotor problems that need to be addressed. Be sure to ask for writing samples produced during actual academic activities.

One of the most important parts of a handwriting assessment is meaningful tasks that reflect the demands of both the curriculum and classroom environment. Simply asking a student to write a few words from dictation or to copy a few sentences from a sample placed in front of him does not provide an accurate estimate of what the student is asked to do in an actual classroom environment when he needs to copy a string of homework assignments presented orally, copy a large amount of information from the blackboard, or mentally compose and write a paragraph or essay. As noted above, some students may pass tests such as the Bender and VMI even though their work samples are illegible.

As with school psychological assessment and learning disability assessments, occupational therapists need to inquire what, if any, medications the student takes, what time of day the student takes the medications, and whether testing is being conducted at a time of optimal medication effect or after the medication may have worn off. If possible, testing under multiple conditions is likely to produce a more accurate understanding of the student's handwriting deficits.

Handwriting Deficits in Specific Disorders

To some extent, the types of handwriting deficits are disorder-specific:

Tourette's Syndrome (TS)

In addition to visual-motor integration deficits, especially fine motor control problems, students with TS may experience impairment in handwritten tasks due to eye, head/neck, or arm tics that interfere with control of the writing instrument (Packer and Gentile 1994). Output may be large, illegible, and dysfluent, with poor use of space and difficulty staying on the lines or in lining up columns of numbers for math calculations.

Attention Deficit Hyperactivity Disorder (ADHD)

Writing samples from students with ADHD look like the inside of their desks. Handwriting is sloppy, disorganized, and chaotic in appearance. Words are not on the line and not within the margins. There can be excessive pressure on the writing instrument. No writing sample from a student with ADHD would be complete without at least a few holes due to heavy pressure on the eraser as the student attempts to correct, and then re-correct errors.

Out of all of the conditions described in this book, ADHD is the one that we have the most research on that refers to handwriting deficits, but unfortunately, much of the research has simply focused on the effects of medications for ADHD on handwriting. Such studies indicate that stimulant medications may improve the legibility or neatness of the handwriting for some students, but may decrease the speed and fluency of writing. The reduced fluency and speed while on medication may be due to the students now paying more attention to handwriting. When asked to close their eyes and/or make a conscious effort to write faster, medicated students wrote more fluently and, at times, automatically (Tucha and Lange 2004, 2001, 2005). There does not seem to be any learning or carryover from medication, however. If the stimulant medication is stopped, the handwriting reverts to its former levels. Because medication does not cure handwriting deficits, students may require remediation even if their handwriting is somewhat better while on medication.

Obsessive-Compulsive Disorder (OCD)

Students with OCD may have perfectionistic tendencies in their handwriting. If the work does not look perfect, they may rewrite or trace over a letter over and over until it looks "just right" or "perfect." Compulsively redoing their written work often interferes with their ability to complete classwork within the allotted time or to complete their homework in a timely fashion.

In some students with OCD, the handwriting may be very tiny (micrographia). The more severe the OCD symptoms, the slower and smaller the handwriting is likely to be. Students with OCD actually exhibit superior performance, however, when they are asked to engage in repetitive motor patterns, i.e., drawing or writing something over and over again (Mavrogiorgou et al. 2001). When patients with OCD were treated for their OCD symptoms, drawing speed improved (Mergl, Mavrogiorgou et al. 2004).

Depression and Bipolar Disorder

Slowed movement (psychomotor retardation) is a common symptom of major depression, and students who are depressed may exhibit significantly slower handwriting [cf. (Mergl, Juckel et al. 2004)]. In contrast, mania may produce more impulsive and illegible writing. Mania may produce worse handwriting than depression (Tigges et al. 2000).

Asperger's Syndrome (AS)

Students with Asperger's Syndrome often have motor clumsiness that is reflected in their handwritten work. Research indicates that no single pattern of handwriting deficits is common to students with AS, however.

Nonverbal Learning Disability (NLD)

VMI and fine motor skills are common deficits in students with Nonverbal Learning Disability. The demands of preschool and kindergarten tasks such as cutting and coloring are difficult for many of these students, and their handwriting may appear illegible and awkwardly produced. As the student with NLD matures, however, their handwriting often improves.

Visual perception and memory are also areas of weakness for many students with NLD. The student with NLD can be physically awkward and slow at learning coordinated sequential motor movements, such as those involved in handwriting. These students may have the type of bilateral coordination problems discussed earlier in this chapter.

Tips and Strategies for Students with Handwriting Issues

Students up to the ages of ten or eleven may benefit from remedial programs for handwriting in terms of handwriting legibility, but improvement in the quality and legibility of handwriting is generally not accompanied by improvement in speed of handwriting or numeral legibility (Case-Smith 2002). Simply using copying exercises with older elementary school students is unlikely to be successful, although students may benefit significantly from re-teaching the letter forms while explaining each form visually and verbally (Karlsdottir 1996).

ADHD

The following are tips from the U.S. Department of Education's guide to educating students with ADHD (U. S. Department of Education 2004). It is important to note that these ideas are specifically referencing students with ADHD-related handwriting issues, and may not be appropriate for students with other disorders.

- Use individual whiteboards. Ask the child to practice copying and erasing the target words on a small, individual whiteboard.
- Provide quiet places for handwriting. Provide the child with a special quiet place to complete his handwriting assignments.
- Teach a trick to space words on a page. Teach the child to use a finger to measure the space to leave between each word in a written assignment.*
- Use special writing paper. Have the child use special paper with vertical lines to learn to space letters and words on a page.
- Provide structured programs for handwriting. Teach handwriting skills through a structured program, such as the Handwriting Without Tears®.**

All Conditions

- Allow more time for handwritten work and reduce the amount to be written at any one time.

---

* A visual editing strip that includes a reminder to use one finger to leave space is depicted in Chapter 19.
** See http://www.hwtears.com/index.html for information on the program.

These two accommodations are presented first and together because we believe that if they are treated as one strategy, many of the problems will be reduced. Reducing the amount of handwritten work may require that the student have a tape recorder, word processor, computer, voice activated software, scribe, or be given hard copies of notes. (See the Assistive Technology section later in this chapter.)

- Practice air-writing. Have the student practice writing their letters and words in the air, using large arm movements.
- Verbalize sequence. Have the students use cognitive cues to learn a verbal sequence by saying the motor sequence for letter formation out loud while forming the letters, e.g., "C is a cup facing right."
- Use wider writing utensils. Provide younger students with wider pencils or pens.
- Provide pencil or pen grips. Choose from the wide assortment of colors, shapes, and sizes of grips available on the market. Your student will know when the grip is correct, and when it drives him crazy and is in the way.
- Allow student to pick their type of writing instrument. Students who keep breaking pencil points from too much pressure on the pencil or who have an obsessive need to keep resharpening the point until it is perfect may find it easier to write with a pen. Allow students to choose the type of instrument that they prefer, and offer them a choice of widths and shapes for the instrument, including the option of utensil grips.
- Introduce cursive early on. Students with handwriting deficits characterized by too much in-air time may produce more legible writing if they are allowed to write in cursive, as it keeps the pen or pencil down on the paper longer and avoids some of the problems with staying on the line. Allow the student to decide whether to use manuscript or cursive.
- Use paper with raised horizontal lines. The tactile cue may help young students stay on the line.
- Do not grade for neatness. If neatness or being able to read the student's work is important, then find another system for recording the student's work.
- Do not penalize for spelling unless it is a spelling test.
- Reduce copying from the board. A significant number of students with the disorders described in this book have VMI impairment that makes copying from the board difficult. When combined with their handwriting deficits, copying from the board can become a huge stressor.
- Provide partial or full copies of lecture notes. Students do not derive any rehearsal or memory benefit from writing notes when they have to think about the how-to of writing. They are also more likely to have difficulty figuring out what to write down, and even if they can figure out what to write and manage to write some of it down, their handwriting is so illegible that they probably will not be able to read their own notes later!
- Provide an agenda or planner that provides adequate space for large, sloppy handwriting or use electronic technology to record assignments. Many schools provide students with planners for school assignments. It is a lovely thought, but many of the planners have distinct drawbacks when it comes to suitability for students with dysgraphia and/or Executive Dysfunction (Chapter 9).

The Dreaded Agenda/Planner

Jared was a high school student with Asperger's Syndrome along with dysgraphia and Executive Dysfunction. All too often, he would open his agenda to look at what was coming up for the day, only to discover that he had a test that he had not studied for, or a big project due that he had not started. Figure 17.1 shows what Jared's planner looked like after a few weeks of use. Trying to encourage him to look ahead, his teacher replaced his existing planner that showed one day at a time with a planner that showed a "week at a glance."

Several problems can be detected in Figure 17.1. On Wednesday's entry for that week, the student actually tried to record his own homework. His handwriting is large, sloppy, contains reversals, and he does not have sufficient space to enter details about his homework assignment. On the next day, he enters "SP" (probably for "spelling"). Other than those attempts, he makes no entries in his planner for the week. He may have felt overwhelmed trying to use the planner because his teacher and mother were also using it for their school-home communications. The planner became so visually cluttered that it was no longer useful to him.

Figure 17.1. Messy Planner

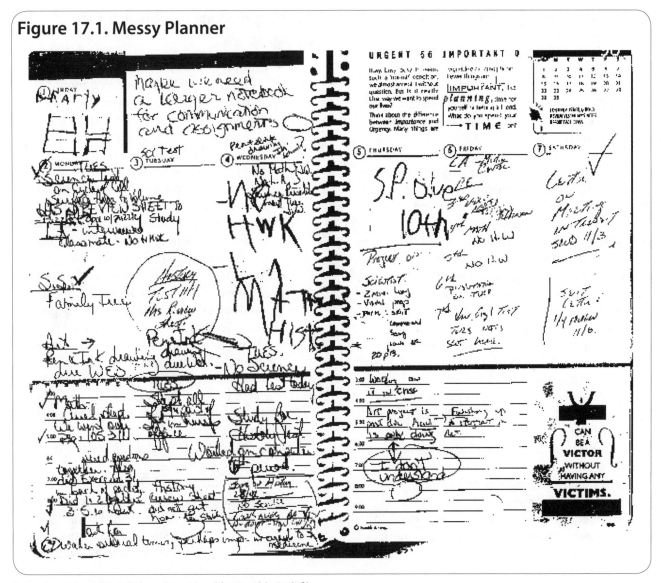

From the author's "Good Ideas Gone Horribly, Horribly Bad" files.

A student's planner or agenda needs to be kept separate from any school-home communication notebook.

When Handwriting Interferes with Calculations

- Allow more workspace for solving math problems. If possible, make sure worksheets leave sufficient space for large, sloppy handwriting and add some lined areas to help the student organize the workspace.
- Use graph paper, lined paper turned sideways, or ruler guides. When using graph paper, make sure that the size of the boxes is adequate for the size of the student's normal writing. Art stores and online merchants sell graph paper with different sized boxes.
- Reduce the number of problems to be done at one time. Handwriting deteriorates as additional problems are done.
- Do not require the student to show his work if mentally performed calculations are accurate. If the student has to think about how to form the numerals to show the work at the same time that he is trying to perform the mental calculations, the student may lose track of the operations and make errors. We are aware that some states have tests that require showing work, but encourage the student's team to explore whether it is possible to obtain an accommodation if handwriting is likely to lead to errors.

- Allow breaks, encourage students to check their work, and conference with the students after they do one or two problems. Do not expect editing to be done simultaneously during math production.
- Allow separate, additional time for editing with use of a math editing strip (Chapter 20).
- Teach cognitive strategies for maintaining a sequence, e.g., order of long division (Chapter 20) to help students preserve sequence if they get distracted while trying to recall how to write numerals.
- Teach cognitive strategies to aid in memorization of math facts (Chapter 20). The automaticity of math facts lessens the impact of handwriting on calculations.
- Allow use of a calculator. Once students have demonstrated that they have mastered the operations and concepts, permit the use of a calculator for additional rehearsal calculations.
- Allow more time for solving and writing out math calculations. Remember that many of these students have significantly slower writing and many also have memory problems that impair their ability to keep track of their computations or to remember the sequence of steps.
- Reduce copying problems from board to paper or from book to paper. The more material the student has to copy over, the more chances to introduce an error in copying due to inability to read handwriting, impulsive errors in copying over operational symbols, etc.
- Give the student partial credit if the operation was successfully carried out even if there are what is referred to as "careless errors." These errors are not "careless" but errors that simply go undetected because the student is busy attending to writing demands and working the math problem. The only way to avoid these errors is to allow time for the use of a math editing strip in conjunction with a set time to edit that is separate, and in addition to, from the time allowed for the work.

Testing Accommodations for Dysgraphia

- Extend time for tests. Break big tests up over days. Specify in the accommodation plan or IEP the longest amount of time the student can be tested at one time and in one day if handwriting is required. Indicate the amount of handwritten responses the student needs to be limited to. If the student requires opportunities to get up and move around, or if he requires a break from writing, indicate how long the break should be in a statement included in the student's testing accommodation plan.
- Accommodate medications in scheduling. If the student is on medication that affects handwriting, schedule testing with medication effects on handwriting in mind.
- Allow the use of word processing, dictation of answers using voice-activated software, or provide a scribe if there is lengthy material to write. In many cases, allowing the student access to a word processor will be the best solution.
- Do not penalize grades for handwriting neatness problems.
- Allow students to circle answers or record answers directly in the test booklet instead of copying them over. If answers involve sentences to be recorded, make sure the test booklet has enough space to allow large, sloppy handwriting.
- Allow alternate forms of testing. Written tests such as essay exams generally underestimate what the student has learned. Allow for oral testing when the purpose of the test is not to assess written expression.
- Ensure that any final work is copied over accurately to test booklet or answer sheet.
- Avoid computer (Scantron) forms for students with writing rituals, e.g., students with OCD. Refer to Chapter 5 for more information.

Assistive Technology

For many years, allowing students to tape record their assignments was considered a high tech solution, but tape recording has drawbacks. For example, it can be difficult to hear the student's voice over the background noise in the room, and locating any one piece of information on the tape later may prove arduous. Working memory deficits make getting information off a tape recorder quite difficult. Such serial processing requirements often discourage students from using their tape recorded notes for studying. An additional limitation of tape recording is that the student does not get to rehearse or demonstrate knowledge of the rules of punctuation and capitalization.

The use of word processors can make a significant difference in the quality of student work and the student's ability and willingness to edit the work. This may be a challenge due to financial considerations and availability of equipment, among other factors (Freeman, MacKinnon, and Miller 2004). Many districts now include keyboarding as part of the curriculum, beginning in the upper elementary grades (Freeman, Mackinnon, and Miller 2005). Students who write slowly and illegibly may also keyboard slowly. That does not mean, however, that trying to remediate handwriting instead of introducing keyboarding is the preferred approach. Keyboards are the electric wheelchairs for these students' hands. Not only are keyboarding skills required for advanced work and business, but research indicates that, on average, keyboarding is faster than handwriting and results in greater text production for 6th grade students (Rogers and Case-Smith 2002).

Determining whether a student requires a scribe, word processor, desktop computer, electronic spellchecker, electronic thesaurus, or a notebook computer requires an assistive technology assessment, as does the determination of whether the student needs to be taught to use any voice dictation software for computer use. Assistive technology evaluators consider the student's visual-motor integration skills, whether the student has any hand tics that interfere with keyboarding or vocal tics that might preclude the use of voice dictation software, whether the student has any compulsions that might be problematic with respect to the use of a computer, and whether the student is so clumsy as to possibly damage or ruin a notebook computer or word processor. Assess the student with respect to:

- What kind of monitor and keyboard does the student require?
- What method of keyboarding will be taught?
- Does the student need an occupational therapist to assess and assist in keyboard instruction?
- What other software needs to be installed on the system to help the student produce quality work?

- What other software might be installed on the system to help the student compensate for Executive Dysfunction (e.g., time management software, calendars, etc.)?
- What other electronic devices will ease the student's difficulty with production?
- Does the student need electronic reference tools such as spell checker or grammar checker?
- Does the computer access to the Internet need to be monitored or blocked for certain areas that can interfere or be harmful to the student?
- What kind of furniture and positioning does the student need?
- If clumsiness is an issue, does the student require a desktop system instead of a notebook or word processor?
- Will the student be allowed to, or encouraged to use a notebook computer on field trips so that he can take notes?

Some schools are quite happy to provide students with AlphaSmart™ word processors, but these devices may not be appropriate for any one student for a variety of reasons, including the amount of material that is displayed in the work screen. If only a few lines of text show in the screen at one time, the student may forget what he wrote at the beginning of the paragraph.* Thus, before any assistive technology evaluation is conducted, make sure the school and parents compile a list of specific questions and concerns that the evaluator needs to address at the end of the evaluation.

When a student's handwriting is sloppy, homework assignments may be copied incorrectly or incompletely into agendas or planners, as exemplified in Figure 17.1. As an alternative to the traditional planner or agenda, we often recommend allowing the student to record their assignments in other ways, such as:

- Entering assignments in a handheld device such as a PDA.
- Sending an email home from the classroom computer with the assignment typed into the body of the email.
- Allowing the student to call home or their own cell phone number to leave a voicemail message with the assignment.

---

* Newer models allow many more lines of text to be displayed than older models.

Homework hotlines or posting daily homework assignments on the web are useful strategies for students who have difficulty getting assignments written down. They also enable absent students to find out the homework and parents to verify what the child's assignments are for the night.

Summary

Handwriting issues contribute to academic problems and to frustration in school settings. Significant fine motor control and visual-motor integration problems contribute to slow and illegible handwriting. For many students with the disorders discussed in this book, medications used to treat the symptoms of their disorders may also produce some improvement in handwriting legibility, but, to date, no remediation program is available that successfully and significantly improves rate, legibility, and fluency once the demands of handwriting in the content area accelerates over time due to curriculum demands. School personnel are encouraged to refer students for assessment of handwriting issues to ensure that they have a fast and functional system for keeping up with classwork and assignments. In many cases, this will entail the use of assistive technology.

Marco, whose classroom teacher was at a loss as to why he wouldn't complete written assignments, finally referred him to the school's occupational therapist. She discovered that Marco had significant handwriting problems so she set up time to work with Marco on his handwriting and gave the classroom teacher suggestions for writing accommodations. Marco's production increased significantly and his grades went from C's to A's.

CHAPTER 18

Language Deficits*

Sean's teacher said that when Sean talked, her head hurt from trying to follow what he was saying. Sean's family reported the same problem. The teacher noticed that Sean's peers would get tired of trying to understand him. It took Sean a long time to admit that he was having trouble figuring out what to say. He would often give up, if his listener had not already given up. Sean said, "I wish it wasn't so hard to speak. It really gets bad when the teacher calls on me in class when my hand is not raised. I get so humiliated when I can't answer the question. I know the answers, but I lose them or can't pull them out in time. My classmates think I'm stupid and forget that I am in the gifted program."

Preview

Language competence is the ability to process and express language in educational and social settings. Language processing and production include the ability to sequence, recall, retrieve, organize, and express information effectively in a timely manner. This chapter covers the language issues associated with all conditions in this book except for Asperger's Syndrome (AS) and Nonverbal Learning Disability (NLD). See Chapter 13 for a description of language issues in those disorders. This chapter will consider each of the major aspects of language and describe how they may be impaired by the disorders covered in this book.

Auditory Perception and Discrimination Deficits

Auditory perception begins when sounds enter the ear and are identified for storage in memory. An example of one of the auditory perceptions is auditory discrimination. It is the perception that allows sounds to be distinguished from each other, such as the difference between the sounds "b" and "d." The disorders described in this book are generally not associated with any primary problems in perception or discrimination, but there may be secondary problems due to symptom interference. An inattentive listener—a student with auditory attention deficits due to symptom interference—may have trouble accurately distinguishing sounds. Symptom interference can affect any auditory function.

Receptive and Expressive Language Disorders

Receptive language refers to the listener's ability to translate verbal information coming in through the ears, process it into meaningful information, and store it in memory. Receptive language is typically not affected by the disorders in this book in the sense of a primary impact, although symptom interference can impair processing and storage.

Expressive language is the ability to pull language out and efficiently use the mouth for speaking or the hands for sign language, gestures, and written expression. Most of the disorders in this book have some impact on expressive language. The problems may not show up on standardized testing unless a time factor

---

* Some of the information in this chapter was adapted from earlier work done by Sharon Cargill, M.A. and Sheryl K. Pruitt, M.Ed. (1988, Staff Development, Parkaire Consultants).

highlights the inefficiency. Given all the time in the world, many of these students can pull the language out eventually, which is one reason untimed tests are often a necessary accommodation for these students.

One aspect of impaired expressive language is word retrieval. In this case, the individual knows the word that is being requested but just cannot access it. For example, if a student says, "You know, that 'whirlybird' up in the sky that is used in the morning to report on the traffic," there is a word retrieval problem in finding the word "helicopter." It is as if the student was in the right drawer but could not efficiently find the right file. In severe cases, students are unable to find any word at all when needed. This can be particularly challenging when faced with a fill-in-the-blank test, for example. To accurately assess the student's knowledge, accompany fill-in-the-blank tests with word banks. Expect that students who have word retrieval problems for a single word will also have rapid naming problems, e.g., naming one or multiple items that start with the letter "b" in a limited period of time. In this population, rapid naming is usually a verbal executive deficit rather than a semantic (vocabulary) deficit in categorization.

Speak privately with the students to ask whether to call on them or whether to wait until they raise their hands. Many students are embarrassed in front of their peers when they cannot retrieve a word quickly and the class has the impression that they do not know the information.

Retrieval deficits and slow retrieval speed can be significant problems when trying to carry on a conversation in the social setting, as peers will not wait long for a social response. One clue that a student is struggling with word retrieval problems is the use of filler words, such as "thing," "umm," or "stuff." Other times, a student may circle around a word (circumlocution) in the file drawer but instead verbalize every other word except the one they were looking for. Socially, these behaviors can be quite embarrassing.

Sentence Formation Deficits

Students may also have difficulty forming sentences due to difficulty finding the correct words, sequencing them appropriately, and then expressing them in real time. Time pressure further impairs sentence formation. Sentence formation deficits impair oral expression, written expression, and social communications with peers.

Impact of Executive Dysfunction on Language: Verbal Executive Abilities and Deficits

The impact of Executive Dysfunction (EDF) on language is similar to other impairments caused by EDF (Chapter 9). This is because the verbal executive functions are a subset of executive functions. Put simply, Verbal Executive Dysfunction is the result of Executive Dysfunction interfering with normal verbal functioning. Verbal Executive Dysfunction, if present, impacts the efficient use of expressive language and social language skills (pragmatics).

Students with Verbal Executive Dysfunction may have difficulty initiating ideas. This creates difficulty answering in real time, if at all. Without an opportunity to brainstorm ideas first, many of these students may be unable to start an oral expression project, e.g., speaking in front of the class.

Difficulty maintaining and limiting a topic may lead to overambitious verbiage and a more rambling, off-topic verbal production. Poor organizational skills and lack of planning may impair the efficiency of oral communication and make it difficult for the listener to understand the student's point. One of our observations is that these students frequently "lose" their listeners because they are not communicating their ideas clearly. To add to the listener's woes, it is often not clear when the student is changing topics.

Students with verbal sequencing and working memory deficits often experience significant impairment in expressing ideas verbally in the appropriate order. The inability to discern cause and effect, as well as the inability to predict consequences and outcomes, reflects the difficulty with sequencing and working memory. These deficits lead to difficulties when the student attempts to communicate thoughts and ideas.

One aspect of executive functions is the ability to shift from one task or set of demands to another quickly and flexibly. A student who is unable to shift verbal sets may get stuck on a topic and have great difficulty changing to another topic. When the teacher wants to shift the topic of discussion or a peer wants to talk about something else, these students may become agitated and/or may be unable to change topics. This is seen in conversations and discussions that require turn-taking.

Students with EDF have poor self-monitoring, which leads to careless errors in speaking and failure to communicate in a way that is meaningful to others.

The inability to edit oral expression leads to poorer quality verbalizations and written work, reduced ability to speak at the appropriate speed and voice level, and inappropriate vocabulary substitutions. Some students cannot speak slowly enough for others to follow and are unaware of how difficult it is for the listener to take in the information at such a rapid rate.

Another verbal executive deficit is the inability to prioritize and know what the primary ideas are. Students frequently use excessive verbiage and include a lot of irrelevant material because they do not know what to leave out and what to include. Many students with EDF also have great difficulty remembering to even think of the needs of the listener.

Verbal Executive Dysfunction is not the only possible explanation for rapid rate of speech. Students with anxiety disorders and students with working memory deficits may also speak too quickly, but for different reasons.

Teacher Behaviors and Reactions to Verbal Executive Deficits

A teacher's internal reactions to the student's communication are often an accurate indicator of whether the student needs remediation for verbal executive deficits, as suggested by the opening vignette in this chapter. Curiosity is key to understanding a student's problems with verbal organization. Once the issue is suspected, the school's speech and language pathologist may help the student to organize and produce appropriate verbalizations. She can also be a great resource for the classroom teacher regarding how to accommodate verbal Executive Dysfunction during oral production tasks in the classroom and how to support peer interactions.

It's easy to take for granted that a person can organize her verbal knowledge, find it, and retrieve it when needed.

Impact of Working Memory Deficits on Language

Working memory (see Chapter 10) involves attention, memory, and executive functioning. When a student's working memory is impaired, she is unable to hold multiple pieces of information in memory while acting on the meaning of the information. This significantly impairs the student's ability to follow oral directions. It also interferes with her ability to hold onto her ideas until she can write them down or express them orally, e.g., holding information in memory until the end of the chapter questions.

Deficits in Pragmatics

By adolescence, effective and efficient verbal and nonverbal social communications, i.e., pragmatics, are very important to social success. One of the leading causes of teenage depression is the failure to be socially successful. If a student has deficits in social communications, intervention is essential.

Although vocabulary is usually a strength for the majority of students with the disorders described in this book, teenage vocabulary changes rapidly and is rarely based on meaningful, contextual cues. The speech and language pathologist can teach the student teenage vocabulary that is crucial to peer communications and acceptance. The speech and language pathologist can also teach the student how to read body language and other nonverbal social communication skills, how to reduce excessive verbalizations, and how to take turns during interactions.

Pragmatic deficits are often found in students with Bipolar Disorder, ASD, and EDF. In other cases, what appears to be pragmatic deficits in social interactions may be secondary to symptom interference or undiagnosed EDF.

Some Possible Indicators for Referring Students to the Speech/Language Pathologist

The following language problems are associated with the neurological disorders discussed in this book. They are mentioned here solely to alert teachers about possible language deficits. The following is **not** a complete language referral checklist:

- Inappropriate word use, e.g., "whirlybird" for "helicopter"
- Word retrieval difficulties, i.e., "I know the answer but can't think of it"
- Nonspecific word use, e.g., "you know… that thing…"
- Unable to memorize facts, e.g., math facts

- Avoidance or no response; says, "I don't know" often
- Repeats directions under breath (i.e., sub-vocalizes)
- Takes extra time before responding
- Trouble understanding cause and effect relationships
- Approaches verbal problems in a disorganized and illogical way
- Difficulty with oral directions
- Difficulty with verbal and auditory sequences
- Difficulty with fill-in-the-blank tests when no word bank is provided

Students are typically referred to speech and language pathologists only if they have articulation issues. Be curious about speech issues, such as excessive verbalization and problems with social communications, and investigate whether a speech pathologist can help. An audiological assessment may also be indicated to help determine if the student has any primary problems with auditory perception or auditory discrimination.

Tips and Tricks for Language Deficits

The following strategies may decrease the effects of the language deficits described above on academic and social performance:

Strategies for Social Language Deficits

- Teach age-appropriate jargon.
- Explain the concepts around social interactions, e.g., the back and forth rhythm that occurs in appropriate conversations.
- Have peers model appropriate social behavior while narrating what is going on for the student. For younger students, role-playing may be very instructive.
- Expand the size and make up of the groups used to practice social events to increase the likelihood of generalization.

Strategies for Following Directions

- Establish a strategy for getting the student's attention before giving directions, e.g., hand signals or tactile cues.

- Give only one direction at a time with a pause or filler in between, e.g., "Take out your book. Good job, John. Go to page forty-four. I see you are on task, Jenny. Go down to problem number three." If the fillers are distracting to students, just pause longer between directions.

If a student cannot maintain eye contact while receiving directions, teach the student to look at the bridge of the speaker's nose.

- Accompany oral discussions or directions with visual stimuli whenever possible.
- Teach students to repeat to themselves oral directions, lists, dates, names, etc. This may help students remember the information.
- Check for comprehension of oral information, especially directions, before letting a student begin a task.

Strategies to Assist Processing

- Use simple and relatively short sentences from eight to ten words in length, modeling speech patterns for the student. Some students need short sentences if they are to be successful in learning.
- Use simple sentence structure whenever possible.
- Use pictures to help students interpret verbal messages, e.g., PowerPoint™ presentations, movies, and photographs.
- Reduce irrelevant information.
- Identify and highlight relevant facts and material. An outline or study guide is very valuable.
- Preview the material to be taught. Students with verbal executive deficits need the overall picture before the individual parts or steps. This strategy increases comprehension and retention of the material.

Strategies to Assist with Word Retrieval

Phonetic cues:
- Say the beginning sound of a word, e.g., say "puh" to elicit the word "pie."
- Say a word fragment containing one or more of the beginning syllables of a polysyllabic word, such as "hippo" for "hippopotamus."

- Give a rhyming word such as "sing" to facilitate recall of the word "ring."
- Position your lips to form the beginning sound of a word, e.g., squeeze your lips together for an "mmm" sound to elicit the word "money."

Associative cues:
- Use an associated word from the same semantic class as a cue, e.g., say "bread and _____," to elicit the word "butter."
- Use the name of a semantic category to elicit the name of a member of that group, e.g., say, "It is an insect" for "ant" or, "It is a fruit" for "apple."

Multiple choice cue:
- Provide multiple choices for cueing, e.g., say, "Is it a house, a tree, or a chair?" to elicit the word "tree."

Sentence completion cue:
- Use the beginning of a sentence familiar to the student to cue a word, i.e., "The cow jumped over the ____."

Strategies for Helping Students Organize Expressive Language

- Teach time concepts such as sequence, and other vocabulary concepts of temporal organization, e.g., then, next, first, second, etc.
- Teach the student the application of the words "first," "second," "next," etc. Have the student use these words to explain the rules of a game or sport. This can help to organize and sequence expressive language.
- Use a flip book or set of cards presented one at a time to help the student sequence oral and written communications, e.g., "What happened first?" "What happened second?" etc.
- Use pictorial cues, such as comic strips, to retell story sequences.
- Have the student record personal stories on tape and review the stories with them. Monitor the student's organization by indicating when the student provides information out of sequence, e.g., "You told me first that you _____, but later, you told me what you did before that."
- Ensure that classroom instructions and presentations are logically sequenced. This facilitates student recall.

Strategies for Helping Students Listen

- Adapt or reduce the structural complexity of all oral material presented.
- Reiterate the nouns at regular intervals in sequences, paragraphs, and lectures in oral sentences featuring a high proportion of pronouns. Do not assume that the student will remember whether "she" refers to Jill or Susan or any other female character.
- Use visual illustration of time sequences during oral presentations, e.g., timelines.
- Make sure that the vocabulary in the lecture has been mastered before giving the lecture.
- Explain implied meanings and intents.
- Cue listener to topic changes.
- Teach the student to ask for clarification as needed.
- Give students a copy of the lecture notes.
- Summarize details in sequential order with a visual guide.

Strategies for Test Taking

- Use a multiple choice format to increase the speed and accuracy of responses.
- Avoid making one of the answers in a multiple choice format the opposite of the correct answer because students with word finding problems may select this choice.
- Use untimed tests to help the student who has to process the question and organize it cognitively before answering.
- Use tape recorded or oral tests to facilitate improvement in performance.

Summary

Inefficient communication often indicates verbal executive difficulties in oral and written expression. Remember that sometimes the student knows the information, but she cannot communicate it. Ask students if they know the material and just cannot "get it out" or if they need the material retaught. The speech and language pathologist is the school's resident expert in this area.

Sean asked his speech teacher to talk to his regular classroom teacher about calling on him in class. Thanks to the discussion, the teacher now only calls on Sean when his hand is raised. Sean says, "I really like my teacher because she listens to my speech teacher when she explains what is wrong with my answering in class. Sometimes the teacher asks me if I know something ahead of time and lets me know she wants me to answer a certain question during the next lecture and I have time to get ready for it. Everyone thinks I have been studying more. They don't know that I have always known it...I just couldn't show them."

CHAPTER 19

Written Expression and Long-Term Projects

Devorah started coming to the therapist's clinic when she was eight years old. She had been diagnosed with severe learning disabilities in basic reading and written expression. Despite the fact that she was gifted, Devorah could not write her name, she could not read, and she could not produce a written document. Devorah had a bad attitude when it came to academics. She wanted to learn but had only experienced failure. Her parents were high-functioning professionals and she, too, wanted to succeed. Devorah was irritable because she was not successful in school and she was pushing people away from helping her at this point. She was afraid no one could help her and she did not want to fail anymore.

Preview

A student can be said to have a learning disability (LD) in written expression when the student's ability to produce a written document is significantly below their potential.[*]

Written expression is one of the two most common LD in students with the neurological disorders described in this book. Although specific statistics are not available on the rate of written expression LD for each of the disorders, one investigator found that 65% of students with ADHD may have a written expression learning disability (Mayes, Calhoun, and Crowell 2000).

---

[*] We realize that different states define learning disability using varying criteria. By looking at processing discrepancies and using multiple measures as well as work samples, the student's team can usually determine if there is a deficit that needs to be remediated.

Definition of a Learning Disability in Written Expression

Written expression is the most complex academic task. Table 19.1 depicts the requisite skills for written expression in the first column. The second column lists the sources of interference that prevent students with neurological disorders from succeeding at these skills. When we consider all the possible sources of impairment or interference, it is not surprising that so many of these students find written expression a frustrating and unsuccessful activity.

Even students without a diagnosed LD in written expression may have tremendous difficulty producing a written document due to interference from symptoms such as writing rituals and thoughts that jump all over the place due to mania. Production for handwritten work may also be affected by pain caused by an inefficient pencil grip or an inability to stabilize posture.

Sometimes school personnel don't realize that a student with OCD who has an "A" grade on his paper was up all night, every night for weeks, having meltdowns over the assignment, creating chaos in the home. If a student is diagnosed with OCD, inquire about how many hours he spends on assignments and whether he is losing sleep over assignments. The Homework Screening Survey, provided in Figure 23.2 and on the accompanying CD-ROM, can facilitate collecting this information.

Table 19.1. Skills and Sources of Interference in Written Expression

Requisite Skills	Interference Factors
■ Handwriting	■ Inattention
■ Letter formation	■ Distractibility
■ Placing letters in space	■ Hyperactivity
■ Visual-motor integration	■ Unstable posture
■ Grammar	■ Disinhibition
■ Spelling	■ Impersistence
■ Goal setting	■ Word retrieval difficulties
■ Organizing	■ Perfectionism
■ Planning	■ Obsessions
■ Sequencing	■ Rigidity
■ Self-monitoring	■ Writing rituals
■ Initiating	■ Anxiety
■ Prioritizing	■ Fears
■ Editing	■ Phobias
■ Executing	■ Major depression
■ Task analysis	■ Mania
■ Time management	■ Sensory defensiveness
■ Shifting flexibly	■ Inability to sleep
■ Using feedback	■ Tic interference
■ Working memory	■ Memory deficits
■ Strategic memory	■ "Storms" or rages
	■ Tracking problems

Major Sources of Impairment in Written Expression

The major sources of impact are from handwriting deficits, attentional issues, Executive Dysfunction, memory issues, and word retrieval issues. Sometimes symptom interference from a specific disorder overwhelms the student's ability to produce a written assignment, e.g., obsessing over writing letters perfectly to the point where the student cannot write a complete sentence.

Handwriting (Graphomotor) Deficits

Students with ADHD, TS, OCD, VMI deficits, and EDF often have significant handwriting issues (see Chapter 17). Because of these issues, students avoid writing assignments and resist editing their work. Addressing handwriting issues is a major component of remediating problems in written expression.

Attention and Distraction

ADHD is frequently seen as the cause of all attention problems in many students (see Chapter 8). Note that a host of other factors may impair attention, e.g., anxiety, tics, mania, depression, obsessions, allergies, family issues, etc. Inability to direct attention to the writing task results in inefficiency. In addition, the lack of automaticity of written expression skills increases stress and thereby causes increased inattention and further exacerbates the difficult process. Many students with written expression deficits do not complete written assignments and are often misunderstood and mischaracterized as being lazy, unmotivated, or oppositional. Problems with attention may have significant impact, particularly when the student has not created a written plan, mindmap, or outline, all of which he may avoid because of handwriting issues.

Executive Dysfunction

Executive Dysfunction (Chapter 9) is the biggest source of impairment in written expression for students with the neurological disorders described in this book. Most students have excellent ideas, but cannot write well in a way that reflects their thoughts. Students with EDF may have one, some, or all of the following deficits that negatively affect written expression.

- **Initiation** deficits make it difficult for the student to get started on the task.
- **Goal-setting** deficits lead to unrealistic goals for the written assignment.
- **Planning** deficits impair the student's ability to plan a paper and complete the task on time.
- Difficulty **prioritizing** results in an inability to recognize main ideas and to write concisely, and leads to spending excessive time on minor details.
- Deficits in **sequencing** results in disorderly thought development.
- Difficulty in **shifting**, i.e., making transitions, leads to excessive information on one topic and not enough information on the rest of the subject matter.
- Deficits in **self-monitoring** lead to careless errors and failure to complete assignments on time.
- Inability to **estimate the amount of time** needed to complete a written assignment is one of the most common reasons for work not being completed and turned in by the deadline.

If students with EDF cannot write without assistance, they will not be able to edit without assistance because editing involves the very same executive skills. Give students strategies for editing and teach them directly to tackle one aspect of editing at a time.

Students with EDF may react poorly to constructive feedback during the writing process because they may not know how to use it. For example, saying, "This is a confusing order and I can't follow it" does not give the student the skill to sequence logically. The student needs specific direct instruction on how to order the material properly.

For many students with EDF, written expression never becomes fluent. One intellectually gifted high school student with EDF told his therapist, "I wish my teachers would understand that it doesn't matter how smart I am—every year I have to start all over again learning how to write. It just doesn't stick."

Some students with written expression problems report that they cannot get started until they get close to the deadline. They say that panic starts to build, adrenalin kicks in, and then they can start to write. They may also claim that they actually write better and produce a better product that way. Tell them that the research does not support this and that even if they are successful now, their system will not work when they take courses that are highly structured and have high work load demands.

Impact of Memory Deficits

Students with the neurological disorders described in this book may have memory deficits (Chapter 10) that impair written expression. Impaired recall and difficulty maintaining ideas make it difficult to hold onto ideas after a reading assignment long enough to incorporate them in a written assignment. These memory problems are compounded by the students' reluctance to write things down due to their handwriting issues. Deficits in working memory also affect editing skills. To address this, place visual reminders of the editing steps on the student's desk.

Impact of Language Impairment

Verbal executive functions involved in expressive language are a subset of executive functions. Students with impaired verbal executive functions may have difficulty recognizing the important ideas, incorporate an excessive amount of irrelevant material, and have difficulty forming sentences. See Chapter 18 for a discussion of language issues in this population.

Other Sources of Impairment

Hyperactivity can limit the amount of time the student can work on a given project before having to move around, while impulsivity may result in the student becoming derailed while writing. This disrupts thought patterns, especially the ability to retain and execute a sequence. These difficulties ultimately slow down the writing process and interfere with efficiency.

Tips and Strategies for Written Expression

See Chapter 17: Handwriting and Visual-Motor Integration Issues for tips and tricks for handwriting issues.

Some students require direct instruction in parts or all of the writing process. Other students may only require tips or strategies to ease production, such as:

- Extend time to accommodate slow production, due to slow processing speed, graphomotor deficits, word retrieval, and other factors.
- Let the student sit in a chair that can roll or rock to allow for movement.
- Show the student a model of the finished product when introducing the project.
- Assign a peer partner who is good at handwriting and organization.
- Protect the student's social relationships with peers on team writing assignments by pitching to the student's areas of strength, e.g., the student with neurological impairments might be very proficient at using the computer.
- Use story starters or have the student brainstorm to help overcome problems with initiation.
- Have the student use a tape recorder or voice dictation software to record written assignments in content subjects (social studies, science, and literature).
- Allow the student to use alternative strategies for notetaking, such as word processing or a notetaking buddy.
- Limit the amount to be handwritten and encourage the use of computer for ease of production.
- Let the student pick the subject to write about when learning new written skills, e.g., when learning to write a term paper, the student picks the topic.
- Do not grade drafts.
- Grade separately for content and mechanics.
- Use computer programs to organize information from the web. Some of these programs can highlight material on the web in different colors and download it in different files.

- Make use of graphic organizers such as editing strips, mindmaps, etc. (Chapters 19 and 20).
- Use cognitive cues for deficit areas, as described below.
- Utilize computer editing tools, as described below.
- Treat editing as a separate subject, allotting time for it. Students with neurological difficulties frequently cannot edit and write at the same time.
- Encourage the student to ask for assistance when editing.

Use the same procedure for teaching writing from year to year. It is hard enough for the students to learn the process one year without having it changed on them the next year. Suggest that the school adopt one consistent writing procedure to use across grade levels and subjects. If the student does use a template, be sure to put the template in the "trick book" (Chapter 28) so that it is available every year if the student forgets the procedure.

Impact of Computers

Computers can offset difficulties with graphomotor problems, attention, impulsivity, visual-motor deficits, editing difficulties, obsessive perfectionism, and organization. Keyboarding is often easier and faster than handwriting, particularly for long assignments. Students with ADHD, OCD, and mood disorders find it easier to sustain their focus when viewing a computer monitor. The color monitor enhances their attention and focus. Editing is less frustrating on the computer due, in part, to software such as spell checkers and grammar checkers. Having a computer highlight an error does not negatively affect the student's self-esteem. Computers also help the student with OCD-related writing rituals and perfectionism because every letter produced by the computer is perfect! This eliminates the need to rewrite imperfect letters. Clinical observations suggest that using the spellchecker increases spelling skills through appropriate modeling of the correct spelling. For students with EDF, word processors can significantly improve the quality of their work and their willingness to edit their work.

Figure 19.1. Mindmap

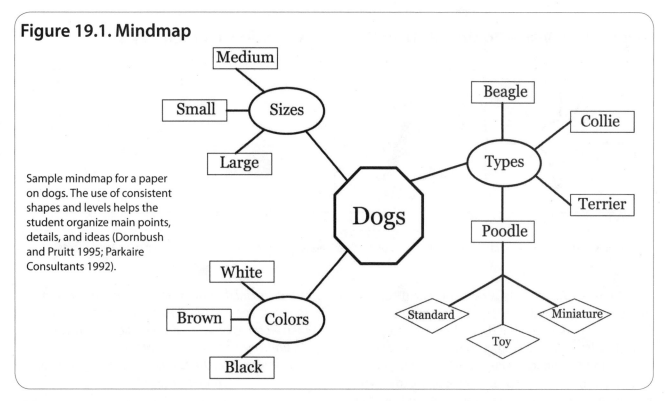

Sample mindmap for a paper on dogs. The use of consistent shapes and levels helps the student organize main points, details, and ideas (Dornbush and Pruitt 1995; Parkaire Consultants 1992).

Mindmapping or Visual Organizers

Use visual strategies to help organize thoughts and materials, such as mindmapping to brainstorm and organize written expression. Computer programs, e.g., Inspiration™ and Kidspiration™, can assist with this. Figure 19.1 is an example of mindmapping a paper on the subject of dogs. Once the mindmap is created, it can be turned into an outline. In our example, the center shape is the level of title, introduction, and conclusion, the ovals are the roman numerals, the rectangles are the capital letters, and the diamonds are the Arabic numbers.

Even with a visual organizer, the student almost certainly needs the help of a teacher, parent, or peer to complete the editing process.

Verbal Cues for Editing Work

Some students are verbal learners and do better with cognitive, verbal cues such as the mnemonics illustrated in Figure 19.2. Place them on the students' desks so they function as visual cues too.

Figure 19.2. Editing Mnemonics: CLIPS* and COPS**

CLIPS

Capitalization
Leave space
Ideas complete
Punctuation
Spelling

COPS

Capitalization
Organization
Punctuation
Spelling

Two mnemonics that help students remember and complete the steps in the editing process.

* Packer 1999
** Schumaker et all. 1981

Figure 19.3. Visual Editing Strip for Written Expression: Elementary Students

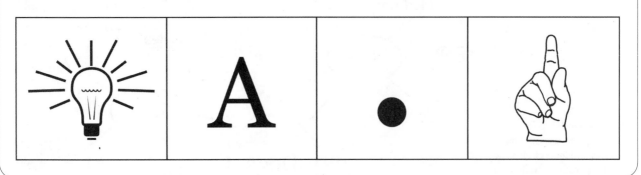

An editing strip that reminds students to check for complete ideas, capitalization, punctuation, and spacing between words (Dornbush and Pruitt 1995).

Figure 19.3 depicts an editing strip for elementary school students. The strip reminds young students to make sure that their ideas are complete, that they have capitalized properly, that they have used punctuation correctly, and that they have left one finger width space between words. With this type of cue, the order does not matter. The student needs to check for all four things, but one at a time, checking off as each is complete (Dornbush and Pruitt 1995).

Figure 19.4 depicts an editing strip that the authors designed for middle school students. The first symbol reminds the student to check for capitalization, the bee reminds them to check spelling, the third cue reminds them to check grammar, the punctuation marks remind them to check punctuation, and the final symbol of a runner reminds them to check for run-on sentences. Other useful editing checklists for written expression can be found in the bibliography. (See Dornbush and Pruitt 2009.) Students and teachers can develop editing strips together, tailored to specific editing problems with each subject. For example, some students may only need the bee and punctuation reminders.

It is crucial that the student check each editing function one at a time when using the editing strip. When working on written expression, follow steps one at a time as mastery is achieved. Start with sentences, then paragraphs, then stories, and finally work up to papers and projects.

Long-Term Projects and Reports

Long-term reports and projects are the bane of some families' existence. Such assignments often result in torturous nights of crying, screaming, and temper outbursts (and that is just the parents' behavior—you should see the children's behavior!). Students rarely start their projects until the night before unless teachers help them break the project down into an orderly sequence of manageable steps and record the steps in their planner. One of the most difficult skills is analyzing tasks, and therefore adult assistance is required. Adults also need to monitor the students' progress on a daily basis to ensure that they are adhering to the schedule.

Figure 19.4. Visual Editing Strip: Middle School Students

See text for description of each visual cue.

Many times teachers will ask parents to assist with monitoring the students' progress on a large assignment without determining if the parents, themselves, are organized enough to provide reliable monitoring assistance. Remember that parents may have executive skills deficits, too, and feel just as overwhelmed as their children. Be sure to send home a model that parents can follow in assisting their children.

Big projects require simultaneous use of multiple executive skills. When a project is assigned, the student with EDF becomes overwhelmed and may forget about the project until reminded that it is due tomorrow, or may be so paralyzed with anxiety that he cannot start the project. When dealing with students, who are likely to become overwhelmed when a big project is announced, speak to them privately the day before and tell them that the project is being assigned tomorrow, but it will be broken down for them into a certain number of homework steps. Assure them that they will be monitored for each step to make sure they are on the right track.

Some students with Executive Dysfunction can take advantage of mindmapping or graphic visual organizers; others may need computer techniques, paper techniques, or a combination. Students who are visual organizers find it easier to create notecards (on the computer or by hand), then lay them out and start to sort, organize, and map the information. Steps for a big project are provided below:

1. Divide the assignment into small parts with a definite time schedule for each part. Ensure that the intermediate deadlines are recorded in the student's daily planner.
2. Print or photocopy research, and highlight main ideas and important details.
3. Reread underlined parts and copy them onto notecards (by hand or using a computer).
4. Make a list of important points and assign a color to each.
5. Create and use a mindmap to outline the project.

Most students with EDF tell us that creating an outline is not only an extra chore, but an actual hindrance to completing the project. Most of them report that they write the paper and then create the outline afterward. If a student can create a mindmap and write the paper from that, a written outline is unnecessary. Consider making the outline optional.

6. Reread notecards and color code.
7. Sort notecards by color.
8. Reread notecards, expand mindmap, and eliminate ideas that do not fit.
9. Check outline or mindmap for balance.
10. Write the first draft on the computer.
11. A few days later, review and proofread the printed draft. Ensure that the reminder to review the work is entered in the planner. Use the spell checker and grammar checker when proofreading.
12. Ask an adult to review editing.
13. Make corrections on computer.
14. Continue to revise until finished editing.
15. Print out final report.

(Dornbush and Pruitt 1995)

Summary

Inefficiency of production is the biggest problem in written expression, and written expression is the most common learning disability for students with these neurological disorders.

Remember Devorah from the beginning of this chapter—the gifted child who was severely learning disabled? Devorah's therapist referred her for a thorough neuropsychological evaluation. The assessment revealed she also had severe visual-motor integration problems and Obsessive-Compulsive Disorder that had not been previously recognized or treated.

Devorah was referred for occupational therapy, learning disability remediation in reading and written expression, education in her disorders, and therapy to help her understand and separate her neurological disorders from her feelings about herself. In time, Devorah realized she was not stupid and could learn using different techniques.

By educating her about her disorders, by providing her with occupational therapy for her visual-motor deficits, and by using academic strategies described in this chapter such as mindmapping, cognitive cues, visual editing strips, and the use of word processors, Devorah became increasingly successful in written expression. By the time she was in middle school, Devorah had made great progress and even won a State of Georgia writing contest! Everyone was proud, but no one was as proud and happy as Devorah and her parents.

The skills and confidence Devorah gained from her remediation led to success in college, a happy marriage, and now a baby. Early academic failure could have kept her from having a successful life. Remediation made all the difference.

CHAPTER 20

Mathematics

Do not worry about your problems in mathematics. I assure you, my problems with mathematics are much greater than yours.
— *Albert Einstein*

Chandler was in the gifted program but whenever he had to do math facts in his head, he would throw up his hands and say, "Would someone please just shoot me and put me out my misery?" No matter how much he tried, he could not memorize his math facts. His teacher, trying to be helpful, suggested that he keep track on his fingers. Chandler looked down at his hands, where his fingers were tapping and moving. "Thanks," he said, "but I don't think that will work."

Preview

If written expression (Chapter 19) is the most common type of academic impairment for students with the disorders described in this book, math calculation may be the second most common academic area of difficulty. The students usually understand the math concepts but are often unable to calculate accurately, efficiently, sequentially, and in an organized manner. Memory for math facts is another common problem. Some children have learning weaknesses in math reasoning, e.g., word problems. This impairment usually does not rise to the level of a learning disability.

Math is very difficult due to the need for precision in exact sequences, and spatial and visual organization. Any difficulty at any point in the calculation process can result in an error. The unforgiving nature of math calculation makes it a great challenge for kids in this group.

Description of Math Difficulties

The following sections describe the impact of specific disorders or types of symptoms on math production.

Handwriting/Visual-Motor Integration and Math

Note: Chapter 17 provides additional information on handwriting and VMI issues.
- Students with ADHD, TS, Asperger's Syndrome, and EDF are more likely to have:
  - sloppy handwriting,
  - poor spacing between digits, and
  - trouble lining up columns of digits.
- Visual-motor integration (VMI) problems lead to errors when copying math problems from a book or the board.
- Visual tracking difficulties cause some students to lose their place and copy math symbols, especially digits, inaccurately.
- Symptom interference in handwriting.

Executive Dysfunction and Math

Note: Chapter 9 provides additional information on EDF.
- Failure to self-monitor may lead to errors in copying digits and operational symbols. It

also leads to problems writing and correcting work simultaneously, and checking work.

- Deficits in prioritizing impair the ability to solve word problems because the student has trouble identifying the important words.
- Deficits in sequencing impair retaining multi-step sequences.
- Difficulties in initiating and completing affect doing math homework.
- Deficits in organization affect all aspects of homework, including math, because students fail to take their math book out of their locker or desk or fail to record the assignment, or fail to pack it in the book bag. If by some miracle the homework gets done, organizational issues interfere with turning in the assignment.

Working Memory and Math

Note: Chapter 10 provides additional information on working memory.

- Reduced working memory capacity can lead to:
  - ❏ Errors in copying, noting digits, or identifying operational symbols. This is particularly evident when transferring information from one source to another (e.g., from the board to paper).
  - ❏ Errors in math reasoning. Holding all the material in a word problem in memory while trying to compare and contrast what information was given is very difficult.
  - ❏ Errors in mental calculations. As an analogy, if the student had a calculator that could only enter five digits before it had to be cleared and the problem required seven digits, the student would likely generate an incorrect answer.
- Working memory deficits interfere with:
  - ❏ Memorizing math facts.
  - ❏ Converting words to the appropriate operations symbols.
  - ❏ Converting units, such as converting inches to feet, cups to pints, etc.
  - ❏ Tracking sequential steps in math calculations

Obsessions and Compulsions and Math

Note: Chapter 5 provides additional information on OCD.

- Compulsions to produce perfect work may lead students with OCD to retrace digits over and over or erase and rewrite until the numbers look perfect. This may mean not finishing work on time.
- Intrusive thoughts/obsessions and compulsions can significantly interfere with tracking mental operations. For example, the student may be driven to mentally recite the lyrics of a song over and over while performing a calculation.
- Obsessions or compulsions may involve particular numbers. For example, the student may have to compulsively count the letters in word problems, or refuse to write certain digits.

Tics and Math

Note: Chapter 4 provides additional information on TS.

- Arm tics or head/neck/eye tics can interfere directly with the student's ability to keep her place in her math calculations.
- The sensory urge build-up that precedes tics for many students can mentally distract them from mental calculations.

Attention Deficit Hyperactivity Disorder and Math

Note: Chapter 8 provides additional information on ADHD.

The cardinal features of ADHD—inattention, hyperactivity, and impulsivity—all impair math production. Students with ADHD may not be able to:

- Sit long enough to complete a multi-step math problem.
- Pay attention when important information is provided.
- Pay attention to details.
- Control the impulsivity that leads to errors in calculation, copying a problem from the board or book, and rewriting work to an answer sheet.

Tricks and Tips for Math

General

- Accommodate handwriting and VMI issues:
  - ❑ Use lined paper turned sideways, graph paper with boxes, or ruler guides to help students line up numbers vertically.
  - ❑ Adjust worksheets to provide larger workspace for large, sloppy handwriting.
  - ❑ Reduce copying from the board or copying questions from a test form.
  - ❑ Give a copy of notes, overheads, or PowerPoint™ slides to assist the student in acquiring the information, or use a proctor to copy data.

- Accommodate attentional or impulsivity issues:
  - ❑ Use color to highlight operational symbols; use a different color for each type.
  - ❑ Teach the student the strategy of highlighting operational symbols.
  - ❑ Use color to highlight important directions.
  - ❑ Reduce the number of problems on a page.
  - ❑ Fold or cover part of the worksheet so that the student sees only one problem at a time.

- Accommodate memory and processing speed deficits:
  - ❑ State directions one at a time; wait for the student to do the step, and then deliver the next direction.
  - ❑ Teach math tricks to students who have difficulty with rote memorization or sustaining focus. (See math facts below.)
  - ❑ Teach cognitive cues for sequential tasks to reduce memory demands.
  - ❑ Check for comprehension of directions, e.g., check the first math problem in an assignment to make sure it is correct. Otherwise, the student may simply rehearse incorrect methods.
  - ❑ Extend time on math classwork, homework, and tests.

- Reduce the number of problems to be done for any one assignment, e.g., every other problem, as long as the student can demonstrate mastery of the math skill. Reducing the number of problems provides the student with time to edit her math work.

- Draw the actions embedded in word problems using pictures or symbols or whatever assists the student in reducing the demands on working memory. Teach this concept to help the student understand how this would apply in other math areas, e.g., geometry proofs.

- Provide a chart of math words that relate to operations and their operational symbols.

- Ask the student to scratch out unnecessary words in the word problems. Check to see if the executive skills make this too difficult for some students and require the teacher to teach which words are important and which ones are not.

- Teach using manipulatives for more concrete, meaningful instruction. This is especially smart when beginning new instruction. Many elementary teachers already use manipulatives but middle and high school teachers frequently do not.

- Incorporate multi-sensory activities.

- Give the student a solved model of the problem that is being taught at the top of each worksheet or homework assignment.

- Make sure that the student has an organized approach for solving a type of math problem and put that approach in the student's "trick" book (Chapter 28) to be readily available the next time it is needed.

- Permit opportunities for movement or breaks, e.g., math games that are fun.

- Use a mastery system to promote success. This means that the student has not mastered the task until she can do it nine out of ten times with checks at three, six, and nine months to see if this is still automatic.

- Allow use of a calculator.

A calculator can be helpful because it decreases demands on memory, and only provides correct answers if the student understands the math concepts. If students do not understand math concepts, using a calculator does not help them.

Specific

- Use cognitive tricks to help the student retain conversion tables. For example, "Kids

Figure 20.1. Math Editing Strip

From (Dornbush and Pruitt 1995)

Hate Doing Most Dirty Chores, Mom!" (Pruitt 1977) is a cognitive trick to remember the order of meters, so that K refers to kilometers, H to hectometers, D to dekameters, M to meters, D to decimeters, C to centimeters, and M to millimeters.

- Provide visual or cognitive cues to help the student maintain the sequence of operations (e.g., "Does McDonald's Sell Burgers?" is a cognitive cue for Divide, Multiply, Subtract, and Bring down—the sequence of steps in long division). (Source Unknown.)

- Teach concepts using concrete, meaningful examples before introducing more abstract concepts, e.g., use a pizza to teach fractions—the student will quickly learn that one quarter is greater than one eighth when offered a choice between the two and seeing the results of the decision. Teach the student that one eighth of a piece means that the top number is the number of pieces left to eat and the bottom number is the number of pieces that the pizza was originally cut into.

Meaning equals memory!

- Have an aide or assistant check that all work has been copied accurately.
- Provide math editing strips to remind students to check and edit their math work.

Figure 20.1 depicts a math editing strip that can be put on students' desks. The first four symbols remind the students to check the operational symbols in their work. The bars remind them to check to see that their numbers line up vertically. The dollar sign reminds them to check for its inclusion and placement of the dollar sign. The decimal point reminds them to check for inclusion and placement of the decimal point. The check mark reminds them to check their computations. Students should check one at a time when using the editing strip.

Figure 20.2 depicts an editing strip that is an adaptation of an old strategy for the order of operations in solving an algebraic equation. The strategy is remembering "**B.B. PEMDAS**" for Braces, Brackets, Parentheses, Exponents, Multiplication, Division, Addition, Subtraction. This serves as both a cognitive and visual strategy.

Math Facts

Despite rehearsal and over-rehearsal, some students are unable to memorize math facts. For these students, use cognitive strategies to teach math facts rather than flash cards. Make use of cognitive strategies for every math fact. For example, consider 7 x 8 = 56. This is one of the hardest math facts for students to memorize. The sequence 7, 8, 5, 6 is meaningless, but the sequence 5, 6, 7, 8 is a very meaningful sequence. Just show this to the student and ask her to remember the numbers just before "9" in

Figure 20.2. Algebraic Visual Editing Strip: B.B. PEMDAS

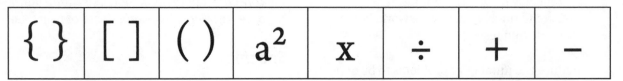

Adapted by Darin M. Bush (1992).

the normal sequence of counting, i.e., "56 = 7 x 8" (Dornbush and Pruitt 1995). These cognitive cues make retrieval of facts significantly more efficient.

Drilling math facts with flash cards is often punitive and inefficient for these students.

Summary

Math calculations are the second most common academic problem experienced by students with the disorders described in this book. Many of these students experience math content deficits such as memory for math facts, and many are unable to get math on paper with accuracy due to handwriting problems, visual-motor integration problems, or symptom interference. In addition, some have significant problems retaining the sequence of operations. Math reasoning may be impaired by deficits in working memory or Executive Dysfunction, e.g., retaining and organizing the information required to solve word problems. Some students will require direct instruction in the use of cognitive strategies to succeed in math, some will require editing cues and modified materials, and many will require extended time and decreased production requirements.

Chandler was taught cognitive strategies to help him memorize math facts. When his teacher taught him the trick for remembering 7 x 8, Chandler actually stood up and applauded. "I'll never forget that one again!" he said. Chandler enjoyed learning other tricks for math facts, and his self-confidence in math increased dramatically. Within a few weeks, Chandler was able to learn all the math facts that he had struggled with for months.

Reading

Kim always tested well in reading assessments. She had a good sight vocabulary and excellent decoding skills. At the same time, she resisted reading in school. No matter how hard she tried and no matter what rewards she offered as inducement, the teacher could not get Kim to willingly read in school.

Preview

Reading is undoubtedly one of the most important skills in the educational setting. Although the rate of reading disabilities in students with most of the disorders covered in this book is no higher than in the general student population, specific aspects of the disorders may interfere with reading and require accommodations.

Description of Reading Difficulties

Basic reading is defined as the ability to decode or sound out words or to memorize and identify sight vocabulary words. Reading comprehension is the ability to understand what is read. Symptom interference is the primary difficulty these students experience.

- ADHD causes inattention to details in reading, impulsive fast reading, distractibility during reading, and being too overaroused and hyperactive to sit still to read.
- Simple motor tics such as eye, head, neck, and arm tics may interfere with the ability to decipher the printed page or to maintain smooth visual tracking of the printed line.

Simple tics may also indirectly interfere with the ability to remember what was read, thereby interfering with comprehension.

- Obsessions and compulsions can cause a multitude of reading difficulties:
  - Obsessive thoughts can interfere with concentration on the written material, reducing reading rate and interfering with comprehension.
  - Hidden rituals such as counting may seriously interfere with reading rate and comprehension. Counting may involve having to count specific letters, or it may involve having to count the number of words, or the number of letters in words, etc., as illustrated in the school impact vignette in the chapter on OCD or as in the case below.

A student was referred to a clinic for reading problems involving decoding and comprehension. During the screening, the therapist asked the student what caused her the most difficulty. She said that it was hard to read and count every third letter at the same time. The therapist asked her if she could stop the counting and she said she got this "yucky" feeling that got bigger and bigger until she started counting again. Her reading problem was not a reading problem; it was OCD.

- Mood disorders can cause over- or underarousal, both of which may interfere with reading. Mania can make it quite difficult to read as thoughts may be racing in the student's head and reading becomes somewhat impulsive. Underarousal can result in slow processing causing great difficulty in being able to persist at lengthy, time-sensitive reading assignments. The slow processing also impedes comprehension.

- Executive Dysfunction (EDF) interferes at the very point of beginning to read if there are initiation deficits. EDF may also interfere with the ability to execute and complete reading activities. The inability to organize and prioritize places excessive demands on memory and interferes with the ability to answer the questions at the end of a chapter.
- Working memory deficits impair the students' ability to hold onto facts while trying to process the information. The inability to float multiple ideas simultaneously interferes with the ability to compare and contrast, thereby interfering with the ability to draw inferences.
- Visual-motor deficits interfere with tracking information while reading. Tracking involves using the fine motor movements of the eye to maintain a smooth, consistent ability to follow each letter, word, and line in an appropriate order without losing one's place. Many students find themselves on the wrong line when reading and, as a result, lose their train of thought.

When it is difficult to sit and listen due to symptom interference, students may benefit from listening to books on tape/CD. This allows the students to be able to listen to their textbooks or engage in pleasure "reading" and not fall behind in their work or in their vocabulary and knowledge development. Sources for books on tape and CD are provided in the Resources section of this book.

Difficulties with Graphic Reading Skills

Graphic reading is the ability to read and comprehend material presented in visual images such as graphs, lines, charts, and maps. There are different types of graphic reading tasks:

- Sequential: flowcharts, timelines, organizational charts, and process charts
- Quantitative: number lines, bar graphs, line graphs, pictographs, and pie charts
- Maps: political, physical, and special purpose maps
- Diagrams: cross sections, blueprints, and machine drawings
- Tables/Charts: row-by-row column matrices

Students with the disorders described in this book tend to have problems with all types of graphic reading tasks. The difficulties are due mainly to symptom interference, including:

- Inability to visualize
- Inability to process too much visual information due to working memory deficits
- Difficulty relating graphic information to text due to working memory deficits
- Inability to attend to visual material
- Inability to stay in precise place on graphic, e.g., tracking, problems or tic interference
- Obsessing about what material has been omitted from a graphic representation due to perfectionist symptoms of OCD
- Executive Dysfunction impact:
  - ❑ Prioritizing what is the most important information in the visual field and what is not and can be ignored
  - ❑ Maintaining the organization and sequencing of the material

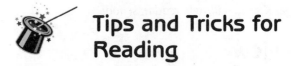

Tips and Tricks for Reading

How to Read a Chapter

Students who have difficulty reading a chapter due to attention problems or other sources of interference may benefit from the following teacher and student strategies:

1. The teacher sets up clear instructional objectives for self and students.
2. The teacher introduces the subject by playing a video or TV program, letting students listen to a tape or CD, do a hands-on project, or some other activity that connects it to students' experiences.
3. The teacher defines the vocabulary and provides a handout with proper spelling and definitions. The teacher will tie in the vocabulary during class discussion.

The students then complete the remaining steps, with guidance from the teacher, as needed, while they are learning this routine:

4. Overview the chapter, story, or book before beginning to read.
5. Look at and discuss all pictures and captions.
6. Read all graphs, timelines, and visual materials.

7. Read the chapter summary.
8. Read the questions at end of the section.
9. Make a list of what he will be looking for as he reads the section.
10. Read each section, making a list of important points in the section while reading it.
11. Answer questions at the end of the section.
12. Cover each section this way.
13. Reread the chapter summary.
14. Answer the questions at the end of chapter.

Adapted from © 1994 M.K. Jennings & S. K. Pruitt, M.Ed., in (Dornbush and Pruitt 1995)

Note that in this sequence of steps, reading the chapter is not the first step. This approach does not make reading classwork or homework take longer because most students who read the chapter first have to reread once they get to the end and realize that they cannot answer the questions.

General Strategies to Teach Graphic Reading Skills

- Draw the students' attention to the graph and provide direct instruction in how to read and interpret it.
- Connect interpretation to students' experience.
- Use direct instruction to teach reading skills:
  - ❏ Determine what graphic information is contained in text. What information is in graphs? How does it relate to the text? What other information could the class graph?
  - ❏ Discuss whether graphs in text are clear or confusing. The class may make up a better display.
  - ❏ Have students choose what they consider relevant, important, or key ideas that can be displayed graphically.
  - ❏ Move away from traditional graphic display forms and create your own. Use maps, webs, and other visual illustrations. Tap into students' creative abilities.

(Jennings 1993)

Reading Strategies for Content Area Classes

General Strategies:

- Make sure that you are testing the material and not symptom interference. For example, ensure that the student's ability to answer a biology question on a test is not confounded by his difficulty reading and understanding the test directions.
- Ensure that the student knows the instructional objective.
- Detect the students' underlying skill deficits, e.g., difficulty with reading and comprehending written directions.
- Provide an overview of books, chapters, and sections to the students so that they understand how the material is organized and how material is emphasized.
- Avoid asking for oral reading.
- Vary rates of presentation.
- Vary levels of sophistication of presentation.
- Vary styles of presentation, e.g., cognitive, auditory, visual.
- Use context cues for decoding and/or vocabulary.

Strategies for Memory and Metacognition:

Students with the disorders described in this book often have working memory or specific types of long-term memory problems. Metacognition is thinking about thinking, i.e., awareness of how we think and learn. Metacognitive strategies are strategies that are not content-specific but refer to an overall approach to learning. To foster greater memory and learning:

- Encourage reading with a pencil, underlining, highlighting, color coding, and making notes in the margins.
- Use cognitive strategies rather than rote memory to teach facts.
- Emphasize logic; do not over-rely on memory. Help students differentiate what must be memorized from what can be figured out.
- Encourage frequent self-testing. Use flashcards, tapes, etc.
- Provide clear, sequenced review sheets for tests. Be sure they are typed, clear, and provide enough white space.

Reading Strategies for Students with Executive Dysfunction:*

- Use directions that are clear and specific.
- Teach the student to highlight key words that tell them what to do.

---

* From (Jennings, 1993)

- Teach the student to number each direction when there is more than one direction in the material to be read.
- Teach the student to follow the directions and not just read them, checking off each step of the directions as it is completed.
- Teach the student how to read and follow directions at the beginning of the year in every course of study.
- Use the same format for directions and questions on tests that are used for every-day classwork.

When creating exams, make sure that they assess whether students know the material, not whether they understand the directions.

Strategies for Prioritizing and Organizing Reading Material:

- Provide a syllabus emphasizing primary ideas.
- Offer a visual organizational strategy (mind-mapping, treeing, webbing) as a tool for notetaking or organizing reading material.
- Give extra help—daily if necessary—with maintenance of notebooks. Model notebook requirements often.
- Teach efficient research skills to relieve some of the homework overload students often feel.
- Integrate the curriculum, where possible, to reduce the amount of reading and to reduce potentially conflicting demands on organization and prioritization.

Strategies to Use When Symptoms Interfere with Normal Reading Ability:

- Avoid asking students to read aloud.
- Encourage use of tape recorders. This is extremely useful for both notetaking and listening comprehension, since it relieves the stress of "having to get every word" the first time.
- Use recorded textbooks.
- Use movies or videos.
- Allow movement while reading and/or listening.

Strategies for Reading Literature, Social Studies, and Any Other Language-Based Subjects:

- Place event or person from the text in time; make a simple timeline.
- Place event or person from the text in space; locate and mark on a map.

- Explore cause and effect. What caused the event from the text to happen or what caused the person to do a certain thing? If two things happen in the same time frame, does one necessarily cause the other or are they simply simultaneous?
- Compare and contrast event or person with others of that time period or in a similar situation.
- Analyze for validity. Do you think this writer is accurate or is his statement an opinion being treated as a fact?

From (Jennings 1993), modified by S. K. Pruitt

Strategies for Reading for Cause and Effect:*

- Teach students that effect may come first in a sentence (e.g., "James got mad when Johnny hit him.").
- Teach students key words or phrases that help them recognize cause or effect. For example, "because" signals that what follows is the cause, whereas "as a consequence" signals that the following material is an effect, and a question that begins with "why" is asking for a cause.
- Have students create their own cause and effect sentences and problems.
- Help the student number sentence parts with #1 for cause and #2 for effect or result.

Summary

When a student is having difficulty with reading, curiosity needs to be your starting place. It is important not to assume that the reading problem is due to a deficit in basic reading skills or reading comprehension. Remember, reading difficulties can also be due to direct symptom interference from a neurological disorder.

Kim's teacher sat down with her one day and asked her what happened when she tried to read. Kim told her, "It's so frustrating. I start to read and then, suddenly, my eyes have missed a line or I wind up losing track of where I was reading." Kim's teacher understood this as having visual tracking problems. She taught her some simple strategies to help her keep her place while reading. Within a few weeks, Kim was reading more in school and actually starting to enjoy reading.

---

* Adapted from (Parkaire Consultants 1991)

CHAPTER 22

Accommodations for Testing and Classroom Assignments

Although Maddiha was obviously very bright, she was failing all of her classes. The school had not given her any accommodations on testing because her eye tics seemed pretty mild and infrequent. When Maddiha's parents requested testing accommodations for her, they were told she was not eligible because her problems were not severe enough.

Preview

Previous chapters described conditions that may directly or indirectly interfere with learning and performance in the classroom. This chapter reviews some of the most frequently needed accommodations in both testing situations and classroom assignments. We do not distinguish between "accommodations" and "modifications" in this chapter, although we recognize that some states *do* make a distinction between what is considered an "accommodation" and what is considered a "modification."

 ## Testing Accommodations

Students with the disorders described in this book may require a variety or combination of testing accommodations, as listed below:

Check for Comprehension of Test Directions

- Highlight test directions.
- Make sure the student understands test directions before starting the test.

Extend Time

Students who are experiencing direct or indirect interference from symptoms may require extended time for tests. The following are examples of symptom interference that may necessitate extended time on tests:

- tics
- obsessive worry
- rituals
- distractibility
- cognitive dulling due to medication
- memory impairment
- word retrieval deficits
- muscle cramps or painful handwriting
- fatigue
- depressed mood

Students with the combined subtype of ADHD with no mood or obsessive-compulsive symptoms may not benefit from extra time if that is the only modification provided. For these students, use extended time in conjunction with checking for comprehension of test directions. Students who require extended time on tests may also require extended time on quizzes. If extended time cannot be provided in the classroom due to other classes coming in, etc., testing in a separate location may be necessary.

Use Flexible Testing Schedule

As with extended time, students with the disorders described in this book may require a flexible testing schedule. Some students (such as those who are depressed) have significant sleep problems and cannot get to school on time in the morning. Students with OCD may be unable to get to school on time in the morning due to interference from significant obsessions and rituals.

Perhaps one of the major—and frequently overlooked—factors requiring flexible testing schedules is medication. Some types of medication "kick in" and "wear off" during the school day, including many of the short acting psychostimulant medications used to treat ADHD. Many of the longer acting stimulants and other classes of longer acting medications do not tend to "wear off" during the school day. Children absorb or metabolize medications at different rates. When a student's medication is wearing off, the student may experience increased activity, agitation, and poorer mood, with more distractibility and difficulty focusing.

Consult with both the student and the parent(s) to determine the best time of day to test the child. This also applies to psychoeducational assessments. Determine how long the student can be tested at any one time and the total amount of testing the student can handle in one day. Break big tests up over a course of days.

Remember that the goal of testing is to determine what the student has learned. By accommodating medication issues, the test evaluates what the student has learned, rather than evaluating her endurance or what she can do under adverse conditions. Symptom interference can cause a student to fail tests, even if she knows the information.

Provide Movement Opportunities and Breaks

Many of the disorders described in this book are associated with the need for increased movement. Students who suffer from hyperactivity, have motor tics, tire easily when writing, or who experience a sense of inner restlessness due to medication may all need opportunities to get up and move around. Students who have significant difficulty sustaining their focus due to ADHD, mood disorder, memory issues, or medication may also require breaks during lengthy testing. In planning for the student, consult with the student, the parents, and other professionals involved with the student to determine how often to provide movement breaks and how long the breaks need to be. One way to provide movement breaks during a test is to divide the test into smaller sections so that the student only gets one section at a time and can take a movement break between sections.

Test in Alternative Location or Setting

Depending on the student's situation, testing in a separate location may be necessary for the student's benefit or the benefit of peers. Any of the disorders described in this book may require testing in a separate location depending on the nature and severity of the student's symptoms. For example, students with tic disorders such as TS may experience a tic exacerbation when they are under the stress of testing conditions. Some will want to stay in the classroom but others may want to be tested where others cannot see or hear the increased tics. For students who have motor tics (but not vocal tics), testing in a separate location can often be avoided by creating a partitioned or screened off area of the room where the student can take the test without peers being able to observe. If students have phonic tics that distract others or that cause them great embarrassment, sending them to a small-group setting will not work, and they will require 1:1 testing. Testing in a separate location might also be necessary when extended time is required but cannot be provided in the regular classroom.

It makes no sense to send a student to a separate location if there are as many students in the separate location as there are in the classroom.

For some students, testing in a 1:1 situation with a proctor who is known to them and with whom they feel comfortable is necessary. Other students may be okay in a small group setting (such as 5:1). In some schools, however, all students who require testing in a separate location may be sent to one classroom at one time, resulting in having ten, twenty, or more students with special needs in the alternate setting. Students who need help understanding test directions, test questions, or copying over test questions or answers may also require testing in a separate location.

Allow Oral Testing

Oral testing as an alternative to written testing may be required for a variety of reasons:

- Students with severe handwriting problems or poor writing endurance may not be able to adequately demonstrate their knowledge if forced to handwrite their answers.
- Students with reading or writing rituals due to OCD may not be able to adequately

demonstrate their knowledge due to symptom interference.

- Students with eye, head/neck, or arm tics may experience direct interference with reading test questions and writing answers. Even students who do not have head/neck or eye tics may experience interference sitting and reading/writing, e.g., students who have severe or forceful leg tics.

Circle Answers or Record Answers Directly in Test Booklet

This type of accommodation may be required for students who have:

- compulsive rituals that prevent them from using computer (Scantron) recording forms where they may get stuck trying to fill in just the first circle perfectly.
- large, sloppy handwriting that does not permit them to record their answers in the available space on the recording form.
- deficits in visual tracking that interfere with putting the answer in the right circle or row.
- deficits in visual tracking or visual-motor integration problems and are likely to miss words or miscopy answers from a scrap sheet to the recording form.

Do Not Penalize for Spelling Errors

Unless it is a spelling test, do not penalize for spelling errors. Encourage students to use an electronic spell checker.

Provide Word Banks or Multiple Choice Format

Students with memory retrieval problems due to OCD, mood disorders, or medication side effects may not be able to retrieve what they know in a timely fashion. Provide word banks for fill-in-the-blank questions or use multiple choice format instead of a fill-in-the-blank format.

Permit Use of Calculator

Students with the disorders covered in this book may experience interference with mental or written math calculations (even when they know the work and correct procedures) due to symptom interference. For example, students with EDF and associated working memory deficits may have difficulty remembering and preserving the sequence of steps in math calculations even when they understand the material being tested.

Allowing a student to use a calculator for a test may seem like bypassing a genuine test of the student's math skills, but remember that the student must have an understanding of the operations and skills in order to be able to use the calculator properly to solve the problems.

Permit Sensory Filtering

Some students with distractibility issues develop their own techniques to help them block out external distractions. These visual or auditory aids may involve the use of headphones playing white noise or familiar music, or allowing the student to wear a baseball cap or pull the hood up on her sweatshirt to serve as blinders.

Many schools prohibit students from wearing baseball caps in school, but if the student is using the cap as a sensory filter, the student's team may wish to permit it as a reasonable accommodation. If the student and parents permit, educating the peers as to why an exception is being made will help address any feelings of unfair or unequal treatment.

Provide a Larger Desk or Additional Space and Additional Blank Paper

- Due to working memory deficits, many students cannot float very much information in memory while taking the test. They may require extra blank sheets of paper so that they can write down their memory tricks after they sit down to take the test but before they start the test.
- Some students require a larger table or desk because they need to keep all papers in front of them since they cannot hold onto the information in memory.
- Some students may need more paper and room for mathematics tests due to the size of some of the student's written production. It can be oversized for some and require extended space.
- Some students may need extra paper and space so that they can draw word problems as they read them.

- For students with deficits in tracking and working memory, copying from a work sheet to the test recording sheet requires enough desk space to display both papers.

Add Adult Assistance

Students may require additional adult assistance for a variety of reasons, such as:
- to check for comprehension of the directions.
- to clarify test questions.
- to write (scribe) for the student.
- to ensure that the student has accurately copied over answers to the test booklet or to copy over the answers for the student.
- to read test questions to the student if tics or compulsions are interfering with reading.
- to proctor the student if the student needs to take a break outside of the classroom during the test.

Permit the Use of Word Processors

Some students experience significant handwriting problems, so any handwritten project underestimates the depth and breadth of their knowledge. Allowing the student to use a word processor or to dictate via voice activation software may enable them to show us what they really know.

Accommodate Handwriting Issues

In addition to the accommodations mentioned previously, other test accommodations may be required, such as:
- modifying materials to allow more space for problem solving and more space for recording answers. Ask the student if wide-lined paper and/or column guides would be helpful.
- reducing the amount to be handwritten at any one time.
- providing additional time that is specifically allocated for proofing and editing written work.
- grading for content, not for neatness.
- ensuring that any work or problem that is copied over to another paper is copied correctly before the student attempts the work.
- ensuring that answers are copied completely and accurately if work is copied from a scratch sheet to final answer sheet.

Allow Alternative Testing and Additional Opportunities to Demonstrate Mastery

Some students need alternative versions of tests to achieve or demonstrate mastery. By allowing students to take alternative versions of tests as many times as needed until they demonstrate mastery or achieve a grade that they are satisfied with, they learn not to give up. Although it may take them a bit longer than their peers to master a particular unit or skill, they gain the satisfaction of knowing that they can do it.[*] Providing alternative versions of tests and allowing students to retake tests also eliminates the need for curving grades.

Remember that we want the student to master the material, not pass or fail a test. Testing can be an open door to point to areas where further instruction is needed as opposed to a stopping point when it comes to instruction.

Reduce Student's Test Anxiety

- Assure students that making a mistake on a test is not the end of the world; they will have more than one opportunity to show us what they know.
- Have students work at an instructional level that ensures success on tests so that their anxiety is replaced with confidence.
- Break tests into smaller pieces so that students only see one small section at a time.

Judy had test anxiety. When she told her teacher, her teacher said, "So did I!" Immediately Judy felt safer, understood, and less anxious. The teacher used this as an opportunity to bond with Judy. The teacher had Judy laughing at their anxiety, and helped her realize that their brains were tricking them into being scared. The explanation and common experience allowed Judy to relax and take the test without as much anxiety.

---

* Leslie spent almost a decade teaching undergraduate statistics. By using a mastery approach, the undergraduate students generally attained much higher levels of understanding and skills than in the typical undergraduate statistics course. Testimonials from the students about how inspiring it was to know that they could achieve top grades if they persisted in their efforts and how much they had learned contributed to the university requiring all undergraduate statistics courses to use a mastery approach.

Having extra time for some students with test anxiety allows them to relax enough not to need the extra time. For others, having extra time is necessary to retrieve information from memory because anxiety has a negative impact on retrieval.

When a student has working memory problems, multiple choice formats can be anxiety producing because the student has to float all of the incorrect answers in memory while searching for the correct answer. Teaching students to cross out incorrect answers reduces the amount of information that they need to hold in memory and therefore reduces anxiety over the task.

Use Accommodations for Classroom Tests as Well as Big Tests

The accommodations required for standardized tests also apply to classroom tests. Unfortunately, in many cases, accommodations are used only for big tests or projects and are not incorporated or provided routinely for all tests. If a student needs more space on a test because of handwriting issues, then they need more space for classroom assignments, too. If a student needs to have the amount of handwritten work reduced on tests, then the student also needs that accommodation on classroom assignments.

All of the accommodations described here for testing may also be required for classroom assignments.

Coordinate with Other Teachers

Having a grade-wide testing calendar for the teachers to use to coordinate their test schedules is an extremely important element of planning. Many students have memory problems that prohibit floating facts for more than one subject at a time. Other students with anxiety get overwhelmed with one test and totally fall apart if they have two tests on the same day. The goal is to measure knowledge and skills and not to measure the student's tolerance for anxiety. Because of this, it is important to adjust and coordinate test schedules.

Summary

Students with neurological disorders almost invariably require at least some accommodations in classroom assignments and testing. Accommodations "level the playing field" for the students so that they have an equal opportunity to learn and to demonstrate their knowledge. By understanding the impact of the students' disorders, the students' team can work with parents, the students, and other professionals to develop a list of necessary and appropriate accommodations.

Although Maddiha's eye tics appeared mild and infrequent to school personnel, they did not know that Maddiha had other tics that she was struggling mightily to suppress so that the other middle school children would not tease her. Throughout the day, she was fighting the need to make snorting sounds and to slap her hand on the desk. The teachers were shocked to find out that Maddiha was spending more time and energy on suppressing her tics than on learning and on the test questions. Once they understood that the fear of embarrassment overrode her ability to focus on tests and to show them what she knew, they realized that she needed to be tested in a separate location where she would not have to fear peer ridicule if she ticced.

CHAPTER 23

Homework Issues

Eric had not done any homework in two years. But because he had not done any classwork, either, his team had started by targeting academic productivity in school. Once Eric was complying with tasks in school and achieving good grades on his classwork, his team decided to tackle the homework issue. In a meeting with Eric's mother, when the team raised the issue of homework, Eric's mother turned pale. "I know homework is important," she said, "but I don't know if I'm ready to deal with all of the fights this will cause. The last time we tried to get him to do homework, we wound up with a lot of holes in the walls." The psychologist reassured her that the team would talk with Eric to help him get on board and that the plan would not require her to nag him or get into any fights with him. Somewhat doubtfully, Eric's mother consented to let the team try to address the homework issue.

Overview of Homework Issues

Homework is important for academic achievement, especially for high school students (Cooper and Nye 1994). One of the major reasons students with disabilities fail in integrated settings is because of problems with homework completion (Epstein et al. 1993; Epstein, Foley, and Polloway 1995). Both students and parents need to understand that homework skills prepare the student for the mundane, routine tasks of independent living such as recording responsibilities, meeting deadlines, and completing uninteresting lengthy projects, such as income tax returns.

Factors contributing to homework problems include the student being unable to work indepen-

dently and inadequate parental support to complete homework assignments (Battle-Bailey 2003). A number of additional factors contribute to homework issues for students with the types of neurological problems described in this book. Figure 23.1 on the next page illustrates the factors that may contribute to homework problems. If a student is experiencing homework difficulties, the school team can interview the parent(s) and/or student about each of these factors to help the team determine which accommodations the student requires.

Many parents and students believe that because the students are so bright and understand the material, they can be excused from homework. Parents sometimes advocate for homework elimination from their child's program, perhaps because the student is tired and symptomatic, and homework becomes a battleground. Even given these objections to requiring homework, homework is essential preparation for independent living.

Medication Issues

Some medications used to treat the disorders covered in this book are relatively short-acting, i.e., they exert their main effect within one hour and wear off several hours later. Other medications remain in the system for longer periods. The implications for homework are clear: If a student is taking a medication to help with focus and the medication has worn off by homework time, the student will likely struggle to concentrate on his homework. This is often the case for students with ADHD who may take their last dose of a psychostimulant medication in school at lunch time to get them through the

Figure 23.1. Factors That Impact Homework

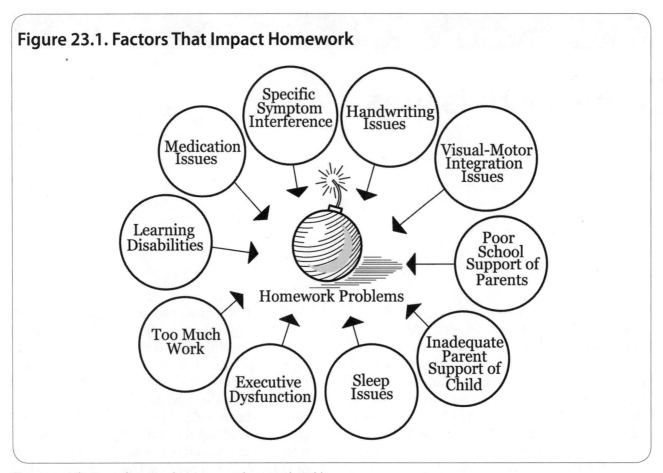

Factors contributing to homework resistance or homework problems.

school day. Although some physicians recommend an afternoon dose to get the student through homework time, many of these medications interfere with appetite and sleep, and parents are understandably reluctant to give them if it means that their child won't eat dinner or sleep at night. School personnel are encouraged to specifically ask parents about the student's ability to focus during homework time.

Along with the possibility that medications may wear off by homework time, some students on stimulant medications suffer what are called "rebound" effects as their medication wears off. If the medication simply wears off, the student is essentially in an unmedicated state. In rebound, the student's symptoms are actually worse than they would have been in an unmedicated state. For example, some students become irritable and weepy as their medication wears off, even though they would not be irritable and weepy if they had never taken the medication. Such rebound effects are likely to interfere with doing homework.

In addition to psychostimulant medications used to treat ADHD, medications used for other conditions can also interfere with homework. The older neuroleptics (e.g., Haldol®) that are still used in some cas-

es to treat tics may produce cognitive dulling. Mood stabilizers for Bipolar Disorder such as variants of lithium can also produce significant cognitive dulling. The newer, atypical neuroleptics that are used to treat tics or mania do not produce as much cognitive dulling. Because medications that cause cognitive dulling tend to be long-lasting medications, students taking these medications require the same accommodations at home for homework as they need for classwork. Finally, some medications can cause drowsiness or lethargy independent of cognitive dulling. Lethargy can interfere with homework completion.

For tips and strategies, see the medication side effects chapter (Chapter 24). Also, consult with the student, the parents, and treating professionals as to necessary and helpful accommodations.

Specific Symptom Interference

Some disorders produce symptoms that can directly interfere with the completion of homework. For example:

- Tics of the head, neck, eyes, or arms can directly interfere with reading assignments at home. Tics can also interfere with the memorization process when students are assigned to rehearse and memorize math facts. Because many students suppress their tics in school and "explode" in tics and emotional behaviors when they get home, homework time may be a time of day when the students' tics are so severe as to make homework an almost overwhelming challenge. Because of the discrepancy in symptom severity between school and home, teachers of students with tics need to specifically inquire about the students' tic frequency and severity in the home in the afternoon, to make appropriate accommodations.

- Obsessions and compulsions (described in Chapter 5) can interfere with homework completion. What might take a student twenty minutes may take hours if a student is "stuck," e.g., counting letters, having to reread material or reading it backwards after reading it forwards, or if there are handwriting rituals that are so severe that the student keeps ripping up his completed work and rewriting it. When the homework assignment is a paper or project, a student with OCD may stay up all night making it perfect.

- Anxiety can interfere with the student's belief that he can handle the work needed to do the homework. Just thinking about a project can produce so much anxiety that the student shuts down and is unable to do the work.

- Inattention and distractibility due to ADHD have obvious implications for starting and completing homework. Additionally, students with hyperactivity may find it difficult or impossible to sit at home and read or to do homework after having struggled to sit still all day in school. Reading may be particularly difficult or frustrating for students who need to move around unless they learn strategies such as rocking while they read or listening to books on tape/CD as they move around. Many students with combined-type ADHD, even with modifications, are unable to read due to hyperactivity independent of any reading disabilities or other issues.

- Students with memory deficits have significant challenges in completing homework. The student may not have retained the class lesson upon which the homework is based. Many parents report having to reteach material before the student can even attempt the homework. If the instructions were only presented orally, the student may not have retained any of the instructions and have no idea what to do. Often, the student will not have remembered to bring home the necessary materials.

  Because of deficits in memorization, students may have to develop strategies at home for remembering large amounts of material. Assuming that the student can even develop such strategies with or without parental assistance, it still requires a tremendous amount of additional time. Once the strategies are developed, the student then has to memorize the strategies.

- Working memory deficits (Chapter 10) that impair students' functioning in the classroom also impair their ability to complete homework. Because attention wanes as the day goes on and because attention is part of working memory, working memory deficits are often worse by homework time.

Because memory is impaired in so many of the disorders described in this book, imagine being a student who has to memorize and study for two or more tests on the same night.

- Processing speed deficits impair the speed and efficiency of homework completion. These students need more time to process homework and the reduced speed creates an inability to hold onto material as they are reading or writing. Just as students with slow processing speed require more time to complete class assignments, they will need more time to complete homework assignments. What may take another student twenty minutes to read and write may take a student with slow processing speed three or four times as long. By conducting a Homework Screening Survey (Figure 23.2 and the accompanying CD-ROM), teachers can find out how long it is taking individual students to complete assignments.

- Students who are depressed may lack the energy to start and complete homework. Additionally, they experience memory problems that interfere with retrieving previously learned information required to do the homework assignments. For many of these students, thinking about homework feels overwhelming because "life is just too hard to deal with right now."

- Students who are hypomanic or manicky may be highly distractible and their racing thoughts do not permit them to slow down enough to develop their ideas. Students who have full-blown mania are almost always incapable of doing any homework until the mania stabilizes, possibly with medication.

- Students with sensory defensive issues may be even more reactive by homework time. For example, for students with auditory defensiveness, soft sounds coming from other parts of the house are magnified to the point where the students cannot concentrate on homework. As another example, cooking smells emanating from the kitchen may trigger emotional outbursts.

- Perseveration, common in students on the autism spectrum, may interfere with the ability to direct attention to an assigned task.

- Many of the disorders described in this book interfere with getting a good night's sleep. Even students who sleep through the night may not derive the same benefits from sleep as their peers. Research has shown that a lack of sleep interferes with both memory and academic performance. Sleep problems have a significant impact on homework completion. Many students with sleep issues come home from school and immediately go to sleep (especially students with mood disorders and those on certain medications). They generally do not wake up until late evening, and are too groggy to work on homework. Even if they are awake enough, their parents are often asleep by then.

- From the stress of the day, many students come home tired, frustrated, and at the end of their rope. The added stress of having to produce homework can trigger a "rage attack" or "storm." Once a storm occurs, whether triggered by homework or another issue, it can last for over an hour, and the child may be unable to function for hours after the storm.

Students who "storm" at home still need to complete homework over the long term, although they may need homework accommodations such as extended time or reduced amount of homework. Once homework is appropriately accommodated, the student needs to complete the homework, even if it cannot be completed that night. Doing homework on weekends without a penalty is a better alternative rather than not doing homework. In our opinion, students need to learn that as adults, they still need to meet their home and work responsibilities even if they are experiencing symptom interference.

That said, there is no question that homework needs to be forgiven in cases of specific severe symptom interference or when students are undergoing medication adjustment and are seriously impaired by symptoms or medication adverse effects.

The same accommodations used in school for the symptoms described in this section and in the individual chapters on the disorders are usually also required for homework. For example, if a student requires adult assistance in school (e.g., scribing, dictation), then homework also needs to be modified based on parental or adult availability to assist the student with homework. If handwriting needs to be reduced in school, it needs to be reduced in homework, etc. Because symptoms tend to worsen in the afternoon and evening after a long day at school, students may require more accommodations than they do in school, e.g., the amount to be handwritten may need to be reduced even further.

Visual–motor Integration Issues

As noted in the chapters on TS and OCD, many of the disorders discussed in this book are associated with varying degrees of impairment in visual-motor integration (VMI). VMI deficits make it difficult for students to accurately copy from a textbook to a notebook. VMI can interfere with students' ability to accurately position work on the page, e.g., to line up numbers properly for math calculations. VMI deficits can also interfere with the ability to visually track during reading and writing. Tracking problems can lead to missed material, the need to reread, and tremendous frustration. Many students with these problems avoid even reading the directions for a homework assignment.

For students with VMI deficits, reducing the amount of copying from one source to another can reduce some of the frustration. Students also need to be directly taught strategies for lining up work and for visually tracking during reading. Do not forget to teach the parents these strategies so that they can cue the student to use them during homework time.

Handwriting Issues

Handwriting issues contribute significantly to homework problems. Students with handwriting issues require accommodations of their homework materials such as those described in Chapter 17. Assigning too much written work is likely to lead to frustration and explosive behavior at home.

Inadequate Support for Parents from School

Almost all studies on homework completion note the importance of parental involvement. Many parents cannot provide adequate support, however, because of poor school-home communication. In many cases, the school does not provide the parents with enough information to enable them to assist the student with homework. Imagine yourself being the concerned and involved parent in the following dialogue with a disorganized child:

Parent: (pointing to an entry in the student's planner) I can't read your handwriting. What does this assignment say?
Child: It says "history slavery."
Parent: What does that mean? Are you supposed to write an essay or a paper or what?
Child: I don't remember.
Parent: Well, when is it due?
Child: I don't know.
Parent: Did the teacher give you any handout for this?
Child: I think so, but I don't remember.
Parent: (searching folders and book bag) Where is it?
Child: I must have left it at school.

Parent: Can you call a classmate to ask for the assignment?
Child: I don't think it will help. I didn't bring my history book home, either.

Or consider this hypothetical interaction with a child in elementary school:
Parent: (unpacking backpack) What is this paper that is partly done?
Child: Um...math.
Parent: Was it classwork or homework?
Child: I don't know.
Parent: Well, are you supposed to finish it in class tomorrow or tonight?
Child: I'm not sure.
Parent: Should we call one of your friends to ask them?
Child: Wait! I just remembered. We did that sheet last month! Where's the sheet for tonight?
Parent: What sheet? I don't see any other sheet in your folder.

If we want parents to support the student in doing homework, then we need to ensure that parents know the assignment, its due date, and any necessary materials.

Tips and Tricks to Improve School-Home Communication

- Screen for homework problems early in the school year. (See Homework Screening Survey in Figure 23.2 and the accompanying CD-ROM.)
- Survey the students about their homework preferences. A reproducible Student Homework Habits Survey is provided (Appendix K) as is a student survey on studying for tests (Appendix L). The Homework Habits Survey can be used by the student to increase self-awareness; by the parents to help the student acquire more effective patterns; and by the teacher, Resource Room teacher, school guidance counselor, or psychologist to help the student develop more effective homework habits.
- Establish a system that lets parents verify daily assignments (e.g., set up a homework webpage that parents can log onto or set up a homework hotline that they can check). For individual communications with par-

ents, arrange to use voicemail or email. Email may be preferable because voicemail may get deleted whereas email can be saved and referred to as necessary.

- Require the use of assignment books or planners, and assist the student in maintaining an accurate and complete planner.
- Ask the parents of younger students to initial each assignment in the planner when it is finished. This way, if the homework is not returned, the teacher will know that it is lost or missing but that it was done. Asking the parents to initial the assignment also increases the likelihood of daily monitoring of homework.
- Give parents specific suggestions for how they can support the homework effort. For example, send home information on how to organize a long-term project with a note to parents explaining that this is how the student is being taught to do it in class. Parents who do not have these skills will not be insulted and will find the information helpful.
- Communicate frequently with parents about homework. Include notification of upcoming big projects with due dates.
- Provide individual weekly notes to indicate any work that is missing.
- Train parents how to support any Behavior Intervention Plan or plan to improve self-management of homework. Research suggests that homework completion and homework accuracy both improve when student training is combined with parental support, particularly in terms of mathematics achievement (Cancio, West, & Young, 2004).
- Screen for organizational problems, using the Organizational Skills Survey in Appendix H.
- Ensure that parents and students have written statements describing homework policies, including policies on missed or late assignments.

It is impossible to overemphasize the importance of screening for homework problems and organizational problems early in the school year. Studies of homework completion for students classified as having emotional and behavioral disorders (EBD) confirm that these students are likely to have significant difficulties in organizing their work, ma-

terials, and time. Their organizational deficits significantly interfere with homework completion (M. Epstein et al., 1993; M. H. Epstein et al., 1995). See Chapter 9 on Executive Dysfunction for a more in-depth discussion of organizational deficits and remediation techniques.

Inadequate Parental Support of Child

Parental involvement in homework takes many forms. It is important that parents create an appropriate workplace and provide structure for the student at home. They also need to provide assistance with homework skills when needed. Just as we, teachers, need to assume the student wants to do well (based on the premise, "I would if I could, but I can't, so I don't" introduced in Chapter 3), we need to give parents the benefit of the doubt. Parents may be unable to provide needed support because of one or more of the following reasons:

- There may be another child in the family with even more intensive needs that is demanding the parent's attention.
- The parent may have the same learning disabilities or challenges as their child and not have the skills to help.
- The parent may not have enough information from the teacher to understand what is expected of the student.
- Some parents may not be motivated to help their child because they have not been educated about the importance of homework to their child's long-term academic success and ability to get a job.

Executive Dysfunction

Executive Dysfunction (EDF) is one of the primary causes of homework failure. Students with EDF often fail to completely record their assignments and frequently do not bring home the materials necessary for completing their homework. If the student does manage to record their assignment and bring home the necessary materials, other aspects of EDF interfere with the homework process. Goal-setting and time estimation are often unrealistic and the simple act of prioritizing homework over play may be impaired. When students do sit down to tackle homework, they may not know how to prioritize assignments correctly. As a result, they may spend hours on a relatively unimportant assignment while neglecting to study for a final examination that counts heavily towards their grade. They may also have difficulty inhibiting behaviors that distract them from staying on task. At other times, they may have difficulty shifting between tasks. Organizing and sequencing work is close to impossible without accommodations or direct instruction in compensatory strategies. Students with EDF may also have difficulty accepting and using feedback from their parents who are trying to assist them with their homework. They may lash out at their parents from the frustration of not being able to use feedback to edit their work, but left to their own devices, students with EDF are generally unable to simultaneously produce and edit their own work. Impairment in time management and self-monitoring results in an inability to task analyze and break large assignments or projects into manageable units. One of the major impacts of EDF on homework is impairment in the ability to create and stick to a plan for a project or paper. (See Chapter 9 for more information on EDF.)

Early screening for organizational deficits and homework problems identifies students who may need accommodations, direct instruction in how to do homework, instruction in self-monitoring, and compensatory strategies.

Because EDF is such a huge issue for so many students with disabilities, establishing excellent school-home support and communication is crucial.

A survey for homework issues is depicted in Figure 23.2 (page 190) that teachers can send home and ask parents to complete. In addition, Appendix H is an Organizational Skills Survey that teachers can send home for parents to complete. See also the study-related student surveys (Appendices K and L). Reproducible copies of these forms are provided on the accompanying CD-ROM.

In addition to the tips and tricks provided in the chapter on EDF, here are some additional tips for helping the student with EDF complete more homework:

- Review the homework planner with the student daily to ensure that all assignments are recorded.
- Use a time estimation tool such as that depicted in Appendix M to help determine whether the student has time issues that may be contributing to homework problems.

- If possible, provide an extra set of books to be left at home.
- Provide a homework website, hotline, or some other way students can obtain the assignment if their planner does not make it home with them.
- Encourage parents to create a structured time and homework routine to reduce problems getting started with homework.
- Provide an alternative method for students to turn in work, e.g., email, fax.

Appendix M provides a worksheet that students can use to estimate time needed for homework and projects. This type of form can also be used as part of a school-based screening for problems that may need to be accommodated when planning for the student. The form in Appendix M is adapted from a form tailored to help a middle school student as part of a plan to get him to complete more homework. At the end of each school day, the student completed this form and reviewed it with school personnel to ensure that he had recorded all of his assignments for the night, including any intermediate goals, and that he had estimated the time it would take him to complete all assignments. The next day, he reviewed the accuracy of his estimates with school personnel and adjusted his estimates for the next day.

Students have two major problems estimating time required to complete homework. Some students cannot accurately estimate how much time each task will really take. Some can, but never add up the time to see how much homework time they need to allow for the night.

Too Much Work

Another factor that contributes to students with neurological disabilities failing to complete all of their homework is that sometimes there is simply too much work. An easy rule of thumb to determine the appropriate amount of time (in minutes) for homework is to calculate ten times the student's grade, e.g., twenty minutes for a second grader, thirty minutes for a third grader, etc. The following are informal recommendations provided by others (Horowitz, 2005):

- Children K to Grade 2: No more than twenty to thirty minutes of homework per day.
- Students Grades 3 to 6: No more than thirty to sixty minutes of homework per day.

Figure 23.2 Homework Screening Survey—Parent Reporting Form

Student's Name: _____   Completed by: _____   Date: _____

ITEM	NEVER	RARELY	SOMETIMES	OFTEN	ALWAYS
My child records all of his or her homework assignments independently in school.					
My child brings the homework planner or recorded assignments home.					
My child brings home the books or materials needed to complete the day's homework assignments.					
My child misplaces or loses schoolwork or homework.					
My child knows and understands the assignment(s).					
My child knows when the assignments are due.					
My child starts homework without reminding or nagging.					
My child leaves homework assignments until the last minute or is late in doing them.					
My child completes the homework without someone sitting with him or her.					
My child can shift or switch easily between homework assignments.					
My child packs up his/her school bag independently and correctly.					
The level of the homework is too difficult for my child to complete independently.					
The amount of homework is too great for my child to complete due to other factors (disabilities, after-school sports, medications, sleep problems, etc.)					
If you have to help your child with homework or supervise your child to make sure the homework gets done, how much time are you spending each day with your child on homework?					
How much time does your child usually spend doing homework each day?					
How often do you fight with your child about homework?					

- Junior and senior high school students: Horowitz notes that there is no recommended timeframe for homework, and it is not unusual for students to spend as long as two and a half hours or more per day on after school assignments (Horowitz 2005).

Although this rule of thumb would suggest that two hours of homework is appropriate for a twelfth grader, to put it bluntly, this is too much for students who are already overwhelmed by symptoms, lack of sleep, and medication side effects. The preceding focuses on the total amount of time and does not address the type of work or skills that are either prerequisite or are being targeted for development.

Learning Disabilities

Many of the conditions described in this book are associated with increased rates of learning disabilities (LD), most notably written expression and math calculations. To improve homework completion for students with learning disabilities, see the chapters in this book on written expression and math calculations for specific tips and strategies that can be adapted for homework. Many of the tips and tricks for VMI deficits in this chapter also apply to students with learning disabilities.

Homework assignments are supposed to be at the level that the student can complete independently, i.e., without help from the parent.

It is not appropriate to routinely assign homework that the student cannot do independently. Use homework to:
- rehearse and strengthen new skills
- apply or integrate previously acquired skills
- foster organizational skills
- foster self-discipline
- foster independence/autonomy
- prepare students for work habits needed in the adult world

Research indicates that providing direct instruction on doing homework independently improves the homework completion of middle school students with LD when the students understand how to do the work (Hughes et al. 2002). Both elements are crucial: ensuring that students know how to do the work assigned, and providing them with instruction on how to work independently.

What are the Consequences for Completing Homework?

If homework is to be meaningful, it must result in timely feedback or grading. Some teachers include homework notebooks or assignments as a percentage of the students' final grade, which generally works against students with disabilities, particularly if they have handwriting problems and if homework completion is not monitored on a daily basis.

Homework needs to be required, but only if it improves skills toward mastery, promotes independent functioning, inspires additional questions or discussion, and leads to something positive for the student. That something positive could be earning a ticket for a class lottery with each completed homework assignment, where a few winners are picked randomly each Friday. Lottery prizes could include a homework pass, pizza, or a coupon to the school store.

Parents can be a wonderful source of support for reinforcing homework completion, but remember that they cannot support the school's efforts if they do not know that there are assignments or when they are due.

Rewarding homework completion and earning class lottery prizes is unlikely to be sufficient. Teachers may also wish to include an accuracy or completeness standard. To encourage accuracy and persistence, adhere to a mastery principle, so that the student resubmits the corrected homework and is then entered in the lottery.

 ## General Tips and Tricks for Helping Students with Homework

- Use meaningful and real life examples or make explicit connections between the assignment and how the students will use that information or skill in their lives.
- If necessary, shorten the length of an assignment rather than omit the assignment entirely.
- Write the assignment on the board and explain it clearly. Provide examples.
- Copy the assignment and email or use a website to send it to parents.
- Assign homework toward the beginning of class.

- When possible, allow the students to start the homework in class and check for comprehension and provide 1:1 assistance, as needed.
- Accommodate handwriting issues in homework assignments (e.g., allow keyboarding or oral recording).
- Use direct instruction to teach study skills. Encourage use of study groups.
- Allow students to work together on homework. Use peer tutors.
- Use direct instruction, if indicated, to teach independence in homework skills.
- Use a homework planner. They have a positive effect on students with LD and average-achieving students with homework problems (Bryan and Sullivan-Burstein 1998). Make sure the planner accommodates large, sloppy handwriting,
- Ensure adequate home-school communication.
- Make sure the students can complete the homework assignment.
- Do not assign more work than the student can accomplish. Coordinate with other teachers to prevent homework overload.
- Remind students of due dates.
- Break big projects into smaller homework units.
- Provide additional 1:1 homework assistance to students.
- Provide feedback, grades, and reinforcers for homework completion.

Summary

Homework is one of the most traumatic and devastating challenges to family life for students with disabilities. Some students with the disorders described in this book require long-term homework accommodations. Others may need shorter term accommodations, e.g., when they are experiencing a symptom flare-up or medication adjustment. For almost all of the disorders described in this book, symptom severity worsens during the afternoon and evening hours.

School personnel are encouraged to screen for homework problems, provide adequate support to parents so that parents can assist their children, and use direct instruction in strategies and skills involved in completing homework and returning it.

After getting his mother's agreement to support our efforts in the home, we met with Eric to ensure that he understood the importance of homework. We also developed a plan with a number of graduated steps that included having Eric record his assignments completely and accurately, estimate the time his work would take, and pack up necessary books and materials. Instead of Eric's parents nagging him about his homework, we placed Eric in charge, and left it up to him to ask his parents for any supports. At all stages, Eric was intimately involved in agreeing to goals, identifying what supports he might need, and establishing a reward contract. Within a few months, Eric went from being a student who had not done any homework in two years to an "A" student who was independently completing and turning in over 95% of his assignments.

CHAPTER 24

Accommodating Medication Side Effects

It was at the end of October when Jeffrey's teacher called the school's consultant. "I didn't know whether to call you or not, but Jeffrey's behavior has been worsening the past two days and I don't know if this is a Tourette's waxing cycle or if there could be something else going on. His behavior is getting worse, and I'm concerned."

The consultant asked the teacher a number of questions to get a clear description of what she had observed and when it had started. The consultant told her that she was exactly right to call and that what she was describing did not sound like a waxing cycle. Her careful observations made the consultant suspect a medication problem. The consultant called the parents, then reported back to the teacher.

Overview

Many students described in this book may be on one or more medications, and the more conditions the student has, the more likely that multiple medications may be prescribed. The school's input to the parents and the treating professionals is critically important in helping determine whether the student's symptoms are so serious as to require medication, or—in a case where there are multiple serious problems—determining which symptoms are the priority for treatment. Prescribing medications for children or adolescents with multiple problems is a juggling act because a medication that helps with symptoms of one disorder may worsen symptoms of another. For example, medications that decrease tics may increase bad moods. Even when a medication is helpful, it might have adverse effects that may interfere with academic functioning or pose health

problems. And in some cases, medication effects can produce or mimic bad behavior, as suggested by the opening narrative. This chapter describes some accommodations that students might need in school due to their medications.

> **Disclaimer:** The information presented in this chapter is provided for informational purposes only and is not a substitute for professional medical advice. School personnel are encouraged to ask the parents to seek advice from the prescribing physician as to what medication accommodations are needed.

Tips and Accommodations for Medication Side Effects

The following accommodations or tips are organized by type of problem:

Fatigue:

- Reduce workload.
- Allow the student more movement breaks and opportunities to get up and walk.
- Reduce the amount of time that the student works on any task in one sitting, unless the student finds the material engrossing and stimulating.

- Seat the student in a brightly lit area.
- Use more interactive and active learning modalities, e.g., manipulatives, electronics, and active exploration.
- Use more peer-based activities.
- Use rehearsal of previous material and delay introduction of new material.

Increased Thirst:

- Allow water bottles in class or whatever fluids the physician recommends.

Dry Mouth:

- Allow water bottles in class or whatever fluids the physician recommends.
- Allow gum or sugarless hard sucking candies.

Visual Blurring:

- Reduce the amount to be read.
- Provide an aide to read to the student.
- Use books on tape/CD.
- Allow tape recorder for notetaking.
- Provide hard copies of notes, a notetaker, or copies of another student's notes.
- Reduce handwritten work.
- Provide copy of board notes.

Frequent Urination, Nausea, Vomiting, or Diarrhea:

- Provide a permanent pass so student can leave the room without having to ask.
- Allow the student to sit near the door to leave quickly and inconspicuously.
- Provide copies of notes missed, a notetaker, or copies of another student's notes.
- Provide discrete assistance in getting caught up due to absences from the room.
- Allow the student to tape record notes.

Always ask the student's parents to keep the school informed of any changes in the student's medication(s), even if the change only occurs in doses taken at home. Additionally, ask the student's parents to inform the school of any side effects that they have detected in the home and that might affect the student's functioning in school.

"Rebound":

When medication wears off during the school day, the student may get more hyperactive, agitated, or irritable than she would have been without any medication. This is called rebound. If a student is experiencing rebound in school:

- Notify the parent(s) so that they can discuss the medication dosing and schedule with the prescribing physician.
- Provide less demanding academic activities during that time.
- Allow more opportunities to move around or engage in activities that are calming.
- Schedule breaks to manage stress or motor excesses.

If the student appears to be experiencing rebound, contact the student's parents and physician (if parents have provided written permission) to inform them.

Loss of Appetite Due to Medications:

Some medications cause loss of appetite, e.g., stimulant medications.

- Contact the parents and physician to inform them if the student is not eating lunch.
- Ask the parent if the student needs to have healthy snacks throughout the day.

Increased Appetite or Significant Weight Gain:

- Consult with parent and physician to determine whether snacking is allowed, and if so, have them define how much snacking.
- Be aware of peer rejection or social issues and provide support.

Cognitive Dulling:

- Allow the use of word banks and other accommodations for word retrieval.
- Allow more time for assignments.
- Extend time for tests.
- Allow tape recording, provide a notetaker, or provide a copy of a student's notes.
- Use story starters to assist student in starting on written expression activities.

Tics Induced by Medications:

- Notify parents and physician.
- See Chapter 4 for how to accommodate tics.

Sudden "Wildness," Agitation, Restlessness, or Inability to Sit after Starting or Increasing a Medication:

- Notify parents and physician <u>promptly.</u>
- Allow more opportunities for movement.
- Allow more opportunity to engage in self-calming activities.
- Schedule frequent breaks.
- Allow student to engage in self-selected engrossing and calming activity.

Hand or Arm Tremor or Muscle Weakness:

- Reduce amount of handwritten work.
- Extend time for handwritten work.
- Allow tape recording, provide a notetaker, or provide a copy of a student's notes.
- Allow use of computer for written expression activities.
- Extend time on tests.
- Do not grade for neatness.
- Reduce copying from the board.

Memory Impairment:

- Allow the use of word banks and other accommodations for word retrieval.
- Allow more time for assignments.
- Extend time for tests.
- Use alternative assessment methods to permit the student to demonstrate understanding.
- Allow tape recording, provide a notetaker, or provide a copy of a student's notes.
- Provide assistance with, and supervision to ensure that assignments are recorded or emailed home.
- Ensure that necessary materials are packed up.
- Provide an extra set of books to be left at home.
- Provide resource room support to review material.
- Conference frequently with student on big projects.
- Ask students if they prefer not to be called on if they have not raised their hand.

Sleeping Problems:

- Allow the student to start the day later.
- Schedule challenging academic courses for mid-morning or later in the morning for older students, if possible.
- Provide home tutoring.
- Ask students if scheduling a highly motivating class for first period might help them wake up; be guided by their assessment of their situations.
- Adjust homework expectations.
- Speak to the physician (with parental consent) about whether to let the student sleep or to try to wake the student if she is falling asleep during class.
- Provide the student with hard copies of all notes and presentations.
- Ensure that all assignments are recorded and necessary materials are packed.
- Allow the student to walk around to see if that helps overcome drowsiness.

Impaired Concentration:

- Seat student near instructor and provide discrete assistance in refocusing.
- Pre-arrange breaks to allow student to get up and move around.
- Allow tape recording, provide a notetaker or a copy of another student's notes.
- Allow use of computer for written expression activities.
- Direct focus by using colorful PowerPoint™ presentations.
- Introduce novelty.
- Use color to enhance focus (see Chapters 8 and 9 for more tips on focusing).
- Extend time for reading and all classwork.
- Adjust work expectations to what student can reasonably complete within available time.
- Extend time for homework.
- Reduce homework expectations, as needed.
- Test student in a separate location.
- Extend time on tests.
- Break testing up over days for large tests.
- Allow alternate means of recording for tests, e.g., provide a scribe, or allow oral testing.
- Allow alternate means for student to demonstrate knowledge.

- Do not penalize for lateness or contract as to how late assignments will be handled.
- Conference frequently with student on big projects.

Difficulty in Speaking Clearly:

- Consult with the student as to whether to be called on or not in class.
- Consult with speech therapist for other strategies for the teacher and the student.

School Phobia:

School phobia is an uncommon side effect of some of the medications used to treat tics, mania, and aggressive behavior. If a student starts having school attendance issues, ask the parent to consult with the physician to see if this might be a medication side effect.

- Do not penalize the student for late attendance or missed classwork.
- Arrange for support in the building when the student arrives at school.
- Send missed assignments to parents for completion at home.
- Extend deadlines for homework and projects.
- Use flexible testing schedule if student cannot arrive at school on time.

Summary

It is often surprising to teachers to learn that medications can cause unusual or problematic behaviors. The students' parents and treating professionals, as well as the school nurse, are an important source of information and support for the teacher.

After Jeffrey's teacher called to report worsening behavior, the school's consultant called Jeffrey's parents to ask whether his behavior had become worse at home. It had. The consultant then asked them when it had started, whether he had been ill recently, or if there had been anything going on that could account for the sudden deterioration in his behavior. When his parents confirmed the teacher's observations and they knew of no explanation, the consultant asked whether Jeffrey's medication had been renewed recently. As it turned out, they had just renewed one of Jeffrey's medications and he had started the new batch the day his behavior started to deteriorate.

At the consultant's suggestion, the parents took the bottle of medication back to the pharmacy to ensure it was the right medication and the right dose. The parents discovered that Jeffrey's medication was part of a bad batch that had been recalled by the manufacturer but was still on the pharmacy's shelves by mistake. The pharmacy immediately gave Jeffrey a new batch of medication. The consultant called Jeffrey's teacher to inform her that Jeffrey might continue to have trouble for a day or so until the medication cleared his system totally, and suggested some interim accommodations until the adverse effects wore off.

The next day, Jeffrey's teacher reported that Jeffrey's behavior was already improving tremendously. Although she thanked the consultant profusely, it was the teacher who deserved the thanks because had she not called to express her concern, who knows how long Jeffrey would have suffered?

Communication.... it makes a world of difference!

PART IV

Behavior

Overview

The disorders described in Part II of this book often have significant academic impact, as described in Parts II and III. Behavioral features associated with these disorders create additional challenges. Increasing knowledge of the student's neurological disorder(s) is the first step in addressing problematic behaviors. The second step is to provide accommodations, as described in previous sections. Implementing the accommodations and suggestions typically reduces or eliminates the majority of behavioral issues associated with these disorders. However, some behavioral symptoms may remain, even after the school has accommodated the student's disorders

Unfortunately, most educators' training programs do not teach adequate behavior modification skills to manage some of the behaviors teachers must deal with on a daily basis. Overworked teach-ers understandably look for simple-to-implement and simple-to-monitor interventions that boost academic productivity and decrease problematic behavior. This section of the book focuses on these sorts of interventions, rather than highly technical details about sophisticated behavior analysis and behavior modification techniques that teachers are unlikely to implement without the necessary support.

In addition to providing simple and effective strategies to manage behavioral symptoms and to promote improved social skills, this section also includes some discussion of what techniques to avoid. We have encountered too many students with disabilities who were harmed by well-intentioned but ultimately damaging plans that unintentionally produced Post-Traumatic Stress Disorder (PTSD), school avoidance or refusal, and depression.

CHAPTER 25

Overview of Problematic Behaviors

*Never underestimate a child's ability to
get into more trouble.*
— Martin Mull

Although students may have a neurological basis for the behavioral symptoms that are observed in school, neurology is only part of the story when it comes to addressing the problems. Multiple factors contribute to behavioral, academic, and social problems in school, as Figure 25.1 depicts.

A student's neurological disorders fall into the category of "Child's Characteristics" in Figure 25.1, which also includes other variables such as whether the student:

- is generally well-nourished
- has had a nutritious breakfast that morning
- is suffering from allergies

Figure 25.1. Factors Contributing to School Behavior Problems

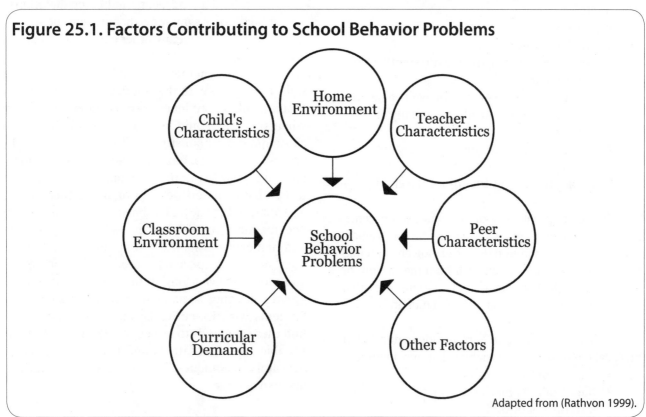

Adapted from (Rathvon 1999).

- has had enough sleep the night before
- has a fundamentally easy or a difficult temperament
- has any particular strengths in sports or creative activities that can be incorporated into assignments to boost motivation for academic tasks and that can help protect the student's self-esteem if there are peer issues
- has been exposed to environmental toxins that may cause behavior problems
- is on any medications
- has missed a medication dose on a particular day or just had medications adjusted

The category "Home Environment" includes multiple variables that may influence the student's behavior in school, such as whether the student has:
- divorced parents
- siblings
- other members of the family who also have neurological or behavioral issues
- additional stresses at home, such as financial difficulties, a death in the family, or job loss for one of the parents
- sufficient structure and consistent routines in the home

"Peer Characteristics" include such factors as whether the peers:
- are too loud
- break the rules
- are perceived to be treated differently than the student
- are generally supportive and well behaved or are intolerant, unruly, or actually harassing the student
- are appropriate role models if they are seated next to the student
- are appropriate as friends for the child

In meetings with school personnel and parents, school personnel often say that a student has friends, but when asked to name one friend or indicate one child who might welcome a phone call from the student or an overture to get together, school personnel are often unable to come up with even a single student.

"Classroom Environment" includes a number of physical environmental variables that may include:
- the size of the classroom
- the likelihood for the student to be uncomfortably hot or cold

- a lot of dust or allergens
- unnecessary noise pollution
- visual overstimulation or worse, a stripped room with nothing interesting in sight
- desks arrangements that may be difficult for the student
- fluorescent lighting
- a group-based behavior management system
- the absence or presence of visual cues and supports for tasks
- space within the room for a student to retreat to tune out distractions or just escape from high levels of stimulation

Altering the environment to support the student is a core element of any support and intervention plan.

"Curricular Demands" include questions about whether the student has:
- any learning weaknesses that make some tasks more challenging
- a fast-paced work load
- handwriting issues
- eye/hand (visual-motor) integration problems that interfere with copying notes or assignments from a book or the board
- Insufficient working memory to meet curricular demands, e.g., multi-step directions
- additional symptoms that prevent the student from meeting other curricular demands

Consider whether the child has the executive skills to keep up with the "hidden" parts of the curriculum. Many students seem to crash and burn when they enter middle school. This is likely because middle school students have multiple teachers and classrooms, have to make more transitions, have to cope with multiple teaching styles, and have to be able to independently organize their books and materials. They also have to be able to use and maintain more complex planners as projects and homework complexity and demands increase. They are also expected to produce longer papers and more involved long-term projects that require greater planning, sequencing, and organizing skills. Students with Executive Dysfunction (Chapter 9) find these demands to be very challenging. Without suitable accommodations and instruction in compensatory techniques, problematic behaviors are likely to emerge.

Some teachers mistakenly believe that because the students look normal, their executive skills are also normal—that is, age-appropriate. Staff may ask that the parents back off and let the student perform independently. This, however, can lead to frustration and acting-out behavior as the student fails due to the impact of EDF. The student can function independently only if teachers use direct instruction on compensatory strategies.

Perhaps the one factor that is too often overlooked in planning for a student is the match between the student's needs and preferences and "Teacher Characteristics." Haim Ginott addressed this very well:

"I've come to the frightening conclusion that I am the decisive element in the classroom. It's my personal approach that creates the climate. It's my daily mood that makes the weather. As a teacher, I possess a tremendous power to make a student's life miserable or joyous. I can be a tool of torture or an instrument of inspiration. I can humiliate or humor, hurt or heal. In all situations, it is my response that decides whether a crisis will be escalated or deescalated and a child humanized or dehumanized."

A supportive teacher who is well organized, has a sense of humor, and can creatively problem-solve with students is often a terrific match for students who have problems with impulsivity, sustaining focus, and mood variability. We have also seen instances where teachers who are very strict but consistent have been good matches for some dysregulated students. There is no "one size fits all" on this. Another teacher trait that is helpful is a willingness to learn about neurological disorders. Asking the parent and the student to describe the best teaching style for the student can often reduce behavioral problems in the classroom.

The factors listed in Figure 25.1 serve as a checklist for factors to consider in arranging a student's functional behavioral analysis (Chapter 26).

Being Proactive, Not Reactive — Look Again!

When it comes to addressing behavioral issues, many educators think in terms of consequences as their first approach. Often, initial plans focus on what a teacher might do *after* a behavior occurs to reward or punish it. In planning for students with neurological disorders, it is more helpful to use an integrated approach that includes looking at all of the possible causes of behavior, such as the approach depicted in Figure 25.1. We start by taking a careful look at each factor, considering its possible role, and then determining what to change *before* problematic behavior occurs.

Closely examine the factors that family and school staff can modify before problematic behavior occurs. Some, but not all, of the child's characteristics may be modifiable, for example:

- School personnel can provide parents with sleep hygiene information (see Appendix J) to assist their child in getting a better night's sleep, which might improve functioning and behavior.
- School personnel can suggest that the student's physician evaluate the student's medication schedule to provide him with better medication coverage during the school day.
- School personnel can give information to parents and students about better nutrition and how it affects the student's functioning and behavior.
- School personnel can incorporate the student's strengths and talents in educational programming.

For child characteristics that cannot be modified by school personnel, school personnel can incorporate some reasonable accommodations. These accommodations may help both improve functioning and reduce the likelihood of problematic behaviors. For example, a common sense solution and accommodation for a student who compulsively sharpens a pencil would be for the teacher to make the pencil sharpener less available, to allow the student to use a mechanical pencil or pen, or to investigate the possibility of using a word processor instead of writing by hand.

Some home environment characteristics may also be modifiable by school personnel to increase academic performance and decrease problematic behavior, including:

- Teaching parents how to organize the student in the home
- Providing parents with information on how to create an appropriate homework environment and structure at home
- Providing parents with leads or resources for the parents who needs treatment themselves

Sometimes it is difficult to help the student if the parent's symptoms interfere. Of course, schools cannot require parents to get support or treatment. Even so, if schools do not somehow assist parents, the school may be less effective in helping the child. Schools that have developed support groups for parents of children with special needs have found that parent networking is an effective means to provide information to parents that is more extensive than schools are permitted to provide. School districts that can arrange parent support groups that meet at times when parents are available (i.e., in the early morning or evening) may be able to reach and help more parents.

- School staff can provide peers with awareness and sensitivity programs that can help them be more supportive of students with disabilities. Peers can also be rewarded or punished based on classroom rules that deal with respect and bullying.
- The physical classroom environment can be easily modified in ways that reduce disruptive or problematic behavior, as described in the chapters on ADHD and Executive Dysfunction.

Without curricular accommodations, many students with the disorders described in this book exhibit more severe behavior problems. Make sure that all learning difficulties have been addressed and all necessary accommodations and modifications have been incorporated. The very first thing we should change or try to change is not what the student does, but what the parents and teachers do before unwanted behavior happens.

One thing that schools can do to improve class behavior is to provide adequate recess time. Recent research shows providing one or more daily recess periods of fifteen minutes or more is associated with better teachers' rating of class behavior in eight- and nine-year-old students (Barros, Silver, and Stein 2009).

In this chapter, we have stressed the importance of using a multiple factors approach to understanding behavior. This approach forms the basis for what is known as a Functional Behavioral Assessment, described in the next chapter.

A teacher's constant task is to take a roomful of live wires and see to it that they're grounded.
— *E.C. McKenzie*

CHAPTER 26

Functional Behavioral Assessments and Behavior Intervention Plans

---

Millions saw the apple fall, but Newton asked why.
— *Bernard Baruch*

Preview

When the U.S. federal law regulating special education was reauthorized in 1997, it revised the way schools were supposed to address disability-related problem behaviors. One of the new requirements was that school districts conduct "Functional Behavioral Assessments" to determine the function of behaviors that interfere with students' ability to learn. The concept is relatively simple: If we find out the *why* underlying an inappropriate behavior we can develop a plan that addresses the why, and teach the student alternative and acceptable behaviors. Like many things in life, the concept is simple but executing it well is not.

What is a Functional Behavioral Assessment?

Functional Behavioral Assessment (FBA) is an approach to understanding behavior. Instead of taking a radical behavior approach that looks only at the environmental consequences of a behavior that might maintain behavior or weaken it, a Functional Behavioral Assessment attempts to identify the biological/neurological, social, emotional/motivational, and environmental factors that contribute to the behavior. FBAs consider the *why* of a student's inappropriate or undesirable behavior, e.g., why does the student start acting out in math class every day,

or why does the student frequently scream at other students in the cafeteria? (See Appendix N.)

The premise underlying an FBA is that behavior serves a function for the student—it either enables the student to avoid or escape something unpleasant (aversive) or the behavior enables the student to obtain something desired. If we can understand what function an undesirable behavior is trying to serve, we can, perhaps, teach the student socially acceptable behaviors to achieve the same goals. We will not judge the goal of the behavior in the sense of saying that the student should not be trying to escape from classwork. Instead, we will focus our efforts on understanding the function that escape serves, and attempt to teach the student acceptable replacement behaviors. For example, can we teach the student to say "I'm frustrated" instead of yelling, throwing books on the floor, or storming out of the classroom because the work is too difficult?

Note that some behaviors may serve functions that we may not be able to determine without the student's ability to verbalize her experience. For example, the student may perform or release a tic to reduce a sensory urge or pressure that is building internally, or a student may be counting in her head compulsively to ward off a terrifying thought that she has not told anyone about.

Consider all of the factors that determine and influence a behavior (see Figure 25.1, Chapter 25). Study or analyze the behavior across settings and conditions to determine its function and what maintains it. Once we have collected sufficient data, we can begin to develop a set of educated guesses (hypotheses) and interventions to consider implementing. Our understanding of, and interpretation of, a student's behavior will lead to our interventions, so it is crucial that we put aside any subjective feelings and let our curiosity about the behavior lead us to asking questions and collecting information—including objective data—to answer those questions.

Even if a teacher or other school personnel never conducts a Functional Behavioral Assessment, it is still important to understand the process. Surprisingly, we have seen one-page FBAs that omit essential information and skip important steps in the process, resulting in ineffective plans. This is an alarming and not infrequent occurrence and shows how frequently the team has misunderstood or underestimated the importance of following all of the necessary component steps.

If a behavior is serious enough to warrant a Behavior Intervention Plan, then it is serious enough to warrant a comprehensive FBA. Ensure that objective data and data from multiple sources are obtained.

All too often, we have seen schools take the approach that the teacher alone or teacher and building psychologist are responsible for coming up with a plan that they develop in the absence of any objective data. At the very least, the school team needs to include all of the student's teachers, the building psychologist, the student's parents, the student, and consultation with any treating professional and related service providers, as well as some objective data.

Steps in Planning and Conducting a Functional Behavioral Assessment

To demonstrate the comprehensive nature of an FBA, we have listed a summary of the steps in an FBA below.* A checklist of steps involved in an FBA is also provided in Appendix N and on the accompanying CD-ROM.

---

* This list is based on material provided by the Center for Effective Collaboration and Practice (CECP). At the time of writing this book, their web address is http://cecp.air.org/center.asp.

- Describe and verify the seriousness of the problem.
- Define and refine the definition of the problem behavior so that it is expressed in *objective and clearly observable terms*.
- Consider the possible functions of the problem behavior.
- Collect data from multiple sources, including interviews with student, parents, and teachers as well as objective data recording, and analyze information to determine agreement.
- Generate a hypothesis statement regarding the probable function of problem behavior.
- Test the hypothesis statement regarding the function of the problem behavior by attempting to look at the behavior while controlling the environment, one variable at a time.
- Develop and implement the Behavior Intervention Plan (BIP).
- Monitor faithfulness of implementation of the BIP.
- Evaluate the effectiveness of the BIP.
- Modify the BIP, if needed.

Remember: Even though FBAs assume that the behavior serves a function and that if we conduct a careful assessment, we can uncover that function, there may be symptoms for which we cannot find a function. Even with our best detective efforts, we may never really identify a clear purpose for some behaviors that are neurological symptoms.

The preceding steps require team members to collect objective data on the problematic behavior under a variety of conditions, compare the behavior under different conditions as part of the process of formulating a hypothesis about the behavior, and collect information from both the student (assuming she's verbal) and the student's parent(s) to get their understanding and observations concerning the behavior. The team then evaluates whether all sources of information, including home, objective recordings across various school settings, teacher and student interviews, and interviews with treating professionals, lead to one clear hypothesis about the function of the behavior. In addition, a well executed FBA includes monitoring the accompanying BIP objectively once it is implemented to determine if it is working, backfiring, or needs other refinements or changes.

The biggest problems we see in school-conducted FBAs are:

- failure to interview all of the teachers, the parents, the student, and the student's treating professional(s) to get everyone's "take" on the problem behavior.
- failure to obtain objective data on the rate, frequency, antecedents, and consequences of the behavior *before* developing a plan.
- failure to include the student to determine her understanding of her own behavior and what positive inducements she thinks might be helpful.
- failure to obtain objective data on the rate, frequency, antecedents, and consequences of the behavior *after* the behavior plan has been implemented.
- failure to review the intervention plan frequently enough to determine its effectiveness.

A therapist was asked to come to a self-contained program for behaviorally disruptive adolescents to observe a particular student. The program used a reward program based on a progressive level system beginning with "unemployed" and going up to "earned a promotion." The student in question, who had TS, OCD, ADHD, BP, and EDF, had been in the program for three years and had never progressed beyond "unemployed." Despite the fact that he was doing so poorly, the school had never reviewed his plan or adjusted it in the three years. It was no surprise to the therapist that the student wanted to drop out of school and did not think he was capable of getting a real job after high school. Remember that if you keep doing what you are doing, you will keep getting what you get. Monitoring the plan for effectiveness and revising it if it is not working are crucial.

Numerous resources are available for those who wish to obtain ready-made forms for completing each of the elements in an FBA. Some forms are freely available on the Internet from the Center for Effective Collaboration and Practice.

Developing the Behavior Intervention Plan

Developing an effective intervention plan requires everyone involved in the planning to consider:

- how to change the environment to reduce the triggers to the undesirable behavior
- how to teach the replacement behavior if skills training is required
- how to ensure that the student gets adequate opportunities to rehearse the replacement behavior
- which positive reinforcers and schedules of reinforcement can be used that are motivating to the student
- whether the teacher and school personnel will have the support they need to faithfully implement and monitor the plan

When developing a student's intervention plan, the team will have to ask itself a number of questions, e.g., which interventions best align with the function of the behavior and the student's current levels of performance, and which is the "least intrusive" and "least complex" intervention likely to produce positive changes in the student's behavior? Selecting appropriate interventions may also include making necessary changes in curriculum or materials, providing any needed related services, and providing peer education or staff development. Teachers may find the suggestions provided by the Center for Effective Collaboration and Practice helpful in developing student BIPs.[*]

The effectiveness of an intervention often depends, in part, on how effective or motivating the positive reinforcers are. Unfortunately, many school personnel arbitrarily determine that "verbal praise" will be the positive reinforcer without ever determining if verbal praise is an effective or motivating consequence for the particular student. In the next chapter, we will describe a variety of behavior modification paradigms that use specific contingencies for delivering reinforcers.

Summary

A Functional Behavioral Assessment is a multidisciplinary effort to identify what function an undesirable or disruptive behavior serves. The goal of the plan is to find an appropriate behavior that can replace the undesirable behavior while serving the same function. The approach may also be used with some neurological symptoms if the team is careful to collect adequate information and monitor the plan objectively.

The assessment must include both quantifiable, objective data that measure the frequency, intensity,

---

[*] At the time of this writing, their materials on BIPs can be found at http://cecp.air.org/fba/problembehavior3/part3.pdf

and duration of the targeted behavior as well as consideration of settings in which the behavior does and does not occur. Objective measures are supplemented by interviews with school personnel, the student, the student's parent(s), and treating professionals, after which the team determines whether the various sources lead to a shared understanding of the function of the targeted behavior.

Once the team has developed its hypothesis as to the function the behavior serves, it develops a behavior intervention plan (BIP) that may include a number of elements such as related services, coaching, a reward-based system, etc. Objective data collection and review will enable the team to determine if the plan is effective or needs revision.

CHAPTER 27

Avoiding Pitfalls in School-Based Behavior Modification Plans*

*It's not easy taking my problems one at a time
when they refuse to get in line.
— Ashleigh Brilliant*

A Functional Behavioral Assessment (Chapter 26) is the basis for developing a Behavior Intervention Plan (BIP). Because some people use the terms "behavior modification plan" and "BIP" interchangeably, it is important to note that neither term refers to merely a set of behavior consequences. In many cases, related services may need to be incorporated in the plan. Both terms, then, also include any necessary environmental supports, accommodations, and remedial services. Consideration of the student's preferences for particular reinforcers will help the team select effective positive reinforcers. Frequent monitoring of the plan to ensure accurate and consistent implementation and frequent reviews will help the team determine whether to continue the plan or modify it.

Over the years, we have noted that all too often, school-based behavior modification plans fail, or, worse, make the student's symptoms worse. This chapter describes some of the pitfalls in school-based planning. Many of the pitfalls described in this chapter would be avoided if schools routinely conducted Functional Behavioral Assessments, but because they do not, teachers need to be aware of the risks and issues.

Considerations

Having the knowledge or skills to design and implement a behavior modification plan does not necessarily mean that a behavior modification approach is appropriate or likely to be effective. Knowing *when* to use these tools is as important as knowing *how* to use them effectively. A few simple examples illustrate that not all behaviors are amenable to behavior modification approaches:

Example #1: Assume that a student has severe seizures. During the seizures, the student's arms and legs may flail. Suppose that in the course of one such seizure, someone standing next to the student got kicked or hit. Would we then say that we will try to modify the student's arm flailing by behavior modification? No. This example probably seems unnecessary because everyone would agree that it is just common sense not to try to apply consequences to involuntary behaviors. But how do we apply that same kind of rational approach to other behaviors that might be symptoms of neurological conditions?

Example #2: Suppose that a student has a spitting tic, which is much more common than teachers might realize. Trying to reward the student for not spitting may only increase stress as the student attempts to suppress the tic to earn the reward. But the teacher could use behavior modification techniques to shape and reward the student for learning to keep a tissue in his hand and using it so that his tic does not impose on others. That approach is socially bene-

---

* Some of the material in this chapter is adapted from two of Leslie's articles that were originally published electronically on www.tourettesyndrome.net: "The Acid Test" and "Pitfalls in School-Based Behavior Modification Plans."

ficial to the student who may have other situations in which he needs to learn how to handle his tics so that they do not irreparably damage peer relationships.

Questions to Consider

Note: In Chapter 2, we explained that many of the problematic behaviors teachers observe in the classroom are actually neurological symptoms. Throughout this chapter, we will use the word "behavior," without implying that the behavior is voluntary.

Whose problem is it?

If the behavior does not significantly interfere with the student's functioning and does not really interfere with the other students' ability to learn, leave well enough alone. Just because a behavior annoys school personnel or parents does not mean that it needs to be targeted for change or is a priority for change.

Are the potential consequences of the behavior so serious, even if the behavior is infrequent, as to warrant intervention?

If the behavior endangers the student or others, if it jeopardizes the student's placement or program, or both, then consider intervention even if the behavior is infrequent. In this case, the more interventions, the better. But consequence-based behavior modification is probably not the first intervention you should try under such circumstances. The first interventions ought to involve changing the environment and what we do before the problem occurs to prevent the serious behavior. The next steps are to assess the student to see if there are unaddressed learning disabilities and to consult with the student's parents to get their understanding of the behavior and their ideas. Behaviors that jeopardize placement need to trigger a Functional Behavioral Assessment. While the FBA is being conducted, use interim supports and strategies to try to reduce the frequency and likelihood of the behavior.

Are we trying to deal with too much at one time?

Students with multiple diagnoses often have a number of problems. We are unlikely to be successful if we try to tackle too many symptoms at once. Prioritize problems and then determine whether to start with the one that is most serious or the one that is most motivating to the student or the one that is most likely to be successful. The important point here is to only start with one problem, not all of them.

"If you chase two rabbits, both will escape."
— Author Unknown

Have we assessed the student thoroughly and are we confident the problem is not indicative of skills deficits that require remediation or accommodations?

If language-based problems might be contributing to the problem behavior, has the team requested a speech and language evaluation? If sensory dysregulation or visual-motor deficits may be contributing to the symptom, has an occupational therapy evaluation been obtained? If not, obtain any additional needed evaluations before developing any behavior modification plan. In some cases, refer the student for a neuropsychological evaluation.

Are accommodations, other therapies, and other agreed upon interventions already in place?

If they are not in place and if the behavior does not jeopardize health, safety, placement, or program, implement all of the accommodations and supports and see what, if any, behavioral problems are left after all of these services are in place. This is particularly important in cases where behavioral acting-out might be due to frustration from a deficit area, e.g., handwriting. Make sure that necessary accommodations and services are in place first.

Would medication be likely or unlikely to help?

School personnel cannot suggest, recommend, or require a student to be on medication. That said, school personnel can encourage a student's parents to discuss the behavioral issues with the student's treating professionals to get their opinion. The treating professionals may recommend helpful accommodations, research-validated interventions, or may even recommend medication.

Do the parents and school agree on the cause of the behavior?

As suggested by the discussion in Chapter 2, if the school and parents do not agree as to what is causing the problem behavior, each will have different ideas about how to address it and the team may not reach agreement as to any plan. If this occurs, and if the parents and treating professionals are saying one thing and the school is saying another, our firm recommendation is that school personnel listen to the parents and treating professionals unless the school has conducted a formal and comprehensive Functional Behavioral Assessment and has obtained objective data to suggest otherwise. Under such circumstances, the school or district may wish to consider an independent evaluation with an outside consultant to guide the team.

A behavior modification plan can be viewed as a behavioral *treatment* when it is applied to a neurological symptom. Before undertaking any attempt to modify a symptom, obtain input from the parents and treating professionals, and obtain parental consent.*

Have we identified a discrete response that we will reward or monitor?

Some processes, like attention, are continuous. If we want to increase on-task time, make sure that the team has a clearly defined "response" that can be measured and rewarded.

Have we conducted a baseline assessment to determine the current rate, frequency, and intensity of the student's behavior so that we can set an appropriate goal as the first goal?

We cannot emphasize too strongly the need for objective data as part of a baseline assessment. Teachers can use a simple A-B-C recording form like the one in Appendix O (and on the accompanying CD-ROM) to collect some objective data. By making A-B-C (Antecedent-Behavior-Consequences) recordings over a period of days and across settings, school personnel are more likely to detect factors that contribute to the problem behavior. They are also more likely to detect when consequences may be maintaining an undesired behavior.

A consultant was reviewing a behavior plan that had been developed by a special education teacher without consultation with the students' parents or treating professionals. The teacher wanted to increase the amount of time that students stayed in their seats, believing that if he could get them to stay in their seats

for longer periods, he could accomplish more with them academically. To that end, he had established a behavior plan whereby the students could earn positive reinforcers (rewards) each time they remained in their seat for twenty consecutive minutes. Any student who remained seated for twenty minutes would earn the reinforcer.

*The plan did not work at all. The main reason it did not work was because the initial goal of twenty minutes was so far beyond the students' abilities that not one student ever earned even one reinforcer! Had the teacher conducted a baseline of the behavior and recorded how long students were actually in their seats before getting up, he might have discovered that the first goal would have been more appropriately set at five minutes.***

Is the student capable of modifying the behavior if we (simply) boost motivation by applying consequences?

If the answer is "No," then do not implement any behavior modification plan until other elements are included in the plan. As Ross Greene, PhD has said, "Motivation makes the possible more possible. It does not make the impossible, possible."

If the student is capable of exhibiting the desired behavior, is the student capable of exhibiting it consistently? What will we do if the student cannot possibly comply with the plan on a given day?

If the student is not capable of exhibiting the desired behavior consistently even with boosted motivation, then any behavior modification plan based solely on applying consequences may produce distress, agitation, and worsening behavior or symptom severity.

As an example of an additional support for a student whose behavior is expected to be quite variable, in-school counseling to help the student understand and accept the nature of his neurologically-based variability may be an important component. Similarly, developing contingencies that allow for a certain number of "failures" or "misfires" without costing the student the reward may be helpful.

During the planning stage, discuss with the student and parents what will happen if the student is having such an awful day that the student feels that he cannot possibly comply with the plan or earn any reinforcers.

---

* Under the federal statute known as the Individuals with Disabilities Education Act (IDEA), a Behavior Intervention Plan requires consent. Even if federal law did not require it, however, or if the reader lives outside the U.S., we strongly recommend schools obtain informed consent for any behavior modification plan. Teachers often believe that they can just implement a behavior modification plan in their classroom without informed consent. We believe that to protect themselves, to protect the student, and to engage more parental support, informed consent needs to be obtained.

** The question of whether or not the plan should have targeted time in seat is another question. In our opinion, a more direct approach of targeting academic productivity is more likely to be successful.

Have we asked the parent whether the student tends to get overaroused or agitated by whatever type of plan we are considering?

Parents often know whether their child does better if he earns rewards for desirable behavior or if he does better if he loses rewards for undesirable behavior. Parents also often know if their child is likely to get too obsessed with the reward system to the point where it is likely to be counterproductive. In our opinion, good planning involves both the student and the parents in the design of the plan.

The student's input is a primary source of information during planning.

Have we designated "reinforcers" or "rewards" without actually collecting data to determine that they are effective rewards for that student?

While something may seem like it would be reinforcing as a reward, do not assume it will be. Use a reinforcer preference questionnaire or talk with the student about possible rewards. Be prepared to change rewards if a potential reward does not appear to be effective when we monitor the plan or if the student earns so many rewards that the reward is no longer effective.

It is also helpful to ask the parents if they know what might work as a reinforcer for the student in school. Remember that we can use an activity as a reinforcer, such as ten minutes of free reading time, extra recess time, extra computer time, etc. In many cases, activities are more effective positive reinforcers than tangible goods such as small rewards. They also have the advantage of being less costly.

If the school cannot provide desirable reinforcers, one creative approach is to ask all students to bring in toys or other materials they no longer want. These items go into the classroom "store" and can be used as reinforcers if the student is willing to work for them. What is one student's trash may be treasure to another student.

Does the plan incorporate immediate reinforcers or only delayed reinforcers?

The most effective way to shape or increase a desired behavior is to reward it every time it occurs and to reward it immediately. In our experience, however, we often see school personnel implementing behavior plans that have contingencies, such as "If you [complete all your classwork] today in school, you'll get a reward when you get home" or "If

you earn [x] number of points every day this week, you will get [this great reward] on Friday." Both of those strategies are unlikely to be successful because they introduce too much delay between the student exhibiting the desired response and the delivery of the reward. At the beginning, provide the reinforcers immediately or quickly after the behavior occurs. Larger rewards for longer time periods (e.g., a whole week) can also be used, but do not neglect to have immediate and effective rewards.

Conference occasionally with the students to see what they find motivating. Set some reasonable limits on choices, but be sure to have something that really motivates them. Remember that reinforcers do not have to be things but can also be activities that the student values. Consider creating a reward "menu" that has a number of choices. Change the reward menu frequently enough that the student does not get bored with the rewards.

Have we established a frequent monitoring system that includes reports from the parents so that we can determine if the plan is backfiring instead of helping?

In some cases, students make extraordinary efforts to suppress symptoms in school so that they can earn promised rewards. Once home, however, they may break down in tears or disruptive behavior from the stress of trying to control themselves in school. Whenever a plan is implemented or a criterion is changed, home-school communication is essential to determine if the plan is really working or just moving the problem to another location, e.g., home, or creating a new problem.

Can those responsible for administering the plan adhere to the plan consistently?

If the answer to this question is "No," do not implement the plan. Assuming, for now, that there are no obstacles to developing a behavior modification plan, we turn to a review of some basic operations and methods in behavior modification.

Simple Operations

The term "behavior modification" is usually understood by school personnel to mean employing consequences for behavior to either teach or strengthen desired behaviors or to weaken or extinguish undesirable behaviors. The "behaviors" can be social behaviors (such as "greets others politely when he enters the classroom") or academic behaviors (such as "checks his work before submitting it").

Note that the emphasis in "behavior modification" as it is usually understood by school personnel is on consequences for overt and measurable behavior that the student exhibits. For example, "sadness" is not "behavior" because it is not a specific behavior that we can observe and measure, but "crying" is an observable "behavior." One of the first challenges school personnel encounter is translating their concerns into specific observable behaviors that can be measured and recorded.

Behavior modification programs rely heavily on "consequences." Consequences actually have two elements to them:

1. Consequences can boost the student's motivation. Teachers and parents routinely use consequences to boost motivation, e.g., "If you finish all your work early, you can play that exciting new computer game!" or "If you grab toys away from others again, you'll have to stay in at recess."

2. Consequences provide feedback or information about the student's behavior. If a student has a plan that calls for getting ten minutes of free time for on-task behavior, telling the student, "You just earned ten minutes of free time" lets the student know that they were on-task for the required length of time. Students with Executive Dysfunction (Chapter 9) do not always understand the cause and effect relationship between their behavior and the feedback involved in getting a consequence. For these students, make the feedback explicit, e.g., "You just spent ten minutes on-task so you've earned fifteen minutes on the computer for play. Good job!"

Table 27.1 provides a summary of four basic approaches to applying consequences in behavior modification.

A few points about the material in Table 27.1 bear special comment:

1. The term "negative reinforcer" tends to confuse people because "negative" generally suggests something that would decrease

Table 27.1. Common Operations in Behavior Modification and Their Effect on Behavior Rate or Strength

Type of Consequence	Operation	
	Delivered or Applied	**Removed or Avoided**
Something positive or valued	*Effect:* maintains or strengthens behavior *Example:* A student starts raising his hand more when raising his hand results in ten minutes of extra recess time. This is called "positive reinforcement."	*Effect:* decreases rate of behavior *Example:* Throwing papers on the floor decreases when throwing is always followed by loss of ten minutes of recess that day. This is called "negative punishment."
Something negative or undesirable	*Effect:* decreases rate of behavior *Example:* Throwing papers on the floor decreases when the student is required to stay after school each day to sweep the floor. This is called "positive punishment."	*Effect:* maintains or strengthens behavior *Example:* Classwork completion increases if a student can avoid being required to stay after school by completing his classwork during class time. * This is called "negative reinforcement."

* This example may sound like punishment for the teacher, but Sherry has used this technique very successfully in the classroom. After a few weeks, the work completion rate had increased significantly to the point where even though the rule remained in effect, incidents of work incompletion were rare.

behavior. A negative reinforcer *maintains or strengthens* behavior by its removal or termination when the desired behavior occurs. The best way to remember this is to know that the term "reinforcer" means that it is maintaining or strengthening behavior.

2. "Positive punishment" refers to what we used to just call "punishment"—decreasing unwanted behavior by applying an unpleasant consequence like having to stay after school, getting sent to the back of the line, etc.

3. Because the removal of something of value to the child can also decrease behavior, it is referred to as "negative punishment." This is when a child loses something of value when inappropriate behavior is demonstrated, e.g., "You will lose X if you do Y."

*We cannot know with certainty whether something is a **reinforcer** or a **punisher** until we actually try it and record its effect on the behavior being targeted.*

A "reinforcer" or "punisher," by definition, is always effective. Saying "I tried positive reinforcement and it did not work" is an example of self-contradiction because by definition, positive reinforcement works. What school personnel or parents may mean to say is something like, "I tried to use [this specific reward] as a positive reinforcer and it did not work to strengthen or maintain the behavior." This type of confusion brings us to a very important point: We cannot know with certainty whether something is a reinforcer or a punisher until we actually try it and record its effect on the behavior being targeted. We may have a good guess that the student would like something or work for it (positive reinforcement), but until we actually implement the plan and *measure* its effect on the behavior, we do not know whether it is a positive reinforcer in that situation.

How and When Do We Reward the Behavior?

Once a student's team has decided to use a behavior modification plan with positive reinforcement, the team needs to consider:

1. Where to set the goal for earning the reward?
2. What to use to try to maintain or strengthen the behavior?
3. How often and when to deliver the reward?

The answers to the first two questions come from the baseline data gathering, where we first gather information on the particular behavior, and from the Functional Behavioral Assessment, discussed in the last chapter. The need for objective data recording is clear when we think about where to set our initial goal. Suppose we want to lose a lot of weight and decide to put ourselves on a reward system. Would our plan be more likely to be effective if we say, "I will give myself the first reward after I lose twenty-five pounds" or would it be more effective if we say, "I will give myself the first reward after I lose three pounds"? When trying to change behavior, the sooner the first reward is provided and the more attainable it is, the better.

Issues of how often and when to deliver rewards are often serious obstacles to effective behavior modification programs in school settings. In the most familiar behavioral modification plans, reinforcers are either delivered *every* time the desired response occurs (a continuous reinforcement or "CRF" schedule) or after some number of responses or amount of time (an intermittent reinforcement schedule). An example of a CRF schedule is: If we are trying to teach Joe to raise his hand instead of calling out, then every time he raises his hand, he would immediately get whatever reward had been designated.

A CRF schedule is the most effective way to increase the frequency of a desirable behavior. Every instance of the desired behavior is rewarded immediately.

When teaching a new behavior or skill, identify approximations to the behavior and reward each and every time the student exhibits the intermediate step to the goal. Do not raise the bar after every successful approximation to the goal, however, raise it gradually.

It does not take much imagination to understand how difficult and time consuming a CRF schedule might be to implement in a regular classroom, particularly if the class includes multiple students with individualized Behavior Intervention Plans. A second concern with CRF schedules is that they increase the chances that the student will get tired of the positive reinforcer because he gets many of them within a relatively brief period of time.

Instead of using a CRF schedule to maintain or increase desired behavior, consider intermittent schedules of reinforcement once the behavior has been well established. An intermittent schedule can be based on a set time or number of responses required to get the reinforcer. An intermittent schedule can be based on time (e.g., every five minutes or on average, five minutes) or it can be based on responses (e.g., every three times or on average, three times).

Given all the demands on a teacher's time, neither a CRF schedule nor an intermittent schedule may sound particularly easy or convenient to use in a classroom. As difficult as it may seem to get started, our experience has been that many teachers can get into the rhythm of implementing a plan relatively effortlessly after the first few days. In other situations, teachers may need assistance, particularly if the class includes a number of students with individualized behavior plans.

Intermittent schedules of reinforcement are particularly well suited once a behavior is established and we want the student to maintain a higher rate of the behavior with fewer reinforcers. For example, suppose that we want to teach Lonny to say "Please" when making a request. At first, we might want to positively reinforce every instance where Lonny says "Please." Eventually, however, once the behavior appears to be established, we want to shift to a less frequent schedule of positive reinforcement. To accomplish that, we might use an intermittent schedule where every third time Lonny says "Please," he gets the reinforcer. When that is well established, we might shift the criterion to every fifth "Please," and so on. Eventually, by gradually increasing the requirement for reinforcement, Lonny will be able to regularly say "Please" without requiring many—or any—external (extrinsic) reinforcers at all.

Other Approaches

The conditioning approaches in Table 27.1 represent the most commonly recognized behavior modification contingencies, but they are not the only ones. School personnel planning a behavior modification approach might wish to consider using other approaches for decreasing unwanted behavior or increasing desired behavior. For now, we will consider just one of the more commonly employed methods in schools—decreasing unwanted behavior by ignoring it.

If a behavior is being maintained by its consequences, then removing the consequences will prob-ably lead to an eventual decrease or elimination of the behavior. When an undesired behavior is allowed to occur but is never followed by a reinforcer or reward, we would expect the rate of the behavior to decrease. This is known as an extinction approach: allowing the behavior to extinguish.

Teachers routinely attempt to use extinction but they may not call it by that name and may just call it "ignoring bad behavior." For example, if a teacher realizes that peer responses or the teacher's own responses to a student's misbehavior are actually maintaining the behavior, the teacher might decide to completely ignore the behavior every time it occurs, and might enlist the help of peers to also ignore the misbehavior.

When using an extinction approach, it is important for teachers to be prepared for the fact that initially the undesired response might *increase* instead of decrease. This is often the case when the teacher or others have been unknowingly and inconsistently reinforcing the behavior in the past. When the reinforcement suddenly stops completely, the student may not realize that the behavior will never again result in reinforcement. The student may persist or increase the rate of the behavior in an attempt to get the reinforcer that was previously associated with the behavior.

The length of time that the behavior persists depends, in part, on how long it takes for the child to realize that the behavior is not going to produce reinforcement. For example, if the first few times we call someone on the phone, he never returns our phone call, we might give up after just the few attempts. But if in the past, our calls were not returned every time but were occasionally returned, we might persist longer before giving up.

Extinction is not the same as active suppression of a response. An active suppression of a response is when a person is consciously trying to not do something. In extinction, the response decreases without the extreme effort and just fades away.

Using an extinction approach to an undesirable behavior is even more effective if it is coupled with providing positive reinforcement for alternative desirable behaviors. For example, if the teacher ignores a student when he impulsively calls out an answer, but calls on him when he raises his hand and says, "Good hand raising," hand raising is more likely to increase than if he just ignored the impulsive "blurts."

Hone Your Use of Praise and Reprimands

Although this chapter has focused on behavior modification, the less sophisticated everyday communications typically have a great effect on student behavior. A simple "tweak" to our verbal communications can often have significant impact.

Verbal praise is more effective if it is contingent on the student's behavior, if it is specific, and if we are sincere. To illustrate the need for specificity, a teacher may know that he is saying, "Good!" to a student because the student completed a sentence, but the student may not know that the "Good" refers to the sentence and may think that he is saying "Good" because he covered his mouth while coughing. Saying, "That's a good sentence" is more effective than a general "Good," especially for students with EDF.

Praise consists of two parts: What we say to the child and what he in turn says to himself.
— *Haim Ginott*

It is even more effective to use attributions in our verbal praise, i.e., refer to characteristics of the student whom we are praising. "You are a great writer" describes the student and not just the sentence he wrote. As such, it helps boost the student's self-esteem in writing sentences and the student may see himself as being a good writer. Using attribution, e.g., "You're being a good organizer" or "You're working hard at organizing yourself," is more effective than trying to persuade the child by saying judgmental things like "You should be more organized" or "You should try harder to organize yourself."

Hone verbal reprimands as well as verbal praise. Reprimands are more effective when we are standing close to the student and using a low voice, audible only to the student. Keep the reprimand short. Although it may be difficult, try to confine the reprimand to just a few words, e.g., "No doodling on your textbook." The student probably does not need an explanation of why writing on the textbook is inappropriate. If the student has Executive Dysfunction and does not understand why the behavior is inappropriate, then we can use the "Instant Replay" technique (Chapter 31) to help him understand the impact of his behavior.

Criticism is more effective when it sounds like praise.
— *Arnold Glasow*

Students with the disorders described in this book have generally encountered a lot of criticism. Anything that sounds like criticism may increase the students' anxiety or lead to feelings of demoralization or worthlessness. How we offer constructive criticism can make a difference. For example, editing is a particularly difficult task for students with Executive Dysfunction. Rather than saying, "This is good, but can you….?" it may be more helpful to say something like, "I really like how you described this character! Maybe you can add more detail so that the reader can really picture what he is doing and thinking."

Summary

Behavior modification offers a number of effective tools that schools can use to help students learn to control undesirable behavior while improving academic and social functioning. To be effective, however, a school plan must be based on a Functional Behavioral Assessment and must ensure that all necessary supports and interventions are in place, including direct instruction in skills if needed. Include provisions to monitor the plan and record data. Make sure the plan provides sufficiently motivating reinforcers in the form of tangible rewards or rewarding activities. Additionally, the plan must set goals that the student can reasonably achieve given the student's current level of functioning.

Sometimes it pays to maintain high expectations. For example, Leslie's son was in a program that involved graduated levels, where Level 3 provided more privileges and opportunities than Level 2, etc. To get to Level 3, however, the students had to maintain a certain number of points for ten consecutive school days. Falling below the required daily points would immediately drop the student back down a level. It took Leslie's son almost a year to reach Level 3 because his behavior was so variable that he generally could not pull even four "good days" together, much less ten. Finally, however, he reached Level 3. He

remained there for all of three days, had one "bad"
day, and dropped to Level 2. His disappointment was
tremendous. Realizing he might stop trying, he was
given in-school counseling to help him understand that
variability was part of what he had to contend with.
With this help, he was able to work his way back up
to Level 3. The next time he lost the level, he was able
to handle it more matter-of-factly and just worked his
way back up. In time, he was able to sustain Level 3,
and the lesson learned about variability enabled him
to persist then and in the future.

We urge our students to try harder so that they
will do better. But if we do better, they will try harder.

CHAPTER 28

School-Wide Positive Behavior Supports and Classroom Group Management

More important than the curriculum is the question of the methods
of teaching and the spirit in which the teaching is given.
— *Bertrand Russell*

Overview

Frequently, well intentioned and well designed behavior intervention plans fail without adequate support for both the student and the teacher. Yet the need for individualized plans may be reduced if the school supports broader plans that reduce problematic behaviors:

> "The school-wide application of positive behavior support (PBS) is a prevention-oriented approach to student discipline that is characterized by its focus on defining and teaching behavioral expectations, rewarding appropriate behaviors, continual evaluation of its effectiveness, and the integration of supports for individuals, groups, the school as a whole, and school/family/community partnerships." (Warren et al. 2006)

Unlike individualized positive behavior support (PBS) plans, school-wide PBS is a multi-systems approach to reducing antisocial student behaviors. Although there is no one set of "cookbook" procedures to follow to implement school-wide PBS plans, the following elements are part of the PBS multi-systems approach:

1. Provide clear definitions of expected appropriate behaviors to both students and staff members.
2. Define problem behaviors and their consequences clearly for students and staff members.
3. Provide regularly scheduled instruction regarding desired positive social behaviors so students can acquire the skills to change behaviors.
4. Provide effective incentives systems that encourage students to behave appropriately.
5. Encourage staff commitment to implementing interventions over the long term and to monitoring, supporting, coaching, debriefing, and providing booster lessons for students to maintain gains.
6. Provide staff training, feedback, and coaching in the effective implementation of the systems.
7. Establish systems for measuring and monitoring the intervention's effectiveness.

Source: (Sprague and Walker 2004)

The first two elements on the list are generally included under "building codes." Most buildings do have such policies and guidelines, but typically students are seldom directly taught the building policies as a lesson with rehearsal and review. In many places, a copy of the policies may be sent home for parents to review with their children and to sign indicating receipt and review. This is not enough. Direct instruction in the school is necessary and helpful. For schools that have not updated their building codes in a while, consider updating goals to include expectations and consequences for dealing with bullying, cyberbullying, and harassment.

The third element in the list contains two important parts: instruction in appropriate skills and assistance to achieve the skills. Some of the instruction can be incorporated into curriculum on a district-wide or school-wide basis, e.g., teach all students conflict resolution. For some students, however, individually administered direct instruction and supports will be required in addition to school-wide instruction to enable the student to adhere to school-wide rules. For example, for some students, teaching them the school-wide expectation of not calling out in class will not be sufficient for them to comply with the rule.

The fourth element in the list, effective incentives and motivational systems, works well both on an individually designed basis and on a group basis. Some principals have tried to inspire particular student outcomes by offering to do ridiculous things if the students achieve some difficult goal. For example, in one high school, the principal agreed to paint his car in the school colors if the students met some school-wide goal to improve attendance. An equally dedicated principal in New Jersey made a bet that his students could not read 10,000 books in a year. When the students won the bet, he paid up by spending a very cold night up on the roof of the school.[*] Making silly bets with students can often be highly motivating for them and can promote academics and appropriate behavior.

Securing commitment to adhering to interventions over the long haul is an important and often overlooked PBS component for students with disabilities. Some issues facing students cannot be completely addressed in a single grading period or even within one school year. Staff planning needs to take a longer view or perspective on how any gains made in the first year will be maintained and how supports will be provided in the future.

As noted in the chapters on Functional Behavioral Assessments and Behavior Intervention Plans, school personnel often require training, feedback, and assistance to plan effectively. Many schools do not have full-time school psychologists, and even when there is a full-time psychologist, her schedule is frequently overloaded with assessments and meetings. Because of this, there may be no way to provide regular in-class observations and supports needed for behavioral interventions. When planning any program, give careful consideration to how to provide adequate support for classroom personnel. It is not reasonable to expect the teacher to teach while simultaneously observing and recording behaviors for each student who may have an individualized plan. Training classroom aides to record can help reduce the burden on the teacher.

Systems for measuring and monitoring the intervention's effectiveness are also required. Remember that one of the essential elements of a Behavior Intervention Plan is that we monitor the plan.

School-Wide Positive Behavior Supports: Specific Strategies

Along with the general elements of a school-wide positive behavior support system described above, the following specific school-wide interventions may decrease behavior problems as well:

1. **Color-code** subjects and stick to the color-coding scheme across all teachers and grades, e.g., science books are always covered in orange across all grades in the district. Color-coding by subject is a great organizational tool and saves a lot of transition time because students can quickly grab and sort by color. Coordinate the color-coding of books and binders with bins in the classroom. Have one to turn in or pick up work and folders for filing other related materials. For students who are color-blind, have an alternative coding/sorting system.

2. Declare one day during the first week of school as a "**Respect Ourselves Day**." Hold a special assembly to teach and review building policies, expectations, and consequences for appropriate and inappropriate behavior. Have individual teachers teach the rules of their class that day. Offer some inducement or motivation for good behavior.

3. Establish a **school-wide zero tolerance** for bullying and for treating students with differences in an unkind way. Administrators

---

* Retrieved from Science Daily on February 25, 2007: http://www.sciencedaily.com/upi/?feed=Quirks&article=UPI-1-20061209-16442200-bc-us-principal.xml

and teachers set the tone for how students are treated. Silence from the adult when something unkind is going on is construed as acceptance and an endorsement of the bullying behavior.

4. **Celebrate diversity!** Schedule an "Embracing Differences" week when students learn about a variety of different disabilities or challenges. Encourage students to help teach these events. Books and videos that may be usefully incorporated in such events or peer education programs are listed on our website at www.challengingkids.com.

5. School districts often have a library of books or materials on specific disabilities, but all too often, the information does not get to the teachers when they need it. Each school can build its own useful library. In addition to any books or pamphlets, create a **"trick book" (a strategy book) about each disorder or disability** where teachers can enter particular strategies that they have used that have been helpful. That way, when a teacher has a student who is diagnosed with a particular disability or challenge, the teacher can consult the "trick book" for that disability.

6. Create a **"trick book" about and for each student** (Dornbush & Pruitt, 1995) in the building. Have teachers note what strategies work well for the student. The "trick book" remains in the school's office or confidential file room, depending on whether the student is classified for special education. Make the "trick book" accessible to the next year's teacher. Do not overlook the wisdom of the teachers that have already discovered "tricks" about the student.

7. **Arrange for staff development** on the disorders covered in this book. Many local support organizations have literature and a speakers' bureau. Also, consider taking advantage of some of the wonderful videos and literature listed on our website at www.challengingkids.com.

When planning for awareness or staff development programs, be sure to include nonteaching personnel who come into contact with students including related services providers, the truant officer, cafeteria personnel, monitors or paraprofessionals, school bus drivers, and bus monitors.

8. Encourage teachers on the same grade level to develop a **common set of expectations or behavior rules** for their classrooms, so that all students in the same grade are held to the same expectations. Each teacher may add some specific rules based on her own preferences and needs, but having a set of developmentally age-appropriate behavior expectations helps ensure generalization across settings (e.g., regular classroom to music, art, PE, etc.).

9. During "diversity" or "awareness" weeks, schedule some **programs for staff and parents** to get together to share information and support. Consider having a panel of parents talk about teacher and school supports they have found helpful when trying to support their child at home. Have a panel of teachers discuss the kinds of supports parents have provided that have enabled teachers to be more successful in the classroom. Provide resources for parents with information on specific disabilities and on how to structure a positive homework environment, how to promote better sleep hygiene (Appendix J), etc., as described in other chapters of this book.

10. Teach all school personnel the "**Instant Replay**" and "**Cooperative Problem Solving**" techniques (Chapter 31) so that no matter which personnel the student has, the student gets the same type of helpful response.

11. Designate some teachers as **Peer Models** who will develop appropriate programs for certain disabilities or behaviors. Let them consult with teachers who are struggling with a student.

At meetings concerning special education students, often five out of six teachers describe a host of problems with the student. Suddenly, the sixth teacher says, "I really cannot believe you are talking about David. He is no trouble in my room and has very good grades, both academically and in conduct. I am so surprised to hear of his struggles in other classes. He is a wonderful student and a pleasure to have in my class." Whenever there is a dramatic difference in reports, investigate what this teacher is doing differently, e.g., consider the curriculum, environment, and teaching style, and consider taking advantage of this teacher's approach.

12. Teach students to use **relaxation techniques**. At home, some students may like a warm bath, or to listen to favorite music, read a book, or have their parent tell them a relaxing bed time story. Some students may need to be taught a technique to use in school, especially if they have an anxiety disorder. (See Appendix G.)

Specific Classroom-Based Strategies and Techniques

Having two or three or more sets of rules or expectations for behavior in one classroom may lead to student protest (e.g., "Why does she get to do this and I don't?"). The principle that each student gets what she needs and "fair does not mean equal" is often impossible to maintain in a classroom, given the often overwhelming multiple responsibilities teachers face. For that reason, and in addition to school-wide supports and strategies, consider implementing effective group-based class plans that might reduce the need for some of the individualized plans.

Teaching the Classroom Rules

Most elementary school teachers teach the rules and have posters reinforcing them in their classrooms. By the time students get to middle school or high school, school personnel often assume that the students know what is expected of them. These assumptions are often not warranted for students with some of the neurological disorders we have described in this book. So, teach the expectations for behavior every school year. Also, schedule some "booster" sessions throughout the year, particularly after long holiday breaks.

For young students, use the "Say, Show, Check" method of direct instruction to teach the rules. Tell the students the rule or expectation, demonstrate it

in action while they comment on it, and have them rehearse or demonstrate the behavior while the teacher observes and provides feedback and reinforcement. To boost motivation for positive participation and attention to this activity, teachers can combine this instructional activity with others described later in this chapter.

Teach and reteach the rules throughout the first week of school. Have a visual poster that states the positive rules. This poster could be usefully placed next to the poster that provides the consequences and any reward system in place.

In developing a poster for classroom rules, we are aware that most teachers have been taught to only list the "Do" rules and not the "Do Not" rules. That said, it is important for some students, who may not generalize or who have EDF, to directly teach what not to do as well as what to do.

If the behavior is important, use direct instruction to teach the expectation and appropriate behavior. Students who do not need the instruction are not harmed by the instruction, and those who do need it, benefit. Combine direct instruction of behavior and social skills with positive reinforcement for participation in the instructional activity. Teach the rules in multiple settings for the benefit of those who have difficulty generalizing.

Token Economies

Token economies are probably the most research-validated and effective group-based behavior management strategy. They can also be used to enhance academic performance.

The use of token economies in schools has been limited, in part, because of the lack of training and support provided to teachers, and, in part, because of a common misperception that using external rewards above the primary grade level might reduce intrinsic motivation. Token economies can still be very effective at the upper grades if the goal is shifted from trying to control the student's behavior to trying to foster greater autonomous and self-determined behavior. Such approaches may raise the difficulty of tasks that students are willing to tackle or attempt (Kamins and Dweck 1999). They may also promote more student-initiated goal setting, self-monitoring, self-evaluation, and strategy use (Zimmerman 2000). When working with older students, the tokens or rewards are made contingent on success, not effort. In developing a reward menu, be sure to include some low cost rewards as well as some bigger rewards that require students to save up for.

For a token economy, establish:
1. a clear set of rules/expectations that will lead to rewards or consequences.
2. which chips or tokens to use.
3. positive reinforcers, or rewards or reward activities that chips or tokens can be "cashed in" for.

Set contingencies based on the group's functioning (e.g., "When everyone has turned in their homework, you will all get...."). When developing the group-based contingencies, events such as Friday pizza parties for the class, extra recess time, and other activities can be motivating for younger students. Keep a visual chart or display that prominently reminds students of their progress toward any group goals. Also, provide individual provisions/rewards (e.g., "Anyone who completes all of her classwork for the day earns...."). With either type of reward system, change the reward menu over time so that students do not get bored with the reinforcers. Teachers may also wish to include positive reinforcers based on group compliance with simple commands such as "Turtle!" (see below).

"Countdown to Free Time"

In this research-validated behavior intervention, the teacher writes the numbers twenty to zero in descending order on the board at the beginning of a selected lesson. Students are told that they can earn free time to engage in rewarding activities by paying attention during the lesson. The maximum amount of free time they can earn is twenty minutes. The teacher informs the students that she will cross off a number every time she has to reprimand one of them for being unproductive or disruptive. The number of minutes of free time left on the board is what the students earn for that day. To prevent the student with these disorders from causing the whole class to lose time or points, consider giving the student three "free passes" so that if she does break the rules, her peers do not resent her for costing them free time or the reward.

The "Countdown to Free Time" method is particularly well-suited to elementary school students. The free time can be provided as a reward that is administered that day. If teachers wish to use the

this technique towards a weekly reward like a class pizza party on Friday, then set the number of points that are needed for the reward, note them on the board, and each day add up the points the class has earned towards the group goal, i.e., a "thermometer" approach.

To most effectively use the Countdown method, use it for only one or two lessons each day. Lessons where the students need to sit and learn new material are particularly appropriate. Simply explain the reward procedure at the outset (e.g., "Right now we're going to learn about _____ and you are also going to have an opportunity to earn _____ (reward)." Be sure to clearly explain what behaviors lead to points or time deduction (e.g., "If you call out without raising your hand, or if you get out of your seat without permission..."). Try to limit unacceptable behaviors to no more than three misbehaviors.

"Turtle!"

For young students, the "Turtle" technique can help if too many students are out of their seats, off-task, or noisy. Use direct instruction (e.g., "Say, Show, Check") to teach the students that when you call out, "Turtle!" they are to freeze and check if they are doing what they are supposed to be doing. The "Turtle!" approach can be used without any rewards or it can be used with a group-based positive reinforcement contingency. For example, a teacher may set up a contingency so that if no more than three students fail to comply with the "freeze," the class earns points towards a group reward. Later on, the contingency can be shifted so that if no more than three students are off-task when the teacher calls out "Turtle!," the class earns points towards the group reward.

Timed Tones

One strategy that has been successfully applied to academic self-monitoring with older students involves using randomly timed tones on a tape recorder. When the tone is sounded, the students are to ask themselves, "Was I paying attention?" and record a "Yes" or a "No" on their individual score sheet or checklist. For this type of application, it may be most helpful to have the tone sound frequently at the beginning of self-monitoring (e.g., sound the tone at thirty-second intervals up to one-and-a-half-minute intervals). As the students learn to monitor themselves for being on-task, they may become more aware of what triggers off-task behavior. Some research suggests that increased awareness may enable them to return to on-task behaviors.

Once the self-monitoring program is producing consistent and successful results, the students can be weaned off the tape recorded tones and the self-recording sheet. Using external rewards to boost motivation may be essential for students with ADHD. Self-monitoring strategies such as the one described here are research-validated methods for increasing the on-task behaviors of inattentive students at both the elementary and secondary school levels (Lloyd et al. 1998).

Note that tones may be distracting for students with ADHD or unpleasant for students with auditory issues.

Need Help? Don't Call Out—Just Turn the Paper Cup Over!

It would be great if some young students would not constantly get up from their desks to come ask for help or if they wouldn't just call out loudly when they need attention or help. An effective and quiet approach to getting help is the paper cup technique. The only materials needed to implement it are small, colored paper cups.

To implement the technique, teach the class (by "Say, Show, Check" instruction) that when they are working and do not need help, they are to leave the cup turned upwards on their desks. If they need help, they should simply turn the cup over (upside down) as a quiet signal that they need help. No calling out, no raising hands—simply turning the cup over. To add some novelty to it, allow the students to decorate their own cups. The paper cup technique also works well when the students are in a clustered desk activity; use one paper cup for the group and any child in the group can reach out to turn the cup over to quietly request assistance.

"Give Me Five!"

The "Give Me Five!" technique can be used to get the students' attention if things are getting disruptive. Using direct instruction, teach the students that when we hold up our hand with outstretched fingers and say, "Give Me Five!" that means the students are to:

- Look at us
- Be quiet

- Sit still
- Have their hands free of any objects
- Listen to us

An alternative approach to "Give Me Five!" is to teach them that "Give Me Five!" means two eyes watching, two ears listening, and one mouth closed.

As with other techniques, combine direct instruction (Say, Show, Check) with positive reinforcement during learning and rehearsal. Also, provide group-based contingencies for compliance with the directions given during activities. Allow for less than perfect compliance so that students with disabilities do not always "cost" the class rewards.

Traffic Controls for Talking

For younger students or those requiring more visual cues and supports, set up a "traffic light" system in the classroom whereby a red light indicates that the students are not to be talking at all during the activity, a yellow light indicates that some talking is allowed if it is to ask a question or answer a question about the activity, and a green light means that talking is permitted during the activity.

Summary

Providing school-wide supports and reinforcement improves behavior and decreases the need for individualized Behavior Intervention Plans. The more consistent teachers are within their own classes and across classes, and the more uniform the standards across settings within a school building, the greater the likelihood that students will generalize positive social and behavior skills. This is especially important for students with Executive Dysfunction.

The real voyage of discovery consists not in seeking new landscapes but in having new eyes.
— *Marcel Proust*

CHAPTER 29

Punishment and Other Aversive Interventions

There is nothing more unequal than the equal treatment of unequal people.
— *Thomas Jefferson*

Punishment refers to reducing a behavior by applying some unpleasant event or consequence when the behavior occurs. By its very nature, punishment is aversive. If it were not, there would be no motivation to decrease the behavior. Punishment is not the only type of aversive event that can decrease unwanted behavior. As described in Chapter 27, removing something that the student values can also decrease an inappropriate behavior. Within educational settings, teachers may attempt to punish inappropriate behavior by having students stay after school, engage in some boring chore (such as writing "I will not talk out of turn" fifty times), or be sent to the principal's office. Very often, the consequences are not intrinsically linked to the behavior or "crime." For students who have handwriting problems due to their neurological disorders, for example, writing sentences is especially inappropriate.

Reparations vs. Artificial Punishment

When dealing with students with the type of neurological conditions described in this book, it is much more effective to use more natural consequences for the behavior to help them understand the connection between their behavior and the consequences. For example, if a student is hitting another student and needs to be removed from the situation, in a calm and neutral tone tell the student, "Because you are having trouble keeping your hands to yourself, you need to sit further away." Use a neutral, matter-of-fact tone that does not suggest that you are trying to punish the student in any way. Similarly, if a student has ripped up papers and thrown them on the floor, have the student pick up the papers and throw them out rather than sending him out of the room.

A reparation technique based on the principle of "You broke it, you fix it" requires the student to restore the environment to its previous state and to go beyond simple restoration as a means to show that the student really wants to repair the relationship.* For example, if a student has thrown papers all over the floor, the student needs to pick up the papers he threw on the floor and then go around the classroom and clean up or tidy even more papers. Teaching the student that they must clean up after themselves, whether in a physical sense or a social sense, is a valuable life lesson. Similarly, if the student has been arguing with the teacher for ten minutes because he is stuck on something, an apology is not sufficient. He needs to help the teacher recover the ten minutes he made the class lose, perhaps by doing some chores for the teacher so that the teacher can get caught up.

The more natural the consequences are, the more likely the student will be to learn what to do if he makes a mistake or loses control. Certainly if a student breaks another student's property by throwing it or breaking it on purpose, he needs to take

* (Pruitt 1995)

steps to repair and restore the relationship with his peer. Sending him to the principal's office does not accomplish that.

When schools and parents adopt a reparations approach to handling problematic behavior, it requires some willingness to not resort to the standard "Go to your room" type of punishment and to carefully reflect on what would be appropriate reparations in each situation as it occurs. Engaging the student in determining what reparations are to be made helps the student see the connection between his behavior, its impact on others, and what he may need to do to repair relationships.

Too Much Punishment

Although punishment may be very effective when used selectively and correctly, the reality in working with students with neurological disorders is that most of them have already experienced enough punishment to last them a lifetime. They may have been punished at home prior to their diagnosis by parents who did not understand the involuntary nature of their symptoms. They may have been punished frequently by previous teachers, or rejected by peers because of their symptoms. For many of these students, the world has been a pretty punishing place, and the last thing they need is more punishment from their teacher.

If we focus on our ultimate goal—to teach the student self-management and responsible behavior—then we can begin to think differently about consequences and punishment. For starters, we begin by taking punishment out of our repertoire of options and explore what we can accomplish by direct instruction in skills and positive supports. If, however, positive supports are insufficient, and positive reinforcement of alternative and desirable behaviors is not effective, then consider using reparations. If that does not seem effective after an adequate trial, consider also taking away something that the student cares about when they exhibit the unwanted behavior. Taking away something the student values or taking away the opportunity to engage in an exciting or rewarding activity are two examples of what may be effective punishment approaches for some students. Some students, however, react poorly to punishment and their behavior problems may increase rather than decrease. Consulting with the student's parents before implementing any such plan is critical as they can probably predict how their child will respond to any punishment being considered.

Some punishment approaches involve both loss of privileges or enjoyable activities and delivery of an aversive consequence such as having to stay after school. Time-out may be considered punishment by some students and is discussed in the next chapter.

Because students with neurological disorders have generally incurred higher than normal rates of aversive consequences for their symptoms and behavior, we strongly discourage using punishment methods unless all nonaversive or less aversive methods have failed.

Using "Aversives"

Perhaps one of the most difficult issues is what to do when a student has a seriously self-injurious or other-injurious behavior and the school and parents agree that something must be done to dramatically and quickly reduce the behavior. Because traditional conditioning techniques generally take time to work and because medications may take time to build up in the system or may not be effective for a particular child, some parents and schools have considered drastic aversive measures such as the use of painful skin shock to punish the symptom or behavior.

The application of aversive stimuli such as painful skin shock poses medical, ethical, and civil liberties issues. If a student's symptom or behavior is so extreme that the school is considering the use of extreme measures, there are at least two points to keep in mind:

- Is there adequately controlled research that supports the use of the proposed intervention for that behavior and for youth with the student's known diagnosis or diagnoses? And is there any long-term research on its effectiveness or possible adverse effects?
- Most schools do not have the necessary psychiatrists and licensed psychologists and nurses in the building full-time to monitor the student's health and safety if these techniques are used.*

In our experience, students with the neurological disorders described in this book do not need nor benefit from these techniques and, worse, may be harmed by them.

---

* Report of the New York State Psychological Association Task Force on Aversive Controls with Children, August 22, 2006.

The use of restraint also raises significant concerns. Because physical restraint is associated with an increased risk of harm, injury, or death,[*] reserve its use to imminent safety emergencies, i.e., to protect the health and safety of the student or others from imminent and serious physical injury. Restraining a developmentally disabled student as a consequence for his behavior to "teach him not to do that" not only violates U.S. federal law[**] but poses significant safety and health risks for the student as well as school personnel.

In the next chapter we consider the use of time-out to decrease undesirable behavior, but before leaving this overview on punishment and techniques designed to reduce behavior by applying consequences, consider this: **"Discipline" means "Training."**

If you punish a child for something he can't control, what have you taught him? If you punish him for the benefit of others, what have you taught them all?
— *Leslie E. Packer, Ph.D., 1999*

[*] The Lethal Hazard of Prone Restraint: Positional Asphyxiation. Protection & Advocacy, Inc., Report #7018.01, April 2002.

[**] 42 U.S.C. § 15009

CHAPTER 30

Time-Out

Phillip was a first grade student with Asperger's Syndrome. He would get stuck on having to be first, and would knock his peers out of his way or race to get ahead of them for all activities. If he could not be first, he would have a meltdown in class. His teacher and aide decided that whenever that happened, he would be removed from the classroom—forcibly, if needed— and taken to the time-out room in the building.

Phillip was so upset by the time-out room that he could not stop talking and worrying about it. And on the very first day of summer camp, Phillip turned to his mother with tears in his eyes and said, "Mommy, will they put me in a time-out room in camp?"

Preview

Time-out from reinforcement ("time-out") is a procedure in which students who have engaged in undesirable or inappropriate behaviors lose the opportunity to engage in rewarding activities. Classroom-wide time-out plans can be an effective group management tool and minimize the risk of students feeling unfairly picked upon or held to different standards. In some cases, an individual student may require a time-out plan that is specific to her problems and disabilities.

Different Types of Time-Out

Different types of time-out procedures can be categorized as follows:
- Student-initiated or student-directed time-out
- Teacher-suggested time-out
- Teacher-directed time-out
- Teacher-directed time-out as planned punishment

In a **student-initiated** or **student-directed** time-out, the student voluntarily initiates the time-out. Young students may be able to initiate a time-out, but this technique is more common as the student matures. That said, there are many older students who may not recognize when they need a time-out and/or may not initiate one. Depending upon the student and the situation, the time-out may be taken at the student's desk or in some preapproved location. Some students may wish to go for a walk inside the building or go to another place in the building, e.g., the student takes a break from the assigned activity and goes to sit outside the counselor's office in order to calm down.

A student-initiated time-out is a potentially valuable self-management tool for students who become dysregulated quickly during academic activities. For easily agitated students who are likely to engage in inappropriate behavior if they stay in the classroom, learning to "take it outside" helps protect others from their symptoms and helps protect their important peer and adult relationships. For some students, such time-outs need to be incorporated in the student's plan and may be supported by counseling services. Help students learn to remove themselves from situations that they cannot handle, and assist them in making a "graceful exit" (Chapter 31). When the student grows up and has a job and family, self-imposed time-out as a self-management tool will help her preserve jobs and social relationships.

For those who are concerned that the student is losing time by taking a self-selected time-out, consider how much time the teacher, the student, and the other students will lose if the student stays in the classroom and becomes disruptive.

If a student seems to be always requesting a time-out during one particular type of academic activity, however, it needs to trigger further assessment by school personnel to consider whether other academic modifications or services are required. A Functional Behavioral Assessment (Chapter 26) can be very helpful when there seems to be too many self-imposed time-outs. In the interim, if a student is requesting a time-out, we recommend that teachers not try to impose a delay or contingency upon leaving. If there is concern that the student is not using time-out appropriately, schedule a meeting to discuss it at another time with the student, parents, or other professionals as needed.

Trying to keep a student in the classroom when she feels that she is ready to "blow" is only inviting trouble. Reduce any anxiety about missing work by letting the student know ahead of time that she will get help getting caught up when she returns.

If a student is struggling with self-control and asks to take a time-out, do not penalize her by taking away opportunities to earn positive reinforcers. In this type of time-out situation, the teacher or aide is encouraged to provide the student with any work missed during the self-imposed time-out so that the student is more likely to take a break to regain self-control.

A **teacher-suggested** time-out can be meaningfully used when a teacher sees that a student is struggling and is about to lose control. The effective use of this type of cue requires a pre-arranged and pre-agreed-upon signal between the student and teacher. The signal lets the student know that not only can she take a break, but that she probably needs to take a break *right now* before she gets into trouble. Remember that it is easier to prevent trouble than to deal with it once it has started. If the teacher can get the student to take a break before matters get out of control, there will be less need to worry about providing time-out as a consequence for bad behavior.

The teacher-suggested time out only works well if the teacher has established a good relationship with the student. If the student does not feel supported by the teacher, the suggestion will not be received in a positive manner.

To encourage the student to comply with the suggestion, make sure the student is not penalized by losing opportunities to earn positive reinforcers. Use positive reinforcement for compliance with teacher-suggested time-outs.

Teacher-suggested time-outs are probably best limited to situations in which the student is likely to get into trouble if she stays in the classroom. As part of the pre-arrangement, however, students need to understand that if they do not cooperate with the suggestion and decide to remain in the situation, then they will be held responsible for their behavior. It is important for the student to always know ahead of time what the consequences are for inappropriate behavior.

Note the significant difference between a teacher-suggested and a **teacher-directed** time-out. In the former, the teacher suggests a time-out, but the student is free to decline (although there may be consequences if she stays in the situation and disrupts the learning environment). In the latter, compliance is not optional. The teacher is politely instructing the student to take a time-out and the student does not have the option to refuse to comply without risking negative consequences for noncompliance. Teacher-directed time-outs can be handled in a calm, non-punitive way, but it is important to realize that they are often experienced as punitive by the student regardless of how the direction is given. For that reason, we talk about some of these techniques as "punitive," but we recognize that teachers may not be intending to be punitive or delivering the instruction in a punitive tone. How the teacher presents the plan to the student can help the student understand that the intention of the plan is not to punish them. The intention is to give them a short break to enable them to refocus, calm themselves, and comply with the expected activity and classroom rules.

If the teacher has a punitive tone or raised voice, the student reacts to that and does not concentrate on what is needed to control her behavior. It is important not to distract the student from looking at her own behavior.

Many students refuse to take a non-punitive time-out when suggested or even directed by the teacher. They do so for a variety of reasons, including becoming obsessively stuck and unable to get themselves out of a situation, having difficulty making a transition quickly, and most often, because they do not want to lose face with their peers by being sent from the room. The use of discreet signals, graceful exits, and sensitivity towards peer issues can help students leave the classroom.

Reserve teacher-directed time-outs for those situations in which the student is likely to get explosive or when her behavior interferes with instruction. Directing a student to leave the classroom because of a symptom that the student cannot control may lead to anger and resentment on the student's part, a feeling of being misunderstood and treated unfairly, and concern for being embarrassed in front of peers. Similarly, if a student is stuck engaging in a compulsive ritual because of anxiety and the teacher directs the student to leave the setting, the student's anxiety level will probably increase even more, raising the risk of explosive or emotional behavior.

If the student cooperates with a nonpunitive teacher-directed time-out, do not penalize the student for any work missed and provide copies of any work the student missed while out of the room. If possible, arrange the situation so that before re-entering the room, the student works with a staff member to review what happened, plan what she will do when she gets back to the room, and then return when she feels she is back in charge of herself.

In a **teacher-directed time-out used as part of planned punishment**, there are consequences for the targeted behavior that involve loss of opportunity to earn positive reinforcers. Whether time-out can even be used as planned punishment as well as the use of special time-out rooms entails additional considerations, described later in this chapter.

On the Necessity of Positive Reinforcement in Time-out as Punishment

For time-out be effective, there needs to be some positive reinforcement system from which the student will be temporarily removed. Removing the student from a boring academic task that does not result in any tangible or desired rewards is not punishment. Removing them from the opportunity to earn a desired reward is punishment. Time-out as planned punishment *generally* does not work if there is no positive reinforcement from which the student is being removed.

Removing the student from an activity that is not linked to the opportunity to earn positive reinforcement is not time-out. It may give the teacher a badly needed break from the student, but when used for such purposes, it is not as likely to be an effective behavior modification tool.

In a typical time-out situation, an undesirable behavior is paired with a time-out consequence. Targeted behaviors typically include behaviors such as calling out without raising your hand or being called upon, distracting others by talking to them when they are trying to work, physically aggressive gestures, and verbal disrespect of teacher or peers. The time-out consequences can be tiered depending on the frequency or severity of the situation:

- The student is allowed to stay at her desk (or wherever she was supposed to be) and listen and watch but the student is not permitted to participate in reinforcing activities.
- The student is moved to another part of the classroom where she can listen and watch, but she is not allowed to participate in the activity or earn any reinforcers.
- The student is moved to another part of the classroom and can neither observe nor participate in the activity.
- The student is removed from the classroom or instructional setting and sent to another classroom.
- The student is removed from the classroom and sent to a time-out room.

When students are removed from the classroom, they may be sent to another classroom, an administrator's office, or, in some schools, a time-out room. When a time-out room is used and the student is alone in the room, we consider this "isolation" and, in our opinion, it is functionally equivalent to "seclusion."*

When students are directed to leave the classroom, it is important to remember that during the time that they are out of the classroom, they are being deprived of their education. If a student is frequently being sent from the classroom—regardless of whether it is to go sit in the hall, to sit in the principal's office or counseling office, or to go to a time-out room—school personnel need to consider the academic and psychological implications of removing the student. Frequent removals or extended amount of time out of the classroom may also constitute a functional change in placement.

---

* Although many schools In the U.S. use time-out rooms, many administrators and teachers do not seem to be aware that federal law 42 U.S.C. § 15009 flatly prohibits the use of seclusion as a planned punishment for students with developmental disabilities in educational programs. For students with developmental disabilities, seclusion may only be used for safety emergencies involving imminent risk of serious injury to the student or others.

As noted previously, teacher-directed time-outs are often experienced as a form of punishment. One way to possibly minimize the likelihood that teacher-directed time-out will lead to worse behavior or disruption is to have the system be part of the classroom-wide behavior plan as opposed to being applied to just one or a few students. Creating a classroom-wide system so that any student who violates the rules is given a time-out will be perceived as fair by most students.[*] This way, all students are held to the same rules, the sense of fairness is intact, and individual students are less likely to feel stigmatized. Classroom-wide plans also have the advantage of reducing the number of individualized behavior plans needed.

Planning an Effective Time-Out Program

As with any behavioral intervention, planning is the key to success. The following steps may be applicable to students in general education. Additional steps and precautions usually apply to students in special education. The following apply to teacher-directed time-outs and not to student-initiated time-outs:

1. Check the school and district policy about the use of time-out as a behavioral intervention.
2. Determine the specific behaviors that result in time-out; define them precisely and in objective terms.
3. Decide whether the student will be given one (and only one) "warning" before time-out is implemented. The warning can be any agreed-upon signal. Some young students find it helpful to have a traffic light configuration wherein the teacher points to the yellow light card on the student's desk that is the warning. A single-warning system can be helpful. It is particularly helpful when combined with reinforcement for alternative and appropriate behaviors. We recommend that teachers do *not* give multiple warnings because students who know that they can get more than one warning will not be as motivated to comply with the first warning.

A lot of teachers use the checkmark on the board system. Regardless of the system, ensure that the student's attention is obtained first. Because students with the disorders described in this book may not be attending or orienting to the board, some other system may be needed for them.

4. Decide how much time the students will have to comply with the time-out direction. For example, if they have one minute to start to get up from their desk and move to the other desk, then what happens if they are still at their desk after that time?
5. Decide how to handle older students who refuse to comply with time-out when given the direction. Will they get a time-out in a more restrictive setting or will they get a choice between complying with the time-out and facing some other consequence such as having to sit in the principal's office during lunch or staying after school, etc.?
6. Determine the length of the time-out for each instance of undesired behavior. Some teachers prefer a fixed amount of time (e.g., five minutes). Some teachers allow the students to remain in time-out longer, at the student's discretion, if they need more time to calm down.

The rule of thumb for teacher-directed time-out is one to two minutes of time-out for each year of chronological age.

7. Determine where the time-out will be implemented. Always begin with the least restrictive setting that is reasonably calculated to be effective.
8. Decide what the student will be doing during the time-out period. Will she be doing classwork if she is not in a time-out room, or will she just be expected to sit and do nothing (not recommended)? Whatever the student does during the enforced time-out period, remember that the time-out activity cannot be more enjoyable or reinforcing to the student than the planned activity.
9. Decide how to handle missed work. Remember that any child who has great difficulty completing work at school does not get better after school as the day goes on. Sometimes the work needs to be completed on a weekend.

---

[*] In some areas, the use of time-out rooms may be restricted to only those students whose individualized education plans incorporate its use for specifically targeted behaviors. Teachers need to consult with their district to determine if it has a policy on the use of time-out rooms for infractions of classroom rules that are not emergency safety situations.

10. Decide what will happen if the student continues to engage in undesirable behavior during the time-out period. For example, will the clock be reset or will the student be placed in the next more restrictive time-out setting?

11. Inform all students' parents of the time-out plan so that they understand its goals and how it is implemented.

Thinking about the preceding issues in the planning stage can save a lot of "on the fly" decision-making and will produce a more cohesive and effective plan. Also, by making these decisions in advance, teachers will be better prepared to explain the system and rules to students and parents. A worksheet to help plan the time-out program is provided in Appendix P with a sample recording form (Appendix Q).

If the student's problematic behavior occurs with other teachers and in other settings, arrange for a team meeting to see if all teachers can use the same plan to address the behavior.

12. If the time-out plan is developed for a particular student, rather than the whole classroom, meet with the parent(s) to review the student's behavior and secure their written consent to use the plan. Ensure that they understand whether the time-out will take place in the classroom or involves removal from the classroom.

13. Keep accurate records showing how often time-out was used, what behavior led to the time-out consequence, how long the student was in time-out, where the time-out occurred (classroom, office), who supervised out of room time-out occurrences, etc. (A data recoding sheet is provided in Appendix Q as well as on the accompanying CD-ROM.)

14. For individualized time-out plans, incorporate some statement as to when and how often the student's parents will be notified if time-out was used. This is especially important for situations in which the child is unable to verbalize what happens to her in school. Parents need to be notified every time a time-out room is used with their child.

15. Parents need prompt notification if there is any injury to the student associated with the use of time-out or time-out rooms.

Keeping accurate records is important for a number of reasons, not the least of which is the need to ensure that the use of time-out is really decreasing undesired behavior. If a student is engaging in misbehavior to escape from a frustrating academic activity, time-out may actually be reinforcing her misbehavior and analysis of the frequency of time-outs and their antecedents helps the teacher determine if time-out is helping or backfiring.

When misbehavior is due to an academic or skills deficit (e.g., if a student does not know to wait to be called upon due to EDF), use direct instruction to teach deficient skills before considering time-out.

Teaching the Time-Out Plan to Students

Once the details of the plan have been determined, make sure the affected students understand the plan. For individual plans, obtain parental consent and meet with the student to teach the plan. If the system is to be used classroom-wide, spend time during the first week of school teaching the system. Give specific examples of the behaviors that will result in time-out, describe the expected cooperation and behavior of the student during time-out, and explain the consequences for noncompliance with time-out. During instruction, be sure to provide examples of alternative behaviors the student can engage in that will not result in time-out.

When teaching students about the time-out plan, include a statement about how quickly they are expected to comply with the direction to go to time-out (e.g., "If I tell you that you are to go to time-out, within one minute, you need to get up quietly and quickly...."). Also review how the student is expected to behave when re-entering the activity or classroom.

Schedule a practice or dry-run of the time-out plan with the student(s). Use "Say, Show, Check" to demonstrate the procedure, including any warnings, and how to return to the activity. Have the student(s) comment on the demonstration and then have them practice with feedback and verbal reinforcement. Give the student(s) an opportunity to ask questions such as, "What happens if I ....?"

As part of teaching the plan, include some discussion of how peers can help when a fellow classmate is sent to time-out. What do the classmates do? Do they ignore the student and just continue with the assigned activity? Do they quietly welcome the student back to the activity when the student returns? The instruction needs to teach what everyone in the classroom needs to do when a student is sent to time-out and when the student returns to class.

Also explain to the students that when a time-out direction is given, the teacher will identify the infraction, but it will not be discussed or explained at that time. The student is expected to comply even if the student disagrees or feels that it is unfair. Tell the student(s) that there will be a meeting later to explain and discuss why there was a time-out.

Because some students may have had negative experiences with time-outs that had been misused by others, it may be helpful to call this something other than "time-out" when talking with students. For younger students, the teacher may want to talk about how even a great car may suddenly have a problem with how it is running and it needs to go in for a tune-up to make sure everything is working smoothly.

For older students, the term time-out may have even more negative connotations. Teachers may wish to tell the students to "go re-boot" instead of saying "time-out" (Hopke, 2007, unpublished). Alternately, tell older students that if they are having trouble working smoothly in class, they may be told to get a "five minute tune-up" during which time they are to check themselves out to see if they have been focusing properly, doing the assigned work, and behaving properly (Packer, 2007, unpublished).

Pitfalls and Handling the Unexpected

If a situation occurs that calls for time-out as per the plan, give the instruction to go to time-out in a neutral, calm voice. Communicating frustration may lead to confrontation. Use a simple directive that conveys both the infraction and where the student should go, e.g., "You did not wait your turn. You're in time-out at your desk for five minutes."

Even if the plan is wonderful and instructions to go to time-out are delivered calmly, prepare for the unexpected. Because teacher-directed time-out is aversive, students with the kinds of disorders described in this book may become more dysregulated when time-out is implemented. Despite clear explanation and their "practice runs," when the time comes that time-out is actually used, they may refuse to cooperate. They may start arguing, challenging authority, or insulting the teacher personally. Remember that this is the student's problem, not the adult's! The adult's job is to help the student restore himself

to calm and to comply with the classroom rules. This is a good time to take a breath and remember that if we lock horns with a dysregulated student, everyone loses. In this one moment, we have the opportunity to model what we want the student to learn: how to conduct oneself in the classroom.

Becoming physical with neurologically impaired, overaroused students usually causes an escalation in behavior frequently resulting in humiliation, harm, and/or further escalation of disrespect for authority.

If a student does not comply with the direction to go to time-out, move close to the student, but not too close, lower your voice, and calmly repeat the direction. If the student is verbally refusing to comply with the direction and is escalating, teachers can give the student a single warning that failure to comply now will result in the next tier of time-out. For example, the teacher might say, "If you do not go to the other desk now, you will be sent to Ms. J's classroom for your time-out."

For safety as well as legal reasons, unless there is an imminent safety emergency, do not lay hands on a student to assist or force them into compliance with time-out without the school administrator's permission to do so, written parental consent to do so, and training and certification in crisis de-escalation techniques and safe restraint methods. While this may seem to be very dramatic advice for dealing with young children, students with disabilities are more at risk for health impairment if they become agitated and are restrained. There is no simple prescription we can provide for how to assist students in complying with a time-out directive as each case is different.

Because students can, and often do, become agitated with time-out, having planned consequences, including consequences for noncompliance, can make a tremendous difference in the effectiveness of the plan. Even when students *do* comply with the time-out direction by going to another location or desk, they may engage in verbal or nonverbal behaviors such as muttering to themselves, making faces, slamming papers down, etc. This type of problem may be prevented by teaching the students how to conduct themselves when they are in time-out. In general, and because some of these behaviors are more for "face-saving" purposes, it is best to ignore the muttering and faces for a while to see if the student then calms down and follows the time-out directions.

If the Plan is Not Working...

When implementing a time-out plan for an individual student, record-keeping helps the teacher determine whether the plan is working or not. A time-out recording form is provided in Appendix Q and on the accompanying CD-ROM.

As with all behavioral interventions that involve unpleasant consequences or removing previously available reinforcers (Chapter 27), it is not uncommon to find that for some students, there is a "honeymoon" effect when the behavior initially improves and then resumes with a vengeance. For other students, behavior may initially worsen and only gradually begin to improve.

If the plan does not seem to be working, consider the following:

- Is the time-out enabling the student to escape from some frustrating activity or setting? If so:
  - ❏ Ensure that necessary academic assessments and supports are in place.
  - ❏ Ensure that there is adequate positive reinforcement for participation in the scheduled activity.
  - ❏ Assign work during the time-out activity that is the same work the student would be doing if not in time-out. Otherwise, the student's misbehavior might be reinforced by escape from the activity.
- Can the student comply with the time-out directive when it is delivered? If the student is obsessive-compulsive and was already stuck and unable to cooperate, telling her to move elsewhere may increase her anxiety and she will not be able to comply with the direction.
- Is there sufficient positive reinforcement for alternative desired behaviors? Is the reinforcer considered positive by the student? Using time-out in conjunction with positive reinforcement for desired behaviors is more likely to be effective than time-out alone.
- Can the student save face with peers when complying with the time-out procedure?
- Apart from any escape from academic frustration, are there any other secondary gains to the misbehavior? Do the students' peers all pay attention to them when they are sent to time-out? If so, and if negative attention is the only kind of attention they can get from peers, this may be part of the problem.

Ensure that the students get positive peer attention for appropriate behaviors.

- Are other teachers using the same plan and observing the same results? If other teachers are experiencing success with the time-out procedure, try to observe the student in their class to see what subtle differences might account for the difference in effectiveness.

If time-out does not appear to be working after a few weeks, or if it seems to be making the problem worse, schedule a meeting with the student, parents, and other professionals to review the situation. For some students, time-out may simply not be an effective approach and other strategies will be required.

Time-Out Rooms

Some schools have specially allocated rooms where students may be sent. In some cases, these rooms may be no bigger than a large closet. Students who are sent to or taken to such spaces are essentially being put in seclusion, even if they are under the watchful eye of school personnel stationed outside the room who can view them through a window in the door.

Time-out rooms pose serious safety, ethical, and legal issues. From a safety perspective, students with disabilities seem to have a higher rate of asthma. If sent to a time-out room, they may become very agitated and experience life-threatening respiratory problems. Similarly, students with some disabilities may be more likely to have cardiac issues. Agitation due to being placed in a time-out room might have tragic and fatal consequences.

Time-out rooms need to comply with the same health department codes for sanitation and ventilation as classrooms or instructional spaces. For students who have storms or meltdowns, the time-out rooms may need adequate padding to ensure that the students cannot hurt themselves. It is important that the rooms are well constructed so that students cannot destroy the room while in the throes of a storm.

Any student who is in a time-out room needs to be under the observation of school personnel, but when a student with known health issues or disabilities is sent to a time-out room, the school personnel monitoring the student need to be able to recognize when a student might be in danger. The media has reported stories about youth who died following placement in time-out rooms because school personnel observing the student thought the student was merely calm or sleeping when they were in respiratory arrest or having other difficulty.

In our opinion, if a disabled student's plan calls for the use of an isolation time-out room, the school needs to obtain written parental consent to the plan. The school or district also needs to obtain medical clearance from a physician attesting that the student has no medical conditions that pose a significant health or safety risk. An evaluation by a mental health professional to determine whether the use of such interventions is likely to cause psychological harm is also indicated, as abused children placed in seclusion may have strong reactions. Qualified clinical personnel also need to be present in the building during any such intervention so that they can monitor the student for physical and psychological safety.

Imagine that a student who is suffering from PTSD due to having been sexually abused and abducted is placed in time-out room because she was getting emotionally dysregulated in class and that she is told she must stay there for twenty minutes. Can being secluded aggravate her PTSD and lead to worsening of problems?

When dealing with students who have emotional or health issues, always seek and obtain clinical clearance from parents and treating professionals before trying to use teacher-directed or involuntary time-out room seclusion.

The preceding concerns do not mean that time-out rooms can never be used productively for students with disabilities. If a time-out room is used as a quiet place for students to calm themselves and then talk with supportive school personnel, and if students are told that they may leave the space at will, it may be beneficial. Some students may even ask to take a self-imposed time-out in the space so that they can calm themselves. Time-out room seclusion may also be necessary and effective for safety emergencies, as long as the students understand that they are free to leave as soon as the emergency has passed. Forcing students to stay in the time-out room for a fixed amount of time is only likely to agitate them and prolong the problem.

Rational and ethical use of time-out rooms needs to be student-centered. If our purpose is to give students a place and time to restore themselves to calm, then we need to reinforce that by allowing them to leave as soon as they have calmed down. When students have accomplished the goal of self-calming, school personnel need to be available to them to escort them calmly back to the classroom and/or to work with them on how they will re-enter the classroom.

For mental health, physical health, and safety reasons, we recommend that federal guidelines for inpatients be adopted by schools. Applying such guidelines, any time a student has been in a time-out room for one hour, they need to be assessed by both a medical professional and a qualified mental health professional to determine if the student's condition is being made worse by the isolation. That said, most students do not need to be in time-out for one hour. If a student is being placed in time-out for one hour on more than one occasion, we recommend a review of her plan.

"But I Have to Go to the Bathroom!"

During the planning stage, plan what will happen if the student says that she needs to go to the bathroom before or during a time-out. Regardless of whether time-out is taking place in the classroom or in a separate location, students need to be allowed to go to the bathroom. Likewise, plan what will happen if the student is in time-out during the time that she would normally be going to get her medication or going to lunch. While a brief delay in getting lunch is not generally particularly problematic from a health standpoint, delaying medication may lead to the teacher forgetting to send the student to the nurse for the medication.

If the student is in time-out during the time that she would be going to the school nurse to get her medication, discuss with the parent how long delivery of the medication can be safely delayed. Some medications need to be skipped entirely if the time for taking it goes beyond a certain point. Regardless of whether medication is missed due to time-out or due to the teacher or student simply forgetting, the parents can ask the student's doctor to give instructions as to what to do when medication is missed at the designated time. To avoid problems, ensure that students get their in-school medication at the designated time, regardless of time-out plans. This prevents health problems, and alleviates the problem of students in time-out obsessively worrying about missing their medication. These students may not be able to calm themselves, thereby needlessly prolonging the time-out.

Summary

Time-out from positive reinforcement may be an effective classroom management plan if there are also opportunities for rewarding activities and positive reinforcers. Applied consistently and nonpunitively on a classroom-wide basis, time-out teaches students the expected rules of conduct in the class and gives students an opportunity to collect themselves, refocus, or calm themselves if they are becoming dysregulated.

Because time-out is generally intended to decrease unwanted behaviors, it is properly viewed as a form of punishment, even if it is not applied punitively. As such, it may produce more dysregulated behavior. Consulting with the students' parents beforehand and maintaining proper records can help school personnel determine whether plans need to be modified, continued, or discontinued. The use of time-out with students with disabilities may entail other legal and medical requirements.

Steve had great difficulty modulating and calming down when over-agitated and aroused by sensory input. Noise and light touch in crowded situations in school made him get agitated, anxious, and begin to escalate his hyperactive behavior. He was taught and he practiced how to remove himself to a time-out place that he helped choose. He was allowed to listen to soothing music through earphones in the library. He also practiced some relaxation breathing techniques that his counselor taught him as he sat there. Steve became so good at self-regulating his behavior that he would simply use a pass and engage in this procedure when needed. He did not abuse this and over time his acting-out behavior diminished and he became more confident in his ability to handle his own overaroused, hyperactive, anxious behavior.

• • •

Emerson hated to go to the time-out room, even though his school called it a "Self-Evaluation Room." When he was in the room, though, he would calm himself and then talk with the school counselor about what had happened and what he might do in the future under similar circumstances. Over time, Emerson was able to learn strategies that would prevent him from getting so out of control that he would need to be sent to the time-out room. One of the strategies he learned was that if he felt that he was "losing it," he could ask to go take a break in the room. Emerson used that technique to his advantage, and learned that calming himself by taking a break from difficult situations was an effective technique for him.

CHAPTER 31

Coaching, Instant Replay, and Cooperative Problem Solving:
Interventions to Promote Better Behavior and Social and Academic Skills

Too often we give children answers to remember rather than problems to solve.
—Roger Lewin

This chapter describes two techniques that school personnel and parents can use to coach successful behavior: "Instant Replay" and "Cooperative Problem Solving." A third technique, the "graceful exit," used to avoid social blunders or poor behavior, follows the description of these two techniques. Selecting which technique to use is a function of the student's awareness of his problems and his ability to engage in solving his own problems.

Symptoms of many of the disorders described in this book impair academic, social, and behavioral skills, but the impact of Executive Dysfunction (Chapter 9) cannot be overstated. EDF needs a more comprehensive instructional plan to teach what is normally viewed as "common sense" when it comes to academic, social, and behavioral issues. The techniques described below are focused particularly on the remediation of this impact.

Coaching

Just as a sports coach may tell a player what to do to be successful, adults in the student's life can coach him as to how to be socially successful in an upcoming situation. Such coaching needs to be provided in as few words as possible and right before the skill will be executed. For example, a student with Asperger's Syndrome might be coached to approach another child, look at the bridge of the child's nose (if eye contact is difficult), and then say, "Hi. Would you like to sit with me at lunch today?" Once the child has done that, the Instant Reply technique described below can be used to review what the child did, how it was received, and what the child will do next time. As another example, if a student is asked to be the recorder for a small-group project but cannot handle being the recorder due to handwriting difficulties, the teacher can coach the student to say, "I cannot write the notes, but I can type them for us." Alternatively, an adult can coach the student to say to peers, "I cannot write, but I can do all the computer graphics for our project" (or whatever skill the student has).

Telling students what to do well in advance of when they will need to use the skill generally does not work well—if at all— because they may not remember the strategy when they need to use it. Because coaching is needed and is more effective at the point of performance, school personnel need to coach behavior in school. What the parent tells the child at home the night before or in the morning before school may not be remembered when it is needed.

If a student requires coaching, do not assume that behaviors rehearsed in one school setting will generalize to another school setting. Providing these techniques across a variety of settings fosters greater acquisition and generalization. When working with students with EDF or ASD, it is especially important to provide coaching for each issue or behavior in a variety of settings. Students with these disorders may not recognize that there is a general rule or principle, and the difference in settings may prevent them from recognizing that they can use the technique or skill across different settings.

Benny, a third grader with Asperger's Syndrome and EDF, was sent to the principal's office for fighting with Sammy in the library. The principal discussed the situation with Benny, and Benny agreed he would not hit Sammy again.

The next day, the principal was surprised to see Benny being escorted into his office by his aide. "What happened?" the principal asked Benny. Benny told him how he and Sammy had gotten into a fight and he had hit Sammy.

"But yesterday you told me that you were not going to hit Sammy again," the principal reminded him.

"I didn't hit him in the library," said Benny seriously. "I hit him in the cafeteria."*

Instant Replay**

Most of us have heard sportscasters say, "Let's go to the Instant Replay" so that what happened can be reviewed. The Instant Replay technique for students is similar. If a student is seriously impaired in terms of knowing what to do to be successful, the Instant Replay technique may help. Use it as a quick review of what happened, and point out what worked or did not work, and what the student needs to do when he enters a problematic situation again.

The technique is used without strong emotion and is informative in tone. Privately tell the student what happened, how the actions of the student socially and emotionally affected the other child and those around them, and what to do next time instead to be successful. This is a nonjudgmental, helpful way of explaining and correcting social mistakes without making the student feel bad about himself. The Instant Replay technique is similar to what Rick Lavoie calls a "social autopsy," but when working with students who have anxiety, obsessions, and/or compulsions, it is a good idea to avoid the word "autopsy," hence "Instant Replay."

The following is an example of how to use this technique. It illustrates a conversation between a teacher and a student after the student tried to join a game in PE and got the entire class in an uproar.

"When you were in PE yesterday and tried to join the game with the other students, it did not work well. You know how you wanted to go next, but other kids were there first waiting their turn? They were being thoughtful of the other kids so that the other students would want to play with them. They got mad that you were trying to break in line ahead of them. So here is how we can fix this problem: From now on in PE, ask the other kids who is the last one waiting for a turn, and then say, "OK, I'll go after him.""

Note that in this example, the teacher provided concrete and clear directions. Abstractions like "cooperate with" or "be nice to" are avoided. Instead, the student is told exactly what to do or say to increase his chances of success.

After the next PE class in which the student tries to join a game, he is supposed to check back in with the teacher who did the Instant Replay with him. If the student forgets to report back to the teacher, it is the responsibility of the teacher to find the student to follow up. The teacher completes the Instant Replay by saying: "OK, your plan was to ask who was last and then go after the last student. How did it work out for you?" After the student reports on his success or failure, the teacher and the student decide whether the student will use that strategy again in the future or whether to revise the strategy. If a student is unable to tell whether the strategy worked well or not, the coach provides that information and feedback, e.g., "When you told them that you would go last, they said 'OK' and Katie even smiled at you. So it seems like your strategy worked and you can use that strategy in PE again."

---

* Adapted from a story one of the authors heard, but sadly, we cannot remember the original source.

** Sherry has been using the term "Instant Replay" in this context for many years. We recently discovered that someone else had the same idea and had actually written a book with the title of "Instant Replay" (Bedford 1974). As they say, "Great minds think alike." Sherry's use of the term and approach was independent of the publication of the book by the same name.

This is another example of when teachers need to lend students their frontal lobes. If the student doesn't remember to seek out the teacher to review what happened, the teacher seeks out the student to complete the Instant Replay.

While coaching is initiated at the point of performance—right before the student is expected to use the strategy—Instant Replay is initiated immediately after the behavior occurs. As such, the Instant Replay technique can also be used to immediately address and correct social blunders, e.g., when a student impulsively does something in class that creates social difficulties. For example, if a student grabs something away from another student, an Instant Replay response would be to say to the student in a calm informative tone, "When you grabbed his pencil, he got angry at you and then did not want to work with you. Go give him back his pencil now, tell him that you are sorry you grabbed it, and offer to help him with his work." Notice that this example includes how the student might make reparations, a technique discussed in Chapter 30. By offering to help him with his work, the student goes beyond just giving back the pencil and tries to repair the relationship.

Instant Replay can also be used spontaneously to reinforce prosocial behavior. For example, if the teacher notices a student spontaneously engaging in a desired behavior, an Instant Replay can be used like this: "Let's review what just happened. Tommy seemed angry when you said you wanted to be the researcher on the team project. You told him that you could both team up on the research. That was great problem solving on your part, and Tommy seemed really happy with you." Similarly, observing a student politely waiting his turn on line, the teacher might say, "I like how you are patiently waiting your turn. You are doing a good job of following the rules." Teachers can also use Instant Replay to follow up on the Cooperative Problem Solving technique intervention described below.

All adults working with students are encouraged to use the Instant Replay technique and provide similar and consistent advice for specified target behaviors so that the students are getting support and direction and can start succeeding. Remember that when many of us were growing up, everyone in the neighborhood and the schools helped every child learn the rules. They also assisted children when they did not understand the negative impact of their behavior on themselves or others. The concept of community support for a student in school is a very important teaching tool. When there is school-wide training as described by Lavoie (1994) and these techniques are used, the school sees significant gains in students becoming more competent. The school can share these techniques with parents who can use these techniques at home to improve skill development.

As suggested above, coaching and Instant Replay can be used to address specific behavioral concerns even if the behavior is a neurological symptom. For example, a student who impulsively calls out without waiting to be called on is pulled aside tactfully by his teacher who engages in an Instant Reply on the impact of his behavior on his peers. The teacher then offers to teach him to use a "Blurt Blocker" technique (Pruitt and Rogers 2001). Using the "Blurt Blocker" technique, the student is taught to casually keep his mouth covered by his hand while listening to the teacher or to have a safe object in his mouth to decrease the likelihood of calling out. A student might also be coached to look like he is casually holding a pen or pencil between his lips. In class the next day, the student is coached (reminded) to use the Blurt Blocker technique right before the teacher starts the lesson. At the end of the lesson, the teacher conducts an Instant Replay to review how the student did.

Cooperative Problem Solving (P.L.A.N.)

If we are not sure whether students are capable of problem solving, we should discuss it with the students. The major pitfalls in this area involve the teacher assuming that the student can problem-solve or cannot problem-solve.

Using the Cooperative Problem Solving program, either the student initiates the interaction by coming to us with a problem, or we initiate the interaction by identifying a problem and asking the student to work with us on solving it. There are four steps to the program:

1. **P**roblem defined
2. **L**ist options
3. **A**ct on one
4. **N**ow evaluate[*]

1. Problem defined.

Keep the statement of the problem short, e.g., "Yesterday, the other kids got angry because you joined the game late and tried to go next. What do you think you could do differently today so that they do not get angry at you?"

---

[*] (Pruitt and Pruitt 2001). Different authors have employed different acronyms to describe a Cooperative Problem Solving approach, but all approaches share the same core steps of identifying the problem, identifying options and picking one, implementing the plan, and then assessing its effectiveness.

2. List options.

When listing options, have the student generate the ideas, if possible. It is more effective to encourage the student to come up with options and then work with the student's list. If he asks us for our ideas, we provide one or two if the student has really tried to generate options but is unable to identify any. It is not necessary for the student to produce an exhaustive list of options. One or two may be more than the student can generate at the beginning.

It is sometimes difficult for adults to resist just giving the student a great idea or solution, but think long-term: We want to encourage the student to come up with options for solving problems for a lifetime. If we always give them better ideas than they can generate, they may simply wait for adults to tell them what to do instead of thinking for themselves. Besides, sometimes the students really do generate better strategies than adults can generate.

Some students with moderate to severe EDF cannot generate specific strategies or solutions when confronted with a problem. In this case, the students need to be taught that their single best strategy is to ask for assistance when needed. Make sure that if they are asking peers, that good peer models have been identified. Teach these students that asking for help is an excellent approach to solving the problem.

After the student has generated an option, ask the student to try to foresee how that option might work out or what obstacles he might encounter. The "Sounds good" or "What will you do if….?" approach may be useful here. Do that for each option they generate.

Adam was always getting sent to the principal's office because he would not do his classwork. The school viewed him as an unmotivated student with disruptive behaviors even though they had been told that Adam was diagnosed with TS, ADHD, and OCD and that his doctors were trying to find a combination of medications to help him focus in school.

Unfortunately for Adam, on the first and only day that he actually wanted to do his work, his teacher did not give him the support he needed. Adam had asked his teacher for permission to leave the classroom so that he could find a quieter place to work and the teacher had said "No." Unable to figure out what else he could do, he started arguing with the teacher. He was sent from the room to the principal's office with a disciplinary referral for arguing with the teacher. Sadly, the teacher had managed to snatch defeat out of the jaws of victory.

When Adam showed up at the therapist's office for his regular visit, he told her the story. The therapist told him that it was terrific that he cared about his work and was trying to find a quieter place so that he could concentrate better. Then the therapist asked him what else he could have done or said when the teacher said "No." For the next twenty-five minutes, there was total silence in the office, other than the occasional prompt to try to think of an option.

Adam had been so impaired that no one had been asking him to solve his problems and he had gotten into the habit of just being told what to do. Because no one had asked him to think about what he could do, he had never learned the skill of problem solving. Rather than just tell him what his options were, the therapist gave him time to think.

After twenty-five minutes, Adam came up with one alternative. The therapist replied, "Great!" Can you come up with another one?" Adam seemed to realize that he could generate ideas, and it took less than five minutes for him to generate another idea. By the end of the session, Adam had a plan for the next school day. He would ask the teacher if he could go somewhere quiet and if the teacher said "No," he would ask the teacher to change his seat or ask the boys sitting near him to be a bit quieter.

That first problem solving session was time-consuming, but after that first session, Adam was able to participate in the process and generate more ideas in less time. His self-esteem improved as he began to see himself as someone who could solve his own problems and he started really looking forward to coming to therapy.

3. Act on one strategy.

Once the student has identified options and picked the one that seems most reasonable or most likely to succeed, it's time to implement the plan. The adult can ask if he needs or wants any reminders or supports to implement his plan. This is particularly important when we are planning something that will not be implemented immediately. The student may need a reminder of what strategy was selected right before he is in the situation. Only provide the reminder, though, if the student requests it.

4. Now evaluate the strategy.

Use the Instant Replay technique. If the student's selected strategy did not work out well, the teacher and student can review the other options the student had identified. The student might also be asked to think about whether there are any other options that might be good in light of what happened with the first strategy. If the student forgot or failed to use the strategy at all, then the adult points that out in a calm, informative tone and asks the student to consider whether any reminders or supports might be needed for the next time.

Dino had come up with a plan to try to remember to do his homework without reminders from his mother. His plan was to take his homework out of his bag as soon as he got home and place it on the music stand in his bedroom so he would see it.

When he met with the therapist the next day, he looked dejected. "The plan didn't work," he said. When asked whether he had forgotten to take it out of his backpack, he said, "Oh no, I remembered that. And I put it on the music stand."

"That's great, Dino," The therapist said enthusiastically. "So what went wrong with the plan?"

"I put something else down on top of the papers," Dino explained.

"OK. So do you want to give up on that plan or maybe just tweak it a bit and try again?"

Dino thought about it and said, "I'll try it again, but now I've got to make sure not to put anything else on the stand."

Teaching Students to Make a "Graceful Exit"

One of the most important skills to teach students who become dysregulated is how to make a "graceful exit."** Being able to remove themselves from situations when they or others recognize that they are becoming overaroused or agitated can help protect the students' relationships with peers and significant people in their lives. The graceful exit system is appropriate to use when the student is experiencing symptoms causing discomfort or embarrassment, when the student needs to calm down due to overarousal, or when the student is close to "losing it" if he stays in the situation.

To train students in making a graceful exit, begin by having a meeting with the student and his parents. This meeting does not need to take place during an Individualized Education Program (IEP) or accommodations planning meeting. Explain to the student and parents that there are times when the student might want to or need to step out of the classroom for a few minutes to self-calm or to avoid "losing it," and that the purpose of this meeting is to come up with a plan for how the student will save face while leaving the classroom.

One technique frequently employed is to provide the student with his own permanent pass that he can use for graceful exit purposes. The student can be offered a choice of colors for the pass, or can even create and decorate the pass himself. Allowing students to choose the color or to decorate the pass helps some students accept the use of the pass. The important thing is for the student to have the pass on him when he is in class so that if he needs to make a graceful exit, he can use it.**

As part of the meeting, the student and teacher(s) need to agree on where the student will go if a graceful exit is used. Encourage the student to think about where in the building he feels that he can self-calm. Designating a place without asking the student whether the student feels that the place feels helpful in self-calming is counterproductive. Some students may prefer to just take a brief walk around the hall or to a specified designation and back.

When a student needs to make a graceful exit, he takes out the pass, places it on his desk so that the teacher can see it when the teacher glances over, and then leaves the classroom for the agreed-upon spot.

Learning to step away from a situation or excuse oneself gracefully is a life skill. As part of any graceful exit training or system, the student may need to be taught some excuses to use when with peers.

- If a student uses a graceful exit system, avoid stopping the student from leaving and do not try to talk to the student at that time.

- If the student is not allowed to use the graceful exit system during tests, that needs to be discussed with the student in advance.

- If a student is using his pass too often in one class, assess whether there are curricular demands or other issues that need to be addressed.

---

* A term adapted by Sherry and described in her earlier book (Dornbush & Pruitt, 1995).

** Make sure that if the student does have an IEP or 504 Plan that the graceful exit plan is included.

As part of the system, establish an agreed-upon cue for the teachers to use if they see a need for a graceful exit looming. The student can be told during the planning meeting that if the teacher sees trouble looming, the student will be given a discreet signal that means "use the graceful exit system." The teacher and student need to agree upon what that signal will be.

At times, the teacher may find that instead of responding quietly and respectfully to the discreet signal, the student balks or grumbles on the way out. Even if the student grumbles on the way out, consider that as compliance and reinforce it. Remember that the priority is to help the student exit the situation before he really loses control and embarrasses himself or becomes disruptive to the class. It is also possible that the student is grumbling because of difficulty changing sets (inflexibility), irritable depression, or other types of symptoms. As part of the student's behavior plan, be sure to use positive reinforcers for compliance with discreet signals.

If the student is unable to comply with the plan, then an assessment needs to be conducted to find out why the student cannot or does not comply, e.g., does the student understand the disorder and its impact, does the student have an anxiety disorder or executive functioning problem that prevents changing from one setting to another, is the student's medication affecting his decision or ability to comply, is there enough positive reinforcement for the plan in place, etc.? A Functional Behavioral Assessment (Chapter 26) is appropriate and necessary if the graceful exit system is not working.

Remember, we are asking the student to do something that his brain is not encouraging him to do. This is often quite difficult but an important skill to master for school and for life.

When using these techniques with children, explain to them that problems are opportunities to learn something new. Tell them that not every strategy will succeed, but that every attempt will teach us something. Sometimes, the people who try the most things, make the most mistakes, and learn from their mistakes turn out to be the most successful.

Summary

Coaching, Instant Replay, and Cooperative Problem Solving represent different levels of support and instruction. In deciding which technique to use, the adult must first determine whether the student is aware that there is a problem, and, if so, whether the student has the ability to engage in a cooperative and interactive problem solving activity. If the student does not recognize that there is a problem or cannot participate meaningfully in problem solving, start with the coaching followed by Instant Replay sequence. If students can identify the problem or can participate in problem solving when a problem is pointed out to them, start with the problem solving technique, and follow up with Instant Replay to review success or failure of the plan. Instant Replay can also be used spontaneously to review a student's behavior. Social skills support may also involve teaching the student techniques such as "graceful exit" or "Blurt Blocker." A student's individualized educational plan should indicate whether school personnel working with the student need to provide coaching, Instant Replay, or Cooperative Problem Solving or a combination of all three. To promote greater success and generalization, the student's parents can be taught these techniques so that they can use them in the home and other settings.

I have missed more than 9000 shots. I have lost almost 300 games. On 26 occasions I have been entrusted to take the game-winning shot—and I missed. I have failed over and over again in my life. And that is precisely why I succeed.
— Michael Jordan

PART V

Other School-Related Topics

Coming together is a beginning. Keeping together is progress.
Working together is success.
— Henry Ford

Overview

The following section reviews the types of services that students with the disorders described in this book might receive as well as the role of service providers. It also describes some issues and strategies for promoting positive school-home collaboration. Finally, it will discuss peer issues in socialization.

CHAPTER 32

School-Based Related Services

Although this book has been written primarily with the classroom teacher in mind, teaching students with the kinds of challenges in this book requires the support of related service personnel and the building administrator. This chapter briefly describes some of the related services typically recommended for students with neurological disorders. Although other services may also be required for any one student, the services below represent the most frequent referrals.

Occupational Therapy

The school-based occupational therapist (OT) is a very important referral because so many of these students have handwriting and visual-motor integration (VMI) issues, e.g., difficulty copying from the board. When assessing students for handwriting issues, the OT can be asked to incorporate a speed test involving a paragraph or some sample that requires more writing than one sentence. Many of these students have poor endurance for writing lengthy passages.

The ability to control the fine motor movements of the eye and accurately track or scan work may also be an issue. A smaller but significant percentage of these students have visual-motor-perceptual deficits. When tracking deficits are combined with handwriting deficits and visual-motor-perceptual problems (Chapter 17), the student's ability to position information on the page with accuracy is impaired, e.g., a student may be unable to line up math problems in the correct columns or to use computer scoring sheets.

Although OT services may be performed as a pull-out service, it is helpful to have the OT also provide services at the point of performance in the classroom. The OT can make specific recommendations to the teacher about accommodations in writing tasks, the positioning of the student, and any necessary modifications in materials and presentation to accommodate for issues with VMI, handwriting, and fine motor skills. Having an opportunity to observe the student in the more typical classroom setting also enables the OT to get a more accurate picture of the student's endurance for activities, fidgetiness, and the student's level of sensory defensiveness.

Additionally, the OT can serve as a resource and provide services for students who experience overreactivity or underreactivity to sensory information. Sensory dysregulation can lead to academic, behavioral, or social problems in the school setting (Chapter 12). Occupational therapy helps the student modify their responses to sensory input. Parents can also be taught to use techniques at home that reduce sensory defensiveness. The OT can provide classroom teachers with a sensory diet for the student, i.e., suggest techniques to reduce sensory-related sources of interference in learning and production, such as avoidance of certain stimuli.*

Some parts of the country have an inadequate supply of assistive technology evaluators. In those areas, the school-based OT may be the professional intimately involved in determining any need for assistive technology such as a word processor or notebook computer. Even when an assistive technology evaluator is available, the OT is usually involved in training the student in keyboarding skills.

---

* See the *Out-of-Sync Child* (2nd edition) for more details on sensory diets (Kranowitz 1998).

Counseling Services[*]

Counseling services may be an important part of a student's program in terms of both self-regulation and social skills. Counselors, such as school psychologists and social workers, also provide support to teachers by educating them about the students' disorders and suggesting accommodations.

School counselors with EDF training and experience in teaching are well suited to run curriculum-based social skills groups. This is because for students with EDF, social problems result from a lack of knowledge, rather than emotional issues, and so require direct instruction. Teaming up with the speech and language therapist, who has social language training, is often quite effective.

In an Internet survey, parents of students with TS reported that the majority of students had not been referred to school psychology or school-based clinical social work services (Packer 2005). In those cases where in-school counseling had been provided, parents generally did not see the service as helpful. This suggests that in-school clinical services may not be helpful if the psychologist or social worker is not adequately trained to work with students with these disorders. However, when the school psychologist or social worker is well trained in these disorders, school-based counseling can be an effective service.

Apart from the contribution school psychologists make by their psychological evaluation of a student, school psychologists can serve other very important roles in the successful education of a student with these challenges, including:

- Direct Services: individual or small-group counseling, i.e.,
  - 1:1 counseling to address interference from obsessive thoughts or compulsive rituals in school
  - 1:1 or small-group counseling to address anxiety issues related to school that, left untreated, may lead to school avoidance or school phobia
  - 1:1 counseling to help the student gain insight into the impact of her neurological challenges on her academic and social functioning
  - 1:1 counseling to assist the student in developing a plan to improve academic and social functioning through altering her behavior. e.g., developing a strategy to become better organized, addressing how to approach peers in social settings, etc.
  - 1:1 or small-group counseling to assist the student in developing self-advocacy skills
  - Identifying meaningful goals and objectives for the student's Individualized Educational Program (IEP)

- Indirect services:
  - Observing the student in the classroom and noting supports that may help the student
  - Using classroom observations to provide suggestions to school personnel as to behavior management strategies
  - Using classroom observations to identify needed accommodations and services
  - Advocating for the student
  - Overseeing and contributing to the development of a Functional Behavioral Assessment and subsequent Behavior Intervention Plan
  - Observing the student and school personnel in the classroom and school settings to monitor accuracy and fidelity of the implementation of any behavior plan
  - Educating school personnel about the nature of the student's disorder(s)
  - Planning and/or participating in a peer education program to increase peer awareness and empathy
  - Locating community mental health support for the student and family

It is important to note that there are research-validated interventions for many of the disorders described in this book, and we encourage school-based clinicians to learn these techniques. Having a student come in just to "talk" about her anxiety or depression may only delay the provision of research-validated approaches such as cognitive-behavioral approaches (CBT) that have been shown to work with children and adolescents in school settings. Some students may need only supportive counseling sessions on an "as needed" basis, but if the student is seriously impaired, a more organized and evidence-based approach is needed.

---

[*] In some parts of the country, these services are provided by the school psychologist or school social worker. In other parts of the country, they may be provided by guidance counselors. From our perspective, the title is not as important as the level of training and experience working with students with these disorders.

Seeing a student for individual help may only demoralize the student if the clinician is not providing an effective intervention. Ineffective interventions may worsen a student's symptoms or discourage the student from trying other strategies.

Figure 32.1 on the next page depicts some generically worded goals and objectives that were adapted for a specific student's school-based counseling services. These provide the psychologist or social worker with goals, objectives, and benchmarks.

If school clinical personnel are not trained in research-validated therapeutic approaches, have the school refer the student to an outside therapist and arrange to work collaboratively. For example, as a consultant, Leslie often works 1:1 with students in the school building while the school psychologist sits in on sessions to learn how to work with the student. Over time, the school psychologist is able to take over the provision of counseling services not only for the one student, but for other students with the same disorders.

School Nursing

Perhaps one of the most neglected school professionals is the school nurse.* The school nurse is rarely invited to team planning meetings on the student, and yet the nurse is one of the professionals that students often feel most comfortable going to if they are having a rough time.

School nurses provide both direct and indirect services. They provide a safe refuge for students who need a place to calm themselves and in many cases, they are the one in the school building who can make the student feel understood, in that the student is not willfully misbehaving but is having a medical problem.

The school nurse can also be a tremendous resource for the rest of the student's team by educating them about the effects and adverse effects of the student's medication(s) and by assisting in peer education programs. In our experience, when the school nurse participates in peer education, the nurse's very presence often effectively conveys to the peers that the student has a medical problem and that they need to have some empathy for their classmate. Even when the teacher is perfectly capable of handling peer education, we recommend including the school nurse to emphasize the medical nature of the student's problem.

_____

* Sadly, some school districts have cut school nurses out of the budget.

Speech and Language Pathology

Chapter 18 described some of the types of language problems students with the disorders covered in this book may experience. Students with these disorders generally are not at any higher risk of having articulation problems, but are at significantly greater risk for having expressive language problems, e.g., word retrieval difficulties, and verbal executive deficits, e.g., difficulties with social language.

School-based speech and language pathologists (SLP) provide both in-class and pull-out services. Both are of value, depending on the student's precise pattern of deficits. A student who is getting particularly frustrated in the classroom and acting out because expressive language is not adequate may require a combination of services.

Speech and language pathologists who can develop social skills groups for students with these disorders can also make a significant difference in the students' pragmatic functioning by their ability to give the students direct instruction, guided rehearsal, and support for verbal and nonverbal social skills. In some settings, the speech pathologist may collaborate with the counselor, psychologist, or social worker to conduct the group.

Although speech and language services are a very important part of programming for students, all too often, students are found not to qualify for speech services because they do well on standardized, untimed tests. They may even perform adequately on speech and language screenings. Even so, the students' classroom performance and behavior are often significantly affected by their inability to communicate effectively in a timely manner and use social language efficiently. When functioning is impaired, a referral to an SLP is in order.

Assistive Technology

Because many of these students are bright, they are often just handed a computer loaded with software. The assistive technology consultant can evaluate students to determine if they need other accommodations, or suggest specific types of hardware and software combinations, furniture, and instruction they may need, based on their specific neurological functioning. Given the extent of the handwriting problems that students experience, as well as other sources of interference with writing tasks such as

Figure 32.1. Sample Counseling Goals and Objectives

Annual Goal	Short-term Objectives
Mark will recognize ways in which symptoms of his TS+ affect his academic functioning in terms of learning, performance, and endurance.	■ Working with his counselor, teacher, and aide, Mark will identify ways in which his tics may interfere with specific activities in the classroom, e.g., whether eye tics slow down his rate of reading or make him lose his place. ■ Working with his counselor, teacher, and aide, Mark will identify ways in which his tics may indirectly interfere with specific activities in the classroom, e.g., whether bouts of tics or his awareness of his tics distract him from listening activities, tire him out, or make him irritable. ■ Working with his counselor, teacher, and aide, Mark will identify ways in which intrusive thoughts and/or compulsions may interfere with specific activities in the classroom, e.g., whether Mark gets stuck on things mentally that interfere with his ability to attend to a lesson. ■ Working with his counselor, teacher, and aide, Mark will identify ways in which impulsivity may interfere with specific activities in the classroom, e.g., whether Mark ever makes mistakes in his work because he did not wait for instructions. ■ Working with his counselor, teacher, and aide, Mark will identify ways in which hyperactivity may interfere with specific activities in the classroom, e.g., whether Mark is unable to complete certain activities because he needs to get up and move around.
Mark will develop strategies to work around or manage interference from his symptoms in terms of learning, performance, and endurance for academic activities.	■ Working with his counselor, teacher, and aide, Mark will identify ways in which he can work around any tics that might be directly interfering with activities, e.g., chunking tasks, alternative methods of production. ■ Working with his counselor, teacher, and aide, Mark will identify strategies he can use when he becomes aware that tics are indirectly interfering with activities, e.g., taking a break to go discharge tics, asking for material to be repeated or provided in hard copy, use of other methods of recording work. ■ Working with his counselor, teacher, and aide, Mark will identify strategies he can use if thoughts and/or compulsions are interfering with specific activities in the classroom, e.g., verbalizing that he is stuck and asking for assistance, taking a break. ■ Working with his counselor, teacher, and aide, Mark will identify strategies for minimizing the impact of any impulsivity, e.g., mental imagery of a red traffic light. ■ Working with his counselor, teacher, and aide, Mark will identify ways to appropriately discharge or manage hyperactivity, e.g., taking a short break to walk around the halls, going for a drink from the fountain. ■ Mark will ask his aide or his teacher for assistance when he is having difficulty maintaining his focus on his work. ■ Working with his counselor, teacher, and aide, Mark will develop strategies that he can utilize to refocus himself when he becomes aware that his attention is drifting.

Mark will recognize ways in which symptoms of his TS+ affect his relationship with his peers and instructional staff.	■ Working with his counselor, teacher, and aide, Mark will identify ways in which intrusive thoughts and/or compulsions may affect his relationship with his peers and instructional staff. ■ Working with his counselor, teacher, and aide, Mark will identify ways in which impulsivity may affect his relationships in school. ■ Working with his counselor, teacher, and aide, Mark will identify ways in which hyperactivity may affect his relationships in school. ■ Working with his counselor, teacher, and aide, Mark will identify ways in which angry outbursts may affect his relationships in school.
Mark will develop and utilize proactive and responsive strategies to minimize the impact of symptoms on his relationship with his peers and instructional staff.	■ Working with his counselor, teacher, and aide, Mark will identify steps he can take when he feels himself getting 'stuck' on a thought that may lead to negative interactions with peers or staff. ■ Working with his counselor, teacher, and aide, Mark will identify and rehearse strategies and responses when he is told "No" to something he wants to do. ■ Working with his counselor, teacher, and aide, Mark will identify strategies he can use when a compulsion may intrude on others or may lead to negative interactions with peers or staff, e.g., counting to ten, or excusing himself from the situation. ■ Working with his counselor, teacher, and aide, Mark will identify strategies for managing impulsive behaviors that may negatively affect peers or staff. ■ Working with his counselor, teacher, and aide, Mark will identify strategies for managing hyperactive behaviors that negatively affect peers or staff. ■ Mark will learn to approach a classmate or teacher and verbalize his recognition of how his symptoms affect them and what he is doing to minimize the impact.

tics or compulsions, conducting a proper assessment of assistive technology needs is essential.

If assistive technology is required, the student's plan may need to incorporate keyboarding skills and/or training in the use of both the hardware and software on the system. See Chapter 17 for some of the questions the assistive technology evaluator can address.

Autism Consultant or Other Consultants

In some cases, the district may need to make arrangements for a consultant to work with the student's team. As we include more students with disabilities in integrated or mainstream settings, it becomes more important to provide teachers with the support of experts in the students' disorders. This is particularly evident when it comes to working with students with Asperger's Syndrome, High-Function-ing Autism (HFA), or Nonverbal Learning Disability who may be in inclusive classrooms. Similarly, although school psychologists have some degree of training and experience in behavioral analysis and developing behavior plans, some cases will require more sophisticated approaches and the district may need a certified behavior analyst, a licensed psychologist, or other healthcare professional with experience in the students' disorders as well as behavioral programming.

Special Education Teacher/ Consultant

Special educators are a resource for regular education teachers in remedial strategies, accommodations, and information on the learning disabilities that are sometimes associated with these neurological disorders. This means that they can consult in the classroom as well as provide pull-out services.

The majority of special education training programs do not have in-depth training on the majority of the neurological disorders listed in this book, so it may be difficult for special educators to pick among their many strategies and tools in developing a plan for a child. Hopefully, the information provided in this book gives special education teachers a greater understanding of the nature of the problem so that they can determine which strategies may work best for their students.

Summary

The concept "It takes a village to raise a child" has become somewhat clichéd, but if ever there was a situation in which it applied, it would be teaching a child with the kinds of neurological challenges described in this book. A regular education teacher simply cannot do everything, and districts may need to provide the teacher and student with the needed supports.

Team means Together Everyone Achieves More!
— Author Unknown

CHAPTER 33

Establishing Positive Home-School Collaboration[*]

Let us put our minds together and see what life we can make for our children.
— *Sitting Bull*

When it comes to teaching students with the disorders described in this book, the image of the "three-legged stool" serves as a starting point. The three legs of the stool are the school, the family, and the student's treatment team. Without all three working together to support the student, the student's ability to flourish is wobbly, at best.

All too often, however, we encounter teachers who are frustrated by the apparent lack of parental support, or cooperating parents who are frustrated by the apparent lack of understanding and support from the teacher, and treatment professionals who may be working closely with the parents but seldom have direct interactions with school personnel.

Four issues generally interfere with establishing positive collaboration between home and school, from the parents' perspective:

- Perceived lack of awareness and professional knowledge of the child's disorder
- Perceived lack of empathy for the child and what the family is going through
- Failure to appreciate the impact of homework on the family
- Inadequate information and communication from the school to the home

Perceived Lack of Awareness and Professional Knowledge

When a child is first diagnosed with one of the conditions discussed in this book, the parents may spend a good amount of time identifying resources on the Internet, reading books, joining mail lists, and finding support from other parents. Over time, they may develop their own expertise in their child's diagnosed conditions. School personnel who do not know anything about the child's disorder(s) or who make statements that suggest a lack of knowledge about the condition may leave the parent feeling that the parent has to teach the teacher. While some parents (and teachers) are perfectly comfortable with the parent sharing information and helping the teacher understand, other parents may experience this type of situation as just one more burden. They want guidance from the teacher. When teachers are not educated about these disorders, parents may feel that they have to become almost professional educators themselves and micromanage what goes on in school. The best antidote is for the teacher to get training or consultation in these disorders. Many districts provide continuing education or staff development for teachers. Ask the district to arrange for staff development or a series of staff developments on these disorders. Teachers can also obtain helpful information from support organizations. A list of organizations is provided in the resources section. Additional resources are listed on our website at www.challengingkids.com.

---

[*] Some of the material in this chapter is based on a presentation given by Leslie at an educators' conference sponsored by the Long Island Tourette Syndrome Association, Inc. in 1998.

The student's parents are often the most reliable source of information as to whether the student is thriving in school or requires additional support. Parents can also tell the educator about the student's strengths so that teachers can teach to the strengths and develop a more integrated and effective educational program.

Here are some statements school personnel might innocently make that create a gap between parents and school instead of building a bridge:

"I do not see any symptoms—or at least, not very many. I wonder if this student really even has [diagnosed condition]."

School personnel need to remember that what they see in the classroom may be only the "tip of the iceberg." For example, most children who have tic disorders do not tic as much in the regular classroom as they do in other environments due to suppression and other factors. Nor do teachers see hidden symptoms such as internal tics, the urge to tic building up, obsessions, or mental compulsions.

Imagine that you are the parent of a child with Tourette's Syndrome and every day your child comes home from school and seemingly explodes in tics and emotional behavior. Now suppose that your child's teacher told you that he does not see any tics in school and wonders whether your child even has TS. What would you think about that teacher? Would you think that the teacher might be unobservant or just not recognizing the signs of TS? Would you think that the teacher had never been taught that symptoms wax and wane and that what goes on in school may be significantly different than what is evident elsewhere?

One way to avoid creating distrust is to say something like, "I know that symptoms can be very different in the home and in the classroom. I just want to let you know that right now, I do not see very many symptoms in the classroom. How are his symptoms at home?"

"He did it yesterday, but he wouldn't do it today. I know he can do it if he just tries harder."

The symptoms of the conditions described in this book may vary from day to day, week to week, or even hour to hour. The fact that students were able to focus or perform yesterday does not mean that they will be able to do it today. Maybe they had a "good neurochemical day" yesterday. Remember that chemistry waxes and wanes and varies from day to day. Or maybe they did not get a good night's sleep last night. How would you feel if you knew your child was trying as hard as he could and someone said that to you? Would you view the teacher as supportive or would you think that the teacher did not understand your child?

The above comments do not mean that all students are always trying their hardest. Sometimes students have given up or are overwhelmed. In other cases, lack of effort or persistence may reflect age-appropriate disinterest or other factors such as an adolescent's greater concern for socialization than academics. But when in doubt, a teacher's best strategy is to start from the premise that the student would do it if he could.

"I understand that you (the parent) are concerned, but I really do not see a serious problem here."

Earlier we referred to the "tip of the iceberg." Educators need to remain ever-aware that what they see in their classroom may be vastly different than what the parent observes in the home, where the student often feels freer to let his symptoms out or where the student may explode after a day of trying to cope with the demands of school. And in many cases, one of the reasons the school does not see a huge problem is because the parent has been helping the student do the homework, organizing and packing up his books and papers, and spending hours with the student each night because he would not get anything done without intensive assistance.

Confronted with a teacher who seems to underestimate the seriousness of their child's disabilities, some parents have considered taking their children off medication or simply not helping them at all for a while so that the school will begin to understand how impaired the child really is. Educators can avoid this type of desperation tactic by simply asking the parent, "How much support do you need to give your child at home for homework and school? Is he able to do any of this independently, and if so, how much?" The Homework Screening tool in Figure 23.2 (and on the accompanying CD-ROM) can be helpful here.

"How can I consider this student disabled when he is performing above grade level?!"

Because children who have neurological disorders follow the same normal curve of intelligence as the rest of the population, they generally manage to stay on grade level. As a result, their needs are often overlooked or misunderstood. All too often, they may have to deteriorate significantly before the school recognizes that they need help. The presence of any intellectual giftedness just compounds the problems further because it may mask detection of learning disabilities that need to be addressed.*

And if you still wonder whether you can consider that student disabled just because he is above grade level, think of Stephen Hawking.** Would anyone suggest that he does not need accommodations or supports just because he is brilliant?

Perceived Lack of Empathy for the Student and Family

Even the most caring teachers may be perceived as lacking empathy by parents who are overwhelmed by their child's problems and who need more support and guidance than they are getting. The section on "sanity-saving premises" (Chapter 3) points out that there is often more than one member of the family who has a particular disorder or related neurological challenges. By reaching out to build a bridge of support to the parents, school personnel also increase the parents' ability to support the school's efforts. For

example, if the school team wants to address behavioral issues such as verbally aggressive behavior towards peers, it helps if the parents support that goal in the home so that there are consistent expectations and consequences across settings. But what if there is another sibling in the home who is even more verbally aggressive or the family is under tremendous stress due to parental separation, job loss, or some other factor? By taking the time to find out what is going on in the home and what supports the parents need, schools can engender greater support from parents and develop more effective programs.

When school personnel simply make requests of parents without inquiring whether the parents can comply, e.g., "Please review math with Sally every day for thirty minutes," the parents may feel that the teacher really does not understand what is going on in the home or how over-taxed the parents are already. A more supportive way for school personnel to make requests or suggestions involves simply asking the parents whether they feel that they can provide the requested or suggested help, or prefacing any request with, "I realize that you already have a lot to deal with at home in terms of helping Sally, so tell me if this is too much for you, but I think it would help if…."

A therapist reported that she once got a phone call from a parent who had received a positive note from her son's middle school teacher. The parent was calling to ask what it meant because it was the first positive note she had ever gotten about her child.

School personnel need to remember that parents need to hear a kind word about their child, even if it means writing a note like, "Jason showed great restraint this week and did not attack any of the other students. We are very proud of him!"

Failure to Appreciate the Impact of Homework on the Family

Homework (Chapter 23) is one of the biggest sources of conflict in the home. It is also one of the biggest sources of frustration parents experience in their relationships with school personnel. In our experience, parents all too frequently report that they simply cannot help their children with homework because:

- The teacher has not provided them with adequate information to understand the assignment and assist with it.

---

* Children who are on or above grade level can often qualify for special education under I.D.E.A. under the federal category "Other Health Impaired" because educational performance involves more than "just grades" and includes behavior, stamina, endurance, and other factors. If they do not qualify under I.D.E.A., they generally can be qualified under Section 504 of the Rehabilitation Act of 1973.

** Stephen Hawking is a well known physicist and mathematician who without accommodations would be unable to communicate and move around due to the advanced state of the neurological disease that has taken his mobility and ability to talk without aids.

- No one has ensured that the necessary books and materials were sent home.
- No one has ensured that the assignment and due date(s) were accurately recorded.
- Parents may have no idea without guidance how to modify homework assignments in light of their child's symptoms or endurance issues.
- Teachers do not coordinate with each other sufficiently and may all assign big tests or projects at the same time.

One of the simplest and most effective ways to establish good school-home cooperation is for teachers to ensure that parents receive adequate information about assignments and tests. Because many students with the disorders described in this book have significant problems with organization and homework (Chapters 9 and 23), teachers cannot assume that any information the student was expected to bring home actually made it home.

Based on our experience, here are some suggestions to prevent confusion and frustration:

- Whenever possible, use the Internet to upload copies of assignments and materials so that parents and students can logon to get the information from home. If additional information is provided in class, e.g., how many pages an assignment is to be or intermediate due dates, that information also needs to be provided on the website.
- Use email, if possible, to allow parents to contact you for clarification on assignments.
- If a student needs accommodations in math homework, give the parents concrete guidelines for how to modify each assignment or type of assignment, e.g., does the student do just even numbered problems, does the parent just reduce the overall number of math problems assigned for the night, or does the parent have the student do a few questions from each section of the worksheet?

One parent, who was also a teacher, contacted a therapist in total frustration. "The teacher told me to use my judgment in modifying his homework, and I did. My son and I decided he'd do his math homework and not his other homework. Then he got into trouble for not having any of the language arts homework done. If she really wanted him to do that homework, she should have said so instead of telling me to use my own judgment."

Many parents tell us that they find it stressful, rather than supportive, if the teacher tells them to use their judgment and that they may encounter more resistance from their child when the child starts arguing, "C'mon, Mom, the teacher said you could decide, so don't make me do this!"

A combination of parental guidance as well as modifications and reductions made by the teacher may be the most helpful approach. Consider offering the following supports:

- If students are using a template or form to complete a writing assignment, ensure that the parents are taught how to use the template and what the student is to do with it.
- If students use editing strips (Chapters 19 and 20) on their desks in school to remind them how to edit their work, send home copies of the editing strips (and post a copy on the website) so that parents can place the same editing strips in front of the students at homework time. If you have taught the students a mnemonic such as "CLIPS" (Chapter 19), inform the parents of the mnemonic so that they can cue the students to use it during homework.
- Ensure that all due dates are clearly written at the top of each assignment.
- Ensure that papers that are to be done or completed in school are marked with a big "C" for "classwork" and that anything that is to be done at home is marked with a big "H" for "homework."
- Coordinate with other teachers so that students do not have too many big projects or tests in the same week. If it is impossible to avoid some overlap, work with parents to come up with a reasonable plan as to extending deadlines and what to attempt first, etc.
- Make an agreement with parents as to what they might do if the student does not understand the homework. Remember, homework is supposed to be practice or independent work, not work at the level of frustration.
- Do not assume that the parent understands the content or how to do the homework. Remember that the student may have inherited the math problem or spelling disability from the parent who is now trying to help him. You can provide such support tactfully by sending home a handout to all parents that says, "I know some of you may have

your own system for doing these problems, but if you would like to use the system I am using with your child in school, here is how I am doing it...."

Other tips and suggestions are provided in the chapter on homework issues (Chapter 23).

Inadequate School-to-Home Information and Communication

As suggested in the homework section, lack of information and communication can strain school-home collaboration and mutual support. In addition to the suggestions above, we encourage teachers to send home weekly notes or emails notifying parents of any missing or incomplete assignments. In many cases, parents are shocked to discover that assignments have not been turned in because they saw their child complete the assignment and pack it up. If they are notified of missing assignments in a timely fashion, they have a better chance of helping their child find the assignment before it gets thrown out or permanently lost.

Another aspect of school-home communication that may become a source of friction is attendance or tardiness. Although some schools now have automated systems that call the student's home on a daily basis to report any unexcused absences or lateness, if such systems are not in place, school personnel need to ensure that parents are notified by email or phone message of their child's attendance issues.

Notifying parents of unexcused absences or cutting classes in a timely fashion is important because the parents and school need to consider why the student is missing classes. Does it indicate that the student is getting overwhelmed and needs more support? Is it indicative of age-appropriate adolescent behavior? Or could it indicate that the treatment plan is failing and that the student's symptoms are spiraling out of control, as may be the case for students with ADHD, OCD, or Bipolar Disorder? If a student with a mood disorder suddenly starts cutting classes, this could flag serious health and safety issues. Notify parents promptly.

Communication is a two-way street. The above suggestions focus only on the school's half of the equation. Remember that parents of students with disabilities are frequently so overwhelmed that unless teachers actively reach out to support them, parents may be unable to support the teachers or the students.

Summary

Without the cooperation of the parents and the teacher, the student's progress goes more slowly, goes backwards, or stops. Without effective and regular home-school collaboration and communication, a student's symptoms may be made worse instead of better, and what would otherwise be doable becomes impossible. The team has to keep its eye on the student as the priority and not get triangulated or at odds with the parents and student's needs. Parents, too, need to learn how to support the school and not allow their child to triangulate them. It is possible for teachers to form a supportive alliance with the parents so that the child cannot triangulate them and damage the ability of the team to work together.

Dan Pruitt has a wonderful way of illustrating the concept of meeting parents where they are and bringing them to where we are as professionals and where the student has to go. He says that you have to think of the parents as being on the other side of the bridge. Our job is to walk across the bridge to where the parents are and assist them to come across the bridge to where we are. The assistance can be figuratively holding their hands or their hearts as we help them across the bridge. The bridge represents the information, recommendations, accommodations, strategies, and medical assistance that are needed for the parents and the teachers to get the students to the other side of each bridge that they encounter (Pruitt 1997).

---

*If kids come to us [educators/teachers]
from strong, healthy functioning families,
it makes our job easier. If they do not come to us
from strong, healthy, functioning families,
it makes our job more important.*
— *Barbara Coloroso*

CHAPTER 34

Social Issues, Peer Rejection, and Peer Education*

---

*"The school is not quite deserted," said the Ghost. "A solitary
child, neglected by his friends, is left there still."*
— *Charles Dickens*

Preview

One of the saddest results of some of the neurological disorders mentioned in this book is difficulty with peer relationships. Peer rejection is very prevalent in this population. Many educators and parents understand the importance of academic success, but sometimes underestimate the importance of social skills for adult success. Social skills affect our ability to marry, create friendships, and often determine our ability to get and maintain a job. Social skills are an important part of preparation for the adult world and schools play a critical role.

Impact of Neurological Disorders on Social Functioning

Stanley Greenspan, M.D. says that impulse control and empathy are necessary for social success. Yet many students with the disorders described in this book have difficulty regulating impulsive behavior, and some are impaired in taking the perspective of others due to deficits in working memory and the executive functions. After all, if a student has trouble holding multiple pieces of information in working memory, she may also have trouble floating multiple perspectives and be unable to hang onto and grasp the perspective of others. Similarly, if a student has deficits due to Executive Dysfunction (EDF), she

may have difficulty sorting and comprehending the information being presented by others. This leads to an inability to hold onto the perspective of others. Thus, EDF and working memory may impair empathy by interfering with the preliminary process of even understanding another's perspective.**

Working memory deficits and EDF obviously contribute to social difficulties. Another impact of EDF on socializing is the student's difficulty in problem solving. For example, if the student has a plan to get together with friends to go to the mall on Saturday and something upsets that plan, the student with EDF may be unable to conceive of other options or solutions.

Visible disorders are always socially challenging. Many students with TS have been publicly ridiculed for their motor and vocal tics. OCD, characterized by inflexibility, obsessions, compulsions, and anxiety, has an obvious impact on socialization. For many students, major depression eliminates the desire to be social. Students with Bipolar Disorder may exhibit chronic irritability and grandiosity that

---

* Much of the material in the social guidelines presented in this chapter are from (Pruitt 1996).

** In Sherry's experience, many students are diagnosed with ASD solely because they are seemingly unable to take the perspective of others (Theory of Mind). It is important to note that some students outside the autistic spectrum can have Theory of Mind or perspective-taking problems without being autistic [cf. research on Theory of mind in Bipolar youth (Lahera et al. 2008)].

causes others to avoid socializing with them. These are just a few examples of the complex impacts that can change a student's normal desire and ability to perform in a social setting. As time goes by and social failure continues, the student may be more likely to turn to drug use, associate with others who engage in risky behaviors, or both. When a student has no friends, it is important for all teachers and staff to monitor that child for depression, hopelessness, and acting-out behavior. If any of these are noted, the parents and school psychologist need to be notified immediately and a referral for help made.

Social deficits isolate students who are then at greater risk of substance abuse and suicide.

Table 34.1 lists some aspects of ADHD, TS, OCD, Mood Disorders, and EDF that affect social-emotional functioning. As this Table suggests, many students have numerous sources of symptom interference that affect their ability to socialize.

The challenges that these students face in socialization can be compounded by the teacher's response to their disorders. The impact of the teacher's attitude toward the social response of the class cannot be underestimated. If teachers ignore peer teasing or harassment, then the students' problems are greatly magnified. The teacher defines the classroom's level of tolerance.

Prepare the path for the child. Begin addressing social deficits by changing the environment. The teacher sets the tone for the class. Seek permission to educate peers so that they can be more supportive and helpful.

Inform students and peers about the impact of neurological disorders on social functioning. If this is done for a particular student, then the student and the parents need to give permission and feel they are ready to disclose the student's disability to peers. A well-done peer education program can frequently minimize social isolation. Changing the environment is generally not sufficient, however. The remainder of this chapter addresses how to remediate social skills deficits.

John was being unrelentingly teased by his peers, and one bully in particular. As his counselors, we asked him if he would allow us to go to his middle school and do a peer in-service on TS using PowerPoint slides. He was very hesitant at first, but we talked it out over several sessions and he finally agreed. We opened with a "bully blaster" line, "We are so excited to be speaking to middle schoolers because unlike kindergarteners, you guys are mature enough not to make fun of a student with a neurological disorder." Since the inservice, John has the support and understanding now of most of his classmates.

Guidelines to Remediate the Impact of Social Deficits

When educating students, it is important to use guidelines to remediate the impact of social deficits. The school is a good place to teach these skills. Have the faculty and staff participate in a school-wide program of improving social skills through training. School-wide techniques such as "Instant Replay," detailed in Chapter 31, give students instant feed-

Table 34.1. Symptoms that Interfere With Social Functioning

Inattention	Being "stuck"	Initiation
Distractibility	Fears	Impersistence
Impulsivity	Phobias	Inability to plan
Hyperactivity	Mood	Disorganization
Motor tics	Chronic irritability	Inflexibility
Vocal tics	Depression	Chronic lateness
Obsessions	Lack of energy	Self-involved
Compulsions	Mania	Hypersensitive
Anxiety	Overarousal	Immaturity
Failure to self-monitor	Underarousal	Inability to use feedback
Medication side effects	Lack of eye contact	

Modified and adapted from (Parkaire Consultants 1995)

back when a social problem occurs. Another strategy that is very helpful is to teach what Richard Lavoie calls the "hidden curriculum" in the school setting (Lavoie 1996). The "hidden curriculum" comprises the skills and knowledge that are normally acquired by awareness of surroundings and others' behavior. EDF leads to a lack of such awareness; so direct instruction is required. For example, a ninth grader with EDF may not know where the ninth graders hang out at the football games or in the school building and needs to be told.

Pragmatic language (Chapter 18) also plays a crucial role in developing satisfying social relationships. Pragmatics can be remediated through a referral to a speech and language pathologist at the school, who can provide direct services to the student and also assist the classroom teacher and parents by providing suggestions and strategies.

As noted in Chapter 8, Russell A. Barkley, Ph.D., has suggested that neurologically impaired students may lag behind their peers in development and may function as if they are 2/3s of their chronological age. The 2/3 rule also applies to social functioning, meaning that a twelve-year-old middle school student may have the social maturity and skills of an eight-year-old. Some students with multiple disorders function at an even lower level and have not even begun to develop the emotional regulation of a four-year-old. This is socially devastating. Many parents note that their children have always seemed to play better with much younger children. Teachers need to adjust their expectations as to the realistic ability of the student to be on the same social level as her peers.

If the social deficits are due to EDF, the skills can be taught using the same techniques used to remediate deficits in learning disabilities and memory disorders. In addition, the techniques described in the chapter on coaching (Chapter 31) may help the student. For some aspects of socialization, problem solving mnemonics can be taught and be very helpful in creating habits in the brain as these techniques are mastered. Some examples are provided in the "Tips and Tricks" section of this chapter below.

Another helpful technique is to provide a social curriculum so the teacher and student have some guidelines for remediating social skill deficits. An example of a teacher and student curriculum is listed in the "Tips and Tricks" section below. The curriculum can be reinforced by setting up successful, positive experiences with the student that other students model.

Are the school and the home establishing similar standards and expectations? As discussed in Chapters 2 and 33, some parents who are overwhelmed by their child's problems are unsure as to where to set limits. Parents who bend over backwards to accommodate their child do not necessarily do their child a favor. Children, regardless of their challenges, need to learn where the line is that they must not cross. If they do not learn where that line is and how not to cross it, they will be impaired socially. Remember, however, that just setting the bar high, without giving the student the necessary strategies and support, is unlikely to succeed.

Figure 34.1. Problem Solving Mnemonics: CLUE, PLAN, and POSE

CLUE*	PLAN**	POSE***
Create a plan	**P**roblem defined	**P**lan
Look at options	**L**ay out options	**O**ptions
Use strategy	**A**ct on one	**S**trategy
Evaluate	**N**ow evaluate	**E**valuate

* (Pruitt 1995)
** (Pruitt and Pruitt 2001)
*** (Pruitt 1995)

Tips and Tricks for Helping Students with Social Deficits

Chapter 31 describes techniques for coaching students in social situations: coaching, "Instant Replay," and "Cooperative Problem Solving." There are a variety of mnemonics available for the steps in the kind of cooperative problem-solving approach described previously, and students can be given a choice of which problem-solving mnemonic they prefer to use. Three such mnemonics are shown in Figure 34.1: CLUE, PLAN, and POSE.

Once the mnemonics are defined for the students, they can be asked whether they would prefer to be cued to use their problem-solving strategy with "What is your CLUE?" or "What is your PLAN?," etc. The remainder of this chapter provides additional tips and strategies for remediating the impact of Executive Dysfunction on social skills.

Teacher (and Parent) Strategies:

Goal setting:

- Have the student formulate a social goal, e.g., "I want Sarah to say 'Hi' to me" or "I want to have a play date with Tony."
- Provide feedback as to whether the goal is realistic.
- Make sure that the student knows how to choose an appropriate friend. If they have not chosen an appropriate friend, suggest someone who would be appropriate (e.g., "I don't think Tony is interested in having a play date, but I noticed that Jamie always wants to eat lunch with you. Maybe Jamie would enjoy a play date with you.")

Planning:

- Teach the students to consider their peers' interests when creating a plan, e.g., "Stephen seems particularly interested in fire trucks. Do you have any fire trucks at home that he might like to play with?" or "What do you think Stephen would enjoy doing?"
- Teach the students how to make a social plan.
- Help the students break the social plan down into steps. Creating a checklist with them that they can use now and in the future will help. Use the same approach as in planning a big project (see Chapter 19), incorporating intermediate deadlines.

Organizing:

- Check for organizational pitfalls in the plan, e.g., if the student wants to invite friends over, has the student created a plan? If the plan requires the assistance of the teacher or parent, one of the first steps in the plan is to ask the teacher or parent for support.
- Find websites and other resources that help with organizing the event that is planned (e.g., for a teen who wants to host a Super Bowl party).

Sequencing:

- Teach how to sequence the execution of the plan. The sequencing can be incorporated in the planning template or checklist. For example, the student needs to ensure that the friend has accepted the invitation to come over before going out and buying any food!
- Help the student to understand that there is an order to social actions.

Prioritizing:

- Remind the student that health and safety of self and others is the prime social priority.
- Help the student understand that paying attention to the feelings of others is a significant priority.
- Teach the student to make sure that her friend has the same priority.

Initiating Conversations with New People:

- Use direct instruction to teach specific greeting skills, as in the example in Chapter 31 where a student with Asperger's Syndrome was coached where to look and what to say when greeting a fellow student.
- Have students practice greeting skills until they have mastered them reliably and successfully.
- Teach the student what subjects would be good and safe for initial conversations.
- Teach conversation starters. For example, a teenager can be taught to ask peers, "Have you seen any good movies lately?" or "What do you like to do on weekends?"
- Explain how to show others that you share their feelings. For some students, direct instruction and role playing may be helpful or necessary.
- Suggest alternate ways to extend an invitation, e.g., email, phone, in person.

Sustaining Relationships:

- Give students strategies for how to pay attention to friends.
- Teach examples of how to compliment peers appropriately.
- Help the students understand the importance and feelings created by sharing.
- Teach the student how to recognize when a relationship needs repair.
- Teach the student how to repair it using the coaching techniques described in Chapter 31.
- Teach manners and the reasons that they are important to help maintain friendships.

Pacing:

- Teach the back-and-forth rhythm of a social conversation, e.g., similar to a tennis match.
- Help the students understand the timing necessary for a successful reciprocal relationship. Timing applies to the back-and-forth of conversations, but it also applies to when to follow-up with a phone call or an invitation and when not to.
- Teach the timing of when to initiate an invitation to a social event.
- Teach the student how much time to allow when extending an invitation, e.g., not waiting until Friday to invite a peer over for Friday night.
- Teach students how to set appropriate deadlines for completing social plans using a planner.
- Help highlight the important holidays and events that occur during the school year in the student's planner so that the student is aware of important events, e.g., so that the student avoids being embarrassed by inviting someone over for "next Thursday," when everyone else realizes that next Thursday is Thanksgiving.
- Keep a calendar in the classroom with reminders of big events, e.g., homecoming.

Inhibiting:

- Provide feedback as to the inappropriateness of any disinhibited verbalizations using the "Instant Replay" technique described in Chapter 31.
- Teach how people feel when interrupted.
- Help the students understand the impact of any uninhibited behavior on their social relationships using the "Instant Replay" technique.
- Help the students understand how their uninhibited behavior affects their safety and the safety of others, e.g., throwing something out of the second story window might hit and hurt anyone standing below.
- Help the students understand how their uninhibited behavior may embarrass them, e.g., "If you have a tantrum on the football field because you did not catch the ball, everyone who sees you having a tantrum or meltdown may be reluctant to hang out with you."

Execution:

- Teach the importance of follow-through in social settings, e.g., "If you tell someone you will call them the following night, she will expect you to call and may be angry or hurt if you do not call." Remind or teach the student to enter such commitments in their agenda or planner ("Write it or Regret It").
- Teach the student strategies for completing social plans.
- Help the student understand the impact of procrastination on social interactions.

Using feedback:

- Teach which facial expressions communicate what message.
- Teach students how to tell if others are interested or bored with what they are saying.
- Teach students how to tell if others are getting annoyed with what they are saying or doing.
- Explain the need to get help with feedback from trusted adults.
- Identify who to ask for help in different social settings.
- Explain, in a nonjudgmental tone to the students, why their behavior was causing a negative reaction in others. Use the "Instant Replay" technique (Chapter 31).
- Teach the student how to use feedback from trusted adults and peers.
- Have the students learn to "people-watch" and specifically to watch others' reactions to negative behavior.

Self-monitoring:

- Explain the impact of bragging and what peer behaviors the student will likely see or hear from others in response to bragging.

- Teach the impact of competition on friends.
- Tell the students when competition is appropriate and teach them what appropriate competition looks like.
- Teach how close to stand to people when talking to them. Teach them to maintain one arm's length from others.
- Help students learn appropriate dress for age-appropriate social settings.
- Provide feedback about whether the student looks clean and neat.
- Teach how others view dirty, unkempt appearance. Teach personal hygiene, if needed.
- Instruct the student in the significance of a good reputation and how to maintain one.
- Help the student to balance her social life with family relationships and grades.
- Teach what gossiping is and the impact of gossip.
- Explain the impact of putting others down and bullying.
- Teach the students how to handle anxiety and anger in a social setting, e.g., the graceful exit (Chapter 31).

Other pragmatics (Chapter 18):
- Teach age-appropriate social expressions and jargon.
- Instruct the student in "feeling" words.
- Teach the student how to read facial expressions.
- Have the students learn self-calming techniques.
- Explain the difference between what is appropriate to say to peers and what is appropriate to say to adults.
- Teach negotiating skills.

Be sure to assess if the skill is there, and whether the symptoms of the disorder make it impossible for the student to use the skill. For example, a student in a mood episode may read facial expressions inaccurately and misinterpret a neutral expression as anger. The student does not need to be taught how to read facial expressions if she normally can read expressions accurately. In this case, she needs to be taught more about her disorder so that she understands that it is impairing her ability to read faces, and she needs to be told which trusted adult or peer she can look to for guidance in interpreting facial expressions.

Student Strategies

Teachers may want to use the following material as teaching tools to share with students.

Goal setting:
- Decide that you want a friend.
- Choose someone to be your friend. If you are not sure who would be a good friend for you, ask an adult you trust.

Planning:
- Make a plan to socialize.
- Join groups with similar interests.
- Find what you and a peer would both like to do as a first outing.
- Get assistance with planning social events.

Organizing:
- Memorize and rehearse social responses for common social occasions.
- Get assistance with organizing social events.
- Check Internet for how to organize different social events.

Sequencing:
- Decide the order in which to implement the steps in your plan.
- Ask for help if the sequence needed to execute the plan is not apparent.

Prioritizing:
- Self-respect and safety come first.
- Your friend's needs count, but so do yours. There is "give and take" in a friendship.
- Make sure you do what you think is right.
- Check your priorities with a trusted adult.
- Make sure you and your friend have agreed upon the priorities.
- See if your plan includes the most important parts.

Initiating:
- Be positive.
- Smile often.
- Learn greeting skills.
- Begin a conversation; learn and rehearse conversation starters for common social settings.
- Show others that you share their feelings.
- Call or email to extend an invitation if it is hard to do so in person.

Sustaining Relationships:

- Pay attention to your friend.
- Include your friend in events that you want to attend.
- Compliment your friend.
- Make sure you share your toys and electronics with your friend.
- Repair relationships when necessary.
- Use good manners to help keep friends.

Pacing:

- Friendships take time to develop and grow; do not go too fast.
- Make sure the person invites you to do things, too.
- Do not forget to call and make plans in a timely manner. Check first to make sure that the date is an open one and not a big holiday or the day before a big test (unless it is a study date).
- Ask someone early in the week if you want to do something with them on the weekend.
- Write down all social appointments or commitments in your planner.
- Pay attention to the future for long range social events, e.g., prom.
- Check your calendar or agenda every night for any social events the next day.

Inhibiting:

- Do not overdo, e.g., talk too much.
- Do not interrupt others when they are speaking.
- Do not make big social decisions in a hurry, e.g., wait twenty-four hours.
- Do not drive too fast. You not only risk your own health and safety and your friend's health and safety, but you may scare your friend and she may not want to drive with you again or her parents may not let her drive with you again.
- If you have done something impulsively that caused problems for others, clean it up and make reparations.
- Do not do what others ask before thinking about it. If you are not sure, ask a trusted adult.

Execution:

- Follow your plan to completion.
- Have deadlines for completing social plans.
- Get help if you find yourself putting things off.

Using feedback:

- Check facial expressions to see how other people feel.
- Get help with feedback from trusted adults.
- Learn strategies for new ways of acting when necessary.
- Observe the social setting continually.
- Watch people to learn about them and to see how others react to their behavior.

Self-monitoring:

- Learn not to brag.
- Do not act competitive with your friend.
- Avoid gossiping.
- Do not bully.
- Do not stand too close to people when you are talking to them, e.g., stand at least one arm's length apart.
- Make sure you are dressed similar to your peers.
- Make sure you are clean and neat, even if your friends do not care. Many teenage girls will not go out with a boy who is dirty, looks messy, or who smells bad.
- Learn the significance of a good reputation.
- Do not let your social life ruin family relationships and grades.
- Do not put others down.
- Use the "graceful exit" strategy when appropriate, such as when you are getting too anxious or too angry.

Other pragmatics (Chapter 18):

- Get help if you do not know age-appropriate social expressions.
- Learn "feeling" words.
- Get help reading faces for the feelings of others.
- Learn how to calm down heated discussions.
- Learn the difference between what you can say to peers and what you can say to adults.
- Get help learning to negotiate when you want to persuade someone to your point of view.

Summary

Successful social skills become one of the foundations of a happy and productive life as an adult. School can affect this deficit in students with neurological disorders. It is possible to add a curriculum for both teachers and students that is practical and easily integrated into the normal classroom routine as well as other school activities. Becoming more successful socially can provide the student with less stress and an ability to better navigate the social setting and the future demands of the adult world.

Marcie is a teenage girl with OCD and major depression. The impact of her disorders was that she became a moral policewoman and frequently chided her peers for breaking school rules. Not surprisingly, her classmates did not want to socialize with her. Her special education teacher met with her and explained how her OCD was causing her to act like a critical parent with her friends. The teacher also explained that the other kids were already fed up with their own parents and did not need another parent. Marcie was surprised to learn that her OCD was the reason that she was having social problems. She started fighting back against her OCD and was able to stop herself from criticizing her peers. Marcie also learned several strategies to repair her broken friendships. Six months later, Marcie turned sixteen and was thrilled that all eight girls that she had invited to her birthday party accepted the invitation.

The *Real* Experts Look Back

In the preface to this book, we shared a bit of our personal stories. Our children are in their twenties and thirties now, and many of the challenges they faced when they were younger are no longer issues for them, but each of them still face challenges.

Since Sherry's children were in school at a time when there was no formal diagnosis for them, they never received special education services and everyone just thought they were not "living up to their potential" as intellectually gifted students. They went through some very hard times with some very difficult teaching situations. In spite of this, they both survived high school. Both went on to attend college but dropped out because of lack of support for the undiagnosed disorders, especially their deficits in executive functioning. Despite all of this, both Sherry's sons are now succeeding in their own way: Jory owns his own business and Darin works in the field of information technology and is a loving father to his young daughter, Julianna—who, not surprisingly, also has neurological disorders.

Leslie's children were both diagnosed, and received—and benefited from—special education. Both of them attended college, but like Sherry's sons, Justin dropped out of college after the first year because of deficits in executive functioning. He now works full-time in an animal hospital and goes to college nights to work on a degree in veterinary technology. He finds it easier to learn "hands-on" and the skills he has gained in the work setting have translated into improved work habits and productivity in his classes. He hopes to eventually become a veterinarian, but realizes that taking numerous courses at one time does not work for him.

Despite some very difficult times in college due to panic attacks and mood swings, Leslie's daughter, Loren, managed to make Dean's List in her last year of college and is currently doing well in a doctoral program in psychology. She also serves as a volunteer hotline crisis counselor for her community after taking 200 hours of training on her own time.

We asked our children to look back on their experiences as students and tell us something positive that a teacher did that made a big difference for them. Here are their responses in their own words:

Jory:

Growing up in the early stages of the awareness of neurological disorders was an interesting experience. I wasn't diagnosed 'til well after high school, so growing up being different was a "bad" thing. In my school, we had the normal people and the "retards." Since my mother taught kids with behavior disorders and LD in school, I knew they were people too, but when I started to tic and no one knew exactly what it was, I had to fight hard to stay "normal." Entering high school, I had never been diagnosed and didn't really even know about ADHD, OCD, or Tourette's. These disorders didn't care that I was a budding teenager trying to get through one of the toughest parts of my life. My high school wasn't equipped to deal with someone who was able to function but not able to concentrate in or out of school.

I spent five years in summer school from eighth to twelfth grade failing seven classes, most of which were English. I didn't learn until much later, that along with the disorders mentioned earlier, I also had a language disorder. The ONLY reason I made it through high school was my Latin teacher, Mr. G. Starting in my freshman year he helped me with Latin but noticed that even though I didn't do my homework and really never picked up on the language, I soaked up Roman history and architecture like a sponge. He was the only one who noticed that the reason I didn't pick up on languages was that trying to learn a language for me was like hitting a brick wall. The information about the language just wouldn't stick, therefore frustrating me, which caused me to become depressed. He let me do other activities within and without the class up to and including joining the Junior Classical League. After three years in Latin with Mr. G. and a trip to the National Junior Classical League Convention, I won a first place National award for a model I built displaying the Watermills of Barbagol. It's been seventeen years and I still remember the name of that model even with a language disorder. You can decide for yourself if he made an impact on me.

Darin:

My mother asked me to talk about teachers I had that were great. Unfortunately for me, they all happened in twelfth grade or later in college. I guess it is a matter of timing. However, I do not believe it is never too late to get a great teacher.

One day I walked into high school English and got the second worst possible news. The worst news is you're going to read Tolstoy. The second worst news is you're going to read Joseph Conrad. I had read "Lord Jim" but I still do not remember a single word of it. Joseph Conrad was brilliant but a little dry. Actually, Conrad is, from the point of view of a seventeen-year-old with ADHD and learning disabilities, incredibly boring. (Sorry, Joe.) In my defense, no one else in my class was excited about reading Joseph Conrad either.

Mr. M., our AP English teacher, walked in a few minutes after the bell rang. He was very theatrical. He arrived late on purpose. He was carrying a box full of books, and began throwing one to each of us the instant he stepped into the room. He certainly woke me up. Our excitement turned to groans as we began to notice the title on the books: "Heart of Darkness." He put the empty box on his desk, and plodded ahead. He picked someone to read, and we started the journey upriver.

After about ten minutes of reading, Mr. M. asked us to stop. He asked us if it was boring. We said, "Yes." He asked us if we would rather watch a movie. A room full of seventeen-year-olds went, "Duh." So he turned off the lights and charged up the VCR. The tape in the player was "Apocalypse Now," directed by Francis Ford Coppola. We were so excited about getting to watch an R-rated movie in class (yes, he had permission) that we totally missed the fact that he had it all queued up and ready to go.

After a few minutes of Jim Morrison singing and helicopters avoiding napalm explosions, the dialogue started. We were all absorbed. Some of us had seen it already, and knew what to expect. Suddenly, Mr. M. jabbed us all in the pause button. "Why do you think he said that?" he asked. "What does that mean?"

We talked about the symbolism and the imagery of one of the most fantastic (but not pleasant) films that has ever been made. We all forgot we were in class. We forgot or did not notice that we were learning. Nobody needed to take notes; we were captivated by the movie and the teacher.

Then the bubble burst. One of the students, who did not have ADHD or EDF, asked Mr. M., "Does this movie have something to do with 'Heart of Darkness'?" "Yes," he answered. We all groaned. We were doing class work! Mr. M. wore a devilish grin and explained to the class, "Coppola made this movie as an adaptation of Conrad's 'Heart of Darkness.' The only major difference is which river, and which war. All the rest is very much the same, especially the names of the characters."

I learned more about Joseph Conrad from Mr. M. and his VCR then I ever learned about any writer or book in the eleven years of school before that. He opened my eyes to alternate ways of viewing written literature. From that moment forward I started to listen to audio books, and watch movies, and allow those adaptations to help me read the actual book, and enjoy it. I went from hating reading to loving reading in a very short period of time. Mr. M. taught me that I could get help picturing the faces and events from great literature. Learning how other people picture the story helped me learn how to do that for myself.

Justin:

There are many different things teachers can do to help encourage their students to learn and behave. Once, one of my homeroom teachers bought a game system that we all loved at a garage sale (she got it cheap). If we (the ENTIRE class) really worked hard at behaving and doing our work, she'd let us stay in the room for lunch period. Rather than go down to the cafeteria, we could stay in homeroom and take turns playing video games. (Pokemon and Magic cards were previously banned from the school cafeteria because it was considered 'gambling.' What did they think we were gambling? "I'll call your chocolate milk, and I raise you two tater tots.")

Now, the catch is, we ALL had to do our best. If even ONE student was causing a problem, we didn't get to stay in homeroom. So, if I saw there was a problem starting with any of my classmates (like two of them butting heads), I'd try and help them work it out. And, in turn, my classmates would do the same. This taught us to try and understand the viewpoints of others, and to help them if they needed it. This took a lot of pressure off of our teacher, and we (the students) became closer friends as a result. Also, during group activities, our grades showed a marked improvement. (For the first time in my life, I got good marks under "Plays Well With Others.")

She was willing to go the extra mile for us, and all she asked was that we do our best. I think, after that, there were maybe three days that we didn't all try to behave our best. There were many other things that she (and most of the other teachers, as well) did to make school an enjoyable learning experience, but this one is the one that stands out in my mind most.

Loren:

When asked to look back at my school career and find a positive experience, I'm faced with a very difficult challenge. Unfortunately, for kids with mood disorders, the bad experiences come to mind much easier and quicker than the good experiences. Yet, if a child is lucky, there can be one teacher that makes all the difference. For me, that teacher is Miss A.

Originally, I started out high school in a regular public school. I was completely mainstreamed and I didn't need any special accommodations. That was until sophomore year began. The end of my freshman year is when everything really started going downhill for me. I was really manicky from Bipolar Disorder and was hospitalized for seven weeks. When I returned to high school, I couldn't stay awake or think in school because of my medications. My mother wanted me in a day treatment program but the district insisted they could handle me. Then one day, a teacher heard me say that I was going to kill a student who had just dumped a bucket of water on my head after I had fallen asleep in class. The teacher thought I was threatening to kill her and didn't believe me when I told her that I wasn't threatening her at all. The teachers and staff didn't think I was fit to be in a public school and I was "suspended indefinitely" after that. Suddenly they were willing to send me to a day treatment program, and I spent the rest of sophomore year at a hospital day program where most of the focus was on therapy and behavior modification. Needless to say, my schoolwork was not a priority.

After completing out the year at the hospital program, I returned the following fall to my old high school. All of the teachers and staff seemed apprehensive about my return due to my behavior the year before. My IEP plan was modified and I started going to resource room first period everyday. The school thought that this would be a good way to help me integrate back into the norms of school, as well as give me a chance to catch up on any work that I might need help with. That is where I met Miss A. Unlike my other teachers, Miss A. seemed like she actually enjoyed having me in her class. She knew what my situation was but didn't seem scared by the possibility that I might have an "outburst," something that my other teachers seem terrified by. Miss A. seemed to know what my strengths were and she applauded me for them. Sometimes the other students would start to annoy me and distract me from my work, so Miss A. would let me sit at her desk to complete what I was working on. Not only was she concerned with my schoolwork, but she truly seemed to care about what was going on in my personal life. She would ask me about my relationships with my family and friends and she always remembered the smallest details. Whenever I was absent, Miss A. showed genuine concern. To sum it up, Miss A. created a warm environment that I always felt welcome in.

After my junior year, my school decided that I didn't need resource room anymore. I felt kind of sad that I was not going to get to see Miss A. everyday but she let me know that I was always more than welcome to stop in and if I needed help with anything she would be there for me. Miss A. always sticks out in my mind because although she had the same information about me that all of the other teachers had prior to entering their classes, she never once judged me or made me feel like I was a "problem" child. After graduation, I have gone back to visit her quite a few times and even though I'm not her student anymore, she still makes me feel the way she did when I was in the eleventh grade. She makes me feel proud of myself and safe.

The four dedicated teachers described above each found a different way to reach and teach students, but they had something in common: They showed respect for and nurtured the children's abilities and created an emotionally safe environment for them. Educators who manage to see the child underneath the symptoms and nurture that child can become famous in the child's life.

A teacher affects eternity; he can never tell where his influence stops.
— *Henry B. Adams*

Glossary of Terms and Acronyms

ADHD—The abbreviation for *Attention Deficit Hyperactivity Disorder*.

Affect—How the student's mood appears. Affect descriptions:
- *blunted*: notable reduction in the intensity of emotional expression
- *flat*: absence or near-absence of any signs of affective expression
- *inappropriate*: mismatch between affective expression and the content of speech or ideation
- *labile*: abnormal variability in affect with rapid and/or abrupt shifts in affective expression
- *restricted or constricted*: mild reduction in the range and intensity of emotional expression

Affective disorder—Characterized by a disturbance of mood; mood disorder.

Agoraphobia—An irrational fear of going out in public places from which escape might be difficult.

Akathisia—Inability to be still; a feeling of inner restlessness. A possible side effect of neuroleptic medications; may be confused with hyperactivity.

Anergic—Without energy.

Anhedonia—Inability to feel pleasure or happiness.

Anxiety—A feeling of worry, uneasiness, or dread.

Anxiety disorders—A group of disorders characterized by excessive, unreasonable, and impairing worry, including fears, phobias, and the like.

APD—The abbreviation for *Auditory Processing Disorder*.

Apraxia—Loss of ability to plan and execute skilled movements and gestures despite having the desire and physical ability to perform them. If mild, referred to as *Dyspraxia*.

Arithmomania—Compulsive mental counting or morbid preoccupation with numbers.

AS—The abbreviation for *Asperger's Syndrome*.

ASD—The abbreviation for *Autism Spectrum Disorder*.

Asperger's Syndrome (AS)—An Autism Spectrum Disorder (ASD) characterized primarily by impaired social relations, communications deficits, and by repetitive patterns of behavior and restricted interests.

Assistive technology—A product, device, or piece of equipment used to maintain, increase, or improve the functional capabilities of a disabled student. Some examples are word processors, speech recognition software, spell checkers, and calculators.

Associated behaviors (or Associated disorders)—The spectrum of behaviors sometimes seen in association with whatever condition is being discussed. For example, if one is discussing Tourette's, the "associated behaviors" referred to are usually obsessive-compulsive behaviors or ADHD-related behaviors.

Attention Deficit Disorder/Attention Deficit Hyperactivity Disorder (ADHD)—The DSM-IV defines this as a condition characterized by: (1) marked inattention or difficulty in sustaining attention and/or (2) impulsivity-hyperactivity. There are three subtypes.

Auditory perceptions—The ability to distinguish the edges of sounds, to distinguish primary sounds, to memorize a sound and blend multiple sounds, and to hold onto enough sounds to understand the whole of what words are being said.

Auditory Processing Disorder (APD)—Impaired ability to discriminate, recognize, or comprehend complex sounds (such as those used in words) despite normal hearing and intelligence. Students with APD have even greater trouble in the classroom where there is background noise and/or reliance on orally presented instruction. Formerly called *Central Auditory Processing Disorder*.

Autism Spectrum Disorder (ASD)—A condition characterized by impaired socialization, impaired communication, and restricted, repetitive, and stereotyped patterns of behavior.

Aversive—Unpleasant, referring to a stimulus or consequence that the individual seeks to avoid.

Basal Ganglia—A group of structures in the "basement" ("basal") of the brain that are intimately involved in involuntary movements and that are involved in pathways to the cortex.

Behavior Intervention Plan (BIP)—A systematic plan to decrease inappropriate or disruptive behaviors or to promote positive behaviors. The plan is based on the results of a Functional Behavioral Assessment.

Behavior modification—The application of conditioning techniques to decrease unwanted behavior, shape desired behaviors, or maintain or increase positive behaviors.

Behavior therapy—A treatment plan that targets a specific behavior or class of behaviors for modification. In behavior therapy, the focus is on observable behavior and not necessarily on any preceding thoughts or feelings.

Biofeedback—A therapy modality in which the individual is given external (usually machine-aug-mented) feedback about some physiological process that he normally would not be able to detect or feel. Neurofeedback is a specific form of biofeedback that relates to brain activity.

BIP—The abbreviation for *Behavior Intervention Plan*.

Bipolar Disorder (BP)—A condition characterized by mood episodes where the person's mood "swings" from the highs of hypomania or mania to the "lows" of depression; formerly known as Manic Depression.

BP—The abbreviation for *Bipolar Disorder*.

CBT—The abbreviation for *Cognitive-Behavior Therapy*.

CD—The abbreviation for *Conduct Disorder*.

Central Auditory Processing Disorder—Refer to *Auditory Processing Disorder*, the current name for this condition.

Chronic—Long-lasting.

Cluttering—The absence of the normal flow of speech due to an inability to plan and organize a response, speaking in rapid spurts, or not being sure what to say.

Cognitive-Behavior Therapy (CBT)—A form of therapy that incorporates changing ideas or thoughts ("cognitions") as well as behaviors.

Cognitive dulling—An adverse effect of some medications involving short-term memory loss (inability to recall recently learned material) and slowed thinking.

Cognitive therapy—A form of therapy where the emphasis is on altering thought patterns to produce improvement in behavior or emotional well-being.

Comorbid condition—A medical condition that occurs along with another medical condition, although one condition does not directly cause the other and they may be occurring together by chance.

Complex tic—Involuntary movement or utterance involving more than one muscle group (complex motor tic) or a linguistically meaningful phrase (complex phonic tic).

Compulsion—A ritualized pattern of behavior often (although not necessarily) associated with irrational, repetitive intrusive thoughts (obsessions). The "hallmark" of a compulsion is that the person has to do it over and over again. Adj.: compulsive: characterized by ritualized nature and the feeling of having to do it over and over again.

Conduct Disorder (CD)—A disorder characterized by disregard for the personal safety of others or disregard for property.

Continuous Reinforcement (CRF)—A conditioning schedule in which every instance of the targeted behavior is followed by a reinforcer (a stimulus that maintains or strengthens the response). Compare to *Intermittent Reinforcement.*

Coprolalia—Involuntary utterances of obscene or socially taboo (inappropriate) statements or words. Coprolalia may be a symptom of Tourette's Syndrome, although the majority of people with Tourette's Syndrome do not have this symptom.

Copropraxia—Involuntary motoric expression of obscene or taboo gestures; may include inappropriate sexual touching. Copropraxia may be a symptom of Tourette's Syndrome, although the majority of people with Tourette's Syndrome do not have this symptom.

CRF schedule—See *Continuous Reinforcement.*

Cyclothymia—A mood disorder characterized by mood episodes that "swing" between hypomania and depressive symptoms (but not major depression).

DCD—The abbreviation for *Developmental Coordination Disorder.*

DD—The abbreviation for *Developmental Disability.*

Declarative memory—A type of long-term memory associated with facts and knowledge. Declarative memory is made up of semantic memory and episodic memory.

Delusion—A belief held despite evidence that it is not true.

Depression—A sustained and somewhat extreme mood of sadness with physical symptoms such as loss of appetite and sleep. Depression can also present as sustained bad ("irritable") mood.

Developmental Coordination Disorder (DCD)—Impairment in performing activities of daily living or academic activities due to motor coordination that is not commensurate with chronological age or intellectual abilities. The deficits are not due to a general medical condition.

Developmental Disability (DD)—A handicap or impairment originating before the age of eighteen that is expected to continue indefinitely and which constitutes a substantial disability.

Diagnostic and Statistical Manual of Mental Disorders (DSM)—A manual published by the American Psychiatric Association in Washington, D.C. that describes the diagnostic criteria for many disorders.

Differential Reinforcement for Low Rates of Behavior—A schedule of reinforcement for decreasing the rate of an undesirable behavior that is occurring at a high rate: The learner only earns the reinforcer if he emits the desired response at a (relatively) low rate (e.g., only out of seat five times in a twenty-minute period if the current rate is seven times). Over time, the criterion would be shifted so that the reinforcer is only provided if he is out of his seat four times in a twenty-minute period, etc.

Differential Reinforcement of High Rates of Behavior—A schedule of reinforcement for increasing the rate of behavior: The learner only earns the reinforcer if he emits the desired response at a high rate (e.g., makes eye contact ten times in a thirty-minute period). If the rate is lower (e.g., nine times in the thirty-minute period), no reinforcer is delivered.

Differential Reinforcement of Incompatible Behaviors (DRI)—A conditioning approach to decreasing unwanted behaviors by ignoring the unwanted behavior and positively reinforcing behaviors that are incompatible with the unwanted behavior. For example, if the student is frequently looking out the window during class, looking out the window would be ignored and an incompatible (and positive) behavior, looking at the teacher, would be reinforced.

Differential Reinforcement of Other Behaviors—A conditioning approach to decreasing unwanted behaviors by providing positive reinforcement if during the specified time interval, the student has not exhibited the targeted behavior. For example, if the student is frequently looking out the window during class, the student might receive a reinforcer every five minutes as long as she is not looking out the window during the five-minute interval.

Double depression—An expression used to indicate that a person has both dysthymia (chronic "blahs" that impair functioning) and episodes of depression.

DRI—The abbreviation for *Differential Reinforcement of Incompatible behaviors.*

DSM—The abbreviation for *Diagnostic and Statistical Manual of Mental Disorders.*

Dysgraphia—Difficulty expressing thoughts in writing or impairment of the ability to write, experienced as a difficulty in automatically remembering and mastering the sequence of muscle motor movements needed for writing letters or numbers.

Dyskinesia—A general term for involuntary movements.

Dysphoria—A state of feeling unwell or unhappy.

Dyspraxia—Impaired ability to plan and execute skilled movements and gestures despite having the desire and physical ability to perform them. See also *Apraxia.*

Dysthymia—A condition in which the person has been in a sustained state of being somewhat or mildly depressed, but the symptoms are not severe enough to meet the criteria for Major Depressive Disorder. Dysthymia may be a precursor to major depression.

EBD—The abbreviation for *Emotional and Behavioral Disorder.*

Echolalia—Involuntary repetition of others' words or phrases. Echolalia may be a complex tic of Tourette's Syndrome, but it may also be a symptom of other developmental disabilities or schizophrenia.

Echopraxia—Involuntary copying or repetition of others' gestures or movements.

EDF—The abbreviation for *Executive Dysfunction.*

Emotional and Behavioral Disorder (EBD)—A special education classification that indicates that the student has a condition in which behavioral or emotional responses in school are so different from his/her generally accepted, age-appropriate, ethnic, or cultural norms that they adversely affect performance in such areas as self-care, social relationships, personal adjustment, academic progress, classroom behavior, or work adjustment. Each state has its own definition and criteria for use of this classification.

Encoding—The processing of physical sensory input into memory storage.

Episodic memory—Memory for autobiographical events. See also *Declarative Memory.*

Etiology—The study of the cause of a disease or condition.

Euphoria—Feeling of well-being or mild elation.

Euthymia—A normal mood state.

Executive Dysfunction (EDF)—A disorder characterized by impairment in the use of the executive functions.

Executive functions—Control processes that involve planning, sequencing, starting and stopping, shifting flexibly, organizing, and keeping an eye on the future.

Explicit memory—A type of long-term memory characterized by the conscious awareness that present experience is linked to a past experience or event, e.g., the student is aware while retrieving an answer to a test question that the answer was rehearsed in a study session.

Expressive language—The ability to use spoken language, gesture, or sign language to communicate with others.

Extinction—A conditioning approach to decreasing behavior in which a formerly reinforced behavior is never followed by a reinforcer; over time, the behavior should decrease or extinguish completely.

Extrapyramidal effects—Side effects of some medications, usually involving tremor or "Parkinsonian" symptoms.

FBA—The abbreviation for *Functional Behavioral Assessment.*

Fine motor skills—The ability to use small muscles to make precise movements such as handwriting or cutting with scissors.

Flight of ideas—A symptom of mania; used to describe the rapid changing, grandiose plans often formulated by those in a manic episode.

Frontal lobes—The largest and most anterior (forward) lobe of each cerebral hemisphere. The frontal lobes are responsible for the control of skilled motor activity, regulating intellectual activity, problem solving, and mood.

Functional Behavioral Assessment (FBA)—A multi-disciplinary approach to developing a hypothesis about the function of an unwanted behavior and the factors that maintain it. An FBA involves both direct and indirect measures and multiple sources of information, including school personnel, parents, student, peers, and others. The FBA leads to the development of a Behavioral Intervention Plan (BIP).

GAD—The abbreviation for *Generalized Anxiety Disorder.*

Generalized Anxiety Disorder (GAD)—Chronic anxiety that lasts six months or more and that pervades a number of aspects of the student's life (such as home and school functioning). Also known as *Overanxious Disorder of Childhood.*

Grandiosity—A symptom of mania; used to describe the larger-than-life feelings of superiority often experienced by those in a manic episode, e.g., the individual who thinks that he will be able to knock Bill Gates out of the competition, even though he has not yet figured out how to turn on his own computer.

Graphomotor—Graphomotor function (handwriting) involves using the muscles in the fingers and hands to form letters easily and legibly and to maintain a comfortable grip on a writing instrument. Graphomotor function is involved in maneuvering a pencil and writing.

Hallucination—A visual, auditory, or olfactory perception that is not based in reality.

Hyperactive—Excessively active.

Hypersomnia—Excessive sleeping.

Hypomania—A mood episode generally lasting a few days that is characterized by a mild degree of mania. In some cases, hypomanic mood episodes are precursors to manic episodes.

IEP—The abbreviation for *Individualized Education Program.*

Immediate memory—Ability to hold incoming information in short-term memory for a very brief time.

Implicit memory—A type of long-term memory where there is no conscious awareness of past events or experience that is being retrieved or that is influencing the present experience. Bicycle-riding, a type of procedural memory, is an example of an implicit memory.

Impulsivity—Being unable to reflect on one's actions before responding.

Individualized Education Program (IEP)—A written plan required by the Individuals with Disabilities Education Act (IDEA) for all students who require and qualify for special education. It includes a description of the student's current level of performance as well as individualized goals, objectives, and a statement of services and supports designed to remediate and accommodate deficits due to the student's disability. The plan must address all aspects of the student's impairment including social-emotional functioning and activities of daily living as well as academic impairment.

Intelligence Quotient (IQ)—A numerical test score that describes the relationship between a child's mental age and chronological age.

Intermittent Explosive Disorder—A condition characterized by explosive outbursts. Not the same as "Rage Attacks" or "Storms" as used in this book.

Insomnia—Difficulty falling asleep or inability to sleep.

Intermittent reinforcement—A schedule of reinforcement in which the reinforcer is not delivered after response, in contrast to a continuous reinforcement schedule.

Involuntary movements—Movements that are not under one's intentional control.

IQ—The abbreviation for *Intelligence Quotient*.

Language—The ability to effectively communicate by receiving information auditorily, in written form, or by gestures, processing and storing the information, and then expressing oneself orally, by gestures, or in written form.

LD—The abbreviation for *Learning Disability*.

Learning disability (LD)—A disorder in a person with normal or superior intelligence in one or more of the basic psychological processes involved in language, reading and comprehending, written expression, spelling, math calculations, and/or math reasoning.

Long-term Memory—The phase of memory processing involving storage of information over a long period of time (e.g., days or years).

"Lumper"—A person who includes associated features under the umbrella of one diagnosis, e.g., saying tics are "part of" Asperger's Syndrome. Compare to "Splitter."

Major Depressive Disorder, Major Depressive Episode—See *Depression*.

Mania—A type of mood characterized by initial feelings of euphoria and well-being, followed by mental and physical hyperactivity and disorganization of thoughts and behavior. Mania may also present as marked irritability. Compare to *Hypomania*.

Manic Depression—An earlier name for *Bipolar Disorder*.

Memory—Refer to *Declarative Memory, Episodic Memory, Explicit Memory, Implicit Memory, Immediate Memory, Long-term Memory, Metamemory, Procedural Memory, Prospective Memory, Semantic Memory, Short-term Memory, Strategic Memory, and Working Memory*.

Metamemory—Awareness of how to use your memory.

Mixed episode—A type of mood episode in which symptoms of both mania and depression are present.

Mood—A combination of an individual's emotional state and overall sense of physical well-being.

Mood congruent—Feelings which are in keeping with circumstances, e.g., feeling sad when someone close dies. We say that something is mood *in*congruent when feelings are not in keeping with circumstances, e.g., feeling happy or giggly when receiving word of a loved one's death.

Motor tic—A brief, purposeless, involuntary movement. May involve one ("simple") or more ("complex") muscle groups.

Myoclonus—Sudden, fast movements or sudden, fast involuntary activity involving groups of muscles, e.g., the leg jerks that many people experience as they fall asleep.

Negative punishment—A conditioning approach to decreasing unwanted behavior by removing something of value to the student when the unwanted behavior occurs, e.g., taking away computer time for hitting another student.

Negative reinforcer—A stimulus that maintains or strengthens a desired behavior by the removal or avoidance of it when the behavior occurs, e.g., a mother keeps nagging her child until he picks up his laundry from the floor, at which point she stops.

Neurofeedback—A type of biofeedback that attempts to alter electrical activity in the brain by providing external feedback.

Neuroleptic—A class of medications that generally target the dopamine neurotransmitter system. Often referred to as antipsychotics, in small doses, these medications are also often used to treat the tics of Tourette's Syndrome (which is not a psychotic disorder) and to treat behavioral symptoms of some conditions (such as "rage attacks").

Neurotransmitter—Any of the chemicals carrying nerve impulses across the synapse (gap) between adjacent neurons (nerve cells). Some of the neurotransmitters most frequently involved in the disorders in this book include serotonin, dopamine, norepinephrine, and GABA.

NLD—An abbreviation for *Nonverbal Learning Disability*.

Nonverbal Learning Disability (NLD)—A disorder characterized by a significantly lower performance IQ than verbal IQ and an inability to interpret the emotions of others, resulting in significant social impairment. NLD is associated with a pattern of cognitive deficits, e.g., concept formation, problem solving, and math. Previously abbreviated NVLD.

NVLD—An abbreviation for *Nonverbal Learning Disability*, no longer used.

Obsession—An unwanted, repetitive, intrusive thought or impulse that is usually experienced as irrational, although children may lack such insight.

Obsessive-Compulsive—Having both obsessive and compulsive features.

Obsessive-Compulsive Disorder (OCD)—A condition characterized by obsessions and/or compulsions that cause significant distress or impairment in an individual's life.

Obsessive-Compulsive Personality Disorder—A chronic condition that may be present in some, but not most individuals who have Obsessive-Compulsive Disorder. Characterized by an inflexible insistence on their beliefs as to how things should be.

OCD—The abbreviation for *Obsessive-Compulsive Disorder*.

Occupational Therapy/Therapist (OT)—The therapeutic use of work, self-care, and play activities to increase development and prevent disability. It may include adaptation of task or environment to achieve maximum independence and to enhance quality of life. OT is also the specialty in treating sensory defensiveness and visual-motor integration problems.

OCs—Obsessive-compulsive symptoms; sometimes referred to as OCb (obsessive-compulsive behaviors). Often, the term may be used to describe the symptoms of a child who may not (yet) meet full diagnostic criteria for OCD.

ODD—The abbreviation for *Oppositional Defiant Disorder*.

Oppositional Defiant Disorder (ODD)—A condition characterized by negative, oppositional behavior.

OT—The abbreviation for *Occupational Therapy/Therapist*.

Overanxious disorder of Childhood—Refer to *Generalized Anxiety Disorder*.

Palilalia—A complex tic characterized by involuntary repetition of one's own words (e.g., repeating "It's five o'clock.")

PANDAS—The abbreviation for *Pediatric Autoimmune Neuropsychiatric Disorders Associated with Streptococcal infections*.

Panic disorder—A disorder characterized by recurrent and unpredictable feelings of utter terror that strike suddenly and repeatedly. The feeling of terror is generally unrelated to anything going on at that moment.

Paranoia—A psychosis characterized by delusions; the delusions are often of persecution or grandeur. Paranoia is usually not accompanied by hallucinations. The adjective "paranoid" may be used to describe an individual who tends to be very suspicious of others, very sensitive to rejection, hostile, and with an inflated sense of self-importance.

PBS—The abbreviation for *Positive Behavior Support*.

Pediatric Autoimmune Neuropsychiatric Disorders Associated with Streptococcal infections (PANDAS)—"PANDAS" is a condition in which a simple infection such as strep throat is associated with acute onset or rapid and dramatic worsening of tics, obsessions, compulsions, or anxiety.

Pediatric Infection-Triggered Autoimmune Neuropsychiatric Disorders (PITANDS)—A disorder characterized by an abrupt and severe worsening of tics or obsessive-compulsive symptoms following an infection or the acute onset of new symptoms following an infection.

Perinatal—Pertaining to the period shortly before and shortly after birth.

Perseveration—Uncontrollable repetition of a particular response, such as a word, phrase, or movement, despite the absence or cessation of a stimulus.

Phobia—Irrational fear of a specific object or situation, generally leading to avoidance of that object or situation, e.g., spiders.

Phonic tic—A generally brief, repetitive involuntary vocalization that may occur in bursts or bouts. Can be simple sounds such as throat-clearing, coughing, grunting sounds (simple phonic tics) or linguistically meaningful phrases or utterances such as echolalia, coprolalia, palilalia (complex phonic tics). Phonic tics are also referred to as vocal tics.

PITANDS—The abbreviation for *Pediatric Infection-Triggered Autoimmune Neuropsychiatric Disorders*.

Positive Behavior Support (PBS)—A framework for selecting, integrating, and implementing evidenced-based practices to improve academic and behavior outcomes for all students.

Positive punishment—A conditioning approach to decreasing unwanted behavior by applying an aversive consequence when the unwanted behavior occurs, e.g., making a student stay after school to complete assigned classwork.

Positive reinforcer—A stimulus that maintains or strengthens a behavior that precedes it. For example, if giving a young student a sticker each time she raises her hand and waits to be called on increases hand-raising, then the sticker is a positive reinforcer for that behavior.

Post-Traumatic Stress Disorder (PTSD)—An anxiety disorder characterized by intense anxiety or fear, heightened startle reflex, and sustained physiological arousal as a result of a prior exposure to a traumatic event that involves actual or perceived threat of death or serious bodily injury. Students with PTSD may react with helplessness or "fight-or-flight" responses if something triggers feelings associated with the original trauma.

Pragmatics—The ability to use language, including gestures and body language, to communicate in social interactions.

Premonitory urges—Sensations immediately preceding an involuntary movement or vocalization; people may report an awareness of an itch or tingling sensation building up in part of their body that will need to be released.

Pressured speech—Rapid, sometimes incoherent speech; a symptom of mania.

Procedural memory—The ability to automatically perform certain sequences that were originally learned through rehearsal.

Prognosis—The expected course of an illness or condition or any prediction of recovery from a condition or illness.

Prospective memory—Memory for the future, i.e., keeping the future in mind.

Psychomotor Agitation—Restlessness.

Psychomotor retardation—Slowing down of movement or actions. Psychomotor retardation may be a symptom of depression.

Psychotropic—Literally means "mind-changing." Psychotropic medications are medications that have the effect of altering mood and/or behavior.

PTSD—The abbreviation for *Post-Traumatic Stress Disorder*.

Punisher—A stimulus that decreases a behavior that precedes it, e.g., if peer teasing always results in that student being sent to the back of the line, and peer teasing decreases, then being sent to the back of the line is a punisher for that student's teasing.

Punishment—A conditioning approach to decrease undesirable behavior whereby an undesirable behavior is followed by either the application of an unpleasant stimulus or consequence or the removal of something valued.

Racing thoughts—A symptom of mania in which an individual's thoughts seem to be sped-up and may come tumbling out of him. The thoughts may all be logical but sped-up, or they may jump from one topic to another without any apparent connection to the listener.

"Rage attack"—A colloquial term used to describe neurologically triggered "fight or flight" responses that are time-limited and out of proportion to the triggering situation. Some people refer to "rage attacks" as "storms" or "meltdowns." Because all of these are colloquial terms and not formal diagnoses, there is no unified set of diagnostic criteria. As used in this book, the term does not include manipulative, naughty, or acting-out behavior.

Rapid cycling—Refers to how quickly an individual switches between a depressive mood state and a manic or hypomanic state in Bipolar Disorder. Some rapid-cycling students may switch over days, others within the day or even the hour.

Receptive language—The ability to translate verbal or gestural information coming in through the ears and eyes, process it into meaningful information, and store it in memory.

Recurrent—Happening again.

Reinforcer—A stimulus or event that, when made contingent on a response or behavior, maintains or strengthens that behavior. Refer to *Continuous Reinforcement, Negative Reinforcer,* and *Positive Reinforcer.*

Remission—A complete absence of symptoms for a period of months to years.

SAD—The abbreviation for *Separation Anxiety Disorder.*

School phobia—Irrational fear about going to school. May be accompanied by physical symptoms such as headache and stomachache.

School refusal—Student-motivated or student-initiated refusal to attend school or difficulty staying in school for the entire day.

Selective mutism—An anxiety disorder characterized by a persistent failure to speak in social situations despite speaking in other situations.

Self-Injurious behavior—Self-inflicted injuries such as skin cutting, skin/scab/nose picking; damage to eye from poking tics or compulsions, etc.

Semantic memory—Memory for vocabulary and facts. Compare to *Declarative Memory.*

Sensory defensiveness—A constellation of symptoms that are the result of feeling alarmed, defensive, or negative about a harmless sensory experience; an overreaction to normal protective senses sometimes appearing as behavior that is irrational. Sometimes referred to as sensory dysregulation. Refer to *Sensory Processing Disorder.*

Sensory diet—The daily total of sensorimotor experiences needed to adaptively interact with the environment. A sensory diet includes alerting, organizing, and calming techniques.

Sensory dysregulation—Refer to *Sensory defensiveness* and *Sensory Processing Disorder.*

Sensory Processing Disorder (SPD)—A neurological disorder associated with impaired processing of information from the senses (vision, hearing, touch, smell, and taste), the sense of movement (vestibular system), and/or the positional sense (proprioception).

Separation Anxiety Disorder (SAD)—An anxiety disorder characterized by significant difficulty separating from major attachment figures such as parents.

Short-term memory—The phase of memory involving temporary storage of information.

Side effect—Any condition caused by a medication other than the effect for which it was prescribed; secondary (usually unwanted) effects of using a medication. Also known as "adverse effect."

Simple tic—An involuntary movement or sound that usually occurs in bursts and that involves only one muscle group or sound.

Sleep hygiene—The practice of establishing good sleep habits.

Slow processing speed—The rate at which a person can take in, act on, and produce information.

Social Anxiety Disorder—A childhood or early adolescence-onset anxiety disorder characterized by a persistent fear of being embarrassed in social situations such as during a performance, when speaking in front of a group, or in any setting in which the student might be observed or judged. Also known as Social Phobia.

SPD—The abbreviation for *Sensory Processing Disorder*.

Spectrum disorder—In a spectrum disorder, the symptoms and additional features can present themselves in a wide variety of combinations. For example, Tourette's Syndrome is said to be a spectrum disorder because some children have "just tics," but the tics range from mild and infrequent to severe and frequent in different children, and some children also have features of other conditions such as Obsessive-Compulsive Disorder, Attention Deficit Hyperactivity Disorder, or a mood disorder.

"Splitter"—A person who uses separate diagnoses for associated disorders, e.g., diagnosing a person with both Asperger's Syndrome and OCD as having two diagnoses instead of just saying "Asperger's Syndrome" and including the OCD in the Asperger's diagnosis. Compare to "Lumper."

Stereotyped—Always occurring in the same ritualized or mannered way.

"Storm"—Refer to "Rage Attack."

Strategic memory—Remembering and using strategies.

Suicidal ideation—Thinking about suicide, suicidal thoughts (but not at the level of making suicide plans).

Symptom—A perceptible change in the body or its functions that indicates disease or dysfunction. Some people use this term only to refer to subjective reports or experiences, and use the term "signs" to refer to objective changes that the observer measures or notes. Other people use the term "symptom" to refer to any kind of perceptible change, regardless of whether it's subjective or objective.

Syndrome—A set or collection of signs and symptoms that usually occur together and that characterize a particular condition or abnormal state.

TBI—The abbreviation for *Traumatic Brain Injury*.

Tic—An involuntary movement (motor tic) or involuntary vocalization (vocal tic), sometimes confused with "nervous habits" or allergy symptoms.

Tourette's Syndrome (TS)—A condition characterized by multiple motor tics and at least one vocal tic, where tics have persisted on and off for more than one year. The name of this syndrome or disorder keeps changing. Currently referred to as Tourette's Disorder in the DSM-IV-TR.

Transient Tic Disorder—A relatively short-lived condition in which the child has one or even a few involuntary movements or sounds that last more than four weeks but less than a year.

Traumatic Brain Injury (TBI)—Physical damage to the brain or to brain function due to a head injury, such as from an automobile accident, a fall, or from physical abuse.

Tremor—Rapid, rhythmic, vacillating movements of limbs.

Trichotillomania—A condition in which one repeatedly or compulsively pulls out his own hair.

TS—The abbreviation for *Tourette's Syndrome*.

TS+—Pronounced "TS Plus," this is a nonofficial shorthand expression introduced by Leslie E. Packer, Ph.D. to denote someone who has Tourette's Syndrome plus features of other disorders such as ADHD, OCD, etc. The other disorders may be present in full-blown form or just as features that do not meet full diagnostic criteria.

Visual closure—Ability to detect the ending of one word or visual form while looking at the next word or form.

Visual discrimination—The ability to distinguish the edges of a visual stimulus.

Visual figure-ground—The ability to find the primary object in the visual field (foreground vs. background).

Visual form constancy—The ability to maintain the shape of a stimulus in visual memory without loss or distortion until it can be encoded for long-term memory or copied onto something (e.g., paper).

Visual-Motor Integration (VMI)—The ability to integrate the visual image of letters and shapes with the appropriate motor response, e.g., to be able to draw/reproduce a shape you have seen.

Visual perception—The ability to interpret visual light information reaching the eyes.

Visual sequential memory—Memory for a series of stimuli (letters, numbers, items) that are presented visually.

Visual single-item memory—Memory for one visual stimulus.

Visual-spatial relations—The ability to accurately position objects in space, e.g., to write the letter "p" on a line so that it looks like a lowercase "p" and not an uppercase "P" or a lowercase "b," "d," or "q."

VMI—The abbreviation for *Visual-Motor Integration*.

Vocal tic—Refer to *Phonic tic*.

Waxing and waning—A naturally-occurring increase (waxing) and decrease (waning) in severity and frequency of symptoms. Usually associated with the tics of Tourette's Syndrome, but symptoms of other conditions may also wax and wane, e.g., OCD, anxiety disorders, and mood disorders.

Word retrieval—The ability to get a specific word out of memory when it is needed.

Working memory—A form of short-term memory that enables us to hold information in mind while we bring forward older information to apply to it, similar to using a temporary workspace to manipulate information prior to long-term storage.

Resources

The resources in this section are organized by topic and follow the sequence of disorders as presented in the book. For some disorders, there are no national organizations specifically devoted to the condition. Because new books and resources frequently appear, we have elected not to include a listing of books here that may be out of date by the time of publication of this book. Instead, updated lists of books, videos, websites, and other resources for peer education and awareness are available on the authors' website at www.challengingkids.com.

Educators or parents who want convenient checklists of accommodations that can be used as part of any planning for a student are encouraged to obtain *Find a Way or Make a Way* (Parkaire Press, 2009, available for purchase at www.parkairepress.com).

Tourette's Syndrome

Tourette Syndrome Association, Inc.
42-40 Bell Blvd., Suite 205
Bayside, NY 11361-2861
Telephone: (718) 224-2999
Website: http://tsa-usa.org

Tourette Syndrome Foundation of Canada
5945 Airport Rd., Suite 195
Mississauga, ON L4V 1R9
Canada
Telephone: (905) 673-2255; (800) 361-3120
Website: www.tourette.ca

Obsessive-Compulsive Disorder

Obsessive-Compulsive Foundation, Inc.
676 State Street
New Haven, CT 06511
Telephone: (203) 401-2070;
Info Line: (203) 874-3843
Website: www.ocfoundation.org

OCD Centre Manitoba, Inc.
100 - 4 Fort Street
Winnipeg, MB R3C 1C4
Canada
Telephone: (204) 942-3331
Website: www.ocdmanitoba.ca

OCD-UK
PO Box 8955
Nottingham
NG10 9AU
United Kingdom
Email: admin@ocduk.org
Website: www.ocduk.org

Anxiety Disorders

Anxiety Disorders Association of America
8730 Georgia Ave., Suite 600
Silver Spring, MD 20910
Telephone: (240) 485 -1001
Website: www.adaa.org

Ottawa Anxiety & Trauma Clinic
Billings Bridge Plaza
Suite 202 - 2277 Riverside Drive
Ottawa, Ontario K1H 7X6
Canada
Telephone: (613) 737-1194
Website: www.anxietyandtraumaclinic.com

Attention Deficit Hyperactivity Disorder

**Children and Adults with Attention-Deficit/
Hyperactivity Disorder, Inc. (CHADD)**
8181 Professional Place - Suite 150
Landover, MD 20785
Telephone: (301) 306-7070
Website: www.chadd.org

**National Attention Deficit Disorder Association
(ADDA)**
15000 Commerce Parkway, Suite C
Mount Laurel, NJ 08054
Telephone: (856) 439-9099
Website: www.add.org

Mood Disorders

Child & Adolescent Bipolar Foundation (CABF)
820 Davis St., Suite 520
Evanston, IL 60201
Telephone: (847) 492-8519
Website: www.bpkids.org

Depression and Bipolar Support Alliance (DBSA)
730 N. Franklin Street, Suite 501
Chicago, IL 60610-7224
Telephone: (800) 826 -3632
Website: www.dbsalliance.org

National Mental Health Association (NMHA)
1021 Prince Street
Alexandria, VA 22314
Telephone: (703) 684-7722
Website: www.nmha.org

Sensory Dysregulation

Sensory Processing Disorder Foundation
5655 S. Yosemite St., Suite 305
Greenwood Village, CO 80111
Telephone: (303) 794-1182
Website: www.spdfoundation.net

Asperger's Syndrome

OASIS @ MAAP
Telephone: (219) 662-1311
Website: www.asperger.org

**Online Asperger Syndrome Information &
Support (OASIS)**
Website: http://www.aspergersyndrome.org

Nonverbal Learning Disability

Nonverbal Learning Disorders Association (NLDA)
507 Hopmeadow Street
Simsbury, CT 06070
Telephone: (860) 658-5522
Website: http://nlda.org

Sleep Disorders and Sleep Hygiene

National Sleep Foundation
1522 K Street, NW, Suite 500
Washington, DC 20005
Telephone: (202) 347-3471
Website: www.sleepfoundation.org

Academic Resources
(Including Learning Disabilities Specific to Disorders in this Book)
Organizations:

Learning Disabilities Association of America
4156 Library Road
Pittsburgh, PA 15234-1349
Telephone: (412) 341-1515
Website: www.ldanatl.org

Learning Disabilities Association of Canada
250 City Centre Avenue, Suite 616
Ottawa, Ontario K1R 6K7
Canada
Telephone: (613) 238-5721; (877) 238-5322
Website: www.ldac-taac.ca

The International Dyslexia Association
40 York Rd., 4th Floor
Baltimore, MD 21204
Telephone: (410) 296-0232
Website: www.interdys.org

Reading/Books on Tape or CD

The National Library Service for the Blind and Physically Handicapped
Library of Congress
Washington, D.C. 20542
Telephone: (202) 707-5100
Website: www.loc.gov/nls

RFB&D: Recording for the Blind and Dyslexic
20 Roszel Road
Princeton, NJ 08540
Telephone: (866) 732-3585; (800) 221-4792
Website: www.rfbd.org

Appendices

Transition Checklist:
The Necessary Steps to Independence

When developing an IEP for a student, the team needs to consider whether the student is prepared for independent living. Use this form to discuss the student's skill levels and help the team incorporate necessary goals and interventions.

Using the Transition Checklist

The transition checklist—the necessary steps to independence—is a guide to assist schools, parents, and students to understand what steps are necessary to successfully leave home. The checklist can help identify skills to be included in a transition plan for students with neurological disorders. Students with Executive Dysfunction are particularly likely to need planning and instruction in some or many of these skills.

The first column in the checklist lists the transition strategy skills and the next four columns are the degree to which these have been accomplished. "Ready to Start" is used when the student has not started the process on the particular skill. "Beginning Skill" means that the student has started developing the skill but has not gotten very far. "Developing Skill" is used when the student is progressing, and "Mastered Skill" means that the student can execute the skill at the level of an independent adult.

The checklist begins by assessing the student's **awareness of his disorder(s)** and the impact they have on his functioning. For some students, you may need more than four rows. In this row, "Mastered Skill" would be checked if the student is able to politely self-advocate to get the necessary accommodations when appropriate.

Medication management involves taking medicine responsibly, knowing how to get more in a timely manner, and being able to and knowing when to contact the doctor.

Students do not always realize that the difficulties in school often relate to difficulties that will affect them in the adult world, e.g., writing a report in business or the tax forms that are due once a year (a long-term project). Having appropriate strategies to overcome these **academic deficits** is important.

Many people are surprised to find out that even gifted students with neurological impairments cannot handle some of the **requirements of daily living**. In the same way that some people need specialized reading strategies to learn to read, many of our students need specialized strategies to become independent in their daily living skills.

One of the daily skills that we decided to include as a separate item is the ability to **travel independently**, e.g., in the community, on business trips. Many of our students do not want to get a driver's license or need to wait until they are older before getting one due to the impact of their neurology on being able to drive safely. Because of this, many students have limited ability to get around independently. They need instruction in public transportation and they need to have a job close to home or near a transportation line. Once they understand that, then many need to learn how to best use the transportation options available in their community. If they need to travel outside of their community, then they may need additional direct instruction, e.g., how long before their flight to arrive at the airport.

As an adult, it is very important to learn to manage use of one's **electronics**. This includes learning to turn off your electronics at inappropriate times, being pleasant when approached while using electronics, and not limiting your social life to only online friends.

Being able to **wake up independently** is also crucial. So many times, students go to post-secondary placements and find that they are unable to wake up independently. All along, they have relied on their parents for this. This inability to wake up independently is one of the leading causes of failure at post-secondary schools and jobs.

Most of the students who have **organizational skill deficits** know it, but awareness of these deficits without specialized strategies is useless. Once the strategies are taught, the next hurdle is to make use of these organizational skills an ironclad rule and eventually a habit.

Many students do not hold onto the present needs beyond "now" and do not see the future. This leads them to not understand the need to manage money until it is too late. Direct instruction of **money management skills** with practice, review, and revision is crucial.

For students with working memory deficits and Executive Dysfunction, there is an inability to hold onto past learning and **remember future plans** while operating in the present. The "now" is all there is. Teaching such students how to **manage time** is a crucial life skill. Poor time management is another area that predicts job loss.

There are two sets of social skills that adults need: those they use to **interact with adult figures,** and those they use to **interact with peers**. Both are important for adult success and happiness. Remember that social skills affect an adult having a family, having friends, and getting and maintaining a job.

Not knowing how to **problem solve** can make life quite difficult. Once students are taught strategies, the strategies must be mastered and put into everyday use.

Some people ask for help too much, but more often than not, students with neurological disorders may ask too little. These students need to be taught when and how to **ask for help** and then make sure they ask for help when it is needed.

Many students grow up and get into trouble because they never learned to have a **respectful attitude toward important adults and others** in their life. They do not get that there are times they should act as if they have respect for someone even if they do not. Many do not even understand why they should have a respectful attitude in the first place. Explaining the impact of disrespectful behavior on themselves and others may be the necessary first step. This needs to be followed by direct instruction in how to act respectfully, modeling respectful behavior, reinforcing respectful behavior, and expecting respectful behavior.

Even when a student grows up and is respectful, having a **positive attitude toward adults and others** has a tremendous impact that the student may not understand. We tend to be friends with, hire, and promote pleasant people. Many neurological disorders influence students to be in a bad mood. Mood and anxiety disorders have a particularly unpleasant impact on a person feeling posi-

tive. The medical information that is taught to these students may allow the student to understand why they are not acting in a positive manner. They then need to be taught and cued to become more positive in their attitude.

Parents and teachers usually understand that students need love and limits. The area that is overlooked more now than in the past is the need for students to learn to **work hard at boring tasks**. The majority of our day as an adult is spent on incredibly unexciting tasks. To be successful, this area is crucial. This is another big impact area on job loss, e.g., not doing the "boring" parts of the job such as paperwork.

There is nothing that grates on human relationships like people who refuse to **take responsibility for their actions, attitudes, and decisions**. This is another big factor when it comes to getting and keeping a job. Parents, unfortunately, tend to put up with this over a long period of time. Husbands and wives may put up with this for a limited time period, but bosses will not! Our students have been wrong so often that they have decided that they cannot be wrong anymore or they truly do not understand that they are wrong. Often, they honestly do not remember that they did what they are being accused of and wind up feeling hurt and defensive because no one believes them.

Transition Checklist

TRANSITION STRATEGIES		Ready to Start	Beginning Skill	Developing Skill	Mastered Skill
Has an awareness of disorders (list each)					
Manages medicine(s)					
Uses appropriate strategies to overcome academic deficits					
Uses sufficient strategies to take care of daily living skills					
Is able to travel independently					
Manages use of electronics					
Wakes up independently					
Uses organizational skills					
Uses money management skills					
Pays attention to the future					
Uses time management skills					
Uses social skills with adults					
Uses social skills with peers					
Uses problem-solving strategies					
Asks for help when needed					
Has a respectful attitude towards adults*					
Has a respectful attitude towards others*					
Has a positive attitude towards adults*					
Has a positive attitude towards others*					
Works hard at boring tasks					
Takes responsibility for actions, attitudes, and decisions					

© 2002, D. G. Pruitt & S. K. Pruitt, revised 2007.

* If the student has deficits in these areas, goals and objectives should be developed that incorporate specifically defined and observable behaviors.

BOLO Guide

If you know or suspect a student has one of the disorders indicated by the columns in the guide below, read down to find out what else you should screen for or inquire about. For each disorder, there are usually a number of other disorders that are likely to "go-together" with it.

Disclaimer: The guide is just that—merely a guide. It does not include every possible disorder a student could have, and it does not include disorders that may occur together in the student by chance.

If a student does have a second disorder or features of a second disorder (which is usually the case), then go to the column for that disorder to see what else you should now screen for.

If a student seems to have features of a number of disorders, we recommend referring the student to a board-certified child psychiatrist for a comprehensive evaluation and diagnosis.

KEY to BOLO Guide

ADHD = Attention Deficit Hyperactivity Disorder	**MOOD** = Mood Disorders
AS = Asperger's Syndrome	**NLD** = Nonverbal Learning Disability
ANX = Anxiety Disorders	**OCD/S** = Obsessive-Compulsive Disorder or symptoms
BP = Bipolar Disorder	**PROC** = Processing Speed
DCD = Developmental Coordination Disorder	**RAGE** = Rage Attacks or "Storms"
DEP = Depression	**SENS** = Sensory dysregulation
EDF = Executive Dysfunction	**SLEEP** = Sleep Problems
HAND = Handwriting	**SOC** = Social, Peer Problems, and Pragmatics
HW = Homework	**TS** = Tics or Tourette's Syndrome
LANG = Language	**VMI** = Visual-Motor Integration
LD = Learning Disabilities	**WM** = Working Memory deficits
MEM = Memory deficits	

	If you know or suspect:										
Then Screen For:	ADHD	ANX	AS	BP	DEP	EDF	NLD	OCD	SENS	TS	WM
ADHD		●	●	●	●	●		●	●	●	●
AS	●					●	●		●		●
ANX	●	●	●	●	●	●	●	●	●	●	●
DCD	●								●		

EDF	HAND/VMI	HW	LANG	LD	MEM	MOOD	NLD	OCD/S	PROC	RAGE	SENS	SLEEP	SOC	TS	Other
●	●	●	●	●	●			●	●			●	●		
●	●	●		●		●		●			●	●	●		Speech Dysfluencies
●	●	●	●	●	●	●				●		●	●		
●	●	●		●	●	●			●	●	●	●	●	●	Eating Disorders; Skin Picking; Trichotillomania; Body Dysmorphic Disorder; Substance Abuse; Autism Spectrum Disorder
●	●	●	●	●	●	●		●		●	●	●	●		
	●	●	●	●	●	●	●	●		●	●		●		Brain Injury
●		●			●	●		●	●	●	●	●	●		Suicidal Thoughts; Substance Abuse
●	●	●		●	●			●		●	●	●	●		Suicidal Thoughts; Substance Abuse
●	●		●		●	●	●	●		●	●	●	●	●	
	●	●	●	●	●	●		●	●		●	●	●		Eating Disorders; School Refusal; Somatoform Disorders; Substance Abuse
●	●	●	●	●	●	●		●	●	●	●	●	●	●	Substance Abuse; Conduct Disorder; Enuresis; Autism Spectrum Disorder

* Diagnosis of DCD is not supposed to be made when a diagnosis of Asperger's has already been made, but we believe that school personnel need to screen for it because of its impact on school functioning.

Classroom Layout Checklist*

Use this reproducible checklist to help you start designing your classroom, materials, and presentations. Then consult chapters on your students' specific disorders to see what other elements you will need to add. Remember: The more you set up in advance that works for the majority of students, the fewer individual accommodations you will have to make. So, go through each chapter in this book to see what you can add classroom-wide to improve academic, behavioral, and social-emotional functioning. Of particular note: You will find many additional helpful tips on routines that will benefit all students in the chapters on Executive Dysfunction and Written Expression.

Classroom Layout and Furnishings
Post the daily schedule in a spot clearly visible to all students. Review it at the beginning of each day.   ■ Include all parts of the daily routine rather than just topics or assignments.   ■ Color-highlight and call attention to important reminders or changes in routine.   ■ Post color-highlighted reminders of intermediate deadlines.   ■ Check off each item on the schedule as it is completed.
Set up different spots in the room where students can go to work if they need to avoid too much visual or auditory stimulation, e.g., set up a study carrel or "office."
Create areas in the room that are shielded and cozy, e.g., a piece of carpeting with bookcases around it and a comfortable beanbag chair for students who need downtime or a place to calm themselves.
Try to have extra desks in the classroom so that students who need to get up and move around can simply take their work to another desk when needed.
Have larger tables or extra desks available to students with memory problems who need to spread out their papers to keep information in front of them.
Have a rocking chair in the classroom for students who need to move while they read and for students who need to rock to calm themselves.
Place cut tennis balls on the feet of the chairs to muffle noise for students who are likely to keep moving their chairs.
Allow sufficient pathways and clear areas in the room so that students can get from their desk to the teacher's desk without coming into close contact with other students.
Set up a computer or word-processing center and a music or multimedia center to facilitate transitions and organization.
Create a desk/table configuration that is easily modified for different types of activities: ■ Use traditional rows of desks for direct instruction of new skills.   ■ Seat students with visual-motor integration problems directly facing the board if they are copying from it.
Have a stash of nonrolling, nonnoisy "fidgets" for students to hold.
Make the classroom visually and intellectually stimulating. If their attention wanders, let it wander to something relevant and interesting. Change displays frequently.

---

* This is an abbreviated version of Packer, LE: *Checklist for Teachers: Creating a Student-Friendly Environment,* which was published electronically at www.tourettesyndrome.net.

Environmental Supports for Organizational Skills

	Use color-coded bins for notebooks, texts, homework submissions, and student work of the same content.
	Designate places for all materials to be kept and use them consistently.
	Provide individual mailboxes that students check before packing up each day.
	Provide each student with a copy of their own schedule on their desk.
	Use task cards, to do lists, and checklists on desks. Teach students to check off each element of an activity as it is completed.
	Provide planners that allow sufficient space for large, sloppy handwriting.
	Provide planners or organizers that foster the student looking ahead.
	Provide alternate (back-up) methods for students to find out the nightly homework assignments if they fail to record them or lose their agenda in a "black hole" on the bus, e.g., homework buddies, websites.
	Provide students with alternate (back-up) methods for returning their homework to school, such as allowing them to email their assignments as attachments or fax them.
	Have students bring in an extra supply of pens, pencils, tissues, or whatever they tend to lose or use up most frequently. Schedule a date on which they all check their "stash" and write notes to replenish. Follow up to see that they have.

Modify Materials, Presentations, and Projects

	Use materials that allow sufficient space for large, sloppy handwriting.
	Color-highlight important directions.
	For multi-step projects, introduce one step at a time, and check for comprehension.
	For multi-step oral directions, give one direction, use a few filler words or pause for a few seconds before giving the next step, etc.
	Provide study guides, outlines, and copies of any overheads.
	Provide a visual organizer (concept map or "mindmap") and a template to help students organize their materials and thoughts for writing tasks. (See Chapters 9 and 19.)
	Use as many modalities as possible in presentations.
	Provide editing strips on the student's desk for sequential tasks (such as math editing strips or proof-editing strips) as illustrated in Chapters 19 and 20 of this book.
	Allocate sufficient time to review and rehearse earlier skills and concepts before introducing new ones.
	Periodically check to ensure students have mastered previously taught skills.
	Explicitly identify goals and subgoals.
	Break presentations into smaller units, e.g., treat a thirty-minute unit as two fifteen-minute units to allow opportunities for movement and student questions.
	Build in numerous intermediate deadlines for large projects. Ensure they are entered into homework planners and reviewed as part of the daily schedule.
	Frequently monitor the students' work pace and work product.
	Hold a prop when presenting new material to foster attention and orientation towards the instructional area.

APPENDIX D

The Animals Inside Me*

I have a spider inside me.
It makes my lips smack.
I have a spider inside me
and it makes me feel black.
     His name is Tourette's.

I have a kangaroo inside me.
It makes me jump up and down.
I have a kangaroo inside me
and it makes me feel brown.
     His name is Tourette's.

I have a frog inside me.
It makes me warty and mean.
I have a frog inside me
and it turns me green.
     His name is Tourette's.

I have an eel inside me
and it makes me slither.
I have an eel inside me
and it makes me shiver.
     His name is Tourette's.

I have a wild horse inside me.
It makes me feel like prancing.
I have a wild horse inside me
and it's always dancing.
     His name is Tourette's.

I have a tiger inside me
and it makes me growl.
I have a tiger inside me
and when I get mad, I go "r-o-w-l!"
     His name is Tourette's.

I'm going to shoot those animals.
I'm going to bring a banana.
I'm going to shoot those animals.
I'm going to wear a bandanna.

And then the puppy inside me
will make me happy and play.
And then the puppy inside me
won't ever run away.
     His name is Justin.

Tic Reporting Inventory

Name of Student: _____ **Date:**_____

Name of Person Completing Form:_____

If the student is on medication(s), indicate the name and dosage of the medication(s):_____

_____

Directions: Please complete this form based on the **frequency** of the tics you have observed in the home/school (circle one) over the last **2 weeks**. Use the last column (Severity) to indicate how severe in intensity the tics appear to you: Use **1**=mild, **2**=moderate, **3**=severe.

Part 1: Motor Tics

	NOT AT ALL	JUST A LITTLE	SOMEWHAT OFTEN	VERY OFTEN	SEVERITY
Motor Tics of the Head, Neck, and Face Region:					
Eye blinking					
Eye rolling or squinting					
Head jerking					
Sticking out tongue					
Snapping head back or to the side					
Brushing or tossing hair out of eyes					
Smelling self or objects					
Smelling self or objects — Describe:					
Grimacing					
Smiling					
Motor Tics of the Shoulder and Trunk Region:					
Shoulder shrug					
Bending over					
Tensing abdominal muscles					
Tensing other muscle groups					
Tensing other muscle groups — Describe:					

	NOT AT ALL	JUST A LITTLE	SOMEWHAT OFTEN	VERY OFTEN	SEVERITY
Motor Tics of the Arms and Legs (Simple and Complex):					
Finger or hand movements					
Describe:					
Arm movements					
Describe:					
Tapping foot					
Kicking					
Jumping or hopping					
Twirling around					
Skipping					
Throwing movements					
Jabbing or poking					
Hitting or punching					
Touching: Objects					
Self					
Other people					
Picking at clothes					
Self-injurious behaviors					
Describe:					
Other Complex Tics:					
Copropraxia: Obscene gestures					
Sexual touching-self					
Sexual touching-others					
Other					
Describe:					
Imitates (echoes): Other's actions					
Own actions					
Other Motor Tics					
Describe:					

Are there any other repetitive and rhythmical movements that the child makes that were not listed above? If so, please describe below. You may use the back of the page if necessary._____

_____

_____

Do the motor tics seem to be embarrassing to the child? Do you think that the tics are interfering with schoolwork? With social relationships? Please explain below or on the back of this page._____

_____

_____

Part 2: Phonic or Vocal Tics

	NOT AT ALL	JUST A LITTLE	SOMEWHAT OFTEN	VERY OFTEN	SEVERITY
Simple Phonic Tics:					
Throat clearing sounds					
Grunting					
Coughing					
Sniffing					
Barking					
Snorting					
Humming					
Squeaking					
Spitting					
Yelling or screaming sounds					
Complex Phonic Tics:					
Animal-like sounds					
Unusual changes in pitch or volume of voice					
Stuttering					
Imitates: Others' sounds or words					
Own sounds or words					
Coprolalia (involuntary): Obscenities					
Racial or ethnic slurs					
Other socially taboo utterances					
Other involuntary utterances	Describe:				

Are there any other repetitive and unusual vocalizations that your child makes that were not listed in the chart above? If so, please describe them in the space below or on the back of this page._____

_____

_____

Do the vocal tics seem to be embarrassing to the child? Do you think that the tics are interfering with school-work? With social relationships? Please explain below or on the back of this page._____

_____

_____

Sleep Survey

Name of Student: _____ **Date:**_____

Instructions: This form is to be completed by the parent or guardian. Please return this to me by:_____

ITEM	RESPONSE
How many hours of sleep does your child usually get each night of the school week?	
What time does your child usually go to bed on school nights?	
What time does your child usually fall asleep on school nights?	
What time does your child usually wake up for school?	
Once your child falls asleep for the night, does he sleep through the night or is sleep interrupted?	
Does your child wake up easily in the morning?	
Do you struggle to get your child up on school mornings?	
Does your child stay up late at night to do homework?	
Does your child sleep in the afternoon after school? If yes, how long does he sleep?	
Does your child maintain the same sleep pattern on weekends or when school is closed for vacation? If no, how is his sleep cycle different?	
Does your child set an alarm clock and wake himself up in the morning?	

Use the back of this page, if needed, to let me know about any of your child's sleep problems that may affect his alertness or mood in school.

Relaxation Techniques

There are many relaxation techniques that work. Some students may find a warm bath, listening to their favorite music, reading a book, or having their parent tell them a bed time story relaxing. But if students are dependent on others to help them relax, or can only relax at home, they may need a technique to use in school when they need to relax themselves. Here are a few simple relaxation techniques that are easy to teach students. How much benefit the students derive from them depends on how often they practice the techniques. The breathing-based technique takes the longest in the sense that it needs to be practiced daily for about fifteen minutes, and even then, it may be a week or more before the student starts to report really feeling relaxed during the exercise. The "Fade to Black" and tense/release techniques tend to produce relaxation more quickly. If students are taught how to relax in school, remember to share the instructions with their parents so that parents can encourage their kids to use the same techniques at home.

Breathing Relaxation Technique Instructions:*

- Get into a comfortable position. Lying down or semi-reclined is best, but this can be done sitting up, too.
- Place one hand over your belly—a few inches below the belly button. Your hand will be giving you feedback as to how you're doing on the breathing.
- Close your eyes and slowly breathe in through your nose. You do not have to take a particularly deep breath; what you are trying to do is take a *slow* breath. As you breathe in, you should feel your belly move out/up against your hand. As you breathe in, your chest should stay relaxed and your belly should move out against your hand (if you're sitting up) or up against your hand (if you're lying down). Your chest should not go up towards your shoulders.
- Once you have inhaled deeply and slowly, hold the breath for a few seconds and then breathe out even more slowly than you in-

haled—but breathe out through pursed lips to keep yourself breathing out slowly.
- As you breathe out, feel your belly come back down and feel your shoulders and neck relax and sag.
- Wait a few seconds and then do another breathing cycle.
- Practice for about fifteen to twenty minutes once a day. If you have time to practice more often, great, but it will still work with a once-a-day schedule. Students can be encouraged to practice this at home at night time, when they are in bed and want to fall asleep.
- If you find yourself getting distracted during the exercise—that thoughts are intruding—you can help focus yourself by thinking "one" as you breathe in and "two" as you breathe out.

Fade to Black Technique Instructions:**

- If your students are having difficulty making transitions because they are "stuck" on activities due to perseveration, compulsiveness, or anxiety, you can try adding in a "fade to black" component.
- Have the students close their eyes and tell them to imagine themselves sitting in a movie theater. Tell them to picture the lights in the theater dimming and then tell them to keep focusing on the screen. Then have them imagine the screen slowly fading to black.
- If you use "fade to black," you might incorporate it in the transition sequence by saying, "It's transition time. Everyone close your eyes and fade to black." You then wait a minute, and say, "OK, now put away _____ and take out _____ to get ready for _____."

Quick Relaxation Technique Instructions:

- Take three deep breaths, breathing out very slowly each time. Tense your fingers or toes (or both!) for five seconds, then relax.

---

* (Packer 1998)

** This strategy is adapted from N. Rathvon: *Effective School Interventions*, Guilford Press, 1999.

Organizational Skills Survey— Parent Reporting Form

Name of Student: _____ **Date:** _____

Instructions: Please answer each of the questions below in terms of your child's organizational skills and return the form to me.

ITEM	NEVER	RARELY	SOMETIMES	OFTEN	ALWAYS
My child keeps his bedroom well-organized and neat.					
My child misplaces or loses personal possessions, including favorite belongings.					
My child is always late for everything, even with reminders.					
My child knows what he's supposed to do each day.					
My child has a good sense of what is important and what isn't.					
My child meets responsibilities in the home without reminders.					
My child makes social plans with peers in advance.					
My child starts nonschool activities or projects but does not finish them.					
My child has trouble getting started on activities without assistance (do not include homework in this category).					
My child is more of a follower than a leader.					
My child can follow three-step directions without forgetting one of them (e.g., "Turn off the lights in your room, come downstairs, and give the dog some water.")					
My child remembers to give me notices from school.					

Mnemonics for Academic Skills or Content

Mnemonic	Use For:
Dirty **M**arvin **S**mells **B**ad* **D**oes **M**cDonald's™ **S**erve **B**urgers? **D**oes **M**cDonald's™ **S**erve **C**heese **B**urgers?	*Sequence of steps in long division:* **D**ivide, **M**ultiply, **S**ubtract, **B**ring down **D**ivide, **M**ultiply, **S**ubtract, **B**ring down **D**ivide, **M**ultiply, **S**ubtract, (**C**ompare), **B**ring down
"SOHCAHTOA" or **O**ne **A**ngry **T**eenager **O**n **H**allucinogenics **S**wore **A**t **H**is **C**lassmates	**S**ine = **O**pposite/**H**ypotenuse **C**osine = **A**djacent/**H**ypotenuse **T**angent = **O**pposite/**A**djacent **O**pposite/**A**djacent = **T**angent **O**pposite/**H**ypotenuse = **S**ine **A**djacent/**H**ypotenuse = **C**osine
Pardon **M**e, **D**ear **A**unt **S**ally **P**lease **E**xcuse **M**y **D**ear **A**unt **S**ally	*Order of operations in math:* **P**arentheses, **M**ultiply, **D**ivide, **A**dd, **S**ubtract **P**arentheses, **E**xponents, **M**ultiply, **D**ivide, **A**dd, **S**ubtract
Every **G**ood **B**oy **D**eserves **F**udge or **E**mpty **G**arbage **B**efore **D**ad **F**reaks **FACE**	*The musical notes represented by the lines on the treble clef:* **E, G, B, D, F** *The musical notes represented by the spaces on the treble clef:* **F, A, C, E**
"ROY G. BIV"	*Colors of the spectrum or rainbow:* **R**ed, **O**range, **Y**ellow, **G**reen, **B**lue, **I**ndigo, and **V**iolet
"FOIL"	*Binomial multiplication:* **F**irst, **O**uter, **I**nner, **L**ast (a + b)(c + d) = ac + ad + bc + bd
King **P**hillip **C**ame **O**ver **F**or **G**ood **S**paghetti	*Order of taxonomy in biology:* **K**ingdom, **P**hylum, **C**lass, **O**rder, **F**amily, **G**enus, **S**pecies
How I wish I could calculate pi	To remember the value of pi to seven places, the number of letters in each word gives the digit's value
My **Ve**ry **E**ducated **M**other **J**ust **S**erved **U**s **N**achos	*Order of the planets from the sun:* **M**ercury, **V**enus, **E**arth, **M**ars, **J**upiter, **S**aturn, **U**ranus, **N**eptune

* This mnemonic © 1982, Parkaire Consultants. Other mnemonics on this page have been compiled by, but not necessarily created by, the authors.

Sleep Hygiene:
DO's and DON'Ts for Establishing Good Sleep Routines

DO:

- get up every day at the same time (one hour later maximum on weekends).
- go to bed at the same time every day, if possible, especially Sunday through Thursday.
- keep the bedroom at the right temperature and humidity (not overly warm*),
- avoid napping, especially after three o'clock in the afternoon. If you must, nap for less than thirty minutes before three o'clock in the afternoon.
- exercise regularly, preferably in the morning or afternoon.
- have a relaxing activity ninety minutes before sleep, such as soaking in a hot bath.
- try to get as much early morning sunlight each day as you can by leaving the blinds open. Try to get at least fifteen minutes of natural daylight between seven o'clock and nine o'clock in the morning.
- get out of bed if you can't sleep and engage in a relaxing activity—but not electronics.
- teach yourself breathing relaxation techniques (Appendix G) or other calming techniques to relax, e.g., yoga.
- check with your doctor if you cannot fall asleep within a reasonable amount of time.

DON'T:

- stay in bed when you cannot sleep.
- sleep outside of the bedroom.
- read in bed or watch TV while lying in bed. Bed should be used only for sleep.
- use electronics like computers, video games, or TV before bedtime, as they are overstimulating.
- drink caffeinated beverages such as coffee, tea, or soda four to six hours before bedtime.
- drink fluids one hour before bedtime.
- eat spicy foods or heavy meals before bedtime.
- exercise strenuously before bedtime.
- have strong sensory input in the bedroom (e.g., loud music, bright lights, very hot temperatures, strong smells).
- use nicotine shortly before bedtime.

For those who are staying up too late and can't seem to wake up on time, you can try adapting an approach known as chronotherapy:

- Estimate the current amount of sleep you are getting each night, then add fifteen minutes.
- Work backwards from wake-up time to determine what time you need to go to bed to get that much sleep
- Go to bed at the new calculated time.
- Get up at wake-up time, no matter what.
- Continue until that pattern is well established; then add fifteen minutes to allow more time in bed.
- Continue with this program until you are getting enough sleep each night (nine hours for adolescents).

For students who can't wake up, parents may wish to try the **Four Alarm Clock System** from *Teaching the Tiger* (Dornbush and Pruitt 1995):

For thirty days, assist your child with the following protocol:

- Purchase two dual alarm clock radios. Place one next to the child or adolescent's bed and the other across the room.
- Set the first alarm on the bedside alarm clock to play music of the child's choosing forty-five minutes before it is time to get up. The child can hit the snooze button as desired.

---

* A lot of children and adolescents with the disorders discussed in this book often report that they keep their air conditioner on all year because they are always hot. Parents of such children and teens should be encouraged to make sure that their kids' bedrooms are cool enough for them to fall comfortably asleep at night.

- Set the second alarm on the bedside clock radio to sound an alarm thirty minutes before it's time to get up. Permit the child to continue to hit the snooze button.
- Set the first alarm on the clock radio across the room to play music on a different station of the child's choice fifteen minutes before it is time to get up. Allow the child to return to the bed after hitting the snooze button.
- Set the second alarm on the clock radio across the room to sound when it is time to get up. Do NOT permit the child to return to the bed after this one has gone off. Have the child start getting ready for school.

For the next thirty days, the child is responsible for utilizing the alarm clock system to wake up alone without help.

- Make breakfast of the child's choosing available for one hour after the designated wake-up time.
- The parents or adult do not wait beyond that hour to assist the wake-up process but continue on with their day and will help get the child to a location as needed if it is convenient to the parent or adult. Consequences for late to school or work are the natural ones that occur for everyone and are sufficient without comment by the assisting adult. True sleep disorders are a medical problem and do not deserve anger or judgment.
- Remember to be clear about "Who owns the problem?" Do not take on someone else's responsibilities—it is insulting and disrespectful to them. It is understandable to want to save people you love from failure, but it is not helpful to them in the long run.

Student Homework Habits Survey

Name of Student: _____ **Date:**_____

1. How do I know what my homework is?
   a. I record it in an assignment book
   b. I record it in a PDA or my cell phone
   c. My teacher records it for me in my assignment book or gives it to me
   d. I call the Homework Hotline
   e. I call/email/IM friends to find out
   f. My teacher emails my assignments to me
   g. My parent(s) find out my assignment(s) for me

2. Do I have what I need to complete my homework, i.e., the assignment and the materials to complete the assignment?
   a. Always or almost always
   b. Usually
   c. Sometimes
   d. Almost Never

3. Do I start my homework without reminders?
   a. Always or almost always
   b. Usually
   c. Sometimes
   d. Almost Never

4. How do I organize my school materials?
   a. Color coded books/folders
   b. Homework folder
   c. None
   d. Other: _____

5. When I start my homework, the order I use is:
   a. Easiest/shortest work to hardest/longest work
   b. Hardest/longest work to Easiest/shortest work
   c. I don't have any consistent method

6. Do I estimate how long each assignment will take me?
   ____Yes   ____No   ____Sometimes

7. When I estimate how long it will take me, am I usually right?
   a. Yes
   b. No, I usually expect it to take longer than it does
   c. No, I usually expect it to take less time than it actually does
   d. Other: _____

8. Do I estimate how long it will take me to do all of my homework and studying for the night before I figure out when to start my work?

    ____Yes   ____No   ____Sometimes

9. When I complete a homework assignment:

    a. I put it in my homework folder immediately
    b. I put it aside until I'm done with all of my homework
    c. Other: _____

10. When I have a big project to do, I break it up into smaller parts and keep myself on schedule.

    ____Yes   ____No   ____Sometimes

11. When I have a big project to do, my teacher(s) or parents break it up into smaller parts for me.

    ____Yes   ____No   ____Sometimes

12. When I have a big project to do, I often forget to work on it until right before it's due.

    ____True   ____False

13. I generally remember to pack up all of my homework assignments without any reminders or help.

    ____True   ____False

14. If I have trouble with my homework:

    a. I give up and put it aside
    b. I call a classmate
    c. I ask a family member to help me
    d. Other : _____

15. On an average school night, how much time do I spend doing homework (in minutes)?

    ____0 ____15 ____30 ____45 ____60 ____90 ____120 ____more than two hours.

16. If I had a magic wand and could get rid of one type of homework assignment, it would be:

    _____

17. My teacher grades my homework or gives me feedback on it.

    ____Yes   ____No   ____Some of my teachers do

18. When homework counts towards my final grade, I take it more seriously and do a better job on it.

    ____Yes   ____No   ____Sometimes

19. I generally know whether I am missing homework or if I am caught up.

    ____Yes   ____No   ____In some classes

20. I generally start my homework:

    a. As soon as I get home from school
    b. Before dinner
    c. After dinner
    d. After 9 p.m.
    e. It varies

Student Survey about Studying for Tests

Name of Student: _____ **Date:**_____

Directions: Circle or highlight the answers that apply to you. There are no right or wrong answers to this survey. Please answer them as honestly as you can.

1. My best time to study for a test is: **Morning   Afternoon   Evening**

2. When do I usually study for a test? **Morning   Afternoon   Evening**

3. Where do I prefer to study for a test? **Bedroom   Kitchen   Family room   Dining room**
   Not in my house   Other:_____

4. Where do I usually study? **Bedroom   Kitchen   Family room   Dining room**
   Other: _____

5. What position do I want to be in when I study? **Sitting at desk   Sitting at table   Lying on floor**
   Lying on bed   Moving around   Other:_____

6. Who do I want to study with? **Alone   Parents   Sibling   Friends   With a tutor**

7. Who do I actually do my best studying with? **Alone   Parents   Sibling   Friends   With a tutor**

8. Do I usually have the books and materials I need to study? **Always or almost always   Usually**
   Sometimes   Rarely   Never

9. If there is more than one subject to study, what do I study first? **Easiest material   Hardest material**
   Shortest material   Longest material   Other:_____

10. What kind of sound environment do I prefer to study in? **Quiet room   Busy or noisy area**
    Music playing   TV on in background

11. What kind of lighting environment do I prefer to study in?   **Brightly lit room   Dim lighting   No preference**

12. What do I need to help me concentrate while I study?   **Food   Drink   Chew on straws/gum**
    None   Other:_____

13. Do I need breaks when I study for a test?   **Yes   No**

14. How do I decide when to take a break when studying for a test?   **After a fixed amount of time**
    When I get to a good stopping point in the material   When I finish studying
    Other: _____

15. When I take a break during studying for a test, how long is the break (in number of minutes):
    5   10   15   20   30   45   60   More than 60

16. How do I study for a test?   **Read   Listen   Talk   Write   Draw   Type   Flash cards**
    Make up memory tricks   Cartoons   Sing   Make up a funny story   Parent quiz
    Other: _____

17. If my teacher gives me a study guide for the test, I use it.   **Yes   No   Sometimes**

Homework Time Estimation Worksheet

Name of Student: _____ **Date:**_____

Directions: Record all of your homework assignments in Column 1. For each assignment, estimate how much time you think it will take you to do. Enter your time estimate in Column 2. Then allow yourself a little extra time and re-estimate the time it will take you to do it. Put your new estimate in Column 3. Two examples are provided to help you understand what to do on this sheet.

Remember to include any work you have to do on long-term assignments or studying for tests in Column 1 when you list all your assignments/work for today.

Add up the estimates from Column 3 (do not include the examples). How much time have you estimated it will take you to do all of your work today if you allow a little extra time? Put your answer here:_____.

Now figure out what time you need to start your homework today so that you can get it all done:_____. Do you really have time to hang out after school or should you go home and start your work immediately?

When you do your homework later, look at the clock before and after you do each activity or assignment on the list and note how long each assignment took you in Column 4.

Bring this form back to school with you tomorrow so we can go over it.

Assignment	Estimated Time To Do	Estimate Including Some Extra Time	How Long It Actually Took Me	Comments (Optional)
Example: Read Ch. 5 in Social Studies Book	20 Minutes	25 Minutes	53 Minutes	
Example: Do three math sheets	20 Minutes	30 Minutes	2 Hours	

Functional Behavioral Assessment Checklist

Name of Student: _____ **Date:**_____

Team Leader:_____ **Grade:**_____

Behavior(s) of concern:_____

_____

Yes	No	Checklist
		1. Is the behavior of concern clearly and <u>objectively</u> defined?
		2. Have replacement behaviors that serve the same function (or result in the same outcome) been identified, along with the circumstances under which they should occur (e.g., when threatened by peer in hallway)?
		3. Have multiple sources of information about the behavior been collected from various individuals (e.g., teachers, parents, classmates, student)? Do at least two separate indirect measures and multiple direct measures agree?
		4. Is the hypothesis statement written in the form of "Under X conditions, the student does Y, in order to achieve Z" so that an intervention plan can easily be produced?
		5. Has the hypothesis been tested by manipulating one variable at a time to determine its impact on the target behavior?
		6. Is the plan aligned with student needs and assessment results?
		7. Does the plan address all aspects of the social/environmental contexts in which the behavior of concern has occurred?
		8. Does the plan address both short-term and long-term aspects of student behavior (and its social/environmental context), including procedures to eliminate reliance on unacceptable behavior?
		9. Does the plan include practical ways to monitor both its implementation and its effectiveness as a behavioral intervention plan?
		10. Does the plan include ways to promote the maintenance and generalization of positive behavior changes in student behavior?
		11. Is the plan consistent with building-wide systems of student behavior change and support?
		12. Can the person(s) responsible for implementing the plan realistically do so? If not, are adequate supports for personnel in place?

Adapted from copyright-free material produced by the Center for Effective Collaboration and Practice: Addressing Student Problem Behavior—Part III: Creating Positive Behavioral Intervention Plans and Supports (1st Edition), 2000 by Leslie E. Packer, Ph.D.

A-B-C Observations and Recording Form

Name of Student: _____ **Observation Date:** _____

Observer: _____ **Class Period:** _____

Observation Time: _____ **Setting:** _____

Target Behavior: _____

Directions: Use this chart to record what task or activity the student was engaging in at the time the target behavior occurred (Activity) and what was going on before the behavior occurred (Antecedent). Describe the behavior and for how long it occurred (Behavior), and what happened after the behavior occurred (Consequences).

Activity	Antecedent	Behavior	Consequences

Time-Out Planning Form

Name of Student: _____ **Date:**_____

Participants involved in planning:_____

_____

1. List the specific and observable behavior(s) that will result in Time-Out:

    (a) _____

    (b) _____

    (c) _____

2. List the informal and less aversive strategies you have already tried without success for the behaviors listed in 1:

    (a) _____

    (b) _____

    (c) _____

3. List the positive reinforcement strategies you have already tried without success for alternative/replacement behaviors:

    (a) _____

    (b) _____

    (c) _____

4. Which type of Time-Out procedure do you plan to start with? Select the least restrictive option from the choices below that might be effective in reducing or eliminating the behavior(s):

    _____ Student will remain in the instructional setting and can watch and listen but cannot engage in activities.

    _____ Student will be removed to another part of the room and can watch and listen but not participate in activities.

    _____ Student will be removed to another part of the room where s/he cannot observe the activity nor participate.

    _____ Student will be removed from the instructional setting to a different setting.

        (a) If selected, identify the other setting (e.g., another classroom, principal's office, Time-Out room):_____.

        (b) If selected, identify who will monitor the student while in the other setting (student must be under direct observation at all times): _____.

5. Are there any behaviors that the student can exhibit while in Time-Out that will shorten the length of the time-out?   **Yes   No**

> If yes, describe: _____

6. What will the student be expected to do while in Time-Out? (e.g., continue working on assigned task, writing about behavior rule that was violated and what would be appropriate behavior)

> (a) _____
>
> (b) _____
>
> (c) _____

7. Will any warning be issued to the student prior to implementing Time-Out?   **Yes   No**

> If yes, what form will the warning take? _____
>
> If yes, how many warnings will be given? _____

8. Is there or will there be a positive reinforcement system in place so that the student earns rewards for appropriate alternative/replacement behaviors?   **Yes   No**

9. Is there or will there be a positive reinforcement system in place so that the student earns rewards for engaging in classroom activities?   **Yes   No**

10. How much time is the student allowed to comply with the "Go to Time-Out" directive (i.e., to get to Time-Out from the time you give the direction to go to Time-Out)? _____

11. If the student *does not comply* with the direction to go to Time-Out, what are the consequences?

> (a) _____
>
> (b) _____
>
> (c) _____

> If the student *does not comply*, will restraint or physical contact be used to remove the student from the setting or classroom?   **Yes   No**

> If *yes*, identify who will be responsible for removing the student:

> (a) _____
>
> (b) _____
>
> (c) _____

> If restraint may be used to remove the student, does the student have any health conditions that would be a contraindication to restraint (e.g., asthma)?   **Yes   No**

> If restraint may be used to remove the student, has the individual who will be using the restraint been trained in crisis de-escalation and safe restraint methods?   **Yes   No**

12. Who will decide when the student can return to the activity or classroom?   **Student   Teacher   Other**

13. What are the criteria for ending the Time-Out?   **Time   Behavior   Both   Other**

> If "time," indicate the minimum amount of time that the student will be in Time-Out _____

If "time," indicate the maximum amount of time that the student will be in Time-Out per incident_____

If "time," is the time recorded from when the student first gets to Time-Out or from when they leave the original setting and activity?_____

If "behavior," what specific behavior(s) must the student exhibit to end the Time-Out?

(a) _____

(b) _____

(c) _____

If "both," indicate the time _____ and behavior_____

If "other," describe:_____

14. How will the student know when the Time-Out is over (e.g., timer set, teacher notification, etc.)

_____

15. What routine should the student follow to re-enter the activity or classroom?

_____

16. Who will be responsible for helping the student re-enter the classroom or activity and get caught up?

_____

17. Identify who will be responsible for monitoring the student while the student is in Time-Out:

In the classroom: _____

In the Time-Out room: _____

Elsewhere (identify location and responsible individual): _____

18. Who will be responsible for maintaining a written Time-Out log or record?_____

19. Has this plan been reviewed with building administration or district administration?   **Yes   No**

20. Have the student's parents given written consent for the plan described in this planner?   **Yes   No**

If no, we strongly recommend attempting to secure written informed consent. In the absence of written consent, the teacher should consult with building and district administration before implementing any Time-Out plan that involves removing the student from the classroom.

Adapted with permission from Behavior management planning sheet: Time-out, Jim Wright, 2004. Retrieved from www.interventioncentral.org.

Time-Out Record

Name of Student: _____

Date	Setting and Activity	Behavior	Time-Out Start Time	Time-Out End Time	Time-Out Location	Comments or Observations

References

Abwender, D. A., P. G. Como, R. Kurlan, K. Parry, K. A. Fett, L. Cui, S. Plumb, and C. Deeley. 1996. School problems in Tourette's syndrome. *Arch Neurol* 53 (6):509-11.

Alfano, C. A., D. C. Beidel, S. M. Turner, and D. S. Lewin. 2006. Preliminary evidence for sleep complaints among children referred for anxiety. *Sleep Med*.

Allik, H., J. O. Larsson, and H. Smedje. 2006. Sleep Patterns of School-Age Children with Asperger Syndrome or High-Functioning Autism. *J Autism Dev Disord* 36 (5):585-595.

Allsopp, M. and C. Verduyn. 1990. Adolescents with obsessive-compulsive disorder: A case note review of consecutive patients referred to a provincial regional adolescent psychiatry unit. *J Adolesc* 13 (2):157-69.

Altindag, A., M. Yanik, and M. Nebioglu. 2006. The comorbidity of anxiety disorders in bipolar I patients: prevalence and clinical correlates. *Isr J Psychiatry Relat Sci* 43 (1):10-5.

American Psychiatric Association. 2000. *Diagnostic and Statistical Manual of Mental Disorders DSM-IV-TR Fourth Edition (Text Revision)*. Washington, D.C.: American Psychiatric Publishing, Inc.

Andres, S., L. Lazaro, M. Salamero, T. Boget, R. Penades, and J. Castro-Fornieles. 2007. Changes in cognitive dysfunction in children and adolescents with obsessive-compulsive disorder after treatment. *J Psychiatr Res*.

Banerjee, T. D., F. Middleton, and S. V. Faraone. 2007. Environmental risk factors for attention-deficit hyperactivity disorder. *Acta Paediatr* 96 (9):1269-74.

Barbe, R. P., D. E. Williamson, J. A. Bridge, B. Birmaher, R. E. Dahl, D. A. Axelson, and N. D. Ryan. 2005. Clinical differences between suicidal and nonsuicidal depressed children and adolescents. *J Clin Psychiatry* 66 (4):492-8.

Barkley, R. A. 1991. New ways of looking at ADHD. In *Third Annual CH.A.D.D. Conference on Attention Deficit Disorders*. Washington, D.C.

———. 1998. *Attention Deficit Hyperactivity Disorder: A Handbook for Diagnosis and Treatment*. New York: Guilford.

———. 1997. *ADHD and the Nature of Self-Control*. New York: Guilford Press.

———. 2003. Attention-Deficit/Hyperactivity Disorder. In *Child Psychopathology*, edited by Mash, E. J. & R. A. Barkley. New York: Guilford Press.

Barros, R. M., E. J. Silver, and R. E. Stein. 2009. School recess and group classroom behavior. *Pediatrics* 123 (2):431-436.

Battle-Bailey, L. 2003. Training teachers to design interactive homework. In *Eric Digest*.

Bawden, H. N., A. Stokes, C. S. Camfield, P. R. Camfield, and S. Salisbury. 1998. Peer relationship problems in children with Tourette's disorder or diabetes mellitus. *J Child Psychol Psychiatry* 39 (5):663-8.

Bedford, S. 1974. *Instant Replay*. New York: Institute for Rational Living.

Bennett, D. S., P. J. Ambrosini, D. Kudes, C. Metz, and H. Rabinovich. 2005. Gender differences in adolescent depression: Do symptoms differ for boys and girls? *J Affect Disord* 89 (1-3):35-44.

Bernstein, G. A., J. M. Hektner, C. M. Borchardt, and M. H. McMillan. 2001. Treatment of school refusal: One-year follow-up. *J Am Acad Child Adolesc Psychiatry* 40 (2):206-13.

Bernstein, G. A., A. E. Layne, E. A. Egan, and D. M. Tennison. 2005. School-based interventions for anxious children. *J Am Acad Child Adolesc Psychiatry* 44 (11):1118-27.

Biederman, J., S. V. Faraone, T. J. Spencer, E. Mick, M. C. Monuteaux, and M. Aleardi. 2006. Functional impairments in adults with self-reports of diagnosed ADHD: A controlled study of 1001 adults in the community. *J Clin Psychiatry* 67 (4):524-40.

Biederman, J., S. V. Faraone, J. Wozniak, E. Mick, A. Kwon, G. A. Cayton, and S. V. Clark. 2005. Clinical correlates of bipolar disorder in a large, referred sample of children and adolescents. *J Psychiatr Res* 39 (6):611-22.

Blenkiron, P. 2006. A mnemonic for depression. *British Medical Journal* 332 (7540):551.

Bloch, M. H., B. S. Peterson, L. Scahill, J. Otka, L. Katsovich, H. Zhang, and J. F. Leckman. 2006. Adulthood outcome of tic and obsessive-compulsive symptom severity in children with Tourette syndrome. *Arch Pediatr Adolesc Med* 160 (1):65-9.

Boldrini, M., L. Del Pace, G. P. Placidi, J. Keilp, S. P. Ellis, S. Signori, G. F. Placidi, and S. F. Cappa. 2005. Selective cognitive deficits in obsessive-compulsive disorder compared to panic disorder with agoraphobia. *Acta Psychiatr Scand* 111 (2):150-8.

Bryan, T., and K. Sullivan-Burstein. 1998. Teacher-selected strategies for improving homework completion. *Remedial and Special Education* 19 (5):263-275.

Burd, L., R. D. Freeman, M. G. Klug, and J. Kerbeshian. 2005. Tourette Syndrome and learning disabilities. *BMC Pediatr* 5:34.

Burd, L., D. W. Kauffman, and J. Kerbeshian. 1992. Tourette syndrome and learning disabilities. *J Learn Disabil* 25 (9):598-604.

Burd, L. and J. Kerbeshian. 1992. Educational management of children with Tourette syndrome. *Adv Neurol* 58:311-7.

Bussing, R., B.T. Zima, A.R. Perwien, T.R. Belin, and M. Widawski. 1998. Children in special education programs: Attention deficit hyperactivity disorder, use of services, and unmet needs. *Am J Public Health.* 88 (6):880-886.

Carlson, G. 2007. Who are the children with severe mood dysregulation, a.k.a. "rages"? *Am J Psychiatry.* 164 (8):1140-1142.

Carter, A. S., D. A. O'Donnell, R. T. Schultz, L. Scahill, J. F. Leckman, and D. L. Pauls. 2000. Social and emotional adjustment in children affected with Gilles de la Tourette's syndrome: Associations with ADHD and family functioning. Attention Deficit Hyperactivity Disorder. *J Child Psychol Psychiatry* 41 (2):215-23.

Carter, A. S., and R. A. Pollock. 2000. Obsessive compulsive disorder in childhood. *Curr Opin Pediatr* 12 (4):325-30.

Cartwright-Hatton, S., K. McNicol, and E. Doubleday. 2006. Anxiety in a neglected population: Prevalence of anxiety disorders in pre-adolescent children. *Clin Psychol Rev.*

Case-Smith, J. 2002. Effectiveness of school-based occupational therapy intervention on handwriting. *Am J Occup Ther* 56 (1):17-25.

CDC. 2005. Mental Health in the United States: Prevalence of Diagnosis and Medication Treatment for Attention-Deficit/Hyperactivity Disorder — United States, 2003. *Morbidity and Mortality Weekly Report* 54:842-847.

Chervin, R. D., J. E. Dillon, K. H. Archbold, and D. L. Ruzicka. 2003. Conduct problems and symptoms of sleep disorders in children. *J Am Acad Child Adolesc Psychiatry* 42 (2):201-8.

Comings, D. E. and B. G. Comings. 1987. A controlled study of Tourette syndrome. I. Attention-deficit disorder, learning disorders, and school problems. *Am J Hum Genet* 41 (5):701-41.

Como, P. G. 2001. Neuropsychological function in Tourette syndrome. *Adv Neurol* 85:103-11.

Conners, C. K., G. Sitarenios, J. D. A. Parker, and J. N. Epstein. 1998. Revision and restandardization of the Conners' Teacher Rating Scales (CTRS–R): Factor structure, reliability, and criterion validity. *Journal of Abnormal Child Psychology* 26 (4):279–291.

Cooper, H. and B. Nye. 1994. Homework for students with learning disabilities: The implications of research for policy and practice. *J Learn Disabil* 27 (8):470-9.

Cunningham, C. E., A. E. McHolm, and M. H. Boyle. 2006. Social phobia, anxiety, oppositional behavior, social skills, and self-concept in children with specific selective mutism, generalized selective mutism, and community controls. *Eur Child Adolesc Psychiatry*.

Currie, J. and M. Stabile. 2006. Child mental health and human capital accumulation: The case of ADHD. *J Health Econ*.

Danielyan, A., S. Pathak, R. A. Kowatch, S. P. Arszman, and E. S. Johns. 2006. Clinical characteristics of bipolar disorder in very young children. *J Affect Disord*.

De Nil, L. F., J. Sasisekaran, P. H. Van Lieshout, and P. Sandor. 2005. Speech disfluencies in individuals with Tourette syndrome. *J Psychosom Res* 58 (1):97-102.

DeBonis, D. A., M. Ylvisaker, and D. K. Kundert. 2000. The relationship between ADHD theory and practice: A preliminary investigation. *Journal of Attention Disorders* 4 (3):161-173.

Deckersbach, T., C. R. Savage, N. Reilly-Harrington, L. Clark, G. Sachs, and S. L. Rauch. 2004. Episodic memory impairment in bipolar disorder and obsessive-compulsive disorder: The role of memory strategies. *Bipolar Disord* 6 (3):233-44.

Dell'Osso, L., P. Rucci, F. Ducci, A. Ciapparelli, L. Vivarelli, M. Carlini, C. Ramacciotti, and G. B. Cassano. 2003. Social anxiety spectrum. *Eur Arch Psychiatry Clin Neurosci* 253 (6):286-91.

Denckla, M. B. 2007. Executive Function: Binding together the Definitions of Attention-Deficit/Hyperactivity Disorder and Learning Disabilities. In *Executive Function in Education*, edited by L. Meltzer. New York: Guilford Press.

Dennis, J. L. and Y. Swinth. 2001. Pencil grasp and children's handwriting legibility during different-length writing tasks. *Am J Occup Ther* 55 (2):175-83.

Dery, M., J. Toupin, R. Pauze, and P. Verlaan. 2004. Frequency of mental health disorders in a sample of elementary school students receiving special educational services for behavioural difficulties. *Can J Psychiatry* 49 (11):769-75.

Dickstein, D. P., J. E. Treland, J. Snow, E. B. McClure, M. S. Mehta, K. E. Towbin, D. S. Pine, and E. Leibenluft. 2004. Neuropsychological performance in pediatric bipolar disorder. *Biol Psychiatry* 55 (1):32-9.

Dirson, S., M. Bouvard, J. Cottraux, and R. Martin. 1995. Visual memory impairment in patients with obsessive-compulsive disorder: A controlled study. *Psychother Psychosom* 63 (1):22-31.

DiScala, C., I. Lescohier, M. Barthel, and G. Li. 1998. Injuries to children with attention deficit hyperactivity disorder. *Pediatrics* 102 (6):1415-21.

Dornbush, M. P., and S. K. Pruitt. 1995. *Teaching the Tiger: A Handbook for Individuals Involved in the Education of Students with Attention Deficit Disorders, Tourette Syndrome or Obsessive-Compulsive Disorder.* Hope Press.

Dornbush, M.P. and S.K. Pruitt. 2009. *Tigers, Too—Executive Functions, Speed of Preocessing, Memory: Impact on academic, behavioral, and social functioning of students with ADHD, Tourette syndrome, and OCD-Modifications and Interventions.* Atlanta: Parkaire Press.

Dudas, R. B., K. Hans, and K. Barabas. 2005. Anxiety, depression and smoking in schoolchildren—implications for smoking prevention. *J R Soc Health* 125 (2):87-92.

Edell, B. H. and R. W. Motta. 1989. The emotional adjustment of children with Tourette's syndrome. *J Psychol* 123 (1):51-7.

Edell-Fisher, B. H. and R. W. Motta. 1990. Tourette syndrome: Relation to children's and parents' self-concepts. *Psychol Rep* 66 (2):539-45.

Egger, H. L., E. J. Costello, and A. Angold. 2003. School refusal and psychiatric disorders: A community study. *J Am Acad Child Adolesc Psychiatry* 42 (7):797-807.

Elia, M., R. Ferri, S. A. Musumeci, S. Del Gracco, M. Bottitta, C. Scuderi, G. Miano, S. Panerai, T. Bertrand, and J. C. Grubar. 2000. Sleep in subjects with autistic disorder: A neurophysiological and psychological study. *Brain Dev* 22 (2):88-92.

Epstein, M., M. Atkins, D. Cullinan, K. Kutash, and R. Weaver. 2008. Reducing Behavior: Problems in the Elementary School Classroom: A Practice Guide edited by National Center for Education Evaluation and Regional Assistance and I. o. E. Sciences.

Epstein, M. H., R. M. Foley, and E. A. Polloway. 1995. A comparison of the homework problems of students with behavior disorders and non-handicapped students. *Preventing School Failure* 40:14-18.

Epstein, M., E. A. Polloway, R. M. Foley, and J. R. Patton. 1993. Homework: A comparison of teachers' and parents' perceptions of the problems experienced by students identified as having behavioral disorders, learning disabilities, or no disabilities. *Remedial and Special Education* 14 (5):40-50.

Faedda, G. L., R. J. Baldessarini, I. P. Glovinsky, and N. B. Austin. 2004. Pediatric bipolar disorder: Phenomenology and course of illness. *Bipolar Disord* 6 (4):305-13.

Frangou, S., S. Donaldson, M. Hadjulis, S. Landau, and L. H. Goldstein. 2005. The Maudsley Bipolar Disorder Project: Executive dysfunction in bipolar disorder I and its clinical correlates. *Biol Psychiatry* 58 (11):859-64.

Freeman, A. R., J. R. MacKinnon, and L. T. Miller. 2004. Assistive technology and handwriting problems: What do occupational therapists recommend? *Can J Occup Ther* 71 (3):150-60.

———. 2005. Keyboarding for students with handwriting problems: A literature review. *Phys Occup Ther Pediatr* 25 (1-2):119-47.

Freeman, R. D., D. K. Fast, L. Burd, J. Kerbeshian, M. M. Robertson, and P. Sandor. 2000. An international perspective on Tourette syndrome: Selected findings from 3,500 individuals in 22 countries. *Dev Med Child Neurol* 42 (7):436-47.

Friedrich, S., S. B. Morgan, and C. Devine. 1996. Children's attitudes and behavioral intentions toward a peer with Tourette syndrome. *J Pediatr Psychol* 21 (3):307-19.

Fuggetta, G. P. 2006. Impairment of executive functions in boys with attention deficit/hyperactivity disorder. *Neuropsychol Dev Cogn C Child Neuropsychol* 12 (1):1-21.

Gallina, N.B. 1990. Tourette's Syndrome children: Significant achievement and social behavior variables (Tourette Syndrome, Attention Deficit Hyperactivity Disorder).

Garland, E. J. 2001. Rages and refusals. Managing the many faces of adolescent anxiety. *Can Fam Physician* 47:1023-30.

Geller, B., B. Zimerman, M. Williams, K. Bolhofner, J. L. Craney, M. P. Delbello, and C. A. Soutullo. 2000. Diagnostic characteristics of 93 cases of a prepubertal and early adolescent bipolar disorder phenotype by gender, puberty and comorbid attention deficit hyperactivity disorder. *J Child Adolesc Psychopharmacol* 10 (3):157-64.

Geller, D. A. 2006. Obsessive-compulsive and spectrum disorders in children and adolescents. *Psychiatr Clin North Am* 29 (2):353-70.

Grills, A. E. and T. H. Ollendick. 2002. Peer victimization, global self-worth, and anxiety in middle school children. *J Clin Child Adolesc Psychol* 31 (1):59-68.

Ha, J. H., H. J. Yoo, I. H. Cho, B. Chin, D. Shin, and J. H. Kim. 2006. Psychiatric comorbidity assessed in Korean children and adolescents who screen positive for Internet addiction. *J Clin Psychiatry* 67 (5):821-6.

Hagin, R. A., R. Beecher, G. Pagano, and H. Kreeger. 1982. Effects of Tourette syndrome on learning. *Adv Neurol* 35:323-8.

Hammerschmidt, S. L. and P. Sudsawad. 2004. Teachers' survey on problems with handwriting: Referral, evaluation, and outcomes. *Am J Occup Ther* 58 (2):185-92.

Harcherik, D. F., J. F. Leckman, J. Detlor, and D. J. Cohen. 1984. A new instrument for clinical studies of Tourette's syndrome. *J Am Acad Child Psychiatry* 23 (2):153-60.

Hazell, P. L., V. Carr, T. J. Lewin, and K. Sly. 2003. Manic symptoms in young males with ADHD predict functioning but not diagnosis after 6 years. *J Am Acad Child Adolesc Psychiatry* 42 (5):552-60.

Himle, M. B. and D. W. Woods. 2005. An experimental evaluation of tic suppression and the tic rebound effect. *Behav Res Ther* 43 (11):1443-51.

Himle, M. B., D. W. Woods, C. A. Conelea, C. C. Bauer, and K. A. Rice. 2007. Investigating the effects of tic suppression on premonitory urge ratings in children and adolescents with Tourette's syndrome. *Behav Res Ther* 45 (12):2964-2976.

Himle, M. B., D. W. Woods, J. C. Piacentini, and J. T. Walkup. 2006. Brief review of habit reversal training for Tourette syndrome. *J Child Neurol* 21 (8):719-725.

Hoekstra, P. J. and R. B. Minderaa. 2005. Tic disorders and obsessive-compulsive disorder: Is autoimmunity involved? *Int Rev Psychiatry* 17 (6):497-502.

Hollander, E., E. Schiffman, B. Cohen, M. A. Rivera-Stein, W. Rosen, J. M. Gorman, A. J. Fyer, L. Papp, and M. R. Liebowitz. 1990. Signs of central nervous system dysfunction in obsessive-compulsive disorder. *Arch Gen Psychiatry* 47 (1):27-32.

Hollenbeck, P. J. 2001. Insight and hindsight into Tourette syndrome. *Adv Neurol* 85:363-7.

Horowitz, S. H. *Research Roundup*. National Center for Learning Disabilities 2005 [cited September 20, 2006. Available from http://www.ncld.org/content/view/577/480/.

Hughes, C.A., K.L. Ruhl, J.B. Schumaker, and D.D. Deshler. 2002. Effects of instruction in an assignment completion strategy on the homework performance of students with learning disabilities in general education classes. *Learning Disabilities Research* 17 (1):1-18.

Hvolby, A., J. Jørgensen, and N. Bilenberg. 2009. Parental rating of sleep in children with attention deficit/hyperactivity disorder. *Eur Child Adolesc Psychiatry*

Hymas, N., A. Lees, D. Bolton, K. Epps, and D. Head. 1991. The neurology of obsessional slowness. *Brain* 114 (Pt 5):2203-33.

Jennings, M.K. 1993. *"Graphic Reading Skills."*

Kamins, M. L. and C. S. Dweck. 1999. Person versus process praise and criticism: Implications for contingent self-worth and coping. *Dev Psychol* 35 (3):835-47.

Karlsdottir, R. 1996. Development of cursive handwriting. *Percept Mot Skills* 82 (2):659-73.

Karlsdottir, R. and T. Stefansson. 2002. Problems in developing functional handwriting. *Percept Mot Skills* 94 (2):623-62.

Kathmann, N., C. Rupertseder, W. Hauke, and M. Zaudig. 2005. Implicit sequence learning in obsessive-compulsive disorder: Further support for the fronto-striatal dysfunction model. *Biol Psychiatry* 58 (3):239-44.

Kearney, C. A. and A. M. Albano. 2004. The functional profiles of school refusal behavior. Diagnostic aspects. *Behav Modif* 28 (1):147-61.

Keller, M. B. 2006. Prevalence and impact of comorbid anxiety and bipolar disorder. *J Clin Psychiatry* 67 Suppl 1:5-7.

Kieseppa, T., T. Partonen, J. Haukka, J. Kaprio, and J. Lonnqvist. 2004. High concordance of bipolar I disorder in a nationwide sample of twins. *Am J Psychiatry* 161 (10):1814-21.

Kostanecka-Endress, T., T. Banaschewski, J. Kinkelbur, I. Wullner, S. Lichtblau, S. Cohrs, E. Ruther, W. Woerner, G. Hajak, and A. Rothenberger. 2003. Disturbed sleep in children with Tourette syndrome: A polysomnographic study. *J Psychosom Res* 55 (1):23-9.

Kovacs, M., H. S. Akiskal, C. Gatsonis, and P. L. Parrone. 1994. Childhood-onset dysthymic disorder. Clinical features and prospective naturalistic outcome. *Arch Gen Psychiatry* 51 (5):365-74.

Kranowitz, C. S. 1998. *The Out-of-Sync Child: Recognizing and Coping with Sensory Integration Dysfunction*. 2nd ed. New York: Berkley Publishing Group.

Kurlan, R. 1998. Tourette's syndrome and 'PANDAS': Will the relation bear out? Pediatric autoimmune neuropsychiatric disorders associated with streptococcal infection. *Neurology* 50 (6):1530-4.

———. 2004. The PANDAS hypothesis: Losing its bite? *Mov Disord* 19 (4):371-4.

Kurlan, R., P. G. Como, B. Miller, D. Palumbo, C. Deeley, E. M. Andresen, S. Eapen, and M. P. McDermott. 2002. The behavioral spectrum of tic disorders: A community-based study. *Neurology* 59 (3):414-20.

Lagace, D. C., S. P. Kutcher, and H. A. Robertson. 2003. Mathematics deficits in adolescents with Bipolar I Disorder. *American Journal of Psychiatry* 160:100–104.

Lahera, G., J. M. Montes, A. Benito, M. Valdivia, E. Medina, I. Mirapeix, and J. Sáiz-Ruiz. 2008. Theory of mind deficit in bipolar disorder: Is it related to a previous history of psychotic symptoms? *Psychiatry Research*.

Langberg, J. M., J. N. Epstein, M. Altaye, B. S. Molina, L. E. Arnold, and B. Vitiello. 2008. The transition to middle school is associated with changes in the developmental trajectory of ADHD symptomatology in young adolescents with ADHD. *J Clin Child Adolesc Psychol* 37 (3):651-663.

Langberg, J. M., J. N. Epstein, and A. J. Graham. 2008. Organizational-skills interventions in the treatment of ADHD. *Expert Rev Neurother* 8 (10):1549-1561.

Laraque, D., J. A. Boscarino, A. Battista, A. Fleischman, M. Casalino, Y. Y. Hu, S. Ramos, R. E. Adams, J. Schmidt, and C. Chemtob. 2004. Reactions and needs of tristate-area pediatricians after the events of September 11th: Implications for children's mental health services. *Pediatrics* 113 (5):1357-66.

Lavoie, R. 1996. *F.A.T. City - How Difficult Can This Be?*: PBS.

Leckman, J. F., E. S. Dolnansky, M. T. Hardin, M. Clubb, J. T. Walkup, J. Stevenson, and D. L. Pauls. 1990. Perinatal factors in the expression of Tourette's syndrome: An exploratory study. *J Am Acad Child Adolesc Psychiatry* 29 (2):220-6.

Leckman, J. F., H. Zhang, A. Vitale, F. Lahnin, K. Lynch, C. Bondi, Y. S. Kim, and B. S. Peterson. 1998. Course of tic severity in Tourette syndrome: The first two decades. *Pediatrics* 102 (1 Pt 1):14-9.

Leslie, D.L., L. Kozma, A. Martin, A. Landeros, L. Katsovich, R.A. King, and J.F. Leckman. 2008. Neuropsychiatric disorders associated with streptococcal infection: A case-control study among privately insured children. *Psychiatry* 47 (10):1166-1172.

Liu, X., J. A. Hubbard, R. A. Fabes, and J. B. Adam. 2007. Sleep disturbances and correlates of children with autism spectrum disorders. *Child Psychiatry Hum Dev* 37 (2):179-191.

Lloyd, J.W., D.P. Hallahan, J.M. Kauffman, and C.E Keller. 1998. Academic problems. In *The Practice of Child Therapy*, edited by Morris, R. J. & T. R. Kratochwill. Boston: Allyn & Bacon.

Luby, J. L., A. K. Heffelfinger, C. Mrakotsky, K. M. Brown, M. J. Hessler, J. M. Wallis, and E. L. Spitznagel. 2003. The clinical picture of depression in preschool children. *J Am Acad Child Adolesc Psychiatry* 42 (3):340-8.

Lyman, F. 1981. The responsive classroom discussion. In *Mainstreaming Digest*, edited by A. S. Anderson. College Park, MD: University of Maryland College of Education.

Maeland, A. F. 1992. Handwriting and perceptual-motor skills in clumsy, dysgraphic, and 'normal' children. *Percept Mot Skills* 75 (3 Pt 2):1207-17.

Mannuzza, S., R. G. Klein, and J. L. Moulton, 3rd. 2003. Persistence of Attention-Deficit/Hyperactivity Disorder into adulthood: What have we learned from the prospective follow-up studies? *J Atten Disord* 7 (2):93-100.

Marcks, B. A., K. S. Berlin, D. W. Woods, and W. H. Davies. 2007. Impact of Tourette Syndrome: A preliminary investigation of the effects of disclosure on peer perceptions and social functioning. *Psychiatry* 70 (1):59-67.

Marsh, R., G. M. Alexander, M. G. Packard, H. Zhu, and B. S. Peterson. 2005. Perceptual-motor skill learning in Gilles de la Tourette syndrome. Evidence for multiple procedural learning and memory systems. *Neuropsychologia* 43 (10):1456-65.

Masi, G., M. Mucci, and S. Millepiedi. 2001. Separation anxiety disorder in children and adolescents: Epidemiology, diagnosis and management. *CNS Drugs* 15 (2):93-104.

Masi, G., G. Perugi, C. Toni, S. Millepiedi, M. Mucci, N. Bertini, and H. S. Akiskal. 2004. Obsessive-compulsive bipolar comorbidity: Focus on children and adolescents. *J Affect Disord* 78 (3):175-83.

Matsuo, M., K. Tsuchiya, Y. Hamasaki, and H. S. Singer. 2004. Restless legs syndrome: Association with streptococcal or mycoplasma infection. *Pediatr Neurol* 31 (2):119-21.

Mavrogiorgou, P., R. Mergl, P. Tigges, J. El Husseini, A. Schroter, G. Juckel, M. Zaudig, and U. Hegerl. 2001. Kinematic analysis of handwriting movements in patients with obsessive-compulsive disorder. *J Neurol Neurosurg Psychiatry* 70 (5):605-12.

Mayes, S. D., S. L. Calhoun, and E. W. Crowell. 2000. Learning disabilities and ADHD: overlapping spectrum disorders. *J Learn Disabil* 33 (5):417-24.

McClure, E. B., K. Pope, A. J. Hoberman, D. S. Pine, and E. Leibenluft. 2003. Facial expression recognition in adolescents with mood and anxiety disorders. *Am J Psychiatry* 160 (6):1172-4.

McLoughlin, G., A. Ronald, J. Kuntsi, P. Asherson, and R. Plomin. 2007. Genetic support for the dual nature of attention deficit hyperactivity disorder: Substantial genetic overlap between the inattentive and hyperactive-impulsive components. *J Abnorm Child Psychol*.

Mehl, R. C., L. M. O'Brien, J. H. Jones, J. K. Dreisbach, C. B. Mervis, and D. Gozal. 2006. Correlates of sleep and pediatric bipolar disorder. *Sleep* 29 (2):193-7.

Mergl, R., G. Juckel, J. Rihl, V. Henkel, M. Karner, P. Tigges, A. Schroter, and U. Hegerl. 2004. Kinematical analysis of handwriting movements in depressed patients. *Acta Psychiatr Scand* 109 (5):383-91.

Mergl, R., P. Mavrogiorgou, G. Juckel, M. Zaudig, and U. Hegerl. 2004. Effects of sertraline on kinematic aspects of hand movements in patients with obsessive-compulsive disorder. *Psychopharmacology (Berl)* 171 (2):179-85.

Moon, S. M. 2002. Gifted children with attention deficit/hyperactivity disorder. In *The Social and Emotional Development of Gifted Children: What Do We Know?*, edited by M. Neihart, S. Reis, N. Robinson, and S. Moon. Waco, TX: Prufrock Press.

Moon, S. M., S. S. Zentall, Grskovic J. A., A. Hall, and M. Stormont. 2001. Emotional and social characteristics of boys with AD/HD and giftedness: A comparative case study. *Journal for the Education of the Gifted* 24 (3):207-247.

Müller-Vahl, K. R., N. Buddensiek, M. Geomelas, and H. M. Emrich. 2008. The influence of different food and drink on tics in Tourette syndrome. *Acta Paediatr* 97 (4):442-446.

Muris, P. and C. Meesters. 2002. Symptoms of anxiety disorders and teacher-reported school functioning of normal children. *Psychol Rep* 91 (2):588-90.

Niehart, M. . 2003. Gifted children with Attention Deficit Hyperactivity Disorder. In *ERIC EC Digest*

Northup, J., C. Broussard, K. H. Jones, T. George, T.R. Vollmer, and M. Herring. 1995. The differential effects of teacher and peer attention on the disruptive classroom behavior of three children with a diagnosis of attention deficit hyperactivity disorder. *J Appl Behav Anal.* 28 (2):227-228.

Ohm, B. 2006. The effect of Tourette syndrome on the education and social interactions of a school-age child. *J Neurosci Nurs* 38 (3):194-5, 199.

Otto, M. W., N. M. Simon, S. R. Wisniewski, D. J. Miklowitz, J. N. Kogan, N. A. Reilly-Harrington, E. Frank, A. A. Nierenberg, L. B. Marangell, K. Sagduyu, R. D. Weiss, S. Miyahara, M. E. Thas, G. S. Sachs, and M. H. Pollack. 2006. Prospective 12-month course of bipolar disorder in out-patients with and without comorbid anxiety disorders. *Br J Psychiatry* 189:20-5.

Owens, J. A., R. Maxim, C. Nobile, M. McGuinn, and M. Msall. 2000. Parental and self-report of sleep in children with attention-deficit/hyperactivity disorder. *Arch Pediatr Adolesc Med* 154 (6):549-55.

Owens, J. A., A. Spirito, M. McGuinn, and C. Nobile. 2000. Sleep habits and sleep disturbance in elementary school-aged children. *J Dev Behav Pediatr* 21 (1):27-36.

Paavonen, E. J., K. Vehkalahti, Vanhala R., L. von Wendt, T. Nieminen-von Wendt, and E. T. Aronen. 2008. Sleep in children with Asperger syndrome. *J Autism Dev Disord* 38 (1):41-51.

Packer, L. E. 1995. Educating children with Tourette Syndrome: Understanding and educating children with a neurobiological disorder. I: Psychoeducational implications of Tourette Syndrome and its associated disorders. New York State Education Dept., Albany, NY.

———. 1997. Social and educational resources for patients with Tourette syndrome. *Neurol Clin* 15 (2):457-73.

———. 1999. A cognitive cue for editing work: The "CLIPS" mnemonic.

———. 2005. Tic-related school problems: impact on functioning, accommodations, and interventions. *Behav Modif* 29 (6):876-99.

———. 2007. *Don't Even THINK About Trying to Wake Me Up in the Morning Syndrome*. PowerPoint.

———. 2002. "Clueless: Understanding Executive Dysfunction." Dobbs Ferry, NY

———. 2002. *"A Little of This, a Little of That Syndrome."* PowerPoint.

———. 2004. Mood Disorders.

Packer, L. E. *Relax!* www.tourettesyndrome.net 1998 [cited. ____] Available from www.tourettesyndrome.net/relaxation.htm.

Packer, L. E. and M. Gentile. 1994. Tourette's Syndrome: A maze of pathologies for unsuspecting OTs. *ADVANCE for Occupational Therapists* 10 (38):16.

Packer, L.E., and C. Wang. 1999. *"Storms."* Powerpoint materials.

Papadimitriou, G. N. and P. Linkowski. 2005. Sleep disturbance in anxiety disorders. *Int Rev Psychiatry* 17 (4):229-36.

Parkaire Consultants, Inc. 1991. Cause and Effects in Reading.

———. 1992. Mindmapping a paper on dogs.

———. 1995. Symptoms That Impact Social Functioning.

Pauls, D. L., K. E. Towbin, J. F. Leckman, G. E. Zahner, and D. J. Cohen. 1986. Gilles de la Tourette's syndrome and obsessive-compulsive disorder. Evidence supporting a genetic relationship. *Arch Gen Psychiatry* 43 (12):1180-2.

Penades, R., R. Catalan, S. Andres, M. Salamero, and C. Gasto. 2005. Executive function and nonverbal memory in obsessive-compulsive disorder. *Psychiatry Res* 133 (1):81-90.

Piacentini, J., M. B. Himle, S. Chang, D. E. Baruch, B. A. Buzzella, A. Pearlman, and D. W. Woods. 2006. Reactivity of tic observation procedures to situation and setting. *J Abnorm Child Psychol* 34 (5):649-658.

Piacentini, J. R. L. Bergman, M. Keller, and J. McCracken. 2003. Functional impairment in children and adolescents with obsessive-compulsive disorder. *J Child Adolesc Psychopharmacol* 13 Suppl 1:S61-9.

Piacentini, J., and S. Chang. 2005. Habit reversal training for tic disorders in children and adolescents. *Behav Modif* 29 (6):803-22.

Piacentini, J., T. S. Peris, R. L. Bergman, S. Chang, and M. Jaffer. 2007. Functional Impairment in Childhood OCD: Development and Psychometrics Properties of the Child Obsessive-Compulsive Impact Scale–Revised (COIS—R). *Journal of Clinical Child & Adolescent Psychology* 36 (4):645-653.

Picchietti, D. L., D. J. Underwood, W. A. Farris, A. S. Walters, M. M. Shah, R. E. Dahl, L. J. Trubnick, M. A. Bertocci, M. Wagner, and W. A. Hening. 1999. Further studies on periodic limb movement disorder and restless legs syndrome in children with attention-deficit hyperactivity disorder. *Mov Disord* 14 (6):1000-7.

Pruitt, D.G. 1997. "Bridges."

Pruitt, D.G., and S. K. Pruitt. 2001. "P.L.A.N."

Pruitt, S. K. 1977. Metric mnemonic.

———. 1987. Storm build-up.

———. 1992. "A Hole in the Wall Syndrome."

———. 1992. "Crasher-Banger"

———. 1992. "Sock Seam Syndrome."

———. 1995. Clueless.

———. 1995. "P.O.S.E."

———. 1995. Reparation.

———. 1996. "Just Right Syndrome."

———. 1996. Teacher and Student Strategies to Remediate the Impact of Executive Dysfunction on Social Skills.

———. 1996. "Three-ring theory."

Pruitt, S. K., and R. Rogers. 2001. Blurt Blockers.

Rathvon, N. 1999. *Effective School Interventions: Strategies for Enhancing Academic Achievement and Social Competence, The Guilford School Practitioner Series*. New York: The Guilford Press.

Reddy, Y. C., S. M. D'Souza, C. Shetti, T. Kandavel, S. Deshpande, S. Badamath, and S. Singisetti. 2005. An 11- to 13-year follow-up of 75 subjects with obsessive-compulsive disorder. *J Clin Psychiatry* 66 (6):744-9.

Reich, W., R. J. Neuman, H. E. Volk, C. A. Joyner, and R. D. Todd. 2005. Comorbidity between ADHD and symptoms of bipolar disorder in a community sample of children and adolescents. *Twin Res Hum Genet* 8 (5):459-66.

Richardson, A. S., H. A. Bergen, G. Martin, L. Roeger, and S. Allison. 2005. Perceived academic performance as an indicator of risk of attempted suicide in young adolescents. *Arch Suicide Res* 9 (2):163-76.

Robert, J. J., R. F. Hoffmann, G. J. Emslie, C. Hughes, J. Rintelmann, J. Moore, and R. Armitage. 2006. Sex and age differences in sleep macroarchitecture in childhood and adolescent depression. *Sleep* 29 (3):351-8.

Roberts, R. E., C. R. Roberts, and I. G. Chen. 2002. Impact of insomnia on future functioning of adolescents. *J Psychosom Res* 53 (1):561-9.

Rogers, J. and J. Case-Smith. 2002. Relationships between handwriting and keyboarding performance of sixth-grade students. *Am J Occup Ther* 56 (1):34-9.

Rucklidge, J. J. 2006. Impact of ADHD on the neurocognitive functioning of adolescents with bipolar disorder. *Biol Psychiatry* 60 (9):921-8.

Samuels, J. F., O. J. Bienvenu, 3rd, A. Pinto, A. J. Fyer, J. T. McCracken, S. L. Rauch, D. L. Murphy, M. A. Grados, B. D. Greenberg, J. A. Knowles, J. Piacentini, P. A. Cannistraro, B. Cullen, M. A. Riddle, S. A. Rasmussen, D. L. Pauls, V. L. Willour, Y. Y. Shugart, K. Y. Liang, R. Hoehn-Saric, and G. Nestadt. 2006. Hoarding in obsessive-compulsive disorder: Results from the OCD Collaborative Genetics Study. *Behav Res Ther*.

Scahill, L., P. J. Lombroso, G. Mack, P. J. Van Wattum, H. Zhang, A. Vitale, and J. F. Leckman. 2001. Thermal sensitivity in Tourette syndrome: Preliminary report. *Percept Mot Skills* 92 (2):419-32.

Schultz, R. T., A. S. Carter, M. Gladstone, L. Scahill, J. F. Leckman, B. S. Peterson, H. Zhang, D. J. Cohen, and D. Pauls. 1998. Visual-motor integration functioning in children with Tourette syndrome. *Neuropsychology* 12 (1):134-45.

Schumaker, J.B., D.D. Deshler, S. Nolan, F.L. Clark, G.R. Alley, and M.M. Wagner. 1981. Error monitoring: A learning strategy for improving academic performance of LD adolescents. Lawrence, Kansas.

Shear, P. K., M. P. DelBello, H. Lee Rosenberg, and S. M. Strakowski. 2002. Parental reports of executive dysfunction in adolescents with bipolar disorder. *Child Neuropsychol* 8 (4):285-95.

Shochet, I. M., M. R. Dadds, D. Ham, and R. Montague. 2006. School connectedness is an underemphasized parameter in adolescent mental health: Results of a community prediction study. *J Clin Child Adolesc Psychol* 35 (2):170-9.

Silva, R. R., D. M. Munoz, J. Barickman, and A. J. Friedhoff. 1995. Environmental factors and related fluctuation of symptoms in children and adolescents with Tourette's disorder. *J Child Psychol Psychiatry* 36 (2):305-312.

Singer, H. S. and C. Loiselle. 2003. PANDAS: A commentary. *J Psychosom Res* 55 (1):31-9.

Sprague, J. R. and H. M. Walker. 2004. Improving School Climate, Safety, and Student Health with Schoolwide Positive Behavior Supports. In *Safe and Healthy Schools: Practical Prevention Strategies*. New York: Guilford Press.

Staton, D. 2008. The impairment of pediatric bipolar sleep: Hypotheses regarding a core defect and phenotype-specific sleep disturbances. *J Affect Disord* 108 (3):199-206.

Stein, D. J. 2001. Handwriting and obsessive-compulsive disorder. *Lancet* 358 (9281):524-5.

Steinhausen, H. C., M. Wachter, K. Laimbock, and C. W. Metzke. 2006. A long-term outcome study of selective mutism in childhood. *J Child Psychol Psychiatry* 47 (7):751-6.

Stokes, A., H. N. Bawden, P. R. Camfield, J. E. Backman, and J. M. Dooley. 1991. Peer problems in Tourette's disorder. *Pediatrics* 87 (6):936-42.

Storch, E. A., A. D. Heidgerken, J. W. Adkins, M. Cole, T. K. Murphy, and G. R. Geffken. 2005. Peer victimization and the development of obsessive-compulsive disorder in adolescence. *Depress Anxiety* 21 (1):41-4.

Storch, E. A., D. R. Ledley, A. B. Lewin, T. K. Murphy, N. B. Johns, W. K. Goodman, and G. R. Geffken. 2006. Peer victimization in children with obsessive-compulsive disorder: Relations with symptoms of psychopathology. *J Clin Child Adolesc Psychol* 35 (3):446-55.

Storch, E. A. and C. Masia-Warner. 2004. The relationship of peer victimization to social anxiety and loneliness in adolescent females. *J Adolesc* 27 (3):351-62.

Storch, E. A., T. K. Murphy, D. M. Bagner, N. B. Johns, A. L. Baumeister, W. K. Goodman, and G. R. Geffken. 2005. Reliability and validity of the Child Behavior Checklist Obsessive-Compulsive Scale. *J Anxiety Disord*.

Storch, E. A., T. K. Murphy, C. W. Lack , G. R. Geffken, M. L. Jacob, and W. K. Goodman. 2008. Sleep-related problems in pediatric obsessive-compulsive disorder. *J Anxiety Disord* 22 (5):877-885.

Sung, V., H. Hiscock, E. Sciberras, and D. Efron. 2008. Sleep problems in children with attention-deficit/hyperactivity disorder: Prevalence and the effect on the child and family. *Arch Pediatr Adolesc Med.* 162 (4):336-342.

Swedo, S. E., H. L. Leonard, M. Garvey, B. Mittleman, A. J. Allen, S. Perlmutter, L. Lougee, S. Dow, J. Zamkoff, and B. K. Dubbert. 1998. Pediatric autoimmune neuropsychiatric disorders associated with streptococcal infections: clinical description of the first 50 cases. *Am J Psychiatry* 155 (2):264-71.

Swedo, S. E., H. L. Leonard, and J. L. Rapoport. 2004. The pediatric autoimmune neuropsychiatric disorders associated with streptococcal infection (PANDAS) subgroup: Separating fact from fiction. *Pediatrics* 113 (4):907-11.

Tallis, F., P. Pratt, and N. Jamani. 1999. Obsessive compulsive disorder, checking, and non-verbal memory: A neuropsychological investigation. *Behav Res Ther* 37 (2):161-6.

Tani, P., N. Lindberg, T. Nieminen-von Wendt, L. von Wendt, J. Virkkala, B. Appelberg, and T. Porkka-Heiskanen. 2004. Sleep in young adults with Asperger syndrome. *Neuropsychobiology* 50 (2):147-52.

The Pediatric OCD Treatment Study (POTS) Team. 2004. Cognitive-Behavior Therapy, Sertraline, and their combination for children and adolescents with Obsessive-Compulsive Disorder. *Jama* 292 (16):1969-1976.

Tigges, P., G. Juckel, A. Schroter, H. J. Moller, and U. Hegerl. 2000. Periodic motor impairments in a case of 48-hour bipolar ultrarapid cycling before and under treatment with valproate. *Neuropsychobiology* 42 Suppl 1:38-42.

Toren, P., M. Sadeh, L. Wolmer, S. Eldar, S. Koren, R. Weizman, and N. Laor. 2000. Neurocognitive correlates of anxiety disorders in children: A preliminary report. *J Anxiety Disord* 14 (3):239-47.

Tucha, O. and K. W. Lange. 2001. Effects of methylphenidate on kinematic aspects of handwriting in hyperactive boys. *J Abnorm Child Psychol* 29 (4):351-6.

———. 2004. Handwriting and attention in children and adults with attention deficit hyperactivity disorder. *Motor Control* 8 (4):461-71.

———. 2005. The effect of conscious control on handwriting in children with attention deficit hyperactivity disorder. *J Atten Disord* 9 (1):323-32.

Tuckman, B. W. 2005. Relations of academic procrastination, rationalizations, and performance in a web course with deadlines. *Psychol Rep* 96 (3 Pt 2):1015-21.

U. S. Department of Education. 2004. Teaching Children with Attention Deficit Hyperactivity Disorder: Instructional Strategies and Practices.

Van Ameringen, M., C. Mancini, and P. Farvolden. 2003. The impact of anxiety disorders on educational achievement. *J Anxiety Disord* 17 (5):561-71.

Van Borsel, J., and M. Vanryckeghem. 2000. Dysfluency and phonic tics in Tourette syndrome: A case report. *J Commun Disord* 33 (3):227-239

van der Wee, N. J., H. H. Hardeman, N. F. Ramsey, M. Raemaekers, V. A. N. Megen HJ, D. A. Denys, H. G. Westenberg, and R. S. Kahn. 2006. Saccadic abnormalities in psychotropic-naive obsessive-compulsive disorder without co-morbidity. *Psychol Med*:1-6.

van der Wee, N. J., N. F. Ramsey, J. M. Jansma, D. A. Denys, H. J. van Megen, H. M. Westenberg, and R. S. Kahn. 2003. Spatial working memory deficits in obsessive compulsive disorder are associated with excessive engagement of the medial frontal cortex. *Neuroimage* 20 (4):2271-80.

Vasa, R. A., R. Roberson-Nay, R. G. Klein, S. Mannuzza, J. L. Moulton, 3rd, M. Guardino, A. Merikangas, A. R. Carlino, and D. S. Pine. 2006. Memory deficits in children with and at risk for anxiety disorders. *Depress Anxiety*.

Verdellen, C. W., G. P. Keijsers, D. C. Cath, and C. A. Hoogduin. 2004. Exposure with response prevention versus habit reversal in Tourettes's syndrome: A controlled study. *Behav Res Ther* 42 (5):501-11.

Verdellen, C. W., C. A. Hoogduin, B. S. Kato, G. P. Keijsers, D. C. Cath, and H. B. Hoijtink. 2008. Habituation of premonitory sensations during exposure and response prevention treatment in Tourette's syndrome. *Behavior Modification* 32 (2):215-227.

Verdellen, C. W., C. A. Hoogduin, and G. P. Keijsers. 2007. Tic suppression in the treatment of Tourette's syndrome with exposure therapy: The rebound phenomenon reconsidered. *Mov Disord* 22 (11):1601-1606.

Voci, S. C., J. H. Beitchman, E. B. Brownlie, and B. Wilson. 2006. Social anxiety in late adolescence: The importance of early childhood language impairment. *J Anxiety Disord*.

Vulink, N. C., D. Denys, L. Bus, and H. G. Westenberg. 2006. Female hormones affect symptom severity in obsessive-compulsive disorder. *Int Clin Psychopharmacol* 21 (3):171-5.

Wagner, A. P. 2005. *Worried No More*. Second ed. Mobile: Lighthouse Press, Inc.

Warren, J.S., H. M. Bohanon-Edmonson, A. P. Turnbull, W. Sailor, D. Wickham, P. Griggs, and S.E. Beech. 2006. School-wide positive behavior support: Addressing behavior problems that impede student learning. *Educational Psychology Review* 18 (2):187-198.

Webb, J.T. and D. Latimer. 1993. ADHD and children who are gifted. In *Eric Digest*.

Weil, M. J., and S. J. Amundson. 1994. Relationship between visuomotor and handwriting skills of children in kindergarten. *Am J Occup Ther* 48 (11):982-8.

Weiss, G, and LT Hechtman. 1993. *Hyperactive Children Grown Up*. New York: Guilford Press.

Wiggs, L., and G. Stores. 2004. Sleep patterns and sleep disorders in children with autistic spectrum disorders: Insights using parent report and actigraphy. *Dev Med Child Neurol* 46 (6):372-80.

Wilbarger, P. and J. Wilbarger. 1991. *Sensory Defensiveness in Children Aged 2- 12*. Denver: Avanti Education Programs.

Wolfson, A. R. and M. A. Carskadon. 1998. Sleep schedules and daytime functioning in adolescents. *Child Dev* 69 (4):875-87.

Woods, D. W. and M. B. Himle. 2004. Creating tic suppression: Comparing the effects of verbal instruction to differential reinforcement. *J Appl Behav Anal* 37 (3):417-20.

Woods, D. W. and B. A. Marcks. 2005. Controlled evaluation of an educational intervention used to modify peer attitudes and behavior toward persons with Tourette's Syndrome. *Behav Modif* 29 (6):900-12.

Woods, D. W., T. S. Watson, E. Wolfe, M. P. Twohig, and P. C. Friman. 2001. Analyzing the influence of tic-related talk on vocal and motor tics in children with Tourette's syndrome. *J Appl Behav Anal* 34 (3):353-6.

Woods, D. W., M. B. Himle, R. G. Miltenberger, J. E. Carr, D. C. Osmon, A. M. Karsten, C. Jostad, and A. Bosch. 2008. Durability, negative impact, and neuropsychological predictors of tic suppression in children with chronic tic disorder. *J Abnorm Child Psychol* 36 (2):237-245

Woods, D. W., M. R. Walther, C. C. Bauer, J. J. Kemp, and C. A. Conelea. 2009. The development of stimulus control over tics: A potential explanation for contextually-based variability in the symptoms of Tourette syndrome. *Behav Res Ther* 47 (1):41-47.

Wymbs, B. T, W. E. Pelham Jr., B. S. Molina, E. M. Gnagy, T. K. Wilson, and J. B. Greenhouse. 2008. Rate and predictors of divorce among parents of youths with ADHD. *Journal of Consulting and Clinical Psychology* 76 (5):735-744.

Zimmerman, B. J. 2000. Self-efficacy: An essential motive to learn. *Contemp Educ Psychol* 25 (1):82-91.

Zinner, S. H. 2004. Tourette syndrome: Much more than tics, part 1: Diagnosis. *Contemporary Pediatrics* 21 (8):22-36.

Zutshi, A., P. Kamath, and Y. C. Reddy. 2007. Bipolar and nonbipolar obsessive-compulsive disorder: A clinical exploration. *Compr Psychiatry* 48 (3):245-51.

Zutshi, A., Y. C. Reddy, K. Thennarasu, and C. R. Chandrashekhar. 2006. Comorbidity of anxiety disorders in patients with remitted bipolar disorder. *Eur Arch Psychiatry Clin Neurosci*.

Index

Page numbers in *italics* indicate figures

About the Authors:

Leslie E. Packer, Ph.D., is a licensed psychologist in New York providing treatment to children and adults with Tourette's Syndrome and other disorders described in this book. She also provides professional development workshops and serves as a consultant to school districts, helping them develop individualized educational programs and behavior intervention plans for students with disabilities. Prior to going into clinical practice 27 years ago, Dr. Packer taught in undergraduate and graduate psychology programs.

Dr. Packer served on the Board of Directors of the Tourette Syndrome Association of Long Island and on the National Tourette Syndrome Association's Education and Advocacy committees. She is the author of the award-winning websites Tourette Syndrome "Plus" (www.tourettesyndrome.net) and SchoolBehavior.com (www.schoolbehavior.com), as well as *Find a Way or Make a Way* (Parkaire Press, 2009). As an advocate for students with disabilities, she was instrumental in her state disseminating information on Tourette's to all school districts, and helped create the first public school program in the country for gifted students with Tourette's Syndrome. Dr. Packer has published numerous articles for both lay and professional audiences, including in *Neurologic Clinics* and *Behavior Modification*. Like her co-author, she is the parent of children with neurological conditions and she draws on both her professional and personal experiences when she presents nationally and internationally.

Sheryl K. Pruitt, M.Ed., ET/P, is the Clinical Director of Parkaire Consultants, a clinic she founded 23 years ago outside of Atlanta, Georgia that serves individuals with neurological impairments of all ages. Previously, Ms. Pruitt conducted a State of Georgia Exemplary Model Learning Disability Program and taught students with behavior disorders in a psychoeducational setting. She served on the Board of Directors of the Tourette Syndrome Association of Georgia and the Scientific Advisory Board of the Tourette Syndrome Association of Georgia and South Carolina. Ms. Pruitt also served on the National Tourette Syndrome Association's Education Committee, and was a member of the Professional Advisory Board for North Atlanta and Central Georgia CHADD. Currently, she is a member of the Professional Advisory Board of the Tourette Syndrome Foundation of Canada and a member of the Senior Advisory Board of the Brad Cohen Tourette Foundation. Ms. Pruitt is co-author of *Tigers, Too* (Parkaire Press, 2009) and *Teaching the Tiger* (Hope Press, 1995), and is a contributing author of the Tourette Syndrome Foundation of Canada's Education Guide on Tourette Syndrome. She teaches a State of Georgia professional learning unit course for teachers on students with neurological impairments. As the mother of two sons with neurological disorders, Ms. Pruitt's national and international presentations reflect both her professional and personal experience. For more information about her clinic, go to www.parkaireconsultants.com.